DISCOVER XIAMEN UNIVERSITY
Strength of the Nation

潘维廉 费 菲 著

XIAMEN UNIVERSITY PRESS

封面题字 王豪杰
责任编辑 施高翔
封面设计 夏 林

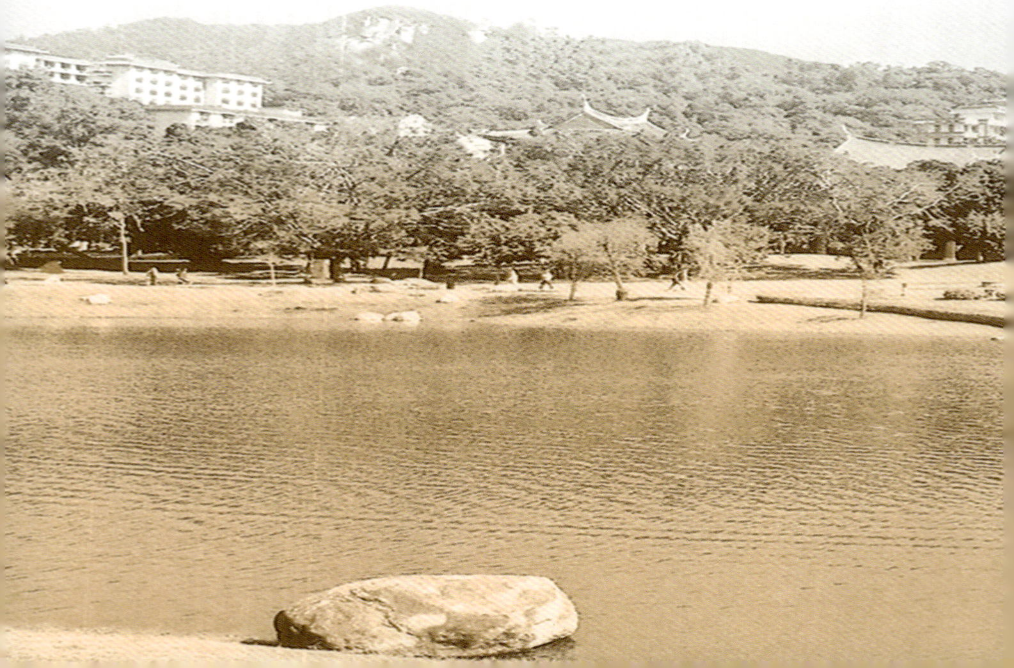

魅力厦大

（第二版）

王豪杰 题

Photo by Mr.Pan Wanhua 摄影：潘万华

Jiageng Complex 嘉庚楼群

处处皆可入画 Gardens Everywhere

Lotus Lake 芙蓉湖

Lotus Dorms 芙蓉楼

Seeing Red? "火"啦!

Gardens Even on Roofs
楼顶花园

国际性大学 An International University

Over 1,600
International Students
1600多名外国学生

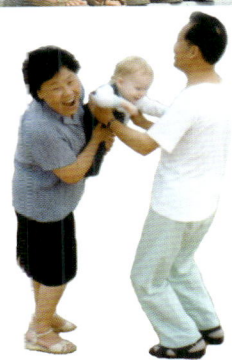

An International Exchange?
国际交流?

Scholars of XMU in Korea
厦大人在韩国
（与仁荷大学学术交流）

China Studies Program("Dr.J")
美华项目

群贤毕至 人才辈出
"Celebrating" Beautiful Minds

December,1992,Jiang Zemin Visited XMU
1992 年 12 月，江泽民同志视察厦门大学

Over 30,000 Students on Campus Today
现有在校学生 30000 多名

Into China, Into the World...
走出校门，走向世界

Over 140,000 Grads Since 1921
1921 年以来培养了 140000 多名学生

"100 Years Cultivate People"
"百年树人"

Fly to the Future

Innovative Education
创新教育

Growing Results in Chemistry
化学研究不断推陈出新

Arts Department
艺术学院

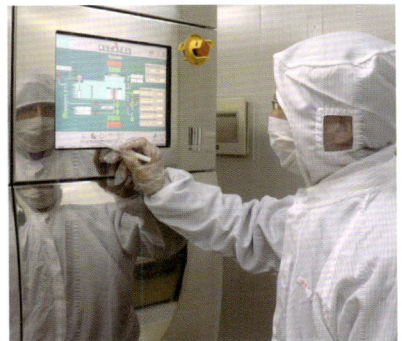 

Small Is Big in Nano-tech
纳米虽"小"，不可忽视

Fly to the Future (Bird-Book Fountain)
飞向未来（如鲲鹏展翅的书形喷泉）

Main Library (almost 4 million books)
校本部图书馆（馆藏图书近 400 万册）

Think Small!
Pen-Tung Sah Ctr.
Small-Seeing Eye
"小"处着眼——萨本栋微机电研究中心前的雕塑

画意能达万言
"A picture's worth ten thousand words..."

XMU Beach
厦大海滨沙滩

Lotus Lake Amphitheatre
芙蓉湖的露天看台

Matt and Friend(1989)
马太和朋友（1989）

4 Seasons of Beauty
四季如画

Lu Xun
鲁迅雕像

积极开展体育运动　A Sports-Minded University

Sino-U.S. Basketball Match?
中美篮球赛？

Be of Good Cheer!
朝气蓬勃！

XMU Basket Wizards
篮球高手

Some Serious Ping Pong!
精彩的乒乓球赛！

World-Class Swim Facilities
世界一流的游泳设施

Students of XMU Qualify in XM Marathon!
厦大学生参加厦门国际马拉松赛

漳州校区
跨海的校区
Zhangzhou Campus

Library 漳州校区图书馆

The New Jiageng Complex 漳州校区的嘉庚楼群

Sports Field 田径场

Mr. Tan Kah-kee "Henry Ford of Asia"
陈嘉庚——"亚洲的亨利·福特"

"我毕生以诚信勤俭办教育公益，为社会服务。"——陈嘉庚

（陈嘉庚先生摄于1905年）

Inspecting School Construction 视察学校建设

Singapore Factory
在新加坡的工厂

Tan Kah-kee and Sun Yat-sen
陈嘉庚和孙中山

Frugal Philanthropist
清贫的慈善家

Tan's "Gamble" Paid off Big!
厦门大学——陈嘉庚的"赌注"回报丰厚

Former Site of Foreigners' Racetrack Becomes...
昔日外国人的跑马场变成了……

...Xiamen University   昔日厦门大学

"When we think of the future days, it is one of the most encouraging things to be seen in the whole of China." (Paul Hutchinson, 1920s)

"当我们展望未来,那(厦门大学)将是全中国最最振奋人心的事物之一。"
(20世纪20年代,保罗·哈钦森)

XMU Faculty, 1926 (Lu Xun in Upper Right)
1926年厦门大学全体教员合影（四排右一为鲁迅）

University of Amoy.

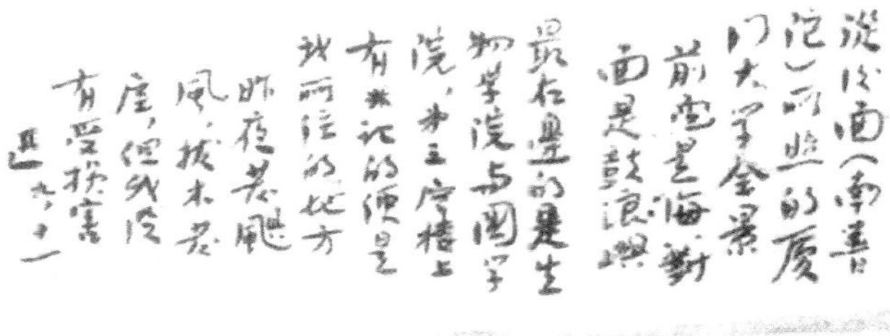

1926 XMU Postcard Mailed by Lu Xun
1926年时的厦门大学全景（鲁迅先生寄给许广平的明信片）

XMU in Exile (Changting XMU)
在长汀办学期间的厦门大学

Changting XMU Dorm Room
长汀的学生宿舍

Tan Kah-kee Toured Changting XMU
陈嘉庚在长汀视察厦门大学

大礼堂：在这古朴的文庙里，曾经有名剧的演出，有名曲的吹奏，也曾经举办过隆重的仪式，轻松的晚会。

嘉庚堂：是个建筑比较考究的大教室，是中西杂志阅览的地方，同时也是学术演讲的中心。

教师之一：轻薄的木板，疏落的树皮，可以遮风，可以蔽日。可是讲解高深的学问也曾是在这个地方。

Changting Today　今日长汀

萨本栋校长与部分师生摄于长汀校门前

50s and 60s Promise and Peril
50年代与60年代的希望与挑战

"Pen in One Hand, Gun in the Other"
"一手执笔，一手拿枪"

Mr. Tan Inspects XMU Construction (1950)
陈嘉庚视察厦门大学的建设工程（1950）

University Classes in a Bomb Shelter
防空洞里的大学课堂

XMU Students on Watch
厦门大学学生在站岗放哨

Mr. Tan and Li Guangqian
陈嘉庚和李光前

外文系民兵进行高射炮兵训练，这是女子射炮班正在进行对空射击操作。

Foreign Language Dept. Girl Students, 1953
(Are Any of Them Big Shots Now?)

1953年外文系的女生

（如今她们当中是否有人成了大炮一样的重量级人物？）

Passing the Reins   "华侨旗帜 民族光辉"

Zhou Enlai Visits
周恩来探望陈嘉庚

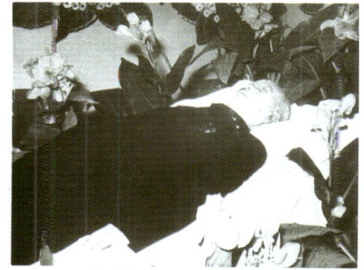

Beijing, Aug. 12, 1961
State Funeral in Beijing
1951年8月12日在北京举行国葬

站在巨人的肩膀上
On Giants' Shoulders

DISCOVER Xiamen University

Caveat This book is not an "official" portrait of XMU but simply our beloved university painted in broad strokes from the perspectives of one foreign teacher and one 3rd year Chinese student. Though not a definitive work, we hope it helps more people better understand our university as we pursue our motto, "Go into the world!"

——The authors

写在前面

这本书并非"官方"文件，而是仅仅从一位美国外教和一个大三学生的个人视角对厦大进行粗线条的刻画，不期待写出什么"巨作"，只希望为母校的"走向世界"尽一份绵薄之力。

——作者

Chapter	Contents	Page

Preface
Part I History
Chapter 1. Intro to XMU,"Strength of the South"　　2
　　Best Home on the Planet/Some of XMU's Many Firsts/
　　How I Got Here/The Foreign "Expert" in China/
Chapter 2. Tan Kah Kee—the Henry Ford of Asia　　16
　　Lee Kongchian(Li Guangqian)/
　　Dr. Lim Boon-keng (Lin Wenqing)
Chapter 3. Dr. Sa Bendong & Changting Xiamen University　36
Chapter 4. Changting Tales　　58
　　Passing the Physical/Shower Disaster/Air Attacks/
　　The Clog Clock/Chicken Picnic/Get Girls with Trilogy/
　　Lu Xun's Laobiao/China—Our Matchmaker
Chapter 5. Great Changes in Xiamen University　　74
Chapter 6. "Reliving History"
　　—An XMU Campus Tour with Zheng Qiwu　　82
Chapter 7. Gifts That Keep Giving: Alumni Contributions　88
　　"XMU Tower"—Building for the New Century—about Cai
　　Yueshi/Everlasting Passion Mr. Shao Jianyin/Midnight Phone Calls Prof.
　　Ge Wunxun /"Return Here to Learn about China !"
　　Mr. Huang Baoxin
Part II Xiamen University Today
Chapter 8. Xiamen University Today
　　Strength of the South, Strength of the Nation　　98
Chapter 9. Tour XMU　　104
　　104 XMU Sites at a Glance!/Wang Yanan/
　　Lin Yutang & Lu Xun Memorials
Chapter 10. XMU—An International University　　154
　　Pioneer in Education for Foreigners/Overseas Education
　　College/Foundation College of Xiamen University/
　　China Studies Program/How Andy met Annie at Xiada
Chapter 11. "It's News To Me" XMU Media　　168
　　XMU News Center/XMU Newspaper/XMU Broadcasting
　　Station
Chapter 12. XMU Activities & Sports　　176
　　New Student Welcome/"Talent Scout" —Ms. Xu Shanna/
　　Sport at XMU/"Xiamen International Marathon"
Part III Departments & Institutes
Chapter 13. Taiwan Research Institute　　190
　　Center for References and Information/So Why Xiamen? /
　　Retiring in Xiamen/Interview with Prof. Chen Kongli Taiwan
　　Research Institute/XMU Campus Life of Taiwan Students Chen Anqi and
　　Zhong Yuanlang/4 Generations of XMU Taiwan
　　Family/Some Taiwan XMU Alumni(1926—1948)

目 录

前 言

第一部分 史海拾贝

第1章 厦大简介——"南方之强" 3
地球上最舒适的家/厦大之最(部分)/我是如何来到这里的/
厦门大学校歌/外国"专家"在中国

第2章 校主陈嘉庚——"亚洲的亨利·福特" 17
李光前/林文庆

第3章 萨本栋和抗战时期的厦门大学 37

第4章 长汀轶事 59
通过体检/洗浴之灾/日机空袭/木屐自鸣钟/公鸡野炊/
"恋爱"三步曲/鲁迅的"老表"/中国——我的红娘

第5章 校园土著话沧桑 75

第6章 "重历历史"——随郑启五老师游厦大 83

第7章 献礼到永恒——校友捐赠 89
"厦大的摩天大楼",迈向21世纪的标志——关于蔡悦诗/
永远的爱——关于邵建寅/午夜电话——关于葛文勋/
"回到这里来学习,学习我们的中国!"——关于黄保欣

第二部分 今日扬帆

第8章 今日厦大——南方之强,民族之强 99

第9章 带你游厦大 104
游览104个景点/罗扬才/郑成功/王亚南/林语堂/鲁迅

第10章 厦门大学——一所国际性的大学 155
留学生教育的先行者/海外教育学院/厦门大学留
学预科学院/"美华"项目/两个美国学生的厦大情缘

第11章 厦大主要媒体 169
校新闻中心/厦大校报/校广播电台

第12章 欢迎来到厦门大学! 177
两次"迎新"/"星探"书记徐姗娜/厦大的趣味运动/
厦门国际马拉松

第三部分 学院一瞥

第13章 台湾研究院 191
文献信息中心/实践交流/为什么选择厦门?/退休在厦门/
访台湾研究院陈孔立教授/台生陈安琪和钟源郎在厦大的求学生活/
彭家四代厦大情/部分在台厦大校友(1926—1948)

iii

Chapter 14. Research School of S.E.Asian Studies Center for
    S.E.Asian Studies Xiamen University   210
Chapter 15. School of Economics   214
    Zhang Xingguo/Luo Yucong
Chapter 16. Wang Yanan Institute for Studies in Economics. 220
    Hong Yongmiao
Chapter 17. School of Management   228
    Prof. Ge Jiashu/Ancient Tales of Business Conquest
Chapter 18. MBA & EMBA Education Center   234
    20 Years of MBA/EMBA/XMU MBA in Alumni's Eyes
Chapter 19. College of Foreign Languages and Culture   248
    XMU's Uncle Beard/The Three Little Pigs Wants to Live Independently/
    SFLC 80th Anniversary Address
Chapter 20. Research Center for Higher Education
    Development   258
    Pan Maoyuan—Father of China's Higher Education Research
Chapter 21. School of Math Sciences   266
    SMS's Beautiful Minds/Chen Jingrun/Lin Qun/Xie Xide
Chapter 22. School of Physics Mechanical & Electrical
    Engineering   276
    Hu Guoqing/Wen H. Ko/Cradle of Chinese Aviation
Chapter 23. College of Chemistry & Chemical Engineering   282
    Lu Jiaxi/Top 50/International Ties
Chapter 24. School of Life Sciences   288
    Lin Shengcai/Tang Chongti/Chen Yiyu/Lin Peng
Chapter 25. College of Oceanography & Environmental
    Science   294
    Cradle of Chinese Oceanography/Zeng Chengkui/He Daren
Chapter 26. Medical College   300
    Ancient Chinese Doctor Tales!
Chapter 27. College of Humanities   304
    Lin Yutang—An "International" Chinese Writer
Chapter 28. School of Journalism & Communication   314
Chapter 29. School of Sinology Research   316
Chapter 30. XMU Arts College   318
    Will XMU's Get Its Own Orchestra? /Chinese European Art Center/
    Professor Tang Sao Yun
Chapter 31. Software School   334
Chapter 32. School of Law   336
    China's 1st Degrees in International law/UN Depository Library
Chapter 33. School of Information Science & Technology   340
Chapter 34. School of Public Affairs   344
Chapter 35. College of Architecture and Civil Engineering   346
Chapter 36. Tan Kah Kee College   348
    Campus Across the Sea
Part IV
    Chapter 37. "Beautiful Minds of XMU"   354

第 14 章　东南亚研究中心暨南洋研究院	211
第 15 章　经济学院	215
行政领导与管理：学术科研的坚固基石——访经济学院党委书记张兴国/罗郁聪	
第 16 章　王亚南经济研究院	221
洪永淼——王亚南经济研究院院长	
第 17 章　管理学院	229
葛家澍教授——中国会计学的传奇人物/古代商业故事	
第 18 章　MBA 和 EMBA 教育中心	235
20 年的 MBA 教育历史/EMBA/校友眼中的厦大 MBA 中心	
第 19 章　外文学院	249
厦门大学的"大胡子伯伯"/三只小猪渴望独立生活/厦大外文学院（原外文系）成立 80 周年庆典上的讲话	
第 20 章　高等教育发展研究中心	259
潘懋元——中国高等教育研究之父	
第 21 章　数学科学学院	267
数学科学学院的"美丽心灵"/陈景润/林群/谢希德	
第 22 章　物理与机电工程学院	277
胡国清/葛文勋/中国航天业的摇篮！	
第 23 章　化学化工学院	283
卢嘉锡/50 强/国际交流	
第 24 章　生命科学学院	289
林圣彩/唐崇惕/陈宜瑜/汪惠耀/林鹏	
第 25 章　海洋与环境学院	295
厦门大学——"中国海洋学的摇篮"/曾呈奎/何大仁	
第 26 章　厦门大学医学院	301
有关医生的经典故事	
第 27 章　人文学院	305
林语堂——一位"国际化"的中国作家	
第 28 章　新闻传播学院	315
第 29 章　厦门大学国学研究院	317
第 30 章　厦门大学艺术学院	319
厦大会拥有自己的乐团吗?/厦门大学艺术学院中国欧洲艺术中心/唐绍云教授	
第 31 章　软件学院	335
第 32 章　法学院	337
中国最早的国际法学位/联合国托存图书馆	
第 33 章　信息科学与技术学院	341
第 34 章　公共事务学院	345
第 35 章　建筑与土木工程学院	347
第 36 章　嘉庚学院	349
跨海到校区	
第四部分　尾声	
第 37 章　厦门大学的"美丽心灵"	355

Apologies

When we set out to write about Xiamen University (XMU) we probably bit off more than we could chew (and maybe more than you can swallow). The problem is that XMU is simply too rich for one book, let alone for a team of two working under such a tight deadline (about 6 weeks) to do the place and the people justice.

Given our lack of time and information, we primarily wrote about those departments and people we were familiar with, and no doubt wrote too much about some areas and not enough about others. Some departments bent over backwards to supply us with information and we wrote more about them, while others offered little or nothing. If you want to learn more about any department, please visit their websites.

Lastly, although we obtained all of our information from official sources, the "facts" and statistics seemed always to change and evolve, even from one week to the next, and sometimes sources from the same bureau conflicted. All that we can say is that if this is reprinted, we will do our best to correct mistakes and omissions and improve it. But again, a team of only two sincerely needs *you*r help! Please E-mail us updated information!

Having said all that, if this book, in spite of glaring weaknesses, gives even a faint glimpse of what makes our XMU great, we will have accomplished our modest goal—to share with the world why we love and respect XMU—the place, the people, and the programs.

Enjoy our home, enjoy XMU!
Dr. Bill & Robin Fei Fei
XMU, March 2006

Praise?   E-mail Bill: amoybill@gmail.com
Complaints?   E-mail Robin: robin_feifei@163.com
Website: http://www.amoymagic.mts.cn (inside China)
           http://www.amoymagic.com (outside China)
           http://www.xiamengaide.com

致歉与感谢！

致 歉

  我们决定写这本《魅力厦大》的时候，其实是决定了写一本不可能完成的书（可能也是您没办法读完的）。因为厦大的魅力实在是无法在区区一本书中全部展现啊，更不用说对于我们这样一个仅有两人的小组、再加上一份几乎没有实现可能性的时间表啦！（为了赶上85周年校庆，完成此书前后只有六个星期！）因此，想要将内容取舍得完全合乎情理、人物刻画得面面俱到，几乎是不可能的。

  时间的紧迫和信息的难以获取，使我们选择了那些我们本身所熟悉的事物，因此难免对于有些方面写得太多，有些方面又介绍得不够。一些院系尽力帮助提供了资料，我们就多用些笔墨来介绍；其他拿不到资料的只好略写。不过，您仍然可以通过书中提供的网址去了解更多的情况。

  还有一点，虽然所有信息全部来源于学校各机构的正式材料，但现实不断发展、数据每个星期都有变化，甚至连出自同一处的资料也会有不一致！那么在这里，我们唯一能说的是：如果本书再版，一定会努力纠正错误和遗漏，并尽全力做到更好！当然，两个人难免势单力薄，因此我们真诚地期待各位的帮助——欢迎通过邮件将最新信息提供给我们！

  最后，此书在许多的不足之外，如果能够向您——亲爱的读者展现哪怕一丁点儿母校的魅力，我们就会因为实现了自己那单纯与朴实得近乎幼稚的目标——与各国的人们分享为什么我们是如此深深地爱着这个地方、这里的人们、这里的一切——而心满意足了！

  那么，爱我们共同的家——厦门大学吧！

潘维廉博士、费菲
2006年4月
于厦门大学

您的表扬请发至：潘维廉　amoybill@amoymagic.com
如有批评，请发至：费菲　robin_feifei@163.com
网站：　http://www.amoymagic.mts.cn（国内）
　　　　http://www.amoymagic.com（国外）

A Letter from our President

"The best place in China is Xiamen, and the best place in Xiamen is Xiamen University," exclaimed a foreigner who has traveled all over China. And on behalf of our large Chinese and foreign community, I warmly welcome you to Xiamen University—China's most beautiful campus, and one of the most international institutes in the country.

XMU was founded in 1921 by Mr. Tan Kah-Kee, the well-known, patriotic overseas Chinese leader who was respected by the late Chairman Mao Tsetung as "the flag of Overseas Chinese and the honour of the Chinese nation". Since day one, our motto of "Pursuing excellence and striving for perfection" has inspired generations of XMU staff and students to overcome difficulties one after another and to achieve success And 85 years of unstinting devotion and hard work has earned XMU the title of "Strength of the South" and a distinguished reputation both at home and abroad.

A pioneer in China's international education and cooperation, we have over 1600 full-time overseas students, as well as over 31,000 Chinese students. Scholars the world over are attracted not only by our excellent academic traditions, superb staff, and advanced research facilities, but also by our idyllic campus on Xiamen Island, the "Garden City." And some scholars not only visit but stay—like Dr. Bill Brown, who has been teaching MBA here since 1988.

校长寄语

"神州美景数厦门,厦门风光看厦大。"一位来华旅游的外国游客曾这样感叹。我谨代表厦大这个中外友人齐聚的大家庭,欢迎各位光临中国最美丽的、最国际化的大学之一——厦门大学。

厦门大学是1921年由被毛主席誉为"华侨旗帜、民族光辉"的爱国华侨领袖陈嘉庚先生创办的。创建伊始,我校便以"自强不息、止于至善"为校训,激励了厦大几代人克服重重困难、获得了极大成功。厦大人85年来的不懈努力和辛勤耕耘使她无愧于"南方之强"的美誉,并在国内外享有很高的声望。

作为中国国际教育与合作的先锋,我校目前有1600名全日制海外留学生,31000名中国学生。来自全世界的专家学者不仅被我校优良的学术研究传统、高素质的教职员工以及先进的研究设备所吸引,而且爱上了坐落于"花园城市"——厦门的诗情画意、风光无限的厦大校园。很多学者不止访问了厦大,还决定留在厦大,从1988年起就在厦大教授MBA课程的潘维廉博士就是其中的一位。

Dr. Brown was XMU's first foreigner to be granted tenure and the first in Fujian Province to receive Permanent Residence, and he received the Friendship Award from Premier Li Peng for his contributions as a foreign expert to China's development. Dr. Brown has long wanted to share with others his deep feelings and unique perspective for XMU, and today he has achieved his dream. I believe that all who read this book, whether they've been to our school or not, or whether they are a student, teacher or worker, will gain a deeper understanding of XMU, as well as a greater reverence and appreciation for Tan Kah Kee, Lim Boon-Keng, Sah Ben Dong, Wang Yanan and other giants upon whose shoulders our university stands.

President Zhu and President Gabriel Buget Ecole Normale Superieure, Paris
朱校长向巴黎高师校长 **Ruget** 教授
赠送学校纪念牌

Finally, I'd like to take this opportunity to express my thanks to Dr. Brown and Robin Feifei for this gift which they have given to our university for its 85th anniversary.

Zhu, Chongshi

President
Xiamen University
March 10, 2006

DISCOVER Xiamen University

潘维廉博士是厦门大学第一位获得永久聘书的教授，也是福建省第一位获得中国永久居留权的外国专家，他还荣获了中国政府为对中国建设做出突出贡献的外国专家而专门颁发的"友谊奖"。长期以来潘维廉博士一直希望能与大家分享他对厦大深厚的感情以及独到的认识，今天他实现了自己的夙愿。摆在我们面前的这本书，饱含着他对厦大的感情，记录着他对厦大的认识。我相信，每一位读完这本书的人，不论他是否到过厦大，是否在这美丽的校园里学习、工作、生活过，都会加深对厦大的了解和热爱，都会加深对陈嘉庚、林文庆、萨本栋、王亚南等先贤的尊敬与崇拜。

借此机会，我要向潘维廉教授和费菲表示我的由衷的感谢，感谢他们把这样一份精美的礼物献给厦门大学85周年校庆。

厦门大学校长

2006年3月10日

Acknowledgments

Thanks to XMU Council Chairman Zhu Zhiwen, University President, Professor Zhu Chongshi, and Vice Council Chairman and Vice President Professor Pan Shimo for their encouragement.

Mr. Wang Haojie, former XMU council chairman, provided the covers calligraphy.

Director Mao Tongwen of ICE (Office of International Cooperation & Exchange) and staff gave invaluable support.

Prof. Wang Haojie, Fovmer Chairman XMU Council, with Yale University President Richard Levin
王豪杰书记与耶鲁大学校长

(Visit the **ICE Site**: http://ice.xmu.edu.cn/en)

Mr. Dai Yan, Vice Director of XMU Dept. of Publicity, let us use his historical black and white photos.

Ms. Lou Hongying, Director of Xiamen University News Center, and the entire XMU Dept. of Publicity, were supportive from the beginning, and provided much direction and valuable materials.

Professor Zheng Qiwu, "Mr. XMU," who has lived his entire life on XMU, provided several articles and gave us an historic tour of XMU.

Ji Yuhua, Uncle Beard, helped edit many sections, and organized grad students to help translate many chapters.

Thank you to Mr. Pan Wanhua, XMU's famous photographer. The beautiful photos in this book are his; the poor photos are ours.

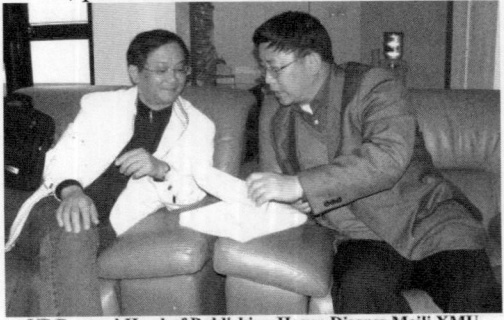

VP Pan and Head of Publishing House Discuss Meili XMU.

衷 心 感 谢

校党委书记朱之文，校长朱崇实，校党委副书记、副校长潘世墨，感谢你们的支持和鼓励！

感谢原校党委书记王豪杰的大力支持，并为本书题写书名！

国际合作与交流处处长毛通文及国际处全体成员，感谢你们真诚地帮助和引导。(ICE 网址 http://ice.xmu.edu.cn/en)

Zhu Zhiwen, Chairman XMU Council with Sun Yafu, Vice Minister of Taiwan Affairs Office of the State Council
朱之文书记与国台办副主任孙亚夫在夏大校园

党委宣传部戴岩副部长，感谢您提供了珍贵的黑白历史照片。

新闻中心主任楼红英老师，以及您所在的厦大党委宣传部，感谢大家从最开始就全力支持本书，并且提供了宝贵的信息和资料。

郑启五老师，被我们成为"厦大先生"，为本书提供了珍贵的资料和文章，并带我们畅游校园。

"大胡子伯伯"纪玉华教授，感谢他帮助对本书进行修改，并组织了研究生翻译小组，从事大量的翻译工作。

潘万华，我们的校园里著名的摄影师，本书中好看的照片是他的，不好看的是我们的！

Miss Lily Zhuang, head of the Foreign Languages Department's Teacher's Affairs Office provided much background material.

Ms. Shi Huixia, of XMU Alumni Association, patiently dropped everything whenever Robin dropped in to share information about alumni.

Chen Jingde and Qin Ji took photos for the cover.

Thanks to these students who helped translate or proofread: Bruce Lee, Xiang Peipei, Li Xichun, Chen Juan, Fei Yadun, Huang Sijiao, Tan Qianqian, Jin Xiaoli, Liu Haiyan, Chenling, Wu Huiyun, Cheng Lin, Li Hongyi, Zhong Mengbo, Liu Gangbing, Zhuang Huiying, Ruan Jing, Gao Zhen.

A special thanks to Xiamen Daily's "Common Talk". (CT), Xiamen Daily's Wednesday English supplement, was the first of its kind in China, and is *the* source for the most up-to-date information on Xiamen. We even referred to CT as we wrote this book to keep abreast of changes at XMU.

A big thanks to Ms. Eunice Chau, of Symphony Company for her great assistance, and the help she has long given us foreigners in Xiamen (including business services, settling in, survival, social connections—and mineral water!). She's also the one to contact for AXE (Association of Xiamen Expatriates). Phone: 581-1621, or 13906028020

Finally, thanks to the many others—far too many to name—who provided materials, photographs, or interviews. We especially thank Jiang Dongming, Director of Xiamen University Publishing, and Shi Gaoxiang, our indefatigable editor. Without XMUP's support we'd have never got this book out in time, so they're the ones to thank (or blame!).

Enjoy our home!   Enjoy XMU!

Dr. Bill Brown & Robin Feifei
Xiamen University,
March, 2006

DISCOVER Xiamen University

庄丽莉，厦门大学外文学院教学科科长，提供不少资料和帮助。

校友总会的石慧霞老师，感谢您的真诚建议，感谢您所提供的关于校友的珍贵资料；也感谢厦大校友总会的支持。

陈敬德和秦骥给我们拍封面的照片。

感谢以下翻译校对本书的同学们： 彭清洪、项培培、李锡纯、陈娟、费亚敦、黄思姣、谭倩倩、金小丽、刘海燕、陈玲、吴慧芸、程林、李鸿艺、钟孟博、刘钢炳、庄慧颖、阮晶、高贞。

特别鸣谢双语周刊的支持和指导！《厦门日报·双语周刊》——厦门日报逢周三出版的周刊，是全国党报首份双语周刊，也是英语厦门新闻的最大来源。 我们甚至在写作此书时还依赖于周刊以保证更新资料、吸引眼球。

非常感谢信而立公司的 Eunice Chau 女士。她给了我们这些在厦门的外国朋友很多帮助（包括商业服务，安置，联络工作—和矿泉水！她也是厦门外籍人协会联络人。电话:581-1621, 13906028020）。

最后，感谢许许多多关心和支持本书的人们！特别感谢厦门大学出版社社长蒋东明和我们孜孜不倦的编辑施高翔，没有他们的帮助,本书不可能及时出版,所以要谢就谢他们吧！（或者批评也批评他们哦！）

那么，爱我们的家，厦门大学吧！

潘维廉博士、费菲
2006 年 3 月
于厦门大学

Why Robin?
By Bill

Over the past couple months I've sometimes had doubts about the wisdom of tackling a book in less than two months, but I did make one decision that was sheer brilliance—asking Robin Feifei to co-author the book.

I first met this Junior in International Business and Economics in 2005 during an extravaganza she helped arrange on Zhangzhou campus, but I had already heard about her from just about every foreigner on campus. Robin seemed to know everyone and be involved in everything, yet she still managed to be first in her department for her first two years and land numerous scholarships ("Study is always my top priority no matter how many activities I'm involved in," she said).

Robin not only speaks English like a foreigner but has impeccable Mandarin, and has won many competitions in both languages. She is president of XMU's Putonghua (Mandarin) Association, and was producer and broadcaster for the university program "English Café" for two years, and since moving to the main campus she's been the anchorperson for the university's TV news center. Robin has written articles for Xiamen Daily's English "Common Talk," represented XMU in the "Model United Nations" in Beijing, and on Feb. 2006, was selected to appear on CCTV10's "Outlook". She's hosted numerous conferences, banquets, and competitions, and worked with various foreign governments (the Philippine government gave her a letter of commendation and this weekend she's helping the Australians!).

Robin has made such brilliant accomplishments in spite of her rather humble background (or perhaps because of it?) Both parents had minimal education; her father works a crane and her unemployed mother cares for her bedridden grandmother, who raised her until she was 16. But Robin's grandfather gave Robin some advice that she obviously took to heart: "Learn more and do more as long as you live." I asked Robin about her goals in life and she said that, short-term, her goal was to give her parents their first plane ride, and to show them how to check in. I would not be surprised if someday Robin *bought* her parents a plane!

This book would have been impossible without the help of a very talented and self-motivated Chinese-speaking co-author, and no one, whether student or teacher, could have done a better job than Robin. In spite of her killer schedule, she did research, interviewed people, wrote articles and chapters, translated from English to Chinese and back again; in short, she contributed much more than her share to making this book possible.

Thank you, Robin! I hope you're next two years are as amazing as the first two, and I look forward to working with you on our next project.

DISCOVER Xiamen University

为什么选择费菲?

潘维廉

在写作本书这段时间里,我有时会怀疑用不到两个月的时间来完成一本书的决定是否明智。但是,我所做的决定中,的确有一个是非常明智的,就是让费菲来做本书的合著者。

第一次与这个国际经济与贸易专业大三的学生见面,是在 2005 年她参加的漳州校区的一个晚会上,但是之前我已从几乎所有的厦大外教那里听说过她。她似乎认识所有的人,参与了一切的活动,却仍然在大一、大二连续两年排名全系第一,并获得过好多奖学金!(她曾经说:"甭管多少社会活动,我觉得学习永远是第一位的!")

费菲不但英语说得就像个老外,而且还说得一口极其标准的普通话,并多次在英语、普通话比赛中获奖。她是"厦门大学普通话协会"的会长;在大学头两年里,还是厦门大学广播电台英语节目的制作人和播音,到本部后还在校新闻中心播音;她为《厦门日报双语周刊》写文章;代表厦大去北京参加"模拟联合国"比赛;2006 年 2 月,还被选去参加中央电视台 10 套"希望英语"节目。她担任过各种论坛、宴会和比赛的主持人,还曾经为不同的外国政府做过工作。(她曾收到过菲律宾政府的表扬信,这个周末又在帮助澳大利亚外宾呢!)

尽管费菲取得了如此成绩,她的家庭背景却并无显赫之处——或者这个家庭背景正是她成功的原因?她的父母都只受过低等教育,她的父亲是一名开吊车的工人,母亲失业很多年,在家照顾费菲卧病在床的外婆———位一直抚养她到 16 岁的老人。幸运的是,费菲一直将她外公的建议铭记于心:"只要活着,就要多学习、多做事。"我问费菲她的目标是什么,她说,因为父母都没有坐过飞机,短期的目标就是带他们去坐一次飞机,并教会他们登机的程序。其实,如果有一天,费菲给她的父母买了一架飞机,我都不会奇怪的!

如果没有这位有才能、主观能动性强、积极肯干又讲中文的合著者的话,我是不可能完成本书的。而且,没有人,不论是老师还是学生,会比她做合著者做得更好。虽然费菲有一张"玩命式"紧张的时间表,她仍然完成了大量的研究、采访、撰写文章和章节、汉英、英汉互译等等工作。总而言之,正是她做了这么多、甚至多于她应该做的二作量,才使本书有了存在的可能!

感谢你,费菲!我希望你在接下来的两年大学生活里,能像前两年那样做得精彩,而且,我等着与你的下一个合作项目。

Our Remarkable Journey
By Robin

It's been an absolute and profound honor working on the book with Dr. Bill Brown, whom I had heard about since entering XMU Sep. 2003, and began to know in person from July, 2005.

When he asked me to "co-author" this book in Nov. 2005, as a junior student and member of "the youngest generation" on the main campus (freshmen and sophomores stay on the Zhangzhou campus)who would have been greatly honored even asked just to "assist" for a book with Dr. Brown, I was completely stunned and extremely thrilled at being entrusted with this great task by someone I had respected who had done all of his previous books on his own, but I was also utterly confused about what contribution I could make to writing about something so extraordinary that no one could hope to express it in a comprehensive way.

Now that we've come to the point where the book is almost completed, and with all I've seen and experienced, I have far more to say than a short introduction can contain, so I'll just try to select the following three points:

The beauty of our university, both externally and within, made material-selection and decision-making extremely difficult. It truly made my heart ache to be forced to leave out a vast amount of the information that constitutes the greatness of XMU. I especially regret that we never got the chance to write the stories of many people, especially those of the Changting period, who were a comfort to XMU during a time of tragedy, and who celebrated with her in her triumph. We also wanted to write about the very many professors who have dedicated their entire lives to our nation's higher education and their academic career, and hundreds of other people who, in different ways, have made XMU the legend she is today.

As a 21- year- old undergraduate student only *beginning* to understand our university's history, I am overwhelmed and humbled, overwhelmed to know I can join in celebrating her great 85th birthday, and humbled by the legacy our predecessors have entrusted to us younger generation.

The more I learned about XMU, the more I realized it was simply impossible to portray this remarkably complex university in only one book—or even in a series of books. Please forgive us for writing about only *parts* of XMU, but had we attempted to show XMU in her entirety, we would have used oceans of ink and reams of paper and still not fulfilled our task..

我们奇妙的旅程

费 菲

我于2003年9月入学，从那时起就已经听说潘维廉教授了，直到2005年7月，才有幸与他认识。能与他合作完成本书，无疑是我莫大的荣幸。

2005年11月，潘维廉教授问我是否愿意与他"合著"本书，我非常地惊讶和兴奋，因为读大三的我不过是校本部的"最小一辈"（大一、大二都在漳州校区），而他对我的要求竟是"合著"而非"协助"！潘维廉博士是我十分敬仰的教授，他又从来都是独自一人写书，现在我被"委以重任"，去刻画一个如此丰满的对象——有着深厚底蕴的厦门大学！我当时并不知道要描绘这样一个没有人能够全面系统地通过文字展现出来的高等学府，自己能够做些什么。

现在书稿成形，回顾走过、看过的点点滴滴，有限的语言远不足以表达我的感受。因此我只选取以下三方面说上一点儿——

厦大之魅力 无论外在还是内在，都使对材料的取舍非常困难。因为极其紧张的时间和有限的篇幅，我们真的不得不忍痛割爱放弃一些组成这"厦大之美"的素材，包括那众多的人物，尤其是内迁长汀时期许许多多陪伴母校走过一路艰难、并与她共同欢庆胜利的校友们；还有那些为国家的高等教育事业和学术研究奉献了一生的老师们；以及无数以各自不同的方式成就了厦大今日辉煌的人……

而我，一个21岁的本科生，经过了本书的写作之后，才算是刚刚开始了解我们的校史，但母校不可抗拒的魅力却已经使我感到卑微和渺小，我们传承了先辈辉煌的遗产，并将有幸为她举杯共庆85岁华诞。

对厦大了解愈多，我就愈发认识到要在一本书、甚至一系列的书里全方位展现这个非凡的整体是不可能之举。所以请原谅我们没有把她写得面面俱到。不过，如果真的有人试图抒写其全部魅力，恐怕是罄尽纸墨也难以完成啊！

Dr. Bill Brown will forever be someone I'll never fully understand. He has constantly impressed and moved me with the many different things he's capable of, his fascinating stories, special intelligence, great character, and what's more, his everlasting deep love for XMU and China...

Most people know him as someone with a great sense of humor who can't open his mouth without cracking a joke. Well, that is entirely true, but what they probably don't know is the tremendous amount of work he accomplishes every day and the very few hours he has to rest.

During the few weeks we spent on the book, he frequently e-mailed me at 2:30 in the morning and then at 6:30am the same day. I cannot express how amazed I was at how `he literally "killed himself" over this book and at the same time fulfilled many other responsibilities in so many different fields. Sp each time I'm overwhelmed by stress and drudgery tasks, I just think of him and his way of working, and that gives me the resolve to "bite the bullet" and move forward....

Every time we did interviews together, they ended up interviewing Dr. Brown instead. People constantly wanted to thank him for his long sacrificial dedication to our university and to China. I personally know many foreigners in Xiamen, including foreign teachers at XMU, and almost every one of them began their understanding of Xiamen or XMU through either Dr. Brown or his books and website, and some even told me that Dr. Brown's achievements and his remarks about the place were the main reason they came here! I am not at all surprised when nationally famous and world-renowned professors shake his hand and don't let go, asking him about his work and family.

I was eager to insert at least one page in this book about him, but as I expected, he refused, saying, "We need to make the book nicer, not destroy it." It seems to me he only measures the significance of his own life by valuing the lives of others.

I'm forever grateful, for his faith in me from the very beginning and for the encouragement every step of the way. And right now I just hope for two things: One, I hope I'll be able to write a book named "Magic Dr. Bill Brown" some day myself when he doesn't have the right to protest as he does now. Two, I hope he can get some rest after "killing himself" over the work to meet the 85th deadline—some " real" rest, with computer shut down and telephone off the hook.

DISCOVER Xiamen University

  潘维廉博士　本身就是一本我永远无法读完的书。他的多才、他的奇妙的经历、他的过人的智慧、他的高尚的人格，还有他对厦大、对中国那永恒而深沉的爱，都会常常让我吃惊和深受感染……

  大家眼中的"老潘"，是个张口就开玩笑、永远风趣幽默的人。当然，这一点儿不假；然而大多数人所不了解的，是他每天超乎寻常的工作量和那少得实在可怜的休息时间。

  在写作本书的这几个星期里，我经常收到他凌晨两点半发来的邮件，同一天的早上六点半又发来一封！对于他这种近乎疯狂的、的的确确是在"拼命"的工作方式，我甚至不能用语言来表达自己的震惊和强烈感受，至于他在完成这许许多多工作的同时又是如何在很多不同方面做出了成绩，更是我永远无法完全了解和体会的。这之后，每次面对任务和压力喘不过气来的时候，我都会想起他的工作方式，然后鼓起勇气、勇敢地向前了……

  每次我们去采访，潘维廉教授都变成了被采访者——大家总是想感谢他长期对厦大、对中国的贡献。我认识很多在厦门的外国人，包括厦大外教，几乎每一个人对厦门的了解都是从潘维廉教授的书和他的"魅力厦门"网站开始的。有些人还告诉我说，潘教授取得的成就和对厦门的评价感染了他们，成为他们离开本国来到这里的直接原因。因此，当我们遇到的那些国内国际知名的教授握住潘维廉博士的手迟迟不肯松开，并殷切地询问他的工作和家庭的时候，我一点儿都不感到惊讶。

  我本很想在本书中专门写上哪怕一页关于他的传记，然而正如我所预料的，他坚持不肯，理由是"我们要让这本书好看些，而不是'摧残'它"。在我看来，他衡量自己人生价值的唯一标准，就是通过珍视他人的价值。

  我永远心存感激，对他从一开始就给予我的信任和成书过程中每一步的鼓励。而现在呢，我有两个愿望——

  第一，我希望有一天自己能写一本"魅力潘维廉"，当然，在他不参与创作因而无权反抗的时候；

  第二，我希望他为85周年校庆前完成本书而严重超负荷地工作之后，能好好地休息一下——关了电脑、拔了电话，"真正"的休息。

Writing in both languages has certainly made the task tougher for us. I usually wrote in English, translated it into Chinese, and then made changes to the English or Chinese, then returned to the translation. And Dr. Brown's writings in English were all translated into Chinese, verified, and sometimes translated back into English. Both my English and Dr. Brown's Chinese are limited, so it was sometimes sheer drudgery, going back and forth between the two languages. And this left us with even less time to interview the people we'd originally intended to write about. I am so thankful for those friends who helped with both the Chinese and English translations. They've probably done a much better job of translating than I could have. Still, because of this frustratingly complex translation process, I sincerely ask for your tolerance and understanding, and promise to spare no effort to improve the book if it's reprinted. At the same time, we would also appreciate whatever suggestions you are ready to make.

In a word, after all I've learned the past couple months, I've fallen in love with XMU and am truly proud to call her "my mother university". And therefore, I humbly ask you to join us on a truly remarkable and, for me, an emotional journey, experiencing the traditions and heritage of our past and the hope of our future, and taking up and passing on the torch so our next 100 year's history will be even greater than that of the past 85 years.

Bill and Robin (photo by Mr. Pan Wanhua)

DISCOVER Xiamen University

用双语写作 显然使原本困难的工作难上加难。我的程序通常是：用英文写作，然后翻译成中文，修改英文或者中文，再回过头去对应着修改译文……潘维兼教授的英文稿被翻成中文后，经过订正，有时又要翻回到英文……我的英文水平实在有限，他的中文也不能完全像中国人一样运用自如。因此这整个过程——在两种语言之间"折腾"来"折腾"去——确实是一份烦琐的工作，有时甚至是折磨！这就使我们能够按原计划进行人物采访的时间更少了。我十分感激那些做了大量翻译工作的老师和同学们，他们出色地完成了任务，比我自己去蹩脚地遣词造句要高明得多！但是，正因为这个双语写作程序的特殊性，我在此真诚地请求您的理解和宽容，如果再版，一定会不遗余力地争取做得更好。同时，如果亲爱的读者们有任何建议，我们都将怀着感激之情虚心聆听。

总而言之，经过了这近两个月，我早已经深深地爱上了能有幸喊一声"母校"的厦门大学了。并且，我诚挚邀请您与我们一同踏上这个奇妙而令人心动的旅程，来经历和感受其历史的深厚沉淀以及未来的光明希望。只有如此，未来的 100 年，才会比逝去的 85 载岁月更辉煌！

Robin in Beijing
(XMU Rep for Model U.N.)

Professor Zheng Qiwu
郑启五老师

A special thanks to Prof. Zheng Qiwu for his guidance, support and contributions. Born in Xiamen on Dec. 7th, 1952, Prof. Zheng has spent his entire life on our campus and knows it perhaps like no other—hence my nickname for him, "Dr. XMU".

From 1954 to 1960, Prof. Zheng attended XMU's kindergarten (XMU's oldest building) and Yanyu Elementary, both of which my sons also attended. Like millions of intellectuals during the Cultural Revolution, Zheng was sent to the countryside and from 1969 until 1972 worked in West Fujian's remote Wuping County. After returning to Xiamen in 1972 he worked in XMU's printing press for two years and as a cook in the English department for four years, but he never abandoned his dream of getting an education.

From 1978 to 1982 he studied in the English Department, and taught in the Taiwan Research Institute from 1982 to 1994. From 1994 until the present he has been an assistant professor and research student mentor in XMU's Population Research Institute.

Professor Zheng has written, at last count, 15 books—and we would have been hard pressed to have written this book without his invaluable advice. Thank you!

郑启五老师

特别感谢人口所的郑启五老师,感谢他的指导和支持。他于1952年12月7日出生在厦门,在厦大校园里长大,对学校的历史和掌故知之甚多。所以我给他的外号是"厦大先生"。

1954到1960年,郑老师还是厦大幼儿园的小朋友呢。(现在的厦大幼儿园所在地是学校里最老的一幢楼,我的两个儿子也在那里上的幼儿园)。和其他许多知识分子一样,"文革"期间,他在偏僻的闽西武平县乡下度过了1969到1972这几年。1972年回到厦门后,他在厦大印刷厂做了两年临时工,之后又在外文食堂做了四年的炊事员。尽管如此,他从未放弃过接受高等教育的梦想。

Prof. Zheng taught us much about XMU

1978到1982年,他在厦大外文系学习,之后的1982到1994年,在台湾研究所授课。1994年至今,他担任厦大人口研究所研究生导师、副教授。

郑启五老师已经出版至少有15本书了吧!我们这一本书的撰写也要感谢他的许多宝贵建议!太谢谢啦!

潘万华 厦门大学党委宣传部秘书,校摄影中心主任。1975年考入厦门大学历史系,1978年毕业至今,在厦门大学从事摄影工作。潘万华在大学期间就对摄影产生了浓厚的兴趣,创作了大量优秀作品,在国内外展出或发表的作品有近千幅,有十几件作品获省级以上金、银、铜牌奖。现任全国高等教育摄影专业委员会常务理事,并协助著名摄影家沙占祥老师在学校开设摄影选修课。

Thank You ICE!

Office of Int'l Cooperation and Exchange (ICE) used to be Office of Foreign Affairs but I think they changed the name because I always joked that their job was to oversee foreigners' "affairs," or that they were Huai Ban (bad affairs) instead of Wai Ban (foreign affairs).

The Cool Folks of ICE!

But I actually prefer the new name, ICE, because now I can call them ICE Agents (which sounds like villains in a James Bond movie).

But for all my joking about ICE, they are the ones who make XMU life possible and pleasant for us Laowai (foreigners)—but it hasn't always been easy for them. For most of the past 18 years, the ICE office was small, cramped, and understaffed (and many of the staff did not even speak a foreign language, which I found strange for folks who were supposed to handle foreigners). But ICE now has a large, modern office, and the large staff is highly trained and highly motivated to lead XMU on her "Go into the World." Thanks in large part to ICE, XMU is indeed going into the world—and it seems that the entire world is coming to XMU as well.

Foreigners used to be so rare on XMU that even I stared at them (though I usually didn't point). But nowadays XMU has dozens of foreign teachers and well over 1600 foreign students. And it seems that not a week goes by that we don't have a foreign delegation or a major international academic conference on campus. Our XMU is truly an international university, with exchange programs with prestigious universities in dozens of countries and regions, but you can be sure that whenever XMU "Walks into the World", it is the agents of ICE who have taken the first step and made it possible. In addition, the Office for Hong Kong, Macao and Taiwan Affairs, which is with ICE, has been instrumental in ensuring that XMU has closer ties with Taiwan than any other mainland university (which I appreciate, since my wife was born in Taiwan, and I lived there as well).

Thank you, ICE, for 18 years of friendship, and for your strong support and encouragement in writing this book.

Dr. Bill

Contact ICE
Phone: (0592)218-6237   Fax: 218-0240
Website: http://ice.xmu.edu.cn/en
E-mail: ws@xmu.edu.cn

DISCOVER Xiamen University

感谢国际合作与交流处!

国际合作与交流处以前叫"外事办公室",我想他们之所以改名,可能是由于我曾戏称他们"坏办",而非"外办",而所谓"外事",还要监督外国人不要出事吧(红杏出墙?)。因为他们常要处理一些外国人的突发状况。实际上我更偏爱这个新名字,因为这样我可以叫他们ICE特工了(听起来像007电影里的角色似的)。

但是玩笑归玩笑,是他们让我们这群老外能在厦大生活工作,并得以如此开心舒适——虽然对于他们来说并不是件容易的事。 在过去18年, 国际合作与交流处还是狭窄、拥挤的小地方,人手紧缺,有些工作人员甚至不会外语(在我看来,从事外事的人不讲外语是件挺奇怪的事情)。但国际合作与交流处现在已经有宽敞而现代化的办公室了,工作人员也都训练有素,正充满激情地帮助着厦大"走向世界"。 感谢国际合作与交流处的努力,厦门大学正走上通向世界的大道,整个世界也在走向厦大。

以前厦门大学的外国教师很少,偶尔见到几个,就连我也忍不住多看几眼(虽然我没有好奇地冲他们指指点点)。但厦大现在已有几十名外籍教师,留学生也已超过 1600 名。几乎每周都有外国代表团来校访问,重要的国际学术会议也接连不断。我们厦大已经是个名副其实的国际型大学,它与世界各地几十个国家和地区的著名大学开展了广泛的交流项目。在厦大走向世界的每一步中,都有国际合作与交流处付出的辛劳。除此之外,国际合作与交流处的港澳台办公室,也使得厦门大学与台湾之间的关系特别紧密,这是内地其他大学所无法比拟的(对此我怀有特殊的感激之情,因为我的夫人是在台湾出生的,我自己也在台湾居住过一段时间)。

谢谢你,国际合作与交流处,为我们 18 年的友谊,也为在本书写作过程中你们所给予的巨大鼓励和帮助。

联系方式
电话:(0592)218-6237 传真: 218-0240
网址:http://ice.xmu.edu.cn/en
电子地址:ws@xmu.edu.cn

Pioneering Xiamen University Press
Thank You XMUP

When I approached Xiamen University Press in 1999 I was surprised they so quickly agreed to publish Amoy Magic in English. And over the years I've come to appreciate not only XMUP's pioneering spirit but also greater professionalism, creativity and efficiency than I have found in most publishing houses I have worked with.

Pioneers XMUP blazed new trails in Fujian by publishing *"Amoy Magic—Guide to Xiamen "* because our province had very little foreign language promotional materials, which is probably why the rest of the world knows so little about Fujian. Although a thousand years ago South Fujian was the start of the Maritime Silk Road and the gateway between China and the world, today when foreigners envision China they think not of Fujian but of Beijing, Shanghai, Canton, or Xi'an.

XMUP Director, Mr. Jiang 蒋东明社长

Most of Fujian's promotional materials have been in Chinese because we have primarily targeted Overseas Chinese (most of whom are from South Fujian), but this strategy is wrong for two reasons. First, many later-generation overseas Chinese don't even read Chinese. Second, as China opens up further to the world, Overseas Chinese account for an increasingly small percentage of foreign investment. So the only way we will deflect foreign investment from Shanghai and Guangdong to Fujian is to promote our province with foreign language materials. Xiamen University Press dared to produce such books, even though the market potential was not very promising and they received no municipal or provincial government support. XMUP has even printed a Chinese version, because to better promote our province Chinese must begin to appreciate it from a foreigner's perspective.

Happily, the publishing of *"Amoy Magic"* did bear some fruit. Readers e-mail me almost daily, and over the past few months I've met several foreigners in Xiamen who had intended on investing in Shanghai or Guangdong, but learned about Xiamen from Amoymagic.com, visited our city, bought *Amoy Magic*, fell in love with our city—and moved here to work, teach or invest.

DISCOVER Xiamen University

开拓创新的厦门大学出版社
(谢谢!)

　　1999年，当我初访厦门大学出版社的时候，我很惊讶他们竟如此干脆就同意出版英文版的《魅力厦门》。这些年来，我不仅欣赏厦大出版社的开拓精神，更钦佩他们的专业素质、创造力以及极高的办事效率。这些优点正是很多与我合作过的出版社所缺乏的。

　　先驱者 厦大出版社出版《魅力厦门》，在福建省开了先河。因为，之前我省几乎没有对外宣传的外语出版物，或许这正导致世界对福建了解较少。虽然，千年之前闽南就成为了"海上丝绸之路"的起点，也是中国和世界交流的门户。然而，今天外国人谈起中国，想到的却是北京、上海、广东或是西安，并非福建。

　　大多数宣传福建的书籍都是中文的，因为我们主要面向海外华人读者（他们大部分是闽南人），但是这种想法是不对的，原因有二：第一，很多华裔子女不懂中文；第二，随着中国的不断开放，海外华人投资者在所有海外投资者中占的比重越来越小。因此，想把原本打算投向上海、广东等地的资金吸引到福建的唯一办法就是大力用外语宣传我省。厦大出版社在没有任何市级、省级政府补贴的情况下，仍然坚持出版了这本市场前景并不是很看好的书，并且还出版了中文版。因为要更好地宣传我省，中国人也要学着从一个外国人的视角来看它。

　　可喜的是，《魅力厦门》的出版收到了较好效果。我几乎每天都能收到读者的电子邮件。过去几个月，我也结识了一些原本打算在上海或广东投资的外国朋友。他们从"魅力厦门"网站上了解了厦门、来到这里、读了这本书，并且喜欢上了厦门这个城市，纷纷到这里来工作、教学或是投资。

...and coming soon, "Beautiful Minds of XMU!"

"*Amoy Magic—Guide to Xiamen*" has not been a great profit maker, even though has been printed 4 times, but XMUP continues to reprint the book because they see the need. XMUP has also published "*Mystic Quanzhou—City of Light,*" "*Discover Gulangyu*" and "*Magic Fujian,*" and will soon publish a couple of other English books we are working on. I hope that eventually XMUP will reap what it has sown!

Professional and Efficient I appreciate not only XMUP's pioneering spirit, but also their professionalism and flexibility. Neither XMUP nor I had ever produced such books so we worked as a team and learned together. My editor Xiao Shi did not take an axe to my book but patiently discussed issues, leading me to make the changes myself, in my own way. I learned much from him and the other members of the staff.

I have also marveled at XMUP's creativity. Xiao Shi suggested the Chinese name 魅力厦门 and since then it has become a slogan used by many government activities (such as the 2004 Xiamen International Marathon, a Xiamen Government DVD,

Editor Shi in HK 施高翔在香港

etc.) XMUP also encouraged me to typeset the book myself, using many of my photos and cartoons. While the books' format is very informal, many readers have expressed their appreciation for the unique style, which is quite unlike other guidebooks.

Over the years I have worked with four other Chinese publishing houses, and while they were all invariably courteous in their dealings, I was frustrated in many areas, from editing to typesetting, and several experiences were downright unpleasant. XMUP as allowed me to be part of the team and given me an opportunity to be creative in my attempts to better promote my adopted home of Xiamen and Fujian. I'm very thankful for XMUP, and I hope that in the future this pioneering publishing house will reap the recognitions and rewards (money would be nice too!) that it deserves for being the first Fujian publishing house to seriously promote our province to foreigners.

Thank you, Xiamen University Press!

《魅力厦门——厦门指南》这本书已经第 4 次印刷了，虽获利有限，但厦大出版社仍坚持要重印，因为他们觉得很有必要。出版社还出版了我的《魅力泉州》、《魅力鼓浪屿》、《老外看福建》等书，很快连同我们现在正在创作的几本英文书也要出版了。我希望终有一天厦大出版社播散的希望的种子能够结出累累硕果。

专业、高效 我不仅欣赏厦大出版社的开拓精神，更钦佩他们的专业精神和工作的灵活性。因为此前厦大出版社和我都没有出版过此类书籍，所以我们共同学习，一起摸索。有时，编辑小施对书中某些内容有不同的看法，他并没有毫不留情地把这些内容删掉，而是耐心地和我一起讨论，引导我用自己的方式进行修改。我从他以及其他的出版社工作人员那里受益匪浅。

厦大出版社无穷的创造力也令我惊叹。小施建议将书的中文名字定为《魅力厦门》，后来这句话竟成为许多政府活动的宣传口号，2004 年的厦门国际马拉松赛，以及厦门市政府的一些宣传光碟都使用它。厦大出版社还鼓励我自己为这本书排版，附上一些我拍摄的照片和自创的漫画。这本书的形式非常随意，许多读者都表示他们非常喜欢这种独特的、与其他旅行指南截然不同的写作风格。

这些年来，我与其他四家中国的出版社也有过合作，虽然，他们对我总是彬彬有礼，然而，从编辑到排版，我常遇到很多麻烦，有几次真的非常不愉快。但是，同厦大出版社的合作让我感到，我是群体的一员，我也能发挥自己的创造力更好地宣传我的"第二故乡"厦门、福建。我由衷地感谢厦大出版社，我希望这家我省出版业界第一个对外宣传我省的、具有开拓创新精神的出版社能够得到应有的赞誉和褒奖。（能赚钱就更好了！）

谢谢你，厦大出版社！

Chapter 1

Intro to XMU, "Strength of the South"

Best Home on the Planet

People laugh when I claim I've the best home on earth but I can prove it!

Best Home China's fascinating past and unparalleled progress today make her the most exciting country on the planet. And China's most interesting province for overseas Chinese and foreigners is Fujian, start of the Maritime Silk Route—an ancient crossroads of commerce and culture that rivaled Alexandria in Egypt. Fujian's most beautiful city (indeed, China's most beautiful) is the "Garden Island" of Xiamen. Xiamen's most delightful location is Xiamen University (XMU), China's most beautiful campus. XMU's most picturesque area is Wu Lao (Five Old Men) Mountains. And perched upon Wu Lao Shan, overlooking historic Xiamen Bay, is our family's home.

Best Job I've not only have the best home on the planet but also the best job. Over recent decades China has bettered the lives of 1/5 of the planet's population. As teachers and students, we are privileged to not just witness but also participate, in a small way, in her economic miracle. And as China's only key university in a special economic zone, XMU has helped pioneer the modern education that has made China's success possible.

Best Family One of the most difficult things about moving to Xiamen was leaving behind family and friends, but our XMU colleagues, students, and neighbors have made us feel at home from day one, and Bill's sons grew up in Xiamen with countless Chinese grandmas, grandpas, aunts and uncles. We have a big family, and that big family is making a big difference not just in China but throughout the world. On the next page are a few ways XMU leads the nation:

The boys with Grandpa Huang

 第1章 厦大简介——"南方之强"

第 1 章

厦 大 简 介
——"南方之强"

地球上最舒适的家

当我说到我拥有地球上最舒适的家时,人们都笑了。但我可以证明这是真的。

最舒适的家 中国光辉灿烂的历史文明和今天无与伦比的社会进步使她成为地球上最令人向往的国家。对于海外华侨和外国人,中国最独特的省份便是福建省,她是海上丝绸之路的起点——中国古代的大门、贸易和文化中心,可与当时埃及的亚历山大城匹敌。福建最美丽的城市(实际上,也应该是中国最美丽的城市)是素有"海上花园"之称的厦门。厦门最美丽的景点就是厦门大学,她是中国最美丽的校园。厦大最独特的风景就是五老峰。在五老峰上有一处寓居,俯瞰久负盛名的厦门湾,那就是我们的家。

最好的工作 我不但有地球上最舒适的家,还有最好的工作。在过去二十年中,中国经济突飞猛进,地球上五分之一人口的生活得到了改善。作为厦大教师,也是学生,我有幸目睹并在极其微小的程度上参与实践了这个伟大的经济奇迹。作为中国经济特区里唯一一所全国重点大学,厦大引领中国的现代教育,为中国的经济建设输送各种人才。

最好的家庭 移居中国时最舍不得的就是家人和朋友。但是来到中国以后,我们从一开始就得到了厦大同事、学生和邻居的热心关怀和帮助,就像回到家一样,丝毫没有让人觉得这里陌生。我们的孩子在厦门成长,他们有无数个爷爷、奶奶、叔叔和阿姨。我们有一个大家庭,这个大家庭以其翻天覆地的变化在中国乃至世界范围内产生着巨大的影响。以下列出的是厦大引领全国的诸多方面:

Some of XMU's Many Firsts
厦大之最（部分）

- China's only key university founded by an Overseas Chinese
  中国唯一一所由华侨创办的重点大学
- China's only key university in a Special Economic Zone
  中国经济特区中唯一一所重点大学
- One of China's most beautiful campus
  中国最美丽的校园之一
- China's largest university auditorium (overlooking the sea)
  中国高校中最大的礼堂（面向大海）
- A "Cradle of modern aviation"
  现代航空学的"摇篮"
- A "Cradle of modern Chinese oceanography" (1st PhD in Oceanography)
  我国海洋科学研究的发祥地（培养了海洋学的第一个博士）
- Mainland China's 1st to award the MBA degree
  授予中国大陆第一批 MBA 学位
- China's leading chemistry department
  中国顶尖的化学系
- China's 1st Institute of Higher Education Research
  中国第一个高等教育研究机构
- China's first modern college for foreigners (OEC)
  中国第一个开展留学生教育的大学（海外教育学院）
- China's pioneer in correspondence education (since 1950s!)
  中国函授教育的先锋（从 20 世纪 50 年代始）
- China's leading mathematicians, including talents like Chen Jingrun.

第1章 厦大简介——"南方之强"
DISCOVER Xiamen University

中国杰出的数学家，包括陈景润等天才

- China's closest university ties with Taiwan.
  中国大陆与台湾联系最紧密的大学
- China's 1st Taiwan Research Center
  中国第一个专门从事台湾研究的研究院
- China's 1st Taiwan research Anthology
  中国大陆第一份专门研究台湾的学术刊物
- China's 1st Institute of S.E. Asian and Overseas Chinese Studies
  中国最早专门从事东南亚和华侨华人研究的学术机构
- China's 1st Anthropology Museum
  中国第一个人类博物馆
- One of China's 1st universities to teach International Law
  中国最早设立国际法专业的大学之一
- One of China's 1st Dept. of Economics and Trade
  中国最早设立国际贸易学科的大学之一
- China's leading economics college
  中国顶尖的经济学院
- China's #1 State Key Laboratory in Physical Chemistry of Solid Surfaces
  中国第一个固体表面物理化学国家重点实验室
- China's only Key Laboratory in Analytical Sciences (the Materials and Life Chemistry)
  中国唯一的分析科学重点实验室（材料和生命化学）

And the list goes on…

How I Got Here (A Sign from the Heavens!)

Many expect some deep, philosophical response when they ask why I chose XMU in 1988, but my answer is rather prosaic: XMU was the only Chinese university then that let foreign students bring families. A far more interesting question is "Why did I come to China at all?" The answer is—I received a sign from the heavens!

I never met a Chinese or ate Chinese food until I was twenty years old. When I was told that one in four people on earth were Chinese I, "That's not true. Our family has 4 people and none of us are Chinese!" But I got *orient*ed quickly when the U.S. Air Force sent me to Taiwan for two years in 1976. That began a decade-long chain of events that led me right to XMU.

Sign From the Heavens As a young Air Force missile systems expert, my only interest in the mainland was as a military target. With hindsight, I'm very thankful that by the 1970s Taiwan and the apocalyptic Yellow Peril were exchanging not weapons but words.

On a bright, spring morning, a batch of mainland propaganda leaflets fell from the heavens like colored snow right onto our Air Force base. I could not read the Chinese so they did not interest me in the slightest—until the Taiwanese police told us, "You'll go to jail if you even touch them!" Forbidden fruit is always sweeter, so I stuffed my pockets with contraband propaganda, raced home, closed my curtains, and studied them secretly. I didn't believe the mainland was as rosy as the photos depicted (Red maybe, but not rosy), but they piqued my curiosity, and I began reading about Chinese history and culture.

I had already fallen for Taiwan and her people, and when I learned that ¾ of Taiwanese were from South Fujian, I decided that someday I'd visit the mainland. I never dreamed that a decade later I'd not only visit but become Fujian Province's first permanent resident foreigner.

第1章 厦大简介——"南方之强"

我是如何来到这里的

很多人问我为什么在 1988 年选择来厦大时,都期待一个深刻的回答。但我的回答很简单:厦大是中国当时唯一一所允许外国学生带家属来的学校。一个更有意思的问题是"究竟为什么要来中国?"答案是:我接到了"天堂来信"!

直到 20 岁,我才见到中国人吃上中国菜。我记得有人告诉我,世界上四分之一的人口是中国人,我说:"不可能!我们家有四口人,但没有一个是中国人!"但很快我就去了东方并开始了解中国,美国空军 1976 年派我到台湾工作二年。此后十年中发生的一系列事情使我最后来到了厦大。

"天堂来信" 作为一个年轻的美国空军导弹系统专家,我对中国大陆唯一的兴趣就是视其为军事目标。后来我知道,感谢 20 世纪 70 年代之前,台湾和"黄祸"之间没有打仗,而是对话。

一个春天的早晨,阳光明媚。我所在的空军基地上空飘下一团来自大陆的传单,就像彩色的雪片。我不懂中文,这些传单一点都没有引起我的兴趣——直到台湾警察告诉我们说,"你们要是碰一下这些传单,就会被抓起来!"人们总是对被禁止的东西充满好奇,我把这些违法宣传单塞进口袋,跑回家,关起窗帘,偷偷地研究起来。我不相信大陆会像照片中拍的那么"玫瑰般"漂亮(红色倒有可能,玫瑰色?不会吧)。这引起了我的好奇心,于是我开始阅读中国历史和文化方面的书籍。

我爱上了台湾岛和岛上的人们。当我知道四分之三的台湾人来自福建的时候,我决定哪天一定要去大陆看看。我从来没有想过,十年后,我不仅去了福建,还成了福建省的第一个永久居住的外国人。

Heard of Xiamen? In April, 1988, right after our second son Matthew's birth, a stranger phoned from Thailand and said, "I hear you're interested in studying Chinese in China. Have you ever heard of Xiamen? Their university has dorms for families..."

"No, never have," I said, "and my wife just had a baby so we can't go anywhere for a couple years. But thanks anyway."

Exactly one week later, a man from Los Angeles, California, phoned and said, "I've heard you want to study in China. Have you ever heard of Xiamen?"

"Yes, I have," I said. "Last week!" I met with him, and 5 months later my wife, two infant sons, and I were in Xiamen University.

Only English Teachers! When I showed up at XMU in 1988 with a PhD in management, half a dozen "China Hands" said China wanted nothing but English teachers, and they suggested I return to the U.S. to get a degree in TESL. So imagine my surprise and delight when I heard that XMU was starting one of China's first MBA programs, and that they did have one foreign teacher. And as "luck" would have it (for me, if not for him), the American teacher left China mid-year because of family issues back home. The Dean asked if I'd take his place. I said, "Let me think about it." And after a good 30 or 40 seconds, I said yes, and we've been here ever since.

It was the right place, and the right time, and I felt so proud to be part of the team that a couple years later awarded China's first MBA degrees on mainland China (beating Nankai University by 6 days). But in 1988, neither XMU nor Xiamen was remotely like the idyllic city and campus we delight in today.

A Poor SEZ XMU may well have been China's only key university in a Special Economic Zone, but China was still a poor country, recovering from decades of difficulties, and XMU's living conditions left much to be desired. Electricity and water were off several days a week (we were once without water for 4 days and I lugged it up the hillside in buckets). When we did have water, it gurgled from the faucet brown, like tea. The air was dirty as well, full of coal soot, and I coughed like a veteran smoker.

Roads were poor, we had only 3 main bus routes, and buses were dilapidated. Black exhaust often billowed through the busses' wooden plank floors and sometimes I looked like a minstrel① by the time I staggered off.

---

① minstrel: a comic who wears black face make-up.

第1章 厦大简介——"南方之强"

听说过厦门吗? 1983年4月,就在二儿子马太出生后不久,一个陌生人从台湾打电话过来,他说:"我听说你想到中国学中文。你听说过厦门吗?那里的大学可以给学生家属提供宿舍……"

"从没听说过,"我说,"我妻子刚生了小孩儿,这两年我们哪都不能去。不过还是要谢谢你啦。"

正好一星期之后,一个洛杉矶的人给我打电话说:"听说你想到中国学习,听说过厦门吗?"

"听说过,"我说,"就在上星期!"后来我跟他见了面。5个月后,我和妻子带着两个幼子,来到了厦门大学!

只要英语老师! 1988年,当我拿着管理学博士的学位来到厦大时,6个"中国通"说中国除了英语老师什么都不要。他们建议我回美国考取一个TESL学位。可以想象,当我听到厦大正要开始设立中国大陆第一批MBA课程、并且有了一个外国老师时,真是又惊又喜。幸运的是那个美国老师由于家中有事,中途回国了(对我来说是幸运的,对他就未必了)。院长问我是否愿意接替他的工作,我说:"让我考虑一下吧。"大约考虑了30多秒后,我说:"好!"从那一刻起,我们再未曾离开厦大。

适当的时间,适当的地点,我成了这个团队的一分子,这让我感到骄傲。两年后我们学院授予了中国大陆第一批MBA学位(比南开大学早6天)。但在1988年,厦大没有我们今天所见到的这个校园漂亮,厦门也没有我们今天所见到的这座城市美丽。

贫穷的特区。 厦大是中国经济特区内唯一的一所全国重点大学,但中国还是一个相当贫穷的国家,刚从几十年艰苦斗争中恢复过来。厦门大学的生活条件很不尽如人意。一周内有好几天要停水停电。(有一次连续4天停水,我只好用提桶从山上提水下来)。装上自来水了,可水管里流出的水是褐色的,像茶一样的颜色。空气也不干净,尽是煤灰,我咳得像个老烟鬼。

街道也很破,当时只有三条公共汽车线路,汽车破旧不堪。黑色气体从汽车的木地板缝冒出,有时我摇摇晃晃地下车,看起来像个黑脸小丑。

Rains transformed our campus' dirt roads into quagmires, with vehicles mired in the mud at the university gates. Though we're an island the drainage was poor and XMU often flooded. After one typhoon, Foreign Affairs (now ICE) spread their documents on the lawn to dry them in the sun. (I was curious to read what they had on me, but I didn't have the nerve to sneak a peek).

Foreign teachers' living conditions were bad, but famous Chinese professors and leaders had it even worse. I often encountered Liu Peng, our MBA Center's Dean, walking home in a robe from the public bathroom a block away. Ji Yuhua, now the nationally famous Uncle Beard, lived in one room, and like other teachers he had built a kitchen of cardboard in the common hallway (replete with padlock on the cardboard door!).

Our 1st "car" in Xiamen

Changed From Within We would have never imagined in 1988 that only a decade later we'd have the idyllic campus we take for granted today, and that Xiamen City would be a garden city recognized internationally for balancing record economic growth with sound environmental preservation.

In 2002, I spent eight months researching Xiamen to help represent her in an international competition for livable cities in Stuttgart[①]. I was awed at what I discovered. Anyone can see that the "Garden City" is indeed one of the most beautiful cities on the planet, but the casual observer does not see the tremendous quality of leadership and planning that made such comprehensive changes possible.

`XMU, like Xiamen City, has undergone not a mere cosmetic makeover but an evolution of purpose and spirit—though I did not have an inkling of the sheer scale of change until we researched this book. We also had no idea of XMU's contributions not just to China but to the rest of the world over the past 85 years. This book only scratches the surface, but we hope it will help you understand, in some small measure, why XMU is not only the Strength of the South but the Strength of the Nation as well.

---

① 国家花园城市比赛 http://www.livcomawards.com/

第1章 厦大简介——"南方之强"

厦大校园的小路大多很脏。下雨的时候，整个校园就成了一片沼泽，车辆就在大门前的泥里抛了锚。排水系统很差，校园里经常会"水漫金山"。有一次台风过后，外事办（现在的国际处）把文件摊开在草地上晒，我很想知道这些文件里是否有关于我的什么信息，但最终也没敢偷看一眼。

如果说外国教师的生活条件很差，那么中国教授和领导的条件就更差了。我经常看到我们 M3A 中心主任刘鹏，身穿浴袍，从公共浴室走好长一段路回家。纪玉华，如今全国知名的"大胡子伯伯"，当时住的是小单间，同其他教师一样，在公共走廊上用纸板搭了个厨房（纸板门上还上了一大堆的锁！）。

从内部开始改变 我们在 1988 年时从没想象过，仅仅十年后厦大会变得今天这样田园般美丽，也没想过厦门市会成为闻名世界的花园城市，既保证了经济增长，又很好地保护了环境。

2002 年，为了准备厦门市参加的在斯图加特举行的国际花园城市的比赛，我用了 8 个月时间考察研究厦门——所见所闻使我震惊！容易发现，这个"海上花园城市"确实是地球上最漂亮的城市之一，然而，不深入探寻怎会知道，这巨变背后蕴藏的是怎样的坚强领导和周密策划啊！

和厦门市一样，厦大的改变不仅仅是表面的，更有追求和精神方面的变化——而我们在写本书之前对比却感受不深，对于厦大在过去的 85 年对中国乃至是对世界的贡献也不够了解。本书仅仅是蜻蜓点水地涉猎一些内容，但我们希望它能帮助人们在一定程度上明白，为什么厦大不仅是南方之强，更是民族之强。

Shannon Matthew Sign Up in Xiamen!

Xiamen University Anthem

Lyrics by Zheng Zhenwen, 1921
Music by Zhao Yuanren, 1921
Translation by Lieng-Huang Lee, 1997

Be strong! Be strong!
Vast sea of learning,
Who'll unveil the nature's mystery?
Lu Jiang deep and long
Let's seek truth to no end,
Hurrah, Master of Southland,
Hurrah, Master of Southland!

Be strong! Be strong!
Misty path of living,
Who'll steer forth the ship of mercy?
Lu Jiang deep and long,
Let's fill with love unbound.
Hurrah, Master of Southland,
Hurrah, Master of Southland!

Note: In Amoy (Xiamen), as the legend goes, the Lu Jiang is the river of herons and was once deep and long. Though no longer deep and long, the Lu Jiang still symbolizes the beautiful Island of Amoy.

第 1 章 厦大简介——"南方之强"

厦門大學校歌

赵元任 曲
郑贞文 词

1=D 2/4

自强 自强 学海何洋洋 谁欤挚鲸
自强 自强 人生何茫茫 谁欤普渡

发其藏 鹭江深且长 致吾知于
驾慈航 鹭江深且长 充吾爱于

无央 吁嗟乎南方之强 吁嗟乎
无疆 吁嗟乎南方之强 吁嗟乎

南方之强   南方之强

(Adopted from "Taiwan XMU Alumni, 1921-1991")

引自《厦门大学台湾校友会》

---

① 厦门的鹭江传说中是白鹭寄居的地方,以前的鹭江又长又深。虽然现在不那么长也不很深了,但鹭江仍然是美丽的厦门岛的象征。

The Foreign "Expert" in China
Teacher or Learner?

(Excerpt from, "*The Problem of China*," by Bertrand Russell (1922)

"When I went to China, I went to teach; but every day that I stayed I thought less and less of what I had to teach them and more of what I had to learn from them. Among Europeans who lived a long time in China, I found this attitude not uncommon, but among those whose stay is short, or who go only to make money, it is sadly rare. It is rare because the Chinese do not excel in the things we really value—military prowess and industrial enterprise. But those who value wisdom or beauty, or even the simple enjoyment of life, will find more of these things in China than in the distracted and turbulent West, and will be happy to live where such things are valued. I wish I could hope that China, in return for our scientific knowledge, may give us something of her large tolerance and contemplative peace of mind....

"Should our lives be spent in building a mansion① that we shall never have the leisure to inhabit?...

"The Chinese answer these questions in the negative, and therefore have to put up with poverty, disease and anarchy. But, to compensate for these evils, they have retained, as industrial nations have not, the capacity for civilized enjoyment, for leisure and laughter...The Chinese, of all classes, are more laughter-loving than any other race with which I am acquainted; they find amusement in everything, and a dispute can always be softened by a joke...

"The Chinese, from the highest to the lowest, have an imperturbable quiet dignity, which is usually not destroyed by a European education. They are not self-assertive, either individually or nationally; their pride is too profound for self-assertion. They admit China's military weakness...but they do not consider efficiency in homicide② the most important quality in a man or a nation. I think that, at bottom, they think that China is the greatest nation in the world, and has the finest civilization."

---

①   building a mansion: accumulating wealth one has no time to enjoy .
②   Homicide: Russel equates war with murder.

第1章 厦大简介——"南方之强"

外国"专家"在中国
老师还是学生？

（摘自《中国问题》，伯特兰·罗素著，1992年）

"我当初来中国是为了教书的，但在中国停留的时间越久，我就越不知道我能教他们些什么，相反我倒是在想我能向他们学些什么。我发现，长时间在中国生活的欧洲人往往都会这么想。但对于那些只在中国生活了较短时间、或者来中国纯粹为了赚钱的人，持这种态度的人少得可怜。这是因为在我们真正重视的东西上中国无法超过我们——军事力量和经济繁荣。但是对于那些崇尚智慧或美感，甚至只是简单地追求生活中乐趣的人们，他们可以在中国更多地找到他们所真正需要的东西。而这些，是他们在纷乱繁杂的西方社会所很难找到的。他们可以在中国过上幸福的生活，因为这些东西也是中国人所看重和需要的。我多么希望，中国可以给予我们她的宽容、博大、平和，就像我们在科学技术方面所给予中国的。

"我们穷尽一生的时间，来积聚我们永远也不会去消费的金钱，值得吗？

"中国人对这些问题的答案是否定的，所以他们必须忍受贫穷、疾病和政治混乱。但是，为了弥补这些不幸，他们保留了文化享受、安逸和笑容，这是工业国家所没有的。我所认识的中国人，无论来自哪个阶层，都比其他任何一个我所知的民族更喜欢笑；他们从每一件事情中享受快乐，一个笑话就可以缓解争端……

"无论来自上流社会还是最底层的中国人，都有着深刻的自我认知，这种认知是欧洲的教育无法融蚀的。正是这种强烈的自我认知，使他们不会孤注一掷、独断专行，无论是个人还是整个国家。他们承认，中国的军事力量还不算强大……但他们并不认为能用最短的时间消灭敌人是一个人或一个国家最重要的品质。实际上，我认为，他们觉得中国是世界上最伟大的国家，有着世界上最先进的文明。"

Chapter 2

Tan Kah Kee
—the Henry Ford of Asia

4 Unique Spirits of XMU

Patriotic Spirit of Mr. Tan Kah Kee (next chapter)

Revolutionary Spirit of Martyr Luo Yangcai (XMU Tour chapter)

Constant Striving Spirit of Sah Bendong during War of Resistance against Japan (see Sah Bendong chapter)

Spirit of Devotion to Science (the late President Wang Yanan (Economics Chapter) and the late Prof. Chen Jinrun (Chemistry chapter)

A Double Portion of Tan Kah-kee's Spirit

Innovative education is of course nothing new at XMU. Our university has pioneered all elements of modern education ever since it was founded in 1921 by the "Henry Ford of Asia," Mr. Tan Kah Kee. This famous Overseas Chinese patriot gave an estimated USD 100 million to education, thanks to his business acumen and frugal lifestyle. But Mr. Tan left us much more than mere money.

Organizational Behavior teaches that organizational cultures often reflect the personalities of their founders, and XMU is certainly no exception. XMU's 85 years of success show it has inherited a double portion of Mr. Tan's spirit and vision for a better China, a better Asia, and a better humanity.

第2章
校主陈嘉庚
—— "亚洲的亨利·福特"

厦大的四种独特精神
◎陈嘉庚先生的爱国主义精神（见本章）；

◎罗扬才烈士的革命献身主义精神（见第九章）；

◎抗日战争期间内迁闽西艰苦办学的自强精神（见第三章）；

◎以王亚南校长、陈景润教授为代表的科学精神（见第九、第二十一章）。

嘉庚精神永示后人
厦大一贯推崇创新教育。自 1921 年被称作"亚洲的亨利·福特"的陈嘉庚建校以来，厦大在现代教育的很多方面走在前列。这位名扬商界、生活节俭的爱国华侨一生倾资约 1 亿美元兴办教育，而他留给我们的却远远超过金钱本身。

"组织行为学"课程中讲，一个集体的性格通常能反映其创建者的性格，厦大当然也不例外。厦大85年来的成功表明，她传承了嘉庚精神，嘉庚精神为我们展现了更伟大的中国、更团结的亚洲和更美好的人性。

Our university's founder, Mr. Tan Kah Kee (Chen Jiageng, 1874-1961), gave an estimated 100 million USD to education but was born into a humble family of merchants in Jimei Village, across from Xiamen Island. Tan worked the fields and the fishnets until he started school at age nine, and in the fall of 1890 moved to Singapore to help in his father's rice shop. His father's business went under in 1904, but the savvy son pulled together enough capital to buy 500 acres of forested land in Singapore and started a pineapple plantation.

The Rubber Magnate Tan rapidly expanded into rice milling, manufacturing, sawmills, real estate, and ocean transport, but it was rubber that really stretched his fortune. He set aside a few acres of his pineapple plantation and eventually had 10,000 acres of rubber trees. His expansion from rubber planting to rubber manufacturing helped create the rubber industry and made him one of the four great Rubber Barons.

By the mid 1920s, the Rubber Magnate's Singapore-based empire employed over 30,000 people, had 150 offices on 5 continents, and did business with 48 countries. But prices plummeted after 1926 and rubber never quite bounced back. Even worse, after Mr. Tan protested Japan's brutal "Jinan Massacre" (May 3rd, 1928), his factory was burned to the ground. Yet even as he struggled through the Great Depression he continued to finance Jimei School, Xiamen University, and Chinese and English schools in Singapore—a feat he managed in part because of his frugality.

第2章 校主陈嘉庚——"亚洲的亨利·福特"

校主陈嘉庚先生（1874—1961）出生在集美社（即现在厦门集美区），他少时从事农渔劳作，直至九岁进入学堂。1890年秋，17岁的陈嘉庚到新加坡协助其父经营米店生意。1904年家道中落，聪明的他筹集了资金在新加坡购置了500英亩林地作为菠萝种植园。

橡胶业巨子

自此，他迅速涉足多个行业——熟米加工业、手工业、伐木业、房地产业以及海运业，然而真正使其获得巨大利润的是橡胶。他预留几英亩菠萝园套种橡胶树，并最终将其扩大到万亩之多。从橡胶种植业到橡胶制造业的拓展有助于他创办橡胶产业，并使其成为东南亚四大橡胶大王之一。

至20世纪20年代中期，总部设在新加坡的橡胶公司雇佣工人达3万多，150家代理商遍布五大洲，并与48个国家建立了贸易往来。但是，自1926年起橡胶价格暴跌，橡胶利润江河日下。1928年4月3日，日军制造了"济南惨案"，陈嘉庚强烈谴责这一暴行，之后，他的工厂被焚为灰烬，这无疑是雪上加霜。大萧条时期他惨淡经营，却一如既往地资助集美学校、厦门大学和新加坡的多所华文和英文学校——这一奇迹在某种程度上源于他的节俭。

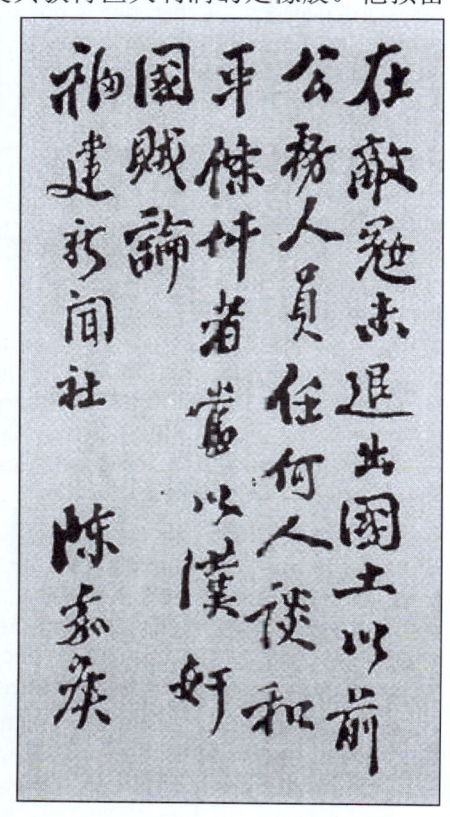

The Frugal Philanthropist

Rich philanthropists generally give but a fraction of their wealth while alive, but leave behind large foundations since the only thing they can take with them when they die is their reputation. But Mr. Tan quite literally gave like a prince and lived like a pauper, subsisting on little more than rice porridge and potatoes, and using the same umbrella and battered suitcases for decades. Other rich Chinese of his day built luxurious villas on nearby Gulangyu Islet, but Mr. Tan contented himself with a simpler home in his native Jimei. As he wrote to a relative, his hometown still had great needs and "I cannot put myself before the community."

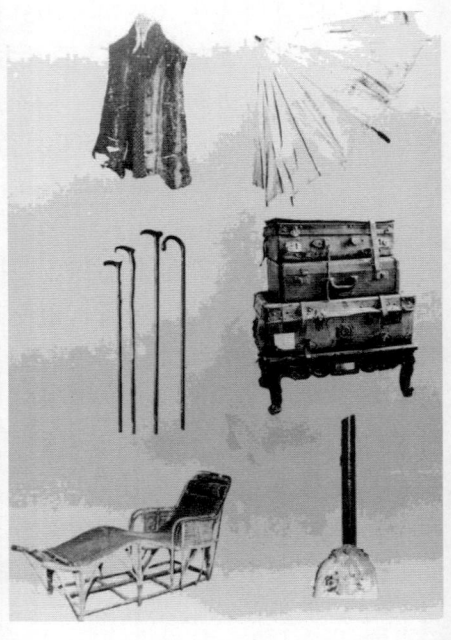

The Japanese destroyed Tan's home in 1938, and when the government offered to rebuild it after Liberation, Tan insisted that war-damaged school buildings be rebuilt first. His home was finally renovated in 1955 and he lived there from 1958 until he moved to Beijing in 1960. Tan's house was restored to its original design in 1980 and is now a museum and meeting place for the Jimei School Committee. The most moving exhibits are the battered suitcases, umbrellas and worn-out shoes that the "pauper millionaire" used for decades.

Mr. Tan's Vision for China Mr. Tan was a social and political reformer from youth. He supported Sun Yat-sen, and at one point accounted for about 1/3 of the Kuomintang's finances (a feat he no doubt regretted when Chiang Kai Shek absconded to Taiwan with his money and everyone else's). But Tan's greatest hope for China was in modern education.

In 1894, at age 21, Tan began a family school in Jimei. In 1912, during the first year of the new Republic of China, Tan returned to China and on January 27, 1913 opened the Jimei Primary School. Between 1920 and 1926 he opened a school a year until Jimei School Village had 11 schools, including a middle school and schools in agriculture, commerce, forestry, navigation, etc. In addition, Jimei School Village's education promotion department donated to more than 70 middle schools and primary schools throughout Fujian province.

第2章　校主陈嘉庚——"亚洲的亨利·福特"

清贫的慈善家

有些富有的慈善家生前施与小部分家财，死后设立大笔基金求得一个好名声，因为只有名誉可以流芳百世。然而陈嘉庚真正做到了倾囊而出，竭尽所有。他像王子般慷慨地施与，却像乞丐般清贫地生活。他甘于每餐只吃番薯和稀饭，甘于一把雨伞和破旧的手提箱一用就是几十年。同时期的富商在附近的鼓浪屿岛上大建豪宅，而他却安于集美老家简朴的住所。正像他给亲戚的信中所说，他的家乡仍然迫切需要资助，"吾未可凌驾于民众之上"。

1938年日本人炸毁了陈嘉庚的家。解放后，中国政府提出重建陈宅，他却坚持战乱中被毁的校舍应优先重建。直到1955年他的住宅才得以修葺，陈嘉庚从1958年起居住在此直到1960年去北京。陈宅于1980年修回原样，现已成为纪念馆和集美学村集会的地方。纪念馆陈列品中最让人感动的是这位"清贫的百万富翁"用了几十年的旧手提箱、雨伞和他那穿了几十年早已破旧不堪的鞋子。

陈嘉庚对中国的期望

陈嘉庚自青年时期起就为社会政治变革而奋斗。他支持孙中山，并一度为国民党提供三分之一的资金支持（当蒋介石携钱财逃至台湾时，陈肯定感到后悔）。但是陈嘉庚先生将对中国最强烈的感情和最殷切的希望寄予了现代教育。

1894年，21岁的陈嘉庚在集美创办了惕斋学塾。他于1912年回国，并于1913年1月27日创办集美小学。从1920年到1926的七年间，他每年开办一所学校，直到集美学村拥有了11所学校，包括一所中学和农业、商业、林业、航海等校。除此之外，集美学村教育促进会还捐资给福建省的70多所中小学，办学兴教。

Supporting Education Abroad Tan also began or funded at least seven schools in Singapore, including Tao Nan (1907), Ai Tong (1912), Chung Fook Girls School (1915), Chung Poon (1915), the Singapore Chinese High School (1918), Nanyang Normal School (1941) and Nan Chiao Girls High School (1947). . His largesse was not limited to Chinese schools. He gave $30,000 to the Anglo-Chinese School in 1919 and $10,000 in 1941 to Raffles College, which later merged with the Medical College and eventually became the University of Singapore.

Xiamen University—the Apple of Tan's Eye In early November, 1920, Mr. Tan offered one million Yuan to start XMU, which began with the Normal and Commerce Departments, and later expanded to five Colleges and 17 departments in Literature, Science, Law, Commerce and Education. Xiamen University captured the imagination of Chinese and foreigners alike. In the 1920s, Paul Hutchinson wrote,

> "This school [Xiamen University] is entirely a Chinese institution, with no foreign teachers and no foreign connections, and right out in a small Chinese village. The course of study is being made very practical... When we think of the future days, it is one of the most encouraging things to be seen in the whole of China."

Mr. Tan emphasized quality education. He sent students abroad, hired teachers from other areas, purchased the latest equipment, and emphasized sports. By the spring of 1937, his financial fortunes had so suffered that he allowed the government to take over XMU, but he continued to subsidize it. Tan wrote to the minister of education that he had had "a fine start and a poor finish," and would "live in perpetual regret." [If only he could see XMU today!]

That same year, XMU relocated to Changting in West Fujian to escape destruction by the Japanese, who had occupied Xiamen. (Read more in the next chapter). The Japanese surrendered in August, 1945, and on October 21, 500 mass organizations in Singapore welcomed Tan's return from a decade of exile in Java. A large meeting in Chongqing on November 18, 1945, celebrated Mr. Tan's safety, and Chairman Mao inscribed a scroll about Tan which read, "Banner of Overseas Chinese, Glory of the Nation."

第2章 校主陈嘉庚——"亚洲的亨利·福特"

支持海外办学

在新加坡陈嘉庚建立或资助了至少7所学校，包括道南学校（1907）、爱同学校（1912）、崇福女校（1915）、崇本学校（1915）、新加坡华侨中学（1918）、南洋师范学校（1941）和南侨女中（1947）。他的慷慨捐赠不只局限于华文

Daonan School (Singapore)

学校，1919年他倾资3万美元资助英华学校，1941年捐资1万美元给莱佛士学院，后来该学院与医学院合并，最终成为新加坡大学。

厦门大学——陈嘉庚的掌上明珠

1920年11月初，陈先生捐资100万元创办厦门大学，最初设立师范和商学两部，后来扩展到文、理、法、商、教育五院十七系。厦门大学实现了海内外人士的共同理想。20世纪20年代，保罗·哈钦森这样写道：

> "这所学校（厦门大学）是一个名副其实的中国学校，没有外籍教师，没有海外关系，而且地处中国一个小村庄。学科设置实用性很强……想到未来，这是整个中国最振奋人心的事物之一。"

陈先生高度重视教学质量。他派遣留学生，从各地聘任教师，购进最新教学设备，注重体育教学。可是，到1937年春，陈嘉庚经济处境已十分窘迫了，只好同意政府接管厦门大学，但他仍旧继续予以资助。他在写给教育部部长的信中，说自己是"虎头蛇尾，为义不终"，并将为之"抱憾终生"。（要是他能看一眼今天的厦大就好了！）

同年，日军占领厦门。为避免日军破坏，厦门大学内迁福建西部的长汀。（详见下章）1945年8月，日本投降，同年10月21日，新加坡500个华侨社团欢迎陈嘉庚结束爪哇的流亡生活回到新加坡。1945年11月18日，陈嘉庚安全返回新加坡庆祝大会在重庆召开。毛主席赠予条幅，题写"华侨旗帜，民族光辉"。

XMU returned to Xiamen after Japan's defeat and the new president and eminent biologist, Dr. Wang Deyao, immediately set out rebuilding and expanding the campus. Tan's vision and money and Wang's leadership paid off. XMU was designated a key national university in 1963 and has been mushrooming ever since.

On October 1, 1949, Chairman Mao invited Mr. Tan to Tiananmen to participate in the ceremony of the founding of the People's Republic of China. Tan settled down in his homeland in 1950 and devoted the rest of his life and fortune to its reconstruction.

Tan's Final Years　During his last years Mr. Tan served in many posts, including Chairman of Returning Overseas Chinese League, Member of the Standing Committee of the National People's Congress, and Vice-Chairman of the CPPCC. He was also responsible for innovations like China's first sea-spanning bridge (the award-winning Xiamen-Jimei bridge), the Jimei Dragon Boat Pool, which has hosted numerous domestic and international aquatic events, and Jimei's 15 storey Nanxun Building, which has a navigational light on the roof to guide fishermen safely home.

Mr. Tan died of cancer in 1961, and after a State Funeral in Beijing, a special train transported his body to his hometown of Jimei. Tan left behind three million Yuan in banks, but the man who gave like a prince and lived like a pauper evidently expected his descendants to do the same—or make their own fortune. He left no money to his family, but gave half a million to Jimei School Foundation, half a million to construct Beijing's Overseas Chinese Museum, and over two million Yuan for education.

Tan's International Legacy　Altogether, Mr. Tan gave an estimated 100 million USD towards education, both in China and abroad, and the Tan Kah Kee Foundation has been awarding a Postgraduate Scholarship since 1983. In 1986, Nobel Prize Laureate Prof. C.N. Yang set up the Tan Kah Kee Inventors' Award, and in 1992, Prof Yang and two other Nobel Prize Laureates, Prof Samuel C.C. Ting and Prof Li Yuan Tseh, together with Prof Chang-lin Tien, former Vice-chancellor of the University of California at Berkeley, and Prof Wang Gungwu, former President of Hong Kong University, set up the Tan Kah Kee International Society Foundation to the advancement of education and culture in the spirit of Tan Kah Kee.

第 2 章　校主陈嘉庚——"亚洲的亨利·福特"

日本投降后,厦门大学回迁至原址。新任校长、杰出生物学家汪德耀立即着手重建并扩建校园。陈先生的远见卓识、资金支持以及汪校长的卓越领导终见成效。1963 年,厦门大学被确定为国家重点大学,并不断成长壮大。

1949 年 10 月 1 日,陈嘉庚先生应毛主席之邀到天安门参加开国大典。1950 年他定居故乡,为重建家乡捐出家财,奉献余生。

陈嘉庚的晚年

晚年的陈嘉庚担任过多种职务,包括中华全国归国华侨联合会主席、全国人大常委会委员和全国政协副主席。他还负责新兴项目的建设,例如中国首座海峡大桥(享誉殊荣的高集海堤),屡次举办国内国际水上活动的集美龙舟池,以及集美 15 层的南薰楼。顶层建有灯塔,引导渔民安全归来。

1961 年陈嘉庚先生因癌症与世长辞。在北京举行国葬之后,由专列将陈先生的灵柩运回故乡集美安葬。陈先生遗留银行存款 300 万元。但很显然,这位像王子一般慷慨施与,却像乞丐般清贫度日的慈善家希望他的子孙后代做与他同样的事情——或是白手起家,自己赚钱。他没有给家人留下一分钱,却将 50 万元充作集美学校基金,50 万元捐作北京华侨博物馆的建筑费,剩余的 200 多万元用于教育。

陈嘉庚留给世界的财富

陈嘉庚累计捐资约一亿美元用于海内外的教育事业。自 1983 年以来,陈嘉庚基金为研究生提供奖学金。1986 年诺贝尔奖获得者杨振宁先生设立陈嘉庚发明奖,1992 杨教授与其他两位诺贝尔奖得主——丁肇中教授和李远哲教授,以及美国加州大学伯克利分校前校长田长霖教授,香港大学前校长王赓武教授共同设立陈嘉庚国际协会基金,发扬陈嘉庚先生的精神,推进文化教育事业的发展。

In 1991, Singapore's president, Dr. Wee Kim Wee, launched the University Endowment Fund in honor of Mr. Tan, and set a goal of raising 1$ billion for education.

On 11 March, 1990, the International Asteroid Center of China named Asteroid 2963 "Tan Kah Kee Star." The naming ceremony was held at XMU.

Lastly, the School of Chemistry in my home state's University of California, Berkeley, has a "Tan Kah Kee Hall." We hope more and more foreigners and Chinese alike will come to understand, and emulate, Tan Kah Kee's spirit of sacrificial giving.

Lee Kong Chian　　Tan Kah Kee was a role model for many Chinese both at home and abroad, including one of XMU's greatest benefactors, his son-in-law Lee Kong Chian (Lee Kong Chian, 1893-1967).

Lee was shivering on a ship deck the first time he saw his future father-in-law. Mr. Tan had announced he was giving blankets to anyone sharing his family surname ("Chen"). Many freezing folk became Chens on the spot! But when Mr. Tan asked one shivering youth why he'd not taken a blanket, he said he wasn't a Chen. Mr. Tan was so moved by his honesty that he announced anyone could have a blanket, regardless of surname.

That honest youth was Lee Kong Chian, who was born in Furong village of Nan'an (just north of Xiamen). Lee joined his father in Singapore in 1903 and studied in the Anglo-Tamil School, Yung Cheng School, St. Joseph's School and Tao Nan Chinese School. He was awarded a scholarship for Nanjing's Chi Nan University in 1908 and returned to China in 1909. In 1911 he attended Beijing's prestigious Qinghua University and then transferred to Tangshan's Railway and Mining College.

After returning to Singapore Lee worked as a teacher in Tao Nan School and Yung Cheng School, and translator for a Chinese newspaper. He joined Tan Kah Kee's Guohua Company in 1915, and while Tan was talking with him one day they overheard others trying to communicate with a foreigner. Lee stepped in and translated, impressing Tan with his abilities and initiative. Tan took the young Lee under his wing, tutored him in business, made him head of the Tan Kah Kee Rubber Company's department, and sealed their partnership forever by giving Lee his daughter in marriage, though the only way Tan could get the humble Li to accept her was by asking someone else to broach the subject!).

第2章 校主陈嘉庚——"亚洲的亨利·福特"

1991年，为纪念陈嘉庚先生，新加坡前总统黄金辉博士创立大学捐赠基金，并确定了为教育筹款10亿美元的目标。

1990年3月11日，中国国际小行星中心将2963号行星命名为"陈嘉庚星"，命名仪式在厦门大学举行。

还有，在美国加州大学伯克利分校的化学学院里，有一座"陈嘉庚楼"。真是希望越来越多的中外人士能够了解他的崇高品格，弘扬陈嘉庚先生无私奉献的精神。

李光前

Photo: SMU 新加坡管理大学

陈嘉庚先生为全世界华人树立了光辉典范。其爱婿李光前就是其追随者之一，为厦大做出了巨大的贡献。

二人初次相见，李光前正蜷缩在甲板上冻得瑟瑟发抖。陈嘉庚已吩咐给所有的陈姓乘客每人发一条毯子。此时天气极冷，乘客早已纷纷冒姓领取。而陈嘉庚看到这个年轻人冻得打战，便忙问他为何不领毯子，他回答说自己不姓陈。年轻人的诚实深深打动了陈嘉庚，于是他吩咐所有的乘客，不分姓氏，都可以领到毯子。

这个诚实的青年名叫李光前，生于南安（厦门北）的芙蓉乡。1903年随父到新加坡。他曾先后就读于英印学堂、养正学堂、圣·约瑟夫学堂和道南中文学堂。1908年获得入读南京暨南学堂的公费资助并于1909年回国。1911年就读于享誉盛名的北京清华学堂，其后转入唐山路矿学堂。

返回新加坡后，李光前执教于道南学堂、养正学堂，兼任一家华文报社电讯翻译，1915年加盟中华国货公司。一天，李光前正在与陈嘉庚交谈，无意中听到有人正试图与外国人交流，他于是上前充当翻译。李光前的才干和主动性给陈嘉庚留下了深刻的印象。陈嘉庚将其收入麾下，授之以经商之道，并聘任他为陈氏橡胶公司经理，后又将女儿嫁给李光前，从此永久"合作"。（陈嘉庚当时可是动用了"媒妁之言"才使出身卑微的李光前接受了自己的女儿！）

Lee launched his Lee Rubber Company in 1931 and was soon known as the Rubber and Pineapple King. One of the richest men in Southeast Asia, he expanded into banking and real estate, and in 1952 became Chairman of the Overseas Chinese Banking Corporation.

Lee donated 10% of the funds needed to set up the University of Malaya in October, 1949, and in 1958 the university awarded Li an honorary degree of law. Lee also set up the Lee Foundation, which between 1952 and 1993 donated over $300 million USD, 75% of which went to education.

In 1962 Lee became the University of Singapore's first chancellor and contributed $1 million Singapore dollars to construct a medical college. Lee funded such diverse institutes as St. Margaret's School, Methodist Girls' School, Kuo Chuan Presbyterian Primary and Secondary School, and the National University of Singapore. He also chaired the Chinese High School from 1934 to 1957 and kept it running in spite of many attempts to shut it down.

Lee gave classes at night while working for the government by day, and when stranded in the U.S. during World War II, he lectured at Columbia University.

Like his mentor Tan Kah Kee, Lee also financed education in his homeland. In 1939 he founded the Guozhuan primary school in his home village of Furong, and in 1943 set up the Guoguang secondary school. Between 1950 and 1954 he contributed towards Tan Kah Kee's Jimei schools and Xiamen University (Lee built the five beautiful granite buildings overlooking the sea).

Lee died in 1967 at age 74, but his entrepreneur spirit and social conscience live on in institutes like the Singapore Management University, which has a Lee Kong Chian School of Business.

1931 年李光前创立李氏橡胶公司,并迅速以"橡胶大王"和"菠萝大王"名扬天下,成为东南亚的巨富之一,后又涉足银行业和房地产业。1952 年他出任新加坡中华总商会主席一职。

1949 年 10 月,李光前捐助了马来亚大学建校资金的 10%。该校于 1958 年授予他名誉法学教授学位。李先生还设立了李氏基金会。该基金会从 1934 年到 1957 年捐资 3 亿美元,其中的 70%用于教育事业。

1962 年,李光前成为新加坡大学首任校长,并斥资 100 万新币建立医学院。他还资助了多所院校,如圣·玛格丽特大学,卫理公会女校、国专长老会中小学、新加坡国立大学。1934 年到 1957 年他任华侨中学董事会主席,不顾重重阻挠坚持办学。

李光前晚间教学,白天在政府供职。二战期间曾滞留在美国,任教于哥伦比亚大学。

和陈嘉庚一样,李光前也资助家乡办学。1939 年和 1943 年,他相继在家乡芙蓉乡建立国专小学和国光中学。1950 年到 1954 年五年间,他为陈嘉庚所建的集美学校和厦门大学不断捐资(厦大建南楼群五座楼的兴建来自李光前的捐资)。

李光前于 1967 年逝世,享年 74 岁。新加坡管理大学设有"李光前商学院"。他的企业家精神和社会责任感永世长存,激励后人。

Tan Kah-Kee and Li Quangqian

Dr. Lim Boon-keng (1869-1957), "Sage of Singapore"
(From *Discover Gulangyu*)

Kipling said East and West would never meet, but they did meet in the 2nd president of XMU, Dr. Lin Wenqing, who was called Sage of Singapore by Chinese and foreigners alike. XMU's founder, Tan Kak Kee, wrote that Lin was "well versed in Western materialistic sciences and Chinese cultural spirit."

Educated first in a Hakka temple and then at Raffles Institution, Lin was the first Chinese awarded the Queen's Scholarship, and earned first class honors in medicine at the University of Edinburgh. But while Westerners admired Lin, the Chinese at Edinburgh spurned him because of his poor written and spoken Mandarin Chinese. According to some sources, English remained his strongest language, and when he gave a speech at Xiamen University in 1926 he had to use an interpreter! But we know that he did master at least Minnan Dialect and Cantonese.

In 1905, Lin set up a private hospital for prostitutes and founded the Anti-Opium Society (ironic, since both his father and China-born grandfather were opium farmers). Lin excelled at business, particularly the rubber industry, shipping and banking, and helped found the Singapore Chinese Chamber of Commerce. A pioneer Chinese financier, he partnered with Huang Yizhu to start the Hefeng Bank and Overseas Chinese Bank. Westerners and Chinese alike sought the Sage's wisdom. He was adviser to the British in the Legislative Council and the Chinese Advisory Board, and attended the coronations of King Edward VII in 1902 and King George V in 1911. Lin really showed his colors during World War I when he raised funds for the Prince of Wales relief fund and for war planes, and in 1918 was awarded the Order of the British Empire.

Lin Wen Qing's Home Gulangyu Home (Photo by Andrea See)

林文庆博士（1869—1957）——"新加坡贤哲"

（摘自《魅力鼓浪屿》）

鲁耶尔·吉卜林说，东、西方永远碰不到一块儿。然而，厦门大学的第二任校长林文庆教授却能将这二者融会贯通。中外人士一致推崇他为"新加坡贤哲"。厦门大学的创始人陈嘉庚评述林文庆时写道："（他）能通西洋物质之科学兼具中国文化之精神。"

林文庆最早就读于福建会馆，而后升入莱佛士学院，成为获得女皇奖学金的第一个中国人。后来在爱丁堡大学学医，获得最高荣誉。正当西方人钦佩林文庆时，爱丁堡大学的中国人却因林文庆蹩脚的汉语笔头和口头表达能力而对他嗤之以鼻。根据某些资料所说，英语仍是他最强的语言。1926年他在厦大做演讲时还不得不靠人翻译呢！但我们知道，他至少懂得粤语和闽南语。

1905年，林文庆开了一家为娼妓治病的私立医院，并创立了"反鸦片社团"（具有讽刺意味的是，他的父亲和出生于中国的祖父竟都是种鸦片的）。林文庆善于经营生意，尤其在橡胶、船运和银行等行业收入颇丰。他还参与创立"新加坡中华总商会"。作为华人金融家先驱，他和黄奕住合资创建"和丰银行"和"华侨银行"。中国人和西方人都推崇这位贤哲的智慧。他当过英国立法院顾问及中国顾问团顾问，出席过1902年爱德华七世和1911年乔治五世的加冕典礼。林文庆在一战期间表现出色，为威尔士王子救济基金和购置战斗机筹款，于1918年获得大不列颠帝国勋章。

In 1900, Lin helped found the Straits Chinese British Association (of which he was elected president twice). He also started the Chinese "Philomathic" Society for the study of Chinese language, Western Music, and English literature, and the Singapore Chinese Girls' School. And perhaps because of his own difficulty in mastering Mandarin, he urged that Chinese children be taught in Mandarin, even going so far as to organize Mandarin language classes in his own home.

Lin was XMU president from 1921 until 1937, but after returning to Singapore he suffered greatly at the hands of the Japanese, who tortured his wife to force him into working for them. In 1949, Lin became the first president of the China Society, and supported that work until his death on New Year's Day in 1957. He left 3/5 of his estate, including his Brush Mountain home, to XMU. The estate is run down nowadays, but still holds a special place in the hearts of those grateful for this man who wrought great change in the lives of Chinese both at home and abroad.

Dr. Lin in a Foreigner's Eyes
(by Averil Mckenzie, Gulangyu resident, 1920s)

"A year previously, Dr. Lim Boon Keng had been appointed President of the new University of Amoy. A graduate in medicine of Edinburgh University, he no longer practiced, but still lived part of the year in Singapore, where he had once done so, and it was there that we first met him and his wife. In Kulangsu, they and their family occupied a house delightfully set in a garden on one of the highest points of the island. A few days after our arrival we ate there. The Lim family's friendship endures to this day, so I cannot, with any certainty, recall of what we talked. I remember the catholic collection of English books on the ground floor, cockroach-scraped and silver-fish-nibbled, as all our books became, but all well-used and alive; and above, the billowing of white curtains, high and airily in white light; Mrs. Lim's dark hair and poised grace against white walls, and the agony of a mouthful of chili sauce which I mistook for tomato.

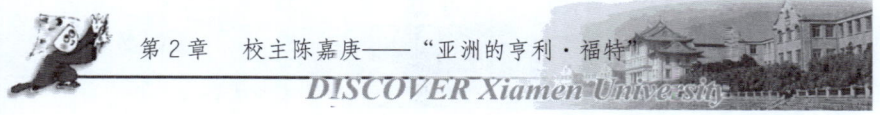

1900年,林文庆参与创立"海峡英籍华人公会",两次当选为该会主席。他还创办了"华人好学社团",开展中文、西方音乐和英国文学等学科的学习活动,还创办了"新加坡华人女子学校"。也许是由于他本人汉语学得不理想,他竭力主张华人应从小开始学习汉语,甚至在自己家里组织汉语学习班。

从1921年到1937年,林文庆担任厦门大学校长。卸任后返回新加坡,却落入日本人之手,深受磨难。日本人拷打他的妻子,逼他为他们做事。1949年,他成为"中华社团"的第一任主席,一直到1957年元旦去世为止。他将五分之三的房产捐给厦大,鼓浪屿笔架山的房子也在捐赠之列。那座老房子如今已经破旧不堪了,但因其主人曾经谋求改善海内外华人的生活,它在对林心存感念的人们心中仍占有特别的位置。

一个外国人眼里的林博士

(摘自《绿姜根》,Averil Mckenzie 著,20世纪20年代鼓浪屿居民)

"一年前,林文庆教授被任命为厦门大学校长。尽管他是爱丁堡大学的医科毕业生,他已不再行医了,但仍像以前那样,一年当中他还是有一段时间在新加坡度过。也正是在新加坡,我第一次见到他和他太太。在鼓浪屿,他家拥有一座舒适的房子,坐落在岛上一制高点的花园里。我们到达几天后在那儿吃了一次饭。我与林家的友谊延续至今,所以我无法准确回忆起那天我们都谈了些什么。我记得,存放在一楼的各种英文藏书已被蟑螂咬出碎屑,也被蠹虫蛀过,就像我们所有的书那样,只不过因主人经常翻阅而显出生气。在高处,白色窗帘在白光中轻快地飞扬。林太太仪态典雅,乌黑的头发与白墙形成鲜明的反衬。还有,我错将辣椒酱当作番茄酱吃了一大口,痛苦不堪。"

"Dr. Lim was short, square, with large, mild brown eyes, but he was a fighter of astonishing range and vigor. Apart from his continuous battle for Western concepts of hygiene against ignorant and superstitious colleagues when he was medical adviser to the Minister of the Interior and Inspector-General of the Peking hospital under the Chinese Government, he had championed any number of causes unrelated to his profession. One of these campaigns had been against pigtails. In this he was not alone but we felt that for him, as a Fukienese, it was particularly appropriate because, for more than two hundred years after the defeat of Koxinga and his supporters in 1683, the Fukienese peasants, forced to be 'tartarized' and to wear queues, coiled these symbols of subjection round their heads and hid them under turbans.

"Dr. Lim had traveled both to widen his own and other people's [views]…As a vigorous advocate for the adoption of kuo-yu, he had gone to Java to preach its benefits to the Chinese schools there. He and Mrs. Lim had explored Europe as well as attending the German, French and Italian medical conferences to which he was officially delegated. He was one of the first to urge his countrymen in Malaya to plant rubber, and was always ready to pursue new ideas offered by friends or books. 'Reading,' he would say, 'and the cultivation of friends are as a fan to the flame of the mind and make it burn more brightly.' He had what I, as a European, can only call a Latin enthusiasm. It was, I suspect, as much for this comprehending eagerness as for his medical skill, that Sun Yat-sen had chosen him as a private secretary as well as physician. But with all his preoccupations for the future of his countrymen he never undervalued his country's past and her perennial philosophy. He had published various books on Confucianism, and a few years after we met, I was to engrave a frontispiece for his translation of the classic Li Sao [Dr. Lim died at the age of 88, in Singapore, shortly after I wrote this chapter]."

第2章 校主陈嘉庚——"亚洲的亨利·福特"

"林教授长得矮矮壮壮,一对棕色的大眼睛流露着温和的神情。但他在诸多领域却是个斗志旺盛的斗士。在担任中国政府内务部医学顾问和北京医院总监时,他坚持用西方的卫生保健观念来反击愚昧和迷信团体。除此之外,他还在一些与他的专业无关的领域尖坚持真理而进行斗争。其中一项是反对留辫子。在这一点上,他并不孤立。但我们觉得,林文庆作为一个福建人,这样做是情理之中的事情。因为,在郑成功和他的支持者们 1683 年失利以后的两百多年里,福建的父老乡亲被迫'满人化'、留长辫,他们将这意味着被异族统治的标志物盘在头上,包裹在头巾里。"

"林教授游历各地,既为开阔自己的眼界,也为扩展别人的视野……作为一个极力推广国语的倡导者,他奔赴爪哇,向那里的华人学校宣传国语的种种好处。他被公派到德国、法国和意大利出席医学会议时,和他太太游历了欧洲。他是第一个力促马来亚的华人种植橡胶的,他也时刻准备探讨朋友或书本所提供的新思想。他说,读书和交友如一把扇子,可以使思想的火苗燃烧得更亮堂。以我作为一个欧洲人看来,他具有一种拉丁式的热情。我猜想,孙逸仙选择他作为机要秘书兼医官,不单是看重他的医学技能,同样也器重他追求真理的那份渴望。他关心国人的未来,从未轻视自己国家的历史及其世代传承的民族哲学。他出版过诸多关于儒家思想的书。在我们认识几年后,我曾打算为他的译作楚辞《离骚》雕刻一幅卷首插图。(在我写完这章后不久,林教授在新加坡去世,享年88岁。)。"

Chapter 3

Dr. Sa Bendong & Changting Xiamen University
By Prof. Zheng Daochuan;
edited by Prof. Zhengqiwu
(a rough translation from the Chinese)

Dr. Sa Bendong, XMU's first president after it became a state university, was a famous physicist, an international engine expert, a preeminent educationalist, and at 35-years-old China's youngest university president—but the Anti-Japanese War broke out across China the day after he became president.

Dr. Sa shouldered the burden of moving XMU several hundred miles from the coast of Fujian to mountainous Changting, in Fujian's far west. Once faculty, students and workers were settled, he labored to lead the university forward under very trying conditions, and by early 1940, our exiled XMU had already won praise as "the most prosperous university east of Calcutta, India". XMU owed its great progress to Sa Bendong, who paid for it with his life. He literally worked himself to death, dying in 1949 at age 47.

萨 本 栋
Sa Bendong
(1937年7月—1945年8月)

From 1940 to 1944, I studied in the Economics Department of Changting XMU. My love for literature brought me into frequent contact with the dramatist Wang Meng'ou, the president's secretary. Wang told me about Sa's overwork, and I saw with my own eyes that Sa stayed in his office very late. Clearly, Mr Sa worked for the University with all his heart and all his strength. I was deeply moved by ten aspects of Dr. Sa's character:

第3章

萨本栋和抗战时期的厦门大学

郑 道 传

（郑启五整理）

作为中国近代著名的物理学家、国际杰出的电机专家与卓越的教育家的萨本栋教授，是厦门大学从私立改国立后的第一任校长，1937年7月6日受命，翌日，抗日战争全面爆发。这位年仅35岁的全国最年轻的校长上任不久，即挑起厦大从福建沿海迁往数百里之外的闽西山区——长汀县的重担，紧接着便是在长汀艰苦的条件下进行一系列的安顿、恢复和发展，校务蒸蒸日上。20世纪40年代初，厦大即获得了海外友人"加尔各答以东最佳大学"的美誉。遗憾的是，萨校长因操劳过度，1949年初不幸英年早逝。时年47岁。

1940—1944年，我有幸就读于长汀厦门大学经济系。由于我爱好文学，与戏剧家王梦鸥先生结下忘年之交。王梦鸥长期担任萨校长的秘书，在与王的交往中，我时常耳闻萨校长呕心沥血办校的事，加上自己的亲眼目睹，就树立了萨校长在我心目中非凡的形象。

1. An Official Who Never Put on Airs   Although the Kuomintang government was thoroughly corrupt at that time, President Sa was an official of integrity. He never put on airs at government meetings or during university speeches. He was a "brief appointment officer" of the second rank under the Kuomintang civil servants system. This system included special appointment officers (first rank), brief appointment officers (second rank), recommendatory appointment officers (third rank) and commissioned officers (last rank). Mr Sa was also the central government supervisor for the Three Pioneers League. In other words, he was a high official, but he was amiable, easy-going and approachable.

President Sa lived a frugal life. He always wore an old gray suit and a pair of out-of-fashion shoes. He was humble and well liked. Whenever and wherever students asked him questions, he always gave a reasonable answer without thinking twice. I remember that Mr Sa lived in a simple cottage with a tiled roof. His cottage had no glass window panes, and were hung with old ragged cloths. His wife did all of the housework for the family of four.

A narrow alley and pebbled path led from his home to his office. I frequently saw him hurrying out very early and returning home very late. Though the university authorized him an old car, he said the maintenance would be too costly and that he should set an example by saving every penny he could for the university. Later, Dr. Sa dismantled the car, removed the engine, studied it closely with other technicians, and successfully converted it into an electric generator. Only because of President Sa did Changting XMU finally enjoy electricity, and students were able to study at night in brightly lit classrooms.

第3章　萨本栋和抗战时期的厦门大学

1.当官不像官

在那时的官场上，摆架子，讲派头，比比皆是。萨校长却不是这样。他时任简任官（国民党政府的文职官员分为特任、简任、荐任和委任等各阶），又是三青团的中央监察，但他平易近人，没有官架子，同学们都说他不像一位简任官。

萨校长衣着平平，常穿一套褪色的布西装，一双老式的旧皮鞋。他为人谦和，路遇师生的提问，总是有问必答，而且耐心细致。至今想起，仍历历在目。他住的是木屋瓦房，用粗夏布替代纱窗，连个玻璃也没有。他一家四口，家务都由他夫人亲自操持。

从宿舍到办公室，要穿过一条小巷和一段卵石镶铺的街道，我常见他手提公文包早出晚归的身影。学校教务处当时给他买了一辆旧轿车，但他坚持不用。当时长汀还没有电，师生都用煤油灯照明，萨校长就亲自提着扳手，带上几个技术人员，把那轿车给拆了，把拆下的发动机改装成用于照明的发电机。从此，厦门大学自己发电，使校园里亮起了明亮的灯光。

厦大华侨同学欢迎陈嘉庚莅汀视察留影
Tan Kah Kee Visits Changting XMU

2. Make XMU in South China as Excellent as Qinghua University in North China.

XMU's retreat to Changting presented President Sa with many difficulties. Buildings were in disrepair, and the remote mountainous location was accessible only by bumpy, narrow village paths. But Mr. Sa did not lose heart. On the contrary, as he explained in a clear and passionate letter to one of his closest teachers, he made it his life goal to improve the situation as quickly as possible and make Xiamen University as excellent as Qinghua University in north China.

Sa adopted two measures to reach this goal. One: recruit first-rate teachers. Two: establish a strict management system with clear rules and regulations in plain words. His philosophy required a first-rate university be strict in 6 areas: strict enforcement of rules and regulations; strict in teaching orders; strict student grade promotions, strict teacher promotions; strict distribution of scholarships, and strict with charity funds and relief funds.

To make sure every new term began on schedule, he stipulated one strict and effective enrolment rule: late enrolment was never tolerated. Students late even 5 minutes late were required to wait until the following year to register. With this draconian but effective requirement, it took only one day for each new semester to get under away in proper order.

President Sa also invented a new "time signal system", inspired by sailors' navigation at sea. A large bell rung sharply on the hour insured that even teachers and students without watches could always begin and end classes on time. This bell-clock system was very popular among both teachers and students and was used in Xiamen University right up until 1949.

2. 要把厦大办成"南方清华"

厦大初迁长汀时,只有孤零零的几间旧房陋屋,散落在断壁残垣之中。学校周遭重峦叠嶂,交通闭塞,条件相当艰苦。但萨校长壮志满怀,在写给他老师的信中曾表示要把厦大办成"南方清华"。

他一是建立了一套严格的规章制度,二是组招了一支精干的教职工队伍。在他的理念中,要办好学,规章制度一定要严,教学秩序一定要好。学生的升留级、教师的晋升,以及奖金、救济金的发放都很严明。

为了保证按时开学,他规定了极为严格的注册制度,注册规定的时间哪怕超过 5 分钟,本学期就不得注册,打回老家做"休学"处理。强烈的时间观念使得学校每每一开学,就立刻走上正轨。萨校长还别出心裁,借用轮船在航行中的"海上报时法",敲打时钟,让大多数没有手表的师生按时作息。厦大的这种报时法一直沿用到 1949年。

Prof. Sah at Tsinghua Univ.

To prevent university leaders' relatives from intervening in university administrative affairs, President Sa made a strict rule that "husband and wife are not allowed to both work in XMU at the same time." For example, when the well-known professor Fu Ying was dean of XMU, his wife, Professor Zhang, was not able to teach at XMU even though she was more than qualified. She taught instead at Yong'an, over 100 miles away from her husband Fu Ying. This rule affected President Sa himself. His wife, Lady Huang, who was a female javelin champion in the 1930s, was allowed to teach PE only for a few months as a substitute during an emergency. After XMU hired a new sports teacher, Lady Huang had to give up the job.

President Sa also focused on improving staff efficiency and simplifying the university organization. The president's office had but 4 staff: a secretary, a stenographer, a clerk and a janitor. The teaching affairs office employed only 5 people: a dean, who also had other duties, an enrolment director, two clerks in charge of teaching affairs, and a janitor. Even key departments such as the university library had only a dozen staff members. The number of staff strictly paralleled institution's size. There was no extra staff during the busy enrolment period; the dean of enrolment had to register students himself. There were no overstaffed offices. Every person overworked, and with high efficiency, largely because of president Sa's excellent management.

Under the leadership of President Sa, the technology department developed into the technology institute, and XMU set up the departments of literature, law, business, science and technology, more or less paralleling North China's Qinghua University. Even then, XMU had already become a unique and large public university in South China's Fujian Province.

第3章 萨本栋和抗战时期的厦门大学

为了避免官场特有的裙带风，萨校长特硬性规定"夫妻不能同校工作"。即使像教务长、知名教授傅鹰这样的学校重要人物也一律对待不得列外。傅教授的夫人张教授只好到远离厦大100多里地的永安去工作。萨校长自己更是以身作则：他的夫人黄淑慎女士是一位体育健将，上世纪30年代曾荣获全国女子标枪比赛冠军。她初到长汀时，义务担任了女生体育的指导，后来学校聘到了专任体育教师，她就立即离岗。

萨校长用人以"精兵"为本。校长办公室只有4个人：一个秘书、一个文书、一个职员、一个工友。教务处为5人，处长是兼职的，下有一个注册主任、两个职员分管教务和学务，再外加一个工友。重要的图书馆也不过十几个人。大小机构，因事设人，没有专门当官的闲职。比如注册主任就要亲自动手给学生注册，不另配职员。在萨校长的精心主持和布置下，人员少，效率高，基本没有人浮于事的情况。

经过萨校长几年的精心打造，1940年厦大的理学院扩建为理工学院，使得学校院系的设置文、法、商、理、工俱全，已初具"南方清华"的态势，成为福建独具规模的国立大学。

Sa Bendong at Changting XMU

3. President and Professor Rolled into One It was well known that Mr. Sa was a president and professor rolled into one. Despite his tight administrative schedule, Mr. Sa also taught several important subjects such as *Calculus, Electrical Principles, General Physics*. He also taught freshman English during a shortage of English teachers, compiled many urgently needed textbooks, and mentored seniors' theses writing. For instance, it was under Dr. Sa's tutelage that Chen Zhongzhu, a senior in the Mechanics and Electronics Department, finished his thesis, *Seven Calculate Meter* 《七股算仪》, which was later lauded highly in the U.S.A.

President Sa wrote his physics class lecture preparations in the ancient but precise and clear Chinese language. Not before or since have physics lecture preparations such as his been accepted as scientific literature. While Dr. Sa's registered students enjoyed his fascinating lectures, many others stood outside his classroom window to audit his talks.

Mr Sa had three strict requirements for his young teaching assistants: a solid foundation in general subjects, expertise in one or two majors, and excellence in foreign languages. For example, Mr. Sa demanded that his calculus teaching assistant, who had earned a very high score in the calculus examination only a few years earlier, take calculus again, take down notes, and finish all exercises, even though his calculus students were required to complete only some of the exercises. Mr. Sa gave his teaching assistants regular lessons and assigned homework and recommended reading.

第3章 萨本栋和抗战时期的厦门大学

3. 是校长，也是教授

"是校长，也是教授"，这是全校师生给萨校长的朴实的评语。萨校长是知名的物理学家，学识渊博。尽管校务极为繁忙，但他坚持不脱离教学工作。他一人承担着好几门重要课程，有微积分、电工原理、普通物理学等，英语教师不够时他甚至顶替大一的英语教师。他还编写了大量的教材，填补了战时教材的空缺，并亲自指导本科毕业生写论文。记得机电系1944级毕业生陈中柱的论文《七段算仪》，就是萨校长指导完成的。该论文的观点后来在美国得到了应用和推广。

萨校长教学，用文言文写讲义，简洁而明了，被学生们私下称为"文理并茂，叹为观止"。他讲课深入浅出，生动风趣，引人入胜。常常吸引了不少学生在窗外旁听。他对教师的要求很严格，特别是对青年助教。他的标准是基础要扎实，专业要精湛，外文要过关。如他手下的微积分助教，在学生时代已经学好了这门课，但萨师要他温故而知新，探测精蕴，并亲自督促检查他们把全部习题作完（学生只要求做其中的一部分）。他还定期给助教们上课，布置参考书目。

Changting XMU Meeting Hall

4. Guarding Students During the domestic revolutionary war, Changting County was an important base for the Red Army, and the remains of revolutionary martyrs like Qu Qiubai are buried at the south foot of North Mountain. Revolutionary banners were still plastered on the walls in towns and countryside, and with memories of the revolution fresh, the entire campus rose up in support of the anti-Japanese war. At that time, three girl students were so outstanding in their anti-Japanese campaign that secret agents of the Kuomintang tried many times to arrest them as leftists and asked President Sa's permission. Dr. Sa sternly rebuked the secret agents and thoroughly protected the three girls.

Miss Chen, for example, enrolled in XMU's economics department in 1943 and was both an ardent student and patriot. President Sa often praised and encouraged her, and she earned high scores and received the *Tan Kah Kee* Prize many times. When the Kuomintang secret agents attempted to arrest her as a leftist, Mr. Sa said to them: "This girl studies very hard, but she is not good-looking. She is depressed because she can't find a boyfriend, not because she's a leftist!" In such ways he protected students from the KMT's secret agents.

Mr. Huang Zhenwu, the Commander-in-chief of the provincial public security bureau, came personally to the campus to arrest some so-called leftist students, but Mr. Sa said sternly, "As president, I'm responsible for caring for my students! As a central government committee member, I am entitled to take charge of the so-called leftist students. As long as they are studying at my university, I will not let you arrest them!" Commander-in-chief Huang had no choice but to leave with his tail tucked between his legs.

第3章　萨本栋和抗战时期的厦门大学

4. 学生的保护神

在国内革命战争时期，长汀曾经是重要的红色根据地。北山南麓还埋有瞿秋白等烈士的遗骨，城镇、农村还多有土地革命时期的红色标语。革命的火种没有熄灭，而抗日的风潮又拍击着厦大的校园。当时有几个女同学表现突出，国民党特务分子就说她们左倾，想拘捕她们，多次向萨校长提出，萨校长总是断然拒绝，并且想方设法编织理由，为她们辩护。

经济系 1943 级的女生陈某，思想进步且学习用功、成绩优异，多次获"嘉庚奖学金"。萨校长很器重这个学生。特务要抓她，萨校长说："这个女生，书念得很好，只是长得比较丑，找不到对象，思想苦闷，不是什么左倾。"一下就把特务挡了回去。省保安司令黄珍吾亲自来校，向萨校长要人，萨校长也不让步，他愤愤地说道："我是一校之长。学生的家长把子女交给我，我有责任加以保护。我是中委，我也有权管这些事，学生在校期间，你们就不能抓！"黄珍吾无可奈何，只得悻悻离去。

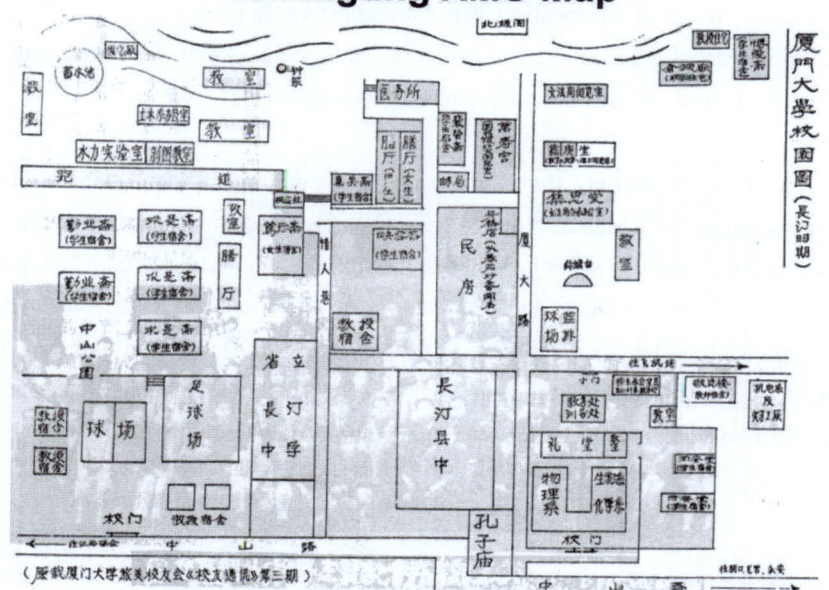

5. Don't Touch the Teachers At that time XMU had two professors who not only looked alike but spoke alike and walked alike. Professor Huang taught science, Professor Yang taught literature. Professor Yang liked poetry and often wrote poems critical of the Kuomintang authorities. In the spring of 1939, Professor Yang published a short poem in a newspaper to criticize Chiang Kai Shek (蒋介石), the then Guomingdang president. The Kuomintang secret police blacklisted Yang as a dissident and, worse, sought a chance to kill him.

On a pitch-dark night, a few secret agents waited in an alley near Changting Hotel to ambush Professor Yang. They saw a figure approaching resembling professor Yang, and attacked like wild bulls. They threw him to the ground, and punched and kicked him.

The next day it turned out they had attacked not Yang but Huang. News of the incident spread like wildfire. The staff was dumbfounded, and President Sa was indignant and immediately protested to the local Changting secret police. The chief officer of the local security bureau promptly apologized to XMU because he feared President Sa and his staff—and he also knew his secret watchdogs often attacked innocent people on spurious grounds.

6. Don't humiliate the Chinese At the beginning of 1944, the Kuomintang's ministry of education invited several foreign experts to lecture in China. President Sa held a banquet in honor of a British scholar who visited Changting XMU, and Secretary Wang asked my classmate and I to accompany him. After the banquet, the Brit arrogantly reproved the Chinese for lacking sanitation, wisdom, science and culture, and concluded with the comment that the Chinese people deserved the humiliation that had been inflicted upon them.

5. 不许殴打老师

当时厦大有两位老师，一位是理科的黄教授，一位是文科的杨教授。两个人的长相和身材举止都很相似。杨教授平时喜欢行文作诗，常常发点对时局不满的牢骚。1939年春，他在报纸上发表了一首对蒋介石有所不满的小诗，结果招来当局的记恨，特务机关准备要暗害他。

一个漆黑的夜晚，几个特务打手埋伏在长汀饭店附近的小巷子里，把单独走来的黄教授误以为是杨教授，便一拥而上，不由分说，就是一阵拳打脚踢。

消息传开，全校哗然，许多师生怒不可遏。萨校长也很生气，立即向长汀有关方面提出抗议。县保安司令部敬畏萨校长的威望，同时感到众怒难犯，害怕事态扩大，不得不向学校认错，并赔偿了养伤费。

6. 不许污蔑中国

1944年初，国民政府教育部特邀几位外国专家来华讲学，其中有一位英国人来到长汀的厦大。萨校长设宴欢迎，王秘书要我和另一位同学作陪。饭后寒暄，那个趾高气扬的英国人老是数落中国人不讲卫生，愚昧无知，科学文化落后，从而得出结论，中国人被欺侮是活该。

Changting XMU Dorm Room

President Sa was indignant at this nonsense and could not hold his tongue. He arose and said, "Not all you said is true. At present China is not very advanced in science because of the corruption of the modern Chinese Government, and also because foreign powers such as Great Britain imposed unequal treaties on China. You know that China created an ancient great civilization and the Chinese people are hard-working and clever." Mr. Sa had hit the nail on the head, and the Brit was speechless.

Soon afterwards at a university meeting, President Sa mentioned the proud Englishman and said, "Though the allied countries have proposed to abolish all unequal treaties imposed on China, we are still haunted by circumstances and the psychological wounds of those treaties. But we at XMU must stand tall and never allow foreigners to humiliate our countrymen."

7. General Advisor of Bomb Shelters The Japanese enemy was dreadful. During the anti-Japanese war, they rained massive bombs upon the mountainous Changting region near XMU. To protect his students, President Sa studied the campus carefully, designed a bomb shelter, and oversaw its construction. He built temporary classrooms near shelters so students could reach safety quickly during attacks by Japanese bombers.

President Sa's first priority was always others' safety. Every time the air-raid siren rang, President Sa stood outside the bomb shelter and directed both students and teachers as they made an orderly rush into shelters. He shouted: "Rush, but don't push!" Staff often pulled him by the arms, urging him into the shelter, but he shrugged them off, saying, "I am president. I should first keep everyone else safe from bombs." Only after everyone else was safe did he enter the bomb shelter. Thus our President Sa exposed himself to danger to ensure others safety.

Sometimes, the Japanese bombing lasted quite long. President Sa asked people in the shelter to stand in line and take turns to go to the cave's opening for fresh air. Under his leadership, people moved orderly and didn't panic. During the bombing, the Japanese obliterated Changting's Shuidong Street, killing and wounding many. However, thanks to President Sa's far-sightedness and wise organization, not one person in nearby Changting XMU was killed or injured by enemy bombs.

萨校长听着听着，忍不住站起身来，他义正词严地指出：老兄讲的情况，尽管有些是事实，但那既是由于近代中国政府的腐败无能所导致，更是由于外国列强把不平等条约强加在中国人民头上造成的。中国是文明古国，中国人民是勤劳和聪慧的人民。萨校长所用的英语言辞准确而锋利，叫那个英国人理屈词穷，气氛一下子十分尴尬。

后来，在一次全校师生的集会上，萨校长针对此事，无限感慨且语重心长地对大家说道："现在，同盟国虽然提出废除不平等条约，但造成这种不平等的客观环境和心理环境依然存在。"

7. 防空总指挥

日寇是极为疯狂的，长汀山区也经常遭到敌机轰炸。萨校长亲自勘察地形，亲自设计，并亲自指导施工，沿着北山山麓开了几个防空坑道，并在坑道附近修了临时教室。这样既保证教学，又保证安全。

每当空袭警报响起，师生们纷纷进洞，萨校长却留在洞外，指挥大家有序进洞。我至今仍清楚地记得他急得满头大汗，喊得声嘶力竭的样子。师生们也很担心他的安全，拉他赶紧进洞。他只是说："你们快走，你们快走！"他就是这样一个不顾个人安危，心系全校师生的防空总指挥。

有时，空袭的时间较长，萨校长就安排洞内的师生们排成长蛇阵，沿着洞壁缓缓挪动，轮流到洞口呼吸新鲜空气。

当时敌机把长汀县城水东街炸得满目疮痍，烧焦的房屋和尸体的臭味经久不散，而整个厦大在长汀期间没有死伤一人，这与萨校长的防空安排与指挥得当是有相当关系的。

8. Farewell Artwork Exhibition for the President On May 7, 1944 a farewell artwork exhibition for President Sa was held in Changting XMU's Great Hall before his departure from Changting. Because I was a senior economics major and quite active, I was chosen to be chairman of this exhibition, which centered on President Sa. The artwork all conveyed teachers' and students' deep love for President Sa, and included Chinese calligraphy by Yuying, Yuyu, He Lisheng, and Chen Sanwei; stonework by San Wei, Feng Yie, and Shi Quan; water paintings by Yi Xiong, Qi Dian and Jin Lai; pencil sketches by Shang An, caricatures and cartoons by Ji Du, as well as many wooden sculptures, innumerable campus photographs, four large murals, the top ten seniors' theses from *Xiamen University Daily*, etc. My own work on display was entitled *President Sa's Merits from His Inauguration Day, July 6, 1937 until Now,* and included piles and piles of telegraphs and letters. The quantity of artwork was uncountable! Everyone just wanted to express their feelings, passion, love, and heart-felt thanks to President Sa.

Just before their departure, President Sa and his wife visited the farewell artwork exhibition with enthusiasm, appreciation and understanding. Mr. Sa wrote movingly in the guestbook, "Artists here are blessed with first-rate skills." His wife wrote, "Rich cultures rely on artists." The two lines of inscription went well together.

The art exhibition was a hit, attracting thousands upon thousands of visitors. It was reported on page 4 of the *Central Government Daily,* Fuzhou edition, dated 18th May 1944.

9. Sorrowful Departure I had a special newspaper clipping on page 3 of the *Central Government Daily* Fuzhou Edition on 15th May 1944. My 400-word anonymous article was entitled, *Special Report on Teachers and Students Seeing off Sa Bendong at Changting.*

The article read, "Dr Sa Bendong, Chinese giant in physics and acting president of XMU, has been invited to the U.S.A to give lectures on our national policy. After the release of this news the entire populace of Changting City was down in spirit and immersed in great sadness. President Sa was scheduled to leave Changting on the 12th of this month. On the morning of the 12th, the wind was blowing and the sun was warm. Changting city and the nearby hills were very beautiful under the cloudless sky. At 6 o'clock, all XMU faculty, staff and students voluntarily stood in a line a few miles long to see off their respected president, Mr. Sa. People from outside of XMU also stood by in the hopes of seeing Mr. Sa with their own eyes. Traffic was jammed as crowds tried to photograph Mr. Sa.

8. 欢送艺展

1944年5月7日,师生员工特在大礼堂举办"欢送萨本栋校长赴美讲学——厦大艺术展览会",身为厦大经济系四年级学生的我担任了这次展览会的主席。展览会内容十分丰富,有余莺、虞愚、何励生、陈三畏的书法;三畏、枫野、世权的金石;一雄、启典、金徕的水墨写生;尚安的铅笔画和纪杜的漫画等,还有许多木刻和校园摄影,以及《厦大一日》的十篇优秀征文。大四学生出版股连夜出版了多达四张的《艺展壁报》。师生们争先拿出自己的特长,抒发对萨校长依依难舍的情感!展览会上最为引人注目的是两张照片,一是萨校长八岁时的旧照,二是萨校长与萨夫人伉俪的结婚照,使整个展览会亲和得像一个其乐融融的大家庭。我别开生面的展品是《萨校长来厦大的前前后后》,选辑了一叠叠的电文和信札,让历史的邮件真切地诉说当年萨师创业的艰辛!

临行前的萨校长和夫人兴致勃勃地参观了展览。在师生们的各种作品前流连忘返。展览会设有一本签名题词本,萨校长的题词"艺术家是天生的",亲切而幽默,且字迹娟秀可人,真是文理全才。萨夫人的题词是:"文化的提高有赖天才的人服务大众"。可谓夫唱妇随。

展览会是成功而轰动的,参观者络绎不绝。事后《中央日报》(福建版)1944年5月18日第4版以近四分之一版的篇幅追发了关于这次欢送展览会盛况的长篇特写。

9. 难分难舍

我存有一份当时厦门大学师生惜别萨本栋校长离汀长汀赴美国讲学的特写剪报,题为《萨本栋离汀时师生惜别速写》(400字),作者不详,刊《中央日报》(福州版)1944年5月15日第3版。全文如下:

> 我国物理学泰斗、现任国立厦门大学校长萨本栋博士,报聘美国讲学,宣扬国策。消息披露,山城鼎沸,萨校长于本月12日自汀启节西行。是晨风和日暖,云彩分明,山城景色,益外清鲜。六时许,厦大全体师生、教职员、校友、工友,队伍整然,浩浩荡荡。横岗下市街,绵延里许不绝,汀市万民拥挤,争仰萨校长伉俪风采,各方争摄三照,交通为之阻塞。

"When he reached the Zhongshan Garden Gate, the President waved his hat to the crowd, a broad smile upon his face. He wore a light green jacket and was in very high spirits. Three girl students from XMU named Yao Cixin, Zhuang Zhaoshun, and Huang Wanxian, bowed deeply to President Sa and presented him with two bunches of flowers and a small university banner. Doctor Zhou Bianming, a linguist and acting dean of the literature college, led in passionate singing and saying goodbye to Mr. Sa. "Have a smooth trip to the U.S.A.!", "May XMU remember you forever!", and "We are forging ahead!" At that moment, the excited crowd sang both the Chinese and American national anthems. One could hear the singing miles away, and as the voices rang in my ears, President Sa left to thunderous applause."

Those tearful but vivid words recorded a departure some 58 years ago, just as moving pictures record moments in time. Those heartfelt words revealed the deep friendship between students and President Sa, who was diligent, hardworking, and loved his career.

10. Do not hand over XMU to factionists

Due to his health, President Sa telegraphed his resignation three times while lecturing in the USA, but all of the students and teachers, from the bottom of their heart, hoped Mr. Sa could stay on as president of XMU, which with President Sa's effort had made such great progress that it was indeed comparable to North China's Qinghua University. But everyone's greatest concerned was Mr. Sa's health.

Chen Lifu, the national education minister, lamented, "Mr. Sa used to be a robust tennis player. But he has worked for XMU University for 7 years and is now very thin and hunched over. As education minister, I will not burden him to toil on at this post…"

In 1945 Mr. Sa's resignation was finally approved and he became chief director in the Central Research Institute. "Who is the right person to succeed me?" he pondered. "Most important is that this person not be a factionalist." It was an open secret that the faculty had Fuzhou factions and Xiamen factions, and Mr. Sa was very leery of factionalism. He banned his staff from speaking dialects in the office. He also told his colleagues that factionalists would not do a good job. He always preferred those who never involved themselves in factional quarrels to hold leadership posts. Wang Deyao, the director of the technology college, always distanced himself from factionalism, so Mr. Sa thought highly of him and recommended him to succeed him as XMU's president.

Epilogue   President Sa was admired and remembered by thousands of teachers and students. Zheng Chaozong, one of his students, wrote in his book *Reminiscences*,

"Mr. Sa lived an easy and comfortable scholar's life, but because of his ardent patriotism, he gave up his comfortable life and accepted the job as president of Changting XMU. He labored there with all his strength and love for 7 years, regardless of his own health. Because of overwork, he passed away at only 47. Mr. Sa's great contributions to the university and his attractive character will never be forgotten by teachers, students, and others."

第3章　萨本栋和抗战时期的厦门大学

抵达中山公园门首，萨校长身着浅绿中山装，精神奕奕，笑容满面，挥帽惜别。当由厦大姚慈心、庄昭顺、黄婉仙三女生进前呈献鲜花两束、小型校旗一面；并由语言学家、现任该校文学院长周辨明博士，引导欢呼，一时中美国歌、声震寰空，"送亚栋呼"、"厦大冲锋呼"、"一帆风顺呼"……旋绕耳际，萨校长伉俪于掌声如雷中登车离汀。"这些珍贵的文字记录如电影胶卷一般，摄下了58年前的那个难分难舍的时刻，显示了一个敬业奉公、鞠躬尽瘁的校长与师生的深厚情谊。

10. 不能把厦大交给热衷搞地方帮派的人

萨校长在美国讲学期间，由于健康等原因，曾三度电呈辞去厦大校长之职。厦大师生当然渴望他能继续留下，浇灌已经亭亭玉立的"南方清华"，但又为他的健康状况深感不安，连当时国民政府的教育部长陈立夫都说："萨本栋本来是网球健将，现在累得又瘦又驼，我是不忍心他再担这副担子了……"

1945年萨校长获准辞去校长职务，被聘为中央研究院总干事。谁来接替厦大校长之职，他是有所考虑的。校为素有福州派和闽南派，这是一个公开的秘密。他虽然是福州人，但始终对地方主义持有戒心。他严禁在办公室内讲方言，并时常告诫同事们不要分这里人那里人的，热衷搞地方主义是办不好事的。他有意选择没有介入地方派性的外省人担任领导职务（当然还要具备其他条件），于是极力推荐没有介入两派之争的理工学院院长汪德耀教授继任厦大校长一职。

尾声

郑朝宗先生后来在《往事漫忆》一文中这样记述这位英年早逝的青年校长："他本是一个养尊处优的学者，只因被爱国之心驱使，便放弃个人的一切而勇挑重担，终至积劳成疾，以身殉职，年仅47岁。他的人格感动了全校的师生，他的贡献至今仍深印在厦大人的心田。"

This passage aptly summarized Sa's great life. He passed away, his wife followed him, and they were buried together on the garden campus of XMU, amidst palm trees and bright flowers. They quietly lay down and listened to the young students' morning reading and evening parties, and the birds' twittering and the people's hearty laughter.

(The author, Zheng Daochuan, was a professor of XMU and consultant of the Xiamen Municipal Civil Alliance. Zheng Daochuan was asked by the National Political Committee to write this article, which was archived in the National Literature and History Archives. At the beginning of 2002, Zheng Daochuan revised and completed the article just before his death with the help of Zheng Qiwu, his son, in order to commemorate President Sa's 100th birthday. This article, Zheng Daozhuan's last, fulfilled his lifetime vow of "pursue excellence, strive for perfection."

第3章　萨本栋和抗战时期的厦门大学

如今萨校长和夫人黄淑慎一同安葬在绿树成荫的厦门大学的校园里，无论是渔舟唱晚，还是百鸟鸣晨，他俩都沉浸在南方之强浓郁的书香里，谛听着男生女生朗朗的笑语欢声……

（**郑道传**，原厦门大学教授、民盟厦门市委顾问。此文原在 1982 年应全国政协文史委之约，写成存档于国家文史档案馆。2002 年初为纪念萨本栋百年诞辰，在病榻上奄奄一息的郑道传在其子郑启五的协助下，重新修订补充完此稿，成为他生前最后的一篇文字，实践了他"生命不息，奋斗不止"的人生誓言。）

Chapter 4

Changting Tales

Passing the Physical Students who did poorly on the required physical exams were limited in how many courses they could take. This rule was to ensure that weaker students took time to rest, but students of course wanted to take as many courses as possible. Over time they found ways to beat the exams, and these 3 strategies were memorized and passed from one generation to the next:

1. **Sleep!** Sleep more, eat less, and refrain from exercise a few days before the exam.
2. **Drink!** Drink as much water as possible so the urine appears clear like water.
3. **Wait!** Wait until most people are finished with their exams before taking your own. It is easier to pass because nurses are less strict when they are anxious to leave.

Shower Disaster Men had no shower facilities, so someone came up with the bright idea of selling tickets to use barrels of hot and cold water. Students yelled "Hot!" or Cold!", and the person on duty served water as needed. But sometimes the barrel handler was careless and gave hot water when students yelled for cold, or cold when they wanted hot. Worse yet, sometimes they left their post while a student was still showering, leaving the hapless scholar stuck inside naked, in freezing winter, with no hot water.

To resolve the problem, students made an unofficial rule that anyone hearing people caught in a "shower disaster" crying for help should come to their aid. Only by everyone helping each other were "shower disasters" finally eliminated.

 第4章 长汀轶事

第4章

长汀轶事[①]

通过体检 每个学生在开学选课前都必须参加体检,如果检查结果表明身体欠佳,该学生就会被限修学分。校方的出发点是体力欠佳者要多休息,却没想过被限修同学的心境如何——他们当然希望修尽可能多的学分了!长此以往,同学们便有了"实战经验",他们总结出了以下"体检三招",并一届届地传承下去:

第一:**睡眠法**——体检前几天,少吃多睡,限制活动,用睡眠来遏制体检出现毛病;

第二:**饮水法**——尿检前夕,大量喝白开水,这样送检尿样就清澈如水;

第三:**拖延法**——体检期间,开头不去,等到大部分人都体检完了再去。这时护士小姐急着下班就不那么严格了,那么也就容易通过了。

洗浴之灾 那时没有淋浴设施,有人想出了个好点子——大家凭票入浴,一票一桶水,不够可补。学生在浴室里喊着调温补水,管理员服务到位。可总有些管理员不那么尽责,他心不在焉时,你要冷水,他给你热水;你要热水,他给你冷水。更有甚者,要是管理员在学生洗澡时溜班,那这些学生可就倒了大霉了:洗澡洗到一半,呼喊着加热水,却没人应答。大冷天的,只能裸身伫候,冻得浑身发抖。

为了解决这个问题,同学们定了个不成文的约定:凡是有人经过浴室附近,遇到这种淋浴之灾,要主动伸出援助之手,为洗澡者解除困难。正是同学们发扬了团结互助的精神,洗浴之灾才得以免除。

---

① 李雪卿:《笃行壮女趣事多多——三忆长汀笃行斋》;曹大廷:《长汀校园生活回忆》;曹祖庆:《回忆长汀日机轰炸》;苏林华:《长汀入学前后——厦大新生谈》。

Air Attacks Japanese planes bombed Changting almost regularly, and every time the siren went off people raced into the air-raid shelter. A student struck by something right after a bomb hit was terrified because he remembered being told that people usually don't feel anything immediately after being wounded by a bomb. He was so frightened that he did not dare look at his own leg, but when he finally did move it, slowly and carefully, he could feel his leg, and so knew it was still there. He was so happy and thankful to discover that he had been hit by bricks, not by the bomb itself.

The Clog Clock It was very difficult to keep track of time for those who lived too far away to hear the class bell and didn't have a watch. But these students soon discovered a foolproof way to tell time—the "clog clock." Each morning, when students heard the heavy thump of clogs pounding the pavement, they knew people were racing to the toilet and that it was time to get up. The same thumping at noon indicated lunch time. In the evening, the sluggish thumping of clogs meant the tired students were getting out of class. And at night, the thumping of hundreds of clogs hitting the floor meant it was time for bed.

The clog clock was accurate, never off, and never broke down.

Chicken Picnic While in Changting, XMU continued to hold sports meets, and one female student recalled winning a live chicken for coming first in the long-distance race. But then as now, squeamish girls would not even touch the chicken, much less kill it, so she had the boys do the fowl deed for her. But it turned out she didn't know how to cook it either. She boiled it with half a bottle of soy sauce, and then she and her friends had a nice picnic of chicken and fresh spring water on the mountaintop behind her dorm. "The chicken was a little too salty," she recalled, "but the water was good".

第4章　长汀轶事

日机空袭　日本飞机经常在长汀轰炸。每当空袭警报响起时，人们便躲进防空洞去。有一个学生，一次空袭来不及躲避，炸弹爆炸后，他感觉有一些东西打在了身上。他想到以往听人说过，人在被炸后，最初都不会感觉到疼痛。他吓得不敢回头去看自己的腿，怕已经被炸伤了，于是先动动看，感到自己的腿部都能活动，知道没有受伤，才放心地坐了起来。后来才发现，是一些地上的砖头被炸后飞起来，打到了他身上。算是上天保佑，保了一命。

木屐自鸣钟　有些学生宿舍离校部远，根本听不见上课的钟声，有手表者又极少，如何做到按时作息，就成了大问题。佢是天无绝人之路，他们从生活实践中琢磨出了一个简单的办法——关注"木屐自鸣钟"。早晨，听到密集而急促的木屐的笃笃声，那是起床如厕盥洗时；晌午，一片震耳欲聋噼里啪啦响，那是去食堂用午膳时；傍晚，拖拖踏踏、断断续续木屐声起，那是疲倦的同学们下课归来；夜晚，耳间地板声声作响，那是上床睡觉时……

"木屐自鸣钟"报时准确，且从不停止，从未坏过。

公鸡野炊　内迁长汀后，厦大还是不时地召开运动会。一个女生回忆起一次参加越野长跑拿了第一名，赢得一只活的大公鸡的情景。不过呢，就像现在一样，"神经兮兮"的女生们是连碰都不会去碰这些"活物"的，更不用说操刀杀鸡了。于是她委托男生搞定那只公鸡。后来的结果是她的烹调技术好像也不太出色，用了半瓶酱油就把它煮了，然后就和几个同学一起到宿舍后面的山上就着清泉野餐。"鸡的味道有点太咸了，"她后来说，"不过山泉倒是不错。"

Get Girls with Trilogy With a boy to girl ratio of 9:1, it was hard to get a girl at Changting, so boys used the "3-Step" strategy they called "Trilogy."

Step 1: Wait in Line to make a date. Boys asked the janitor of the girls' dorm to pass a message that he wanted to see a girl, but sometimes the girls asked the janitor to lie to the boys and say they were not in. The boys, in turn, learned to tip the janitor, and have her shout out the girl's name and ask her to please come downstairs. In order to avoid disturbing the others, the girl would give in and come out to meet the boy.

Step 2: Set the "Hook" After the first date, the boy spared no effort in finding excuses to see the girl again. One of the best strategies was "borrow the notebook." Borrowing it and returning it gave him two more chances to see her, and sometimes he inserted a small note between the pages saying, "Would you like to take a walk with me to discuss that question the teacher raised?"

Step 3: Success! After many dates and many discussions, some of these campus couples did start a life together. Those marriages were especially precious and valued by both because of the difficult but memorable times.

(Huang Baoxin of HK met his wife in Changting! See chapter 7)

And here's a tale of how Lu Xun got a lover! (not at Changting, though).

Which step is he on?

"恋爱"三步曲 长汀时期,男女生人数大概是 9∶1,可见那时追到一个女生有多难了。于是男生采取了"三步走"战略,被称为"交友三步曲"。

第一步:排队约会。男生们请传达室的大嫂传喊某女生,但是有时候女生会请大嫂跟男生说"就说我不在"。后来,有的男生也学会了给小费,请大嫂再度传喊某女生下来。为了避免影响别人休息,某女生也只好出来见那个男生了。

第二步:愿者上钩。第一次约会之后,男生又会不遗余力地设法再见那个女生。其中一个最好的办法就是"借听课笔记",一借一还就增加了两次见面的机会。有时候男生还会在笔记里夹上一张纸条,上面写着"愿意一起去散散步,讨论一下老师提出的那个问题吗?"

第三步:开花结果。经过了很多的约会和讨论之后,的确有一些"校园夫妻"过起了他们自己的生活。那段艰难而又难忘的岁月,使得他们的结合更加珍贵,彼此也更加珍惜。

(香港校友黄保欣就是在长汀遇到红颜知己,见第七章)

下面是一则关于鲁迅先生追女生的故事(不过倒是不在长汀)

Lu Xun's Laobiao Cousin and Lover!

By Bruce Lee

"Lao Biao" traditionally means "cousin," and Lu Xun was a Chinese literary genius praised by Chairman Mao Zedong, the first president of the People's Republic of China, as a modern literary giant, great thinker, and social revolutionary. Chinese often associate Lao Biao with Lu Xun because Lu Xun redefined the meaning of Lao Biao while he was in XMU.

Lu Xun was invited to teach literature in XMU for four months, from September 4, 1926 to January 16, 1927. But he was ostracised by his contemporaries because of his critical view of the then Kuomintang government. One of the few people who actually had close contact with Lu Xun was a female student, Xu Guangpin, who later became his wife. It was while romancing Guangping that Lu Xun expanded the word "Lao Biao" (cousin) to include the meaning of "girlfriend."

Miss Xu often visited Lu Xun's room and helped him wash clothes and do dishes. Although their relationship wasn't public at the time, it was proper. One day, Lu Xun's colleagues dropped by his room without warning and recognized Miss Xu. "Ah, this girl had intimate relations with Lu Xun!" they thought, and they hoped to get Lu Xun to confirm it with his own mouth. They didn't make a fuss, and with feigned nonchalance they asked Lu Xun, "Who is this young girl, my friend?" Totally surprised by the question, the usually eloquent Lu Xun became tongue-tied and stammered, "She is, is…er…" At last Lu Xun managed to whisper with a shy curl of his lip, "She is, …er…my Lao Biao." (That is, "she is my cousin."). Lu Xun's thin face flushed as his colleagues exploded with laughter. One reason Lu Xun was so embarrassed was that he had had an arranged marriage and he hadn't dismissed her legally. From then on, Miss Xu, the so-called Lao Biao, was actually his new girlfriend.

When Lu Xun married Miss Xu several years later, those colleagues didn't forget "Lao Biao" episode and asked Lu Xun on the wedding: "Hi, Old Brother, isn't your bride your so-called Lao Biao?"

This time around Lu Xun gave a firm reply. "Yes, now she is not only my Lao Biao but also my lifetime wife." His friends laughed and gave him a thunderous round of applause.

Afterwards, the expression "Lu Xun's Lao Biao" spread quickly and became a hot news item on the XMU campus, and an interesting episode in modern Chinese literary history. His colleagues accepted Lao Biao's new meaning of girlfriend, boyfriend, or newly married husband or wife, and even today, people often use the term Lao Biao to refer to a secret lover.

And next…see how I got *my* girl!

鲁迅的"老表"
——"表亲"与文学巨匠鲁迅

"老表"在中文里的本义是指表亲,如表兄弟、表姐妹。鲁迅先生是一位中国现代文学大家。毛主席曾说过,鲁迅是伟大的文学家、思想家和革命家。然而,鲁迅和"老表"有什么联系呢?原来,鲁迅先生在厦门大学任教期间,赋予了"老表"以新的内涵。

1926年9月4日至1927年1月16日鲁迅在厦门大学教授文学纲要期间,曾经猛烈抨击国民党政府,遭到同事的排挤。当时他只和几个人的关系比较密切,其中有一位女学生——许广平小姐,后来成了他的妻子。正是因为他们在这期间的热恋,"老表"才有了新的内涵:女朋友。

许小姐经常去鲁迅先生的住处帮他做些日常琐事。当时他们已经开始恋爱,但还未公开。有一天,鲁迅的几个同事突然光临,认出了恰好也在那里的许小姐。那几个同事猜想这位小姐和鲁迅先生的关系一定非同一般,并想得到鲁迅先生的亲口证实。他们并未大惊小怪,只是故作平静地问道:"老弟,这位小姐是……?"鲁迅被问住了,平时能言善辩的他变得支支吾吾,半天挤出一句:"她是……是……我的……我的……老……老表。"鲁迅的脸红了,同事们相视而笑。鲁迅之所以对他与许小姐的恋情难以启齿,其中一个原因是因为他当时并未与父母安排的结发之妻离婚。自那以后,许小姐就成为鲁迅先生新的女朋友。

几年后,鲁迅与许小姐结婚了。在婚礼上,鲁迅的那几位同事还对"老表"之事不依不饶,打趣他说:"嘿,鲁迅老弟,那位老表怎么成新娘了?"这次,鲁迅先生镇定自若,说:"许广平小姐不仅是我的老表,也是我的终生伴侣。"同事们都笑了,并给予鲁迅雷鸣般的掌声。

从此,"鲁迅的老表"这个说法传遍厦大校园,风靡一时,成为中国现代文学史上一段有趣的插曲。同事们接受了"老表"这个说法,它成了男女朋友,新郎新娘的代名词。直到今天,人们还常常用"老表"指代地下情人呢!

下面,看看我是怎么追到我的"心上人"的吧!

China—Our Matchmaker

(Were it not for our mutual interest in China, I'd have neither met nor married my "Made in Taiwan" blond haired, blue-eyed wife!
      Here's the story…)

China
Our Matchmaker

In 5th grade I was forced to sing in the girls' section of the chorus because I had a bell-like soprano—the highest voice in school. Other boys taunted "Bill's a girl!", and I prayed for puberty, and a "manly" voice. My prayers were answered all too soon. The bell cracked, usurped by an ungainly, adolescent alto, but now that adolescence was upon me with a vengeance I no longer disdained the company of sweet sopranos. I struggled to belt out those high notes that used to come so easily, but my vocal contortions were in vain. The upper octaves were denied me and I was unceremoniously expelled from Eden.

Oh, for the old days of prearranged marriage, when boys never agonized over asking a girl for a date. What if she says no? And almost as bad—what if she says yes? Do you take her to dinner, a movie, a ballgame, skating? Do you hold hands? Dare you kiss her? If so, on cheek or lips? How embarrassing to steel yourself for a goodnight kiss and then, betrayed by doubt, end up shaking hands as if concluding a business transaction.

Even sitting with a girl is a trial calculated to cow Hercules. You muster the courage to inch your arm nonchalantly around her shoulder, eyeing her sidewise, taking stock. If she smiles, you're home free, but if she frowns, you jerk your arm back as if it had acted of its own volition, clasp your clammy palms together, and prattle inanely about the weather. And if she should countenance your advances, what next?

By age 25, as intimidated as ever by the fairer sex, I swore off girls. With an iron will, I ignored the pretty coeds and glued my eyes to my textbooks. My world shrank to the confines of my dorm room, classrooms, library and cafeteria. My steely resolve lasted all of—two weeks. On Easter Sunday, 1981, a couple I had known in Taiwan invited me and a couple dozen youth to their home for dinner. My fate was sealed.

第4章　长汀轶事

中国——我的红娘
潘维廉

（若不是出于对中国共同的兴趣，我可能永远也不会娶到我那金发碧眼，美丽动人的台湾太太。故事是这样的……）

小学五年级的时候，我被逼在合唱队女声部唱歌。因为我那清脆如银铃般的"女高音"是全校最高亢的。男同学都开我的玩笑，"比尔是个女孩！"那时，我是多么盼望青春期的到来啊，我就可以拥有一副男人味十足的嗓音了。我的愿望实现得太快了，悦耳的银铃碎了，取而代之的是沙哑的、变声期嗓音。而现在，青春期像报复我似地离我远去了，我也不讨厌那些拥有银铃般嗓音的日子了。我声嘶力竭地想把那些原来易如反掌的高音唱上去，但白费功夫。高八度是没有希望了，我就这样随随便便地被逐出了伊甸园。

很久以前，婚姻都是父母做主的，男孩根本不用发愁怎么约会女孩。现在就不同了，要是她不同意怎么办？就算她同意了也未必是好事，接下来又该怎么办呢？是请她吃饭、看电影、看球赛，还是去滑冰？是牵手好呢，还是不牵好？要不要亲她一下，如果要的话，哪儿好呢，嘴唇还是脸颊？下定决心要在约会结束的时候吻她一下，但最终还是犹豫了，竟以握手告终，搞得就像商人谈成生意似的。太窘了。

单单和女生坐在一起，即使对大力神赫拉克勒斯也是个挑战，别说是一般人。你鼓起勇气慢慢地、装作漫不经心地把手臂搭在她的肩上，从侧面察言观色。如果她微微一笑，那你胜券在握；但要是她皱眉头，你得马上把那"不听话"的手抽回来，紧张地搓搓潮湿的手掌，望着天空，赶紧傻乎乎地说："今天天气不错哦！"若是她对你的行为表示鼓励呢，接下来怎么办呐？

到了25岁，我已被追女生的折磨吓倒了，于是决心"戒掉"女生。我以"钢铁般"的意志，"两眼不见如花女，一心只读教科书"，整天就穿梭于宿舍、教室、图书馆、食堂四点之间。我"坚定"的决心足足持续了——两个星期。1981年的复活节，在台湾结识的一对夫妇邀请我和另外几个年轻人去家中做客。我的命运就在此刻注定了。

No sooner had I crossed their threshold than my eyes were riveted to a young blue-eyed beauty with waves of flaxen hair cascading down her white and blue ski jacket. Mesmerized, I sauntered past her with studied indifference but covertly memorized every inch of her face and form; in my nonchalance I nearly walked into a wall.

I ached to introduce myself, but she was besieged by bolder young men the entire afternoon. By evening I was still a nonentity in her eyes, until my friend told everyone how the county rescue team had tried to rescue me from halfway up a 300 meter cliff the night before, and when their flashlight failed, I rescued one of them instead. My Venus eyed me curiously. "Great," I thought. "Now she thinks I'm a nut."

Then our host asked her, "Sue, did you know Bill lived in Taiwan and wants to go to China?"

"Really?" she exclaimed. "When were you in Taiwan?"

My mouth went dry, my heart pounded. Don't blow it, Bill. Keep cool. Count the years on your fingers and toes. "Oh, from June 1978 to June 1976," I said. "No, '76 to '78. Have you been to Taiwan?"

"I was born and raised there!" she laughed. "But from June 76 to June 78 I was in the States, so we missed each other!"

The ice broke and I plunged beneath, never in this life to resurface.

For hours we discussed our mutual interest, China. When Sue said she planned to visit her parents at Christmas, I deftly conjured up excuses for me to visit Taiwan as well. "Let's go together." And when I overheard she was having car troubles, I gallantly loaned her my car. I roller skated to school anyway—and it gave me an excuse to see her again.① But I needn't have worried; she agreed to attend a free campus concert on Friday night.

The five days loomed over me like eternity but when the momentous day arrived, we hit it off as if we'd known each other forever, right up until time to say goodbye; then I froze. Timidly, I gave her a friendly hug goodnight; she reciprocated with a kiss that sizzled my socks.

My "Made in Taiwan" Blonde!

---

① See Changting Stories. XMU males used the same strategy—with notebooks!

第4章　长汀轶事

刚跨进大门，我的目光就定格在一个年轻美女身上，再也移不开了。她有着碧蓝深邃的眸子，一头亚麻色的秀发如倾泻的瀑布一般，披散在白蓝相间的滑雪衫上。我像被催眠了一般，却强作镇定地从她身边走过，她的一颦一笑、一举一动都深深地印在我的心间。虽然，装得和没事儿人一样，我还是差点撞到了墙上。

我特想和她说话，但整个下午她周围都有群大胆的家伙。眼看就到了晚上，她看都没看我一眼，直到我朋友跟在场的人们讲，前一天晚上县里的救生员想把我从 300 米高悬崖的半山腰救出，他们的手电却没电了，反而是我救了一个队员的命。我的女神好奇地转向我，"这下可好"，我暗想，"现在她以为我神经不正常了！"

接着，这家的主人说："苏，你知道吗？比尔曾在台湾呆过，还想去中国大陆呢？"

"真的？"她很惊讶。"你是什么时候去台湾的？"

我突然口干舌燥，心跳加速。比尔，别搞砸，慢慢来，装酷一点儿。扳指头算算有几年，手指头不够就上脚趾。"哦，是从 1978 年 6 月到 1976 年 6 月，"我说，"不不，是从 1976 年到 1978 年……你去过台湾吗？"

"我就生长在台湾啊！"她笑着说。"可惜，1976 年 6 月到 1978 年 6 月这段时间我在美国，我们刚好错过啊！"

这是我们之间意义深刻的"破冰对话"，从此，我就一头钻到这"冰"的下面，此生再也没有"上岸"了。

说起共同的兴趣——中国，我们一谈就是好几个小时。当苏说她打算圣诞节去看她的父母时，我立刻就编了也要去台湾的理由，"那我们一起去吧。"后来，我无意中听到她的车坏了，便毫不犹豫地把我的车借给了她——反正我后来用旱冰鞋也"蹭"到学校了。而且，这样一来，我就有借口和她再见面了①。其实，我是不用担心啦，她答应了周五晚上和我一起听免费的校园音乐会。

五天的等待对我来说比一个世纪还要漫长，当那个"历史时刻"最终来临的时候，我们却好似已相识多年。告别时，我犹豫了，只害羞地给了她一个朋友的拥抱；而她，却回吻了我。那一吻，让我幸福得天旋地转。

---

① 请看"长汀轶事"一文。厦大的男生当时也常用这一招，不过把车换成笔记本而已。

The ice was not only broken but melted. From that date until our marriage in Taiwan ten months later, we saw each other every single day.

The following night we attended a free dinner with African grad students, but freebie dates can't last forever. Sooner or later I had to put my money where my heart was. For our third date in as many evenings, I invited Sue out to dinner and she showed up in a stunning evening dress and heels, expecting that, like her previous boyfriend, John, I'd take her to a fine restaurant. John was a smartly dressed gentleman who gave her flowers, opened doors for her, took her to elegant restaurants. The consummate gentleman, John was everything I was not.

After years of crushing conformity in the military, I now reveled in playing student and dressing however I felt. I grew a patchy beard and wore ragged, holey army-surplus clothes—a decade before it was fashionable to pay high prices for new clothes that looked old.

Fortunately, Sue overlooked my slovenly exterior. She also ignored my seeming poverty when I took her to a cheap fast food place rather than a nice restaurant. John spent more money parking his car than I spent on dinner.

Good old John: I met my predecessor the next Sunday at Sue's church. Although he'd already found another girl, the sight of my arms around Sue rekindled his flagging ardor. Sue squirmed awkwardly in John's warm embrace as he and I stared daggers at one another. If looks could have killed, blood would have flooded the church aisles.

To Sue's chagrin John started haunting her apartment, and I was relieved when she finally exorcised him—until I realized how serious our relationship was becoming. Cold feet!

I knew, of course, I'd never find a more perfect match. American girls born and raised in Taiwan and interested in moving to China don't just grow on trees. And fewer yet would put up with someone like me. Sue was definitely one of a kind, but I told her frankly that I did not think she could cope with the simpler lifestyle we'd probably face in China.

She repeatedly reassured me, "Whatever you do, I'll do."

I was unconvinced. One evening, in the dorm parking lot, I began to list all the reasons I thought we could never marry. As she listened silently, eyes moist, I mentally kicked myself. Then out of the blue I blurted, "Since we're visiting Taiwan in December, maybe we could get married there?"

To this day I've no idea how this most unromantic of marriage proposals leaped straight from my heart, bypassed my brain, and dove off my tongue. Sue merely laughed, "You're joking, aren't you?"

第 4 章 长汀轶事

　　至此，我们之间的那层"冰"不但"破"了，而且完全融化了。从那天起，直到 10 个月后在台湾结婚，我们每天都见面。

　　第二天晚上，我们参加了非洲毕业生的免费晚宴。佢是，免费约会不是长久之计啊，迟早我都得自己为心上人花线的。我们第三次约会的时候，我请苏吃饭。那天她穿了一件迷人的晚礼服，高跟鞋，还以为我会像他的前男友约翰那样请她去高级餐厅。约翰是个穿着讲究入时的绅士，给她送花，帮她开车门，带她去高消费的餐厅。和这样完美的绅士相比，我简直一无是处。

　　过了几年时时处处强调一致的军队生活之后，我倒喜欢穿得随便一些，像个学生，穿得很寒酸，留着参差不齐的胡子。如今，花大价钱把新衣服搞旧已成为时尚，殊不知十年前，我就已经在穿到处是洞的乞丐装了，那还是我当兵时留下的衣服。

　　幸运的是，苏并不介意我的不修边幅。我没有带她去高级餐馆，而是吃了便宜的快餐，她也并不在意我是不是很穷，约翰请她吃饭时花的停车费比我请的晚饭还贵。

　　哦，我可怜的约翰！接下来的周末我在苏的教堂看到了这位"前任"。虽然，他已经交了新的女朋友，但是我搭在苏肩头的手臂还是让他妒火中烧。我和他对视，我们的目光像锋利的剑，直刺对方。苏对于约翰热情的拥抱也显得非常尴尬。如果目光能杀人，教堂的过道上早已是血流成河了。

　　令苏气愤的是，约翰开始频繁地往她的公寓逛荡。当苏最终把他赶走的时候，我松了一口气。直到那时，我才意识到，我们已经离不开对方了——我退缩了。

　　当然，我当时已经很清楚，苏就是我生命中所寻找的另一半。这世上还真有生在台湾、长在台湾、热爱中国的美国女孩儿。而且，竟然还被我追到了。苏真的是我爱的类型，但是我直言不讳地告诉她，我觉得她恐怕无法适应到中国后要面对的简朴生活。

　　她却不断地承诺："无论你做什么，我都跟着你。"

　　但我仍然迷茫。一天晚上，在宿舍停车场，我开始罗列我们不能结婚的理由。她静静地听着，眼里含着泪，我则心如刀割一般地痛。突然，我不假思索地说："既然十二月我们要去台湾，在那儿结婚怎么样？"

　　时至今日，我仍然搞不懂，这句极不浪漫的求婚辞是怎么从心里跳出来、绕过大脑的加工、飞过舌头的阻拦、从嘴里蹦出来的。当时，苏只是笑了笑说："你是开玩笑的，是吧？"

Frankly, I was as surprised by the proposal as she was—but to have her laugh in my face was a bit much. "No, I'm serious!" I protested.

Her eyes widened. "Yes, I'll marry you!"

Many of Sue's former classmates participated in our Dec. 1981 wedding in Taipei's Christ College, but I remember little about the ceremony. I was in shock and might have abandoned Sue at the altar had her father not had my air tickets. And doubts continued long afterwards, but we worked through them over the years, one by one, and our marriage is stronger for it.

Too many marriages, built upon mere infatuation and raging hormones (which I well relate to!), fail because they lack growth, commitment, and sacrifice. Sue's best quality is her capacity for sacrifice.

True to her vow of "for better or for worse," Sue never complained about my grad student's Spartan lifestyle, so I was happy when my small company flourished and a six-figure income gave us a better lifestyle than she'd expected when she married me. But my heart was still on China, and the more we lived the so-called American Dream, the more I doubted she could give all up for China. Or for that matter—could I?

In 1987, I hesitantly asked Sue, "What would you think of selling our business now and moving to China?" My timing was not the best. Sue was nursing one baby and about to have another. But more confident than I, she assured me, "If you feel its right, let's go."

Within a year we'd burned our bridges and, with two young sons, moved to Xiamen. It was a stressful transition, but we've never regretted it. Life in China has been more rewarding than we could have ever imagined.

Looking back, from 5th grade chorus to marriage was an awfully long row to hoe, but it was well worth the harvest! I could not imagine life with anyone but my "made in Taiwan" wife, or anywhere but in China!

Arranged marriages might indeed have their advantages—such as sparing us insecure males the agonies of dating. But who on earth could have ever arranged such an unlikely marriage as mine? Such marriages aren't arranged, they're made in heaven.

And since it was our mutual interest in China that brought us together, you might say that China was our matchmaker! Thank you, China!

第4章　长汀轶事

说实话，我当时的吃惊程度决不比她小，但是看到她笑，我有点承受不了，马上反抗说："不，我是认真的。"

她睁大双眼："好的，我嫁你！"

苏的很多同学都参加了我们1981年12月份在台北基督学院举办的婚礼，但是关于当时婚礼的情形我几乎什么都不记得了。我当时神情恍惚，若不是苏的父亲拿走了我的机票，我可能真会把她一个人丢在礼堂跑掉了。对未来的许多迷惘在婚礼后很久都未消失。但随着岁月流逝，我们已逐渐地将迷茫和困惑解开，婚姻也因此而愈发坚定了。

如今，太多的婚姻建立在冲动和狂热之上（这一点我深有体会），大多失败了。因为它们缺乏成长、承诺和一个有点过时的词——牺牲。这是我妻子最令人敬佩的美德：她勇于牺牲。

坚守着自己"不论贫穷或富有"的结婚誓言，苏从来没有抱怨过我简朴的生活方式。当我原有的小公司发达之后，六位数的收入让她过上了比嫁给我时预想得好得多的生活，这当然使我非常骄傲。但是我的心仍在中国，我们逐渐实现了所谓的"美国梦"，我更担心了，"她舍得丢下这一切去中国吗？我舍得吗？"

1987年，我踌躇了很久，终于问她："我们结束这里的生意，搬去中国，你觉得怎么样？"我问的时机不对，苏当时要照顾孩子，而且马上要生第二个小孩儿了。但是，她却比我更坚定地说："如果你认为应该，我们就走。"

一年内，我们"破釜沉舟"，带上两个年幼的儿子移居厦门。这个生活的巨大转变压力困难重重，但我们却从不曾后悔，在中国生活之精彩、回馈之丰富是我们当时所未曾想象的。

回首往事，从小学五年级到结婚真是一段辛苦的耕耘，但却是值得的，因为我的收获是苏！无法想象，如果不是我这位"台湾制造"的妻子，如果生活的土地不是中国，那生活会成为什么样子！

包办婚姻是有些好处，比如说可以省去我们这些信心不足男人的约会之苦。但是究竟是谁"包办"了我们这段看似不可能的姻缘呢？这样的婚姻，恐怕无人能够包办，而是一生一世彼此注定啊！

是我们对中国的共同兴趣让我们走到了一起。所以，或许可以说，中国才是我们的红娘。

谢谢你，中国！

Chapter 5

Great Changes in Xiamen University

By Professor Zheng Qiwu
(a rough translation of the Chinese)

My father and mother taught in Xiamen University all of their lives. I'm a real "Campus Native", as I was born here and brought up on campus in the 1950s, though back then XMU was not like a university at all. My little companions and I often played "war" in the vegetable fields on campus. We climbed to the top of Five Peak Mountain nearby and peered through a homemade telescope rolled from a large eucalypt leaf to get a bird's eye view of XMU. All we saw were rows of dilapidated classroom buildings, a small meeting hall, and some teachers' houses scattered here and there, all surrounded by large vegetable patches and fields. Only two or three dirt paths meandered between the fields and houses, and the whole campus looked more like a large farm than a university. It smelled like one too. Professors with textbooks tucked under their arms rubbed shoulders daily with farmers hauling excrement for fertilizer. The entire campus was redolent of excrement and rotten cabbage.

At that time the coast outside the campus was a complete wilderness of shrubs and bushes teeming with chirping crickets hidden inside. My little companion and I used to play in that wilderness and catch crickets. The entire campus vanished behind the cover of bushes swayed by sea winds.

第 5 章
校园土著话沧桑
郑启五

父亲和母亲在厦门大学当了一辈子的教书匠,上个世纪 50 年代我土生土长在那个校园里,算得上是一个正宗的"校园土著"。其实那时的厦大校园令人很没有校园的感觉,我和小伙伴玩"打野战",常常趴在五老峰腰的巨石上,用大叶桉的树叶卷成的"望远镜"鸟瞰厦大,只见几列瘦瘦的教学楼、宿舍楼、家属楼与成堆的农舍茅屋犬牙交错,或散落在荒山脚下,或跻身于田头地边,三两条蚯蚓的土路像细细的白线勾连其间,校园几乎全是大片大片的菜园子,夹着讲义的教授与挑着大粪的菜农天天擦肩而过,空气中总是淡淡飘散着被粪尿沤烂的包菜叶发出的青酸,还有老黄牛慢悠悠地甩着尾巴。现在回味起来,昔日的厦大可真像是一家荒郊野岭中的"菜农学府"。

我们还常常跑到海边的草岗野地捉蟋蟀,海风掀动着寂寞的灌木丛,四下一片地老天荒。从那里几乎发现不了校园的踪影。

XMU Students on Guard

XMU's first five teaching buildings along the hilltop were the only distinctive features among the ordinary farms. It was within the shadow of those five great buildings that my parents told me XMU's history. They spoke to me of the spirit of our founding father, Mr. Tan Kah Kee, who sold his own property to finance our school. They also praised the great people of the 1920s like Lu Xun and Lin Yutang. They recalled the difficult period of the anti-Japanese war when XMU had to move to mountainous Changting County. They told those stories again and again to make sure I remembered them. They also said to me that they named me "wu" (which means "five" in English) in order to celebrate both the completion of XMU's first five teaching buildings and the setup of New China's first five-year plan.

Indeed, XMU prospered at the dawn of New China in the 1950s, and Mr. Tan Kah Kee envisioned building the five majestic buildings of the Jiannan complex, but soon afterwards the tension escalated between the Mainland and Taiwan. As Xiamen and nearby Taiwan-occupied Jinmen exchanged cannon fire, heavy bombs rained daily on Xiamen. The shrill bomb siren haunted the campus and we had to hide in damp bomb shelters for hours on end.

The war strangled XMU's development, and from the late 1950s until 1976, unending political campaigns swept the entire nation. XMU suffered a disastrous academic recession. The teachers, including my parents, were ousted from their posts and put in water buffalo huts. For quite a long time I carried rice to my parents in an aluminum pot. Students stopped studying and became "Red Guards." No one took care of the teaching buildings, including the first five grand buildings. The building walls were covered with political slogans and black ink scribbles. Once gorgeous buildings became shabby and shattered.

Buffaloed

第 5 章　校园土著话沧桑

只有跑到大礼堂等五幢楼房前才能抒发厦大人的骄傲。从小父母亲就常在这五座楼下对我"忆苦思甜",追忆校主陈嘉庚毁家办校的壮举,还有鲁迅、林语堂等大师在原始校园的足迹,抗战期间为躲避日寇的铁蹄而内迁闽西山城长汀时的木屋岁月,并反复深情地谆谆告之:我名字中的"五"字就是为了欢呼新中国的第一个五年计划和新厦大这五幢楼房的建设而取的。

的确,建国之初,厦门大学拥有过一段阳光明媚的日子,校主陈嘉庚老人拄着手杖亲自敲打,敲出了这五幢建筑雄健的风光,飞檐加红瓦的中式楼顶,玻窗加圆柱的西式楼身,别具一格地雄踞在海岸的坡地上,让所有进出厦门港的巨轮都肃然起敬。然而,海峡两岸剑拔弩张,厦门金门炮声不断,制约了校园的发展,幼年的我不知多少回在凄厉的警报声中抓着小板凳紧跟大人们躲进潮湿的防空洞里。

更可恨的是上世纪 50 年代后期开始了没完没了的政治运动窒息了学科的建设。许多老师(包括我的父母)被整、被斗、被关……少年的我日复一日惊惊颤颤提着铝锅去给"牛栏"里的父母送菜饭。十年"文革"把整个校园折腾得满目疮痍,连厦大人引以为骄傲的那五幢楼也是白墙涂黑墨、门窗被砸烂……

Ready for Class!

The football field became a sweet potato field. It was very difficult for the nation to recover from the Cultural Revolution. Fortunately, Deng Xiaoping, the chief architect of Chinese construction, came to power a third time. Mr. Deng gave first priority to science, technology and education. My parents, the intellectuals in cow-huts, returned to work in the educational arena. The intellectuals helped XMU enter another golden era of prosperous construction, and set her goal to become South China's strongest university.

In 1978, the third session of the 11th Communist Party Central Committee opened another page in New China's history. And as our nation developed, so did our university. We resumed recruiting students from all over the nation, and I was fortunate to pass the university entrance examination at 25 years old and become an XMU student. I had long dreamed of becoming a college student, even while laboring as a temporary worker, pig feeder and student cafeteria cook. How delighted I was when my dream came true! My parents gave me a big hug, their eyes brimming with tears of joy and congratulations.

Our university resumed her campaign to become the "strongest campus in South China." In 1978, XMU had only 10 departments; now we have 46 departments, 18 research institutes and 13 state-level advanced subjects. We expanded our university rapidly not by absorbing other colleges but through our own construction. Every year our university made breakthroughs in its fields of study, and new building groups sprang up like mushrooms during the spring—especially the new "Five Jiageng Buildings" facing beautiful Furong Lake, which marked the grandeur of the University's 80th anniversary.

第5章 校园土著话沧桑

堂堂的上弦场居然密密麻麻种满了喂猪的地瓜、菜瓜……"文革"后拨乱反正举步维艰,幸有第三次复出的邓大人重拳出击,在教科文领域快刀斩乱麻,救我千万"臭老九"及其子女于苦海之中。饱经磨难的厦门大学知识分子群体终于抖落了满身的枷锁,在天风海涛

Our son Shannon with cows on XMU in 1990!

之中奏响了"南方之强"搏击勇进的雄浑乐章!

最是那1978年,十一届三中全会掀开了中国历史崭新的一页,改革开放势不可挡,校随国运,人随国运:这一年学校先后迎来了恢复高考后的第一、第二届大学新生,我也做梦般地跻身其间。本"校园土著"在历任校园临时工、猪场饲养员、食堂伙头军之后,于25岁高龄终成厦大学子,老父母与我相拥而泣,喜泪横流……

再没有形形色色的政治运动,再没有五花八门的精神包袱,我真正以个中人的角度全身心地感受着从此如日中天的厦门大学在展翅翱翔的发展中迎面扑来的祥和之风,面向大海,春暖花开,我们厦大与厦门特区的建设比翼双飞。年年都有新突破,岁岁皆有大手笔(大概再没有人会把校园新楼司空见惯的基建与子女的取名进行兴奋的挂钩);芙蓉湖澄碧的涟漪早已轻轻地荡去"菜农学府"的旧影,新五座的"嘉庚楼群"隆重地顶托起80年校庆的辉煌,从1978年屈指可数的10个系3000余师生的"菜园学府",扩建至现在的18个学院46个系108个科研机构3万多师生的国家重点高等学府,山光海气,地灵人杰,14余万厦门大学毕业生在全国和世界各地尽显才华,为人类的文明与进步而孜孜不倦……

More impressively, the third "5 Jiageng Bldgs." are under construction at the new campus in Zhangzhou City across the bay. They will be the most modern, advanced and best equipped to face the 21st century.

My parents, former professors, are old now, and enjoying their happy retirement. And I, former temporary laborer, tutor graduate students. I am very happy to follow in my parent's footsteps. In my spare time, I climb the Five Peak Mountains, which I used to climb as a child, and through my handmade "leaf telescope" I gaze from the peak upon what is now an incomparably beautiful garden-like campus: the old Five Jiageng Buildings, the new Five Jiageng Buildings, two rippling lakes, rows of trees, and rows of dormitory buildings. The farm-like campus has long vanished.

From the peak I can also see our new campus in Zhangzhou City across the bay, where we are building the third Five Jiageng Buildings. When they are completed, we teachers will cross the sea by boat and lecture in Zhangzhou. Oh, how wonderful that will be! We're the first campus in China to have expanded across both land and sea, and because of XMU, Xiamen City and Zhangzhou City are connected more closely. More beautiful and grander than ever, our University stands to the west of the Taiwan Strait, in the southeast of Mainland China, in the eastern hemisphere. When I think of it, my heart is both peaceful and, at the same time, ambitious for the future.

Thoughts fly afar

Oh, my thoughts fly afar! After having overcome so many difficulties, our Xiamen University must have a brilliant future!

第5章 校园土著话沧桑

身为教授的父母正安享着幸福的晚年，我也成了厦门大学讲坛上的研究生导师，子承父业，其乐融融。人到中年我再次爬上儿时的山头，左眺右望阅不够厦门大学的满园春色，爬了这个山头，又爬了那个山头，气喘吁吁的"校园土著"企盼着像儿时一样鸟瞰厦大全貌的企图总是一再落空，校园依山傍海全方位地扩展，用树叶"望远镜"便可将其尽收眼底的岁月已化作一抹遥远的夕照！啊，厦门大学，你再也不是沧海边那个农教混杂的田庄。千楼竞秀风情万种！

啊，给我一个望远镜吧，我还要远眺海湾那一边的厦门大学漳州新校区，嘉庚老人上个世纪之初的梦想已加倍化地为眼下中国第一座跨海湾大学的辉煌，海湾那边仿佛近在咫尺的新的大学城正在拔地而起，又是一排陈嘉庚风格的现代巨建依山傍海，但更加端庄、更加俏丽而雄伟。"校在海上，海在校中"，我每每乘着高速快艇去上课，胸海和大海一同浪花滚滚，心空宁静而致远！

白鹭翩翩蓝天翔舞。厦门因为有了厦大，而大师云集，高徒荟萃，藏龙卧虎，在五个特区大家庭的比试和竞争中显得神闲气定，饱有学术的厚重和文化的底蕴，发展后劲十足；厦大因为坐拥厦门大港而海阔鱼跃，八面来风，气势如虹，啸傲神州！啊，我的饱经沧桑的厦门大学，我的蓬勃发展的厦门大学，我的前程无量的南方之强！

— 81 —

Chapter 6
"Reliving History"
An XMU Campus Tour with Zheng Qiwu

This title occurred to me while reading Hillary Clinton's "Living History," because I could not find a better way of expressing how I felt on this tour, especially given the four people on it: Zheng Qiwu, Dr. Brown, Gary, and myself. Zheng Qiwu has spent his entire life, from birth, *in* the university. Dr. Bill, as Professor Zheng said, is the "representative" of current Sino-US (or at least XMU-US) relations. Gary Proctor, another American teacher, well represents foreigners who are doing their best to understand and appreciate Chinese people and history And finally, as an XMU undergraduate I am one of the young generation eager to take the torch passed to us by XMU's founding father and his successors, and to make it shine brighter in a larger world.

Prof. Zheng started life in 1952 in the small apartment, Danan #10 and then moved to Guo Guang Building 3, # 17, so our history tour began there. Professor Zheng must surely be a great teacher, because he peppered his "history lesson" with not just facts and stories but passion, wisdom, and a sense of responsibility.

We visited the oldest building on campus, which was built around 1900 even before the university existed. It is now a kindergarten, and Dr. Brown's own two sons attended it (now one is in college, and he hopes his grandsons will attend XMU kindergarten too!). I thought, "The oldest building is now a place for the youngest, and most are university staff...the cycle of life."

At the Fengting buildings, Zheng told us that in the 1950s Tan Kah kee's son-in law, Lee Kong Chian, invested USD $500,000 to build the three Furong buildings, three Guoguang buildings, and three Fengting buildings. "It takes a whole village to raise one child", Hillary said in one of her speeches; it took the effort of Tan Kah Kee's entire family to get the university started, (his brother, son-in-law etc.), but it is going to take the strength of all of us, through many generations, to make XMU prosperous.

We passed some Longyan ("dragon eye" fruit) trees along the road and Prof. Zheng said that the name fits the trees perfectly because he used to climb them as a child, and the "dragon's eyes" have witnessed change, revolution, and reform of the university up until the present.

第6章

"重历历史"

——随郑启五老师游厦大

想到这个题目是因为我正在阅读希拉里·克林顿的《亲历历史》，除此之外我找不到更好的方式来表达这次校园之旅的感悟了，特别是有幸与郑启五老师、潘维廉教授、加里·普罗克特三位同行。郑启五老师——一位从出生至今五十余年生活在校园里的"老厦大"，潘维廉教授——像郑老师所说的，"当代中美关系"（至少也算是"厦大—美国关系"）的代表；加里·普罗克特——美国外教，很好地代表了那些正在尽力去了解和感受中国历史和人民的外国人；而我——厦大年轻一代中的一员，渴望着从陈嘉庚先生和其他无数先辈手中接过火炬，并使其在更广阔的世界里放出更璀璨的光芒。

郑启五老师1952年出生，当时居住在大南10号，后搬入国光317号，那里自然也就成为我们重温历史之旅的起点。郑老师不愧是位出色的教授，他在教授这堂"历史课"时激情洋溢，史实和故事的讲述中处处闪现着他的睿智和责任感。

我们来到了校园里最古老的房子——现在的厦大幼儿园托儿部。它建于上个世纪初，比厦大本身的历史还要久。潘教授的两个儿子就是在这里上的幼儿园（如今大儿子已经上了大学，他希望他的孙子们将来也能上这个幼儿园！）。最古老的建筑却成为最年轻的生命嬉戏的乐园，而且绝大多数正是学校教工子女……生命的轮回啊！

走到丰庭楼群时，郑老师告诉我们，1950年，陈嘉庚先生的女婿李光前出资50万美元建了芙蓉一、二、三，国光一、二、三以及丰庭一、二、三。我想起希拉里在一篇演讲中说："培养一个孩子需要全村人的努力。"厦大早已人才辈出，而其当年的创立则倾注了陈嘉庚先生全家人的心血，那么，她今天的繁荣却将需要数代人的共同努力和不懈追求！

我们沿途经过几棵龙眼树，郑老师说，他小的时候经常爬到树上去偷摘果实，此树恰如其名，像"龙的眼睛"，见证了学校的沧桑变化。如今的学校，楼多了，树少了，已很难想象那曾经树木遍地、水果满山的情景，那种"都市里的村庄"的感觉已经不复存在了。不远处便是厦大学生在1954—1979年间自己动手挖的防空洞（学生挖防空洞，又是厦大在全国独一无二之处），这段记忆全都铭刻在了龙眼树的年轮上，这些树，如同世人，也在低头沉思着那段走过的艰难岁月吧……

Now that XMU has more buildings and fewer trees, it is hard to imagine it was once covered with fruit trees and called an "urban village." While standing between big old dragon eye trees and air-raid shelters dug by students between 1954-1956 (a rare student activity at that time in China!), I felt

Lessons in a Bomb Shelter

that the trees, like people, were contemplating the tough times they'd survived.

We visited the well kept old villa, Da Nan #3, which was built in the 1930s. It's now the home of Prof. Zheng's friend, Yang Mingyi, whom Dr. Brown calls "Senior Uncle Beard" because his beard is even longer than that of famous XMU professor "Uncle Beard" (Ji Yuhua). Given Yang's age, he could be my "grandpa," and when he shook hands with Gary, my "American grandpa", I felt that even though they could not speak each other's language, they both knew what it was like to experience history. Later, Prof. Zheng said the Changting XMU campus was close to the American military airport, and Chinese students and American soldiers became friends and played basketball together. I thought of then and now, and reflected on Dr. Brown's first letter to me, in which he wrote, "The best thing you and I can do is to help the rest of the world better understand China, so let's work on that." As Prof. Zheng noted, from Sa Bendong's day until now, both Chinese and foreigners have been helping XMU carry out this task.

We visited the statues of Lu Xun and President Sa Bendong, and also saw a statue of Zheng Chenggong (Koxinga), who fought against the Dutch for Taiwan in the Ming Dynasty. Even though Koxinga lived 350 years ago, Dr. Brown said, "I've met him!" Of course, that was because Bill played a bad guy (the last Dutch governor) in a movie about Koxinga. So I took this funny picture of Dr. Brown on bended knee before the statue, and we all laughed and said "Victor and victim!" Dr. Brown said he had surrendered to Koxinga, and afterwards they had Chinese fast food!

We cannot discuss XMU architecture without mentioning the "four fives"—four groups of buildings, with five buildings in each group. The four groups are: Qun Xian #1— #5 (built in 1921); Shang Xianchang #1—#5 (finished in 1955); Jiageng #1—#5 (2001) and Jiageng #1—#5 on Zhang Zhou campus (2003). (But this may change to "five fives" because Dr. Brown keeps expanding his mountainside apartment!).

第6章 "重历历史"——随郑启五老师游厦大

郑老师带我们拜访了他的老朋友杨明宜先生。杨先生居住的是校园内建于上世纪 30 年代的老别墅——大南 3 号楼，如今这栋房子依然保存完好。潘教授见面便称呼杨先生为"老大胡子伯伯"，没错，他的胡子确实比厦大的"大胡子伯伯"（著名教授纪玉华）还要长。以杨先生的年纪，一定能做我的爷爷了。因此，看着他和被我称作"美国爷爷"的加里握手，我想对于两位曾远隔外万水千山却共同经历历史的老人，虽然语言不通，那种饱经沧桑的感受必定是相通的。后来，郑老师谈起内迁长汀时厦大与美军机场为邻的往事，说当时厦大学生同美国士兵建立了深厚的友谊，还一起打篮球……从那时形成的跨国情谊，到面前这一中一美两位老人长长的握手，我不禁转头看看潘教授——18 年来为使这友谊之树更加枝繁叶茂而不辍耕耘的美籍专家，他给我的第一封信中的句子再一次涌上了我的心头："你我生命中能做的最伟大的事情，就是让世界了解中国，让我们一起努力吧！"如郑老师所说，无论是萨本栋，那位在抗战期间远赴美国为厦大筹集资金的校长，还是今天的潘维廉教授等众多外籍专家，都肩负这个跨越国界的藩篱与偏见的鸿沟的神圣使命，并为此全力以赴。

我们瞻仰了鲁迅像、萨校长伉俪墓，又来到民族英雄郑成功的雕像前。虽然，郑成功生活的时代距今已有 350 年，但潘教授却兴奋地说："我见过他！"原来，他在电影《郑成功》中扮演了荷兰最后一任总督。他屈膝跪在雕像前，做投降状，我连忙按下快门，将这有趣的一幕拍下。潘教授还说他向郑成功"投降"之后，他们还共进了中式快餐！

I surrender--again!

既然谈到厦大建筑，我们就不能不提"四个五"——四组楼群，每组有五幢楼组成（一主四从）。这四组楼群分别是：群贤 1 号—5 号楼（建于 1921 年）；上弦场 1 号—5 号楼（完工于 1955 年）；本部嘉庚 1 号—5 号楼（2001 年）以及漳州校区嘉庚 1 号—5 号楼（2003 年）。（但是这个可能很快要变为"五个五"了。因为潘教授正在他自己山上的房子里搞扩建呢！）

We visited the majestic granite buildings of the Shang Xianchang group. Prof. Zheng said that they are not very tall, but because they are perched upon the hill like tigers, they can be seen from afar and are the first sight to greet visitors arriving by ship. The centerpiece is XMU's most photographed building—the largest university auditorium in China even today.

The grand auditorium and the four buildings flanking it face the sea, and have watched the sun rise and set for over half a century. The splendid scenery brought to mind lines from a drama I had been practicing as part of the 85h anniversary celebration. When asked why he selected this spot to found a university, Tan Kah Kee said, "Backed against the majestic Wu Lao (Five Old Men) Mountain, facing the awesome ocean, to the west of Nan Putuo Temple and east of Huli Hill Fort, no other place is more perfect than here for a university. This is also where Koxinga trained his soldiers, and I hope this will help students keep in mind that they have the responsibility to complete the work begun by their ancestors."

We ended our trip at where the university started—the first set of five building near the west gate which Tan Kah Kee built himself. We looked at the inscribed cornerstone, which Prof. Zheng said is the single most important spot on the campus but usually overlooked. I touched the cornerstone, and revered the statue of Tan Kah Kee which is in the square right in front, and I was inspired and moved by the stories behind each one of those buildings, by my university's long history and indomitable will to survive. Prof. Zheng said no other university in China had to overcome so much—the Japanese in the 30s and 40s, bombing by the Kuomintang in the 50s, the dark days of the Cultural Revolution in the 60s and 70s. But the university has survived because of people like Prof. Zheng, who has devoted his entire life to her and accompanied her through joy and misery, happiness and suffering, all the way to the present—and still love her as they always have. It's no wonder that Dr. Brown calls Prof. Zheng "Mr. XMU!"

People throughout China say XMU is "One of China's most beautiful campuses," and this is definitely the truth, but there's more to XMU than outward beauty. I am humbled by her greatness, both past and present, and by her hopes for the future. We have been entrusted with the continuing legacy of many generations, and today's tour was truly a chance for me to relive history with one who lived it and two who are helping make it today. I hope that my own generation will carry the torch even higher, that it may burn brighter—for China and for the world.

第6章 "重历历史"——随郑启五老师游厦大

于是我们便来到了宏伟的花岗岩建筑，这"四个五"之一的上弦场楼群。郑启五老师说这些建筑虽然不算高，但是依山而建，如同猛虎一般，人们从海上乘船驶来，第一眼看见的就是它们——这也是陈嘉庚先生当年的意图。中心一幢，便是校内最常上镜的建筑，也是迄今为止中国大学中最大的礼堂——建南大礼堂。

这"一主四从"均面海而建，经历了半个多世纪沧桑。眼前这壮观的景象让我想起正在排练的一部为85周年校庆献礼的话剧《诚毅人生》中的台词。在被问及为何要将厦大选址于此时，陈嘉庚先生感叹道："这里背靠雄伟的五老峰，面向壮阔的大海，西临南普陀寺，东接胡里山炮台，建大学非此地莫属。这里曾是郑成功操练大军的地方，在这里创办大学，可以继承先烈遗志，继往开来！"

我们此行的结束地，却是厦大的起点——由陈嘉庚先生亲建的、毗邻西校门的第一个"一主四从"楼群——群贤楼群。郑老师说那块奠基石应该算是整个校园最具重大意义的标志，却常常被忽略。俯身轻抚奠基石，抬头仰望位于广场正前方的陈嘉庚雕像，我心怀崇敬，被这一幢幢建筑后面隐藏的故事，被母校悠久的历史以及顽强的生存意志所深深地打动。郑老师动情地说，中国没有哪个大学像厦大这样经历了如此多的磨难：上世纪三四十年代的日军侵略，五六十年代金门守军的炮轰，六七十年代"文化大革命"的浩劫……但是你看，她却显示出无限生机，原因是有许许多多把自己毕生的精力献给了厦大，和她同甘苦，共患难，一路走到今天，对厦大的深情挚爱至死不渝的人——郑启五老师本人就是其中之一，无怪乎潘维廉教授称他为"厦大先生"！

众所周知，厦大校园是全国最美丽的校园之一，但是厦大拥有的不仅仅是美丽的外表。我们个人因她历史和现实的伟大、因她未来前途的光明而备感创业艰难、重任在肩。而今天的校园之旅，特别是与一位亲历历史以及两位正在帮助她书写今天历史的人结伴同游，更使我深切体会到这遗产的弥足珍贵。我期待我和我的同龄人能够高举这火把，让它燃烧得更旺，照亮中国，更照亮世界。

Chapter 7

Gifts That Keep Giving: Alumni Contributions

Generations of people have left their beloved mother university after graduation, but their hearts have remained. The years have grayed their hair and deepened their wrinkles but not hindered their endeavors to help XMU develop in any way they can. And it is with their continuous assistance, generous gestures, and most importantly, their remarkable emotional influence and spirit, that our university has been able to make tremendous progress on her way to academic prominence.

As one digs into the history behind our campus facilities, one is stunned by the countless stories told of alumni—of the long and yet incomplete list of their contributions, and of their capacity to love their mother university.

"XMU Tower" —Building for the New Century
—about Cai Yueshi

The 21-story "Song'en lou", XMU's tallest building and landmark as she strides into the 21st century, was built in 2001. This building, and the nearby Jianwen Building, was endowed by Mrs. Cai Yueshi and her husband, Mr. Ding Zhengzeng. Mr. Ding has passed away but Ms. Cai, an industrialist in Thailand and XMU graduate, carries on their shared philanthropy.

Cai Shiyue was born in a Christian family in Jinjiang, Fujian, and when she was little she went to Manila with her father. When the war with Japan broke out in 1937 they moved to Shanghai, and then back to Jinjiang in 1945. Cai was recommended for admission to XMU but she didn't go because by that time XMU had moved to Changting, which her family thought was too far from home. The following year, Cai took the exam and was accepted once again.

第7章 献礼到永恒——校友的捐赠

第7章

献礼到永恒
——校友的捐赠

一代又一代厦大人毕业离开了母校，然而他们的心却永远留了下来。许多年过去，他们或许已两鬓斑白，但为厦大的发展而尽己所能付出的不懈努力却从未有丝毫减少。也正是有了他们慷慨解囊，不断帮助，最重要的是，有了他们的精神和思想的巨大感召，我们的学校才能在奔向优秀院校的道路上大踏步前行。

当我们试图挖掘校园楼群设施背后潜藏的故事时，不禁被强烈地震撼了：那长长的、却又永无尽头的捐资兴学的名单，那关于我们的校友说也说不完的故事，那对于母校刻骨铭心、至死不渝的挚爱……

"厦大的摩天大楼"，迈向21世纪的标志
——关于蔡悦诗

完工于2001年的21层"颂恩楼"，是学校里最高的楼，也是厦大迈向21世纪的标志。这座高楼和不远处的"建文楼"都是由泰国实业家、厦大校友蔡悦诗、丁政曾夫妇捐资兴建的。丁先生已经过世了，但蔡女士(大家亲切地称她为"蔡大姐")却仍在他们共同的捐资兴学之路上前行。

蔡悦诗出生在福建晋江的一个基督教家庭，年幼就随父亲移居马尼拉。1937年抗日战争爆发后，她随父母定居上海，1945年又回到晋江。她后来被保送到厦大，但是当时厦大迁到长汀办学，她觉得长汀离家太远，就没有去。第二年自己再考，再次进了厦大。在厦大读了一年以后，她来到上海沪江大学。注册、交费后，上了十天课就决定回厦大了，因为她已经习惯了在厦大"国立化"的生活，要改变实属不易。在厦门大学她认识了丁政曾，后来两人走到了一起。回忆起往事，蔡大姐开玩笑道："那个时候我要是不回来，现在不晓得是哪一家的老太太了。"

After one year at XMU, she transferred to Shanghai Lujiang University, a Christian University, where she registered, paid the tuition and stayed in class for only ten days before deciding to return to XMU because she was used to the routine at XMU, a national university, and found it difficult to change. At XMU she met Ding Zhengzeng, her future husband. Recalling the old times she joked, "If I had not returned then, who knows whose wife I would have become?"

Those who attended XMU's 80th anniversary ceremony still remembers vividly Cai's remarks. When asked to give a speech she said:

> "Back in high school we talked about, if my memory serves me right, something a former Yale president said. 'Don't ignore the A and B students, as they will return as professors. Don't look down upon the C and D students, as they will donate for building more buildings for the university.' "A and B students contribute their intelligence in the academic arena, and help build our university's prestige, while C and D students may not have as many academic achievements but are successful in business and donate money to help with buildings and other facilities. Of course, there are people like Huang Baoxin and Huang Keli whose contributions were both in "software" and "hardware". They, together with other alumni who dedicate themselves to their own field, all deserve our high respect."

Everyone present applauded her remarks.

Cai, who is about to turn 80, returns home to XMU regularly and does not ever want to miss a celebration.

Everlasting Passion
Mr. Shao Jianyin

Mr. Shao Jianyin, an alumnus who now lives in the Philippines, has done far more than just donating for Yi Xuan Guan. He and his wife Lin Yanzhen have worked together constantly to raise funds for different activities at XMU. They contributed to "Pen-Tung Sah Education and Scientific Research Foundation" (PESRF) and also raised US$300,000 for it.

Mingpei Stadium, Cai Qingjie Lou, Ziqin Lou and others were named after the alumni who endowed them. These benefactors were influenced by Shao, who was President for five years of CKSC, a college in the Philippines, and four had been his students. They were all inspired by his giving personality, deep love for his university and his efforts to support her growth, and they helped build close ties between XMU and that college.

第7章 献礼到永恒——校友的捐赠

当时参加了厦大80周年华诞庆典的人们还清楚地记得蔡大姐在她演讲中讲到的话:"回忆当年高中时,大学生之间流传着这么几句话,如果我没记错的话,应该是当时美国耶鲁大学校长的话。他说:'你们不要疏忽成绩A和B的学生,他们将来可能回到母校当教授。你们也不要小看成绩C和D的学生,他们日后会回来给学校捐建大楼。'……那些A和B的学生把他们的智慧财产献给母校。他们回到母校,肩负培育下一代的重任,同时也凭借他们在学术上的成就,提升母校声誉……至于那些C和D的学生,由于精力充沛,活动力强,在商场上较占优势。他们没有智慧成果可夸耀,只能献上金钱供学校改善教学环境和增添先进设施……当然,很多人,比如我们的黄保欣学长、黄克立学长,他们的捐献是全面的,既有智慧又有实体。还有我们许多默默耕耘的同学,他们在各自的岗位上尽心竭力,发挥他们的作用,这是最值得我们佩服的……"

在场的人对她的话报以热烈的掌声。

蔡大姐如今快80岁了,但仍然"常回家看看"。她从不愿意错过学校的任何一个庆典。

永远的爱
——关于邵建寅

菲律宾校友邵建寅先生所做出的贡献远不止捐建"亦玄馆"。邵先生和夫人林彦珍女士始终不停地为学校募集资金。他们不仅自己为"萨本栋教育科研基金会"捐款,还为其募集了30万美金。

邵先生的精神也影响了其他许多校友。捐赠明培体育馆、蔡清洁楼、自钦楼、祖营楼的四位厦大校友分别是佘明培、蔡清洁、许自钦和洪文炳,他们在菲律宾中正学院(CKSC)时都曾经是邵先生的学生——邵先生在那里当过五年的院长。几位学生被邵先生无私奉献的人格魅力、对母校的热爱和他为其发展所心甘情愿付出的一切所鼓舞。大家还通过共同努力,帮助厦大和中正学院建立了紧密的联系。

Shao's dedication to XMU is so deep that he now has a new hobby: touring XMU campus. He visits the campuses often and has brought his family to show them about at least five times! Every time people he knows in the Philippines visit Xiamen, he insists they see XMU, and he contacts friends on campus and suggests they escort his Filipino friends around campus, and he reminds the "tour guide" not to miss certain places that he thinks his friends should see. And Shao never loses track of construction, on either the Zhangzhou or Xiamen campus. Every time he hears of some new project under way, he immediately jumps a ferry to Zhangzhou campus, like a child, full of enthusiasm and eager with anticipation.

Midnight Phone Calls
Prof. Ge Wenxun

The significance of alumni's endeavors to support their university goes far beyond money. Together they have created a certain ethos for the whole community. People have been inspired and come to realize that after many years, their hearts still belong with their mother university, giving rise to a spirit in which people do their best to contribute in different ways, all of which are equally appreciated.

Prof. Ge Wenxun matriculated in 1946 and has lived in the US for many years. Although he's been living far away, his heart has never left XMU. When the Pen-Tung Sah Micro-Electro-Mechanical Systems Research Center was established, he collected information, translated it into English, and compiled a brochure that he could distribute to people when he attended international meetings, forums or even class reunions. He raised funds for "Pen-Tung Sah Education and Scientific Research Foundation" at meetings, parties and from doctoral students. Whenever he met excellent professors, scientists, or promising students, he told them about XMU and encouraged them to come to work here. He always takes time out of his busy schedule to write letters to family members, former classmates, friends, colleagues, or other professors to encourage them to help with XMU's progress….

第 7 章　献礼到永恒——校友的捐赠

邵先生对母校的热爱之深，使他养成了一个习惯：参观厦大。他会经常回来看看校园，仅带着全家人参观学校就不少于 5 次！每次有他的菲律宾朋友到厦门来，他都会请他们务必来看看厦门大学，然后还会打电话给在厦大的朋友，请他们当"导游"，陪着菲律宾客人参观校园，并特意提醒千万不要漏掉了某些"必看"的地方。比如漳州校区大型漂亮的图书馆。无论是本部还是漳州校区搞了什么新的建设，邵先生从来都知道，每次听说漳州校区那边某个新的建筑已开始施工的时候，他都会像个小孩子一样跳上开往校区的船，是那么的充满热情、渴望和憧憬……

午夜电话
—— 关于葛文勋

校友们为支持母校发展所做的努力，其影响力远远超过金钱本身。他们已经为社会树立了一种捐资兴学的风尚，让更多的人们备受感动和鼓舞，使他们意识到，离开了许多年之后，他们那颗心仍旧属于厦大，属于挚爱的母校，在这种精神的影响下，更多的人尽全力奉献自己的力量，方式不同，却同样让人感激、使人感动。

葛文勋教授 1946 年进入厦大，现已经在美国居住多年。他虽然身在万水千山之外，却不忘经常回来看看母校。萨本栋微机电研究中心成立的时候，他主动地搜集资料，翻译成册，然后就随身携带着，利用参加国际会议、开论坛或者是同学聚会的机会，分发给大家并向大家介绍。他在各种场合为萨本栋教育科研基金会募集资金，包括带领博士生募捐。无论在哪里接触到杰出的教授、科学家或者出色的年轻人，他都会不失时机地向他们介绍厦大并鼓励他们来厦大工作。他还会经常写信给亲戚、老同学、朋友、同事等等，请他们也为厦门大学的发展做出一份贡献……

Ge is over 80 years old, but still does research in his lab all day and then returns home each evening to pursue other ends. Because of the time difference, when people from the Alumni Association in China call him in the morning, it is evening or late night in the U.S. Yet he is always happy to talk with them, even at the end of a long day. His wife says, "Phone calls late at night are usually from XMU!"

Ge has kept a unique habit for many years. Every time he returns to XMU, either the day he arrives or very early the next morning, he visits President Sa's tomb on campus and sits there for a while, quietly and peacefully, recalling the difficult but memorable times of his life, the hardships the university survived, and the president who led them to fight their way through the war, a teacher and president of his lifetime. When Ge leaves, he picks some little yellow flowers that grow by the tomb and gravely wears them on his suit. This has become his routine—visiting his highly respected and forever remembered professor, talking with him quietly in his heart, or maybe even telling him about the latest difficulties that he has conquered, both in the academic field and in his life. He then takes his leave, with tiny yellow flowers on his suit shining in the rays of the sun, eyes moist and heart humbled, but proud...

"Return Here to Learn about China!"
Mr. Huang Baoxin

Huang Baoxin graduated from XMU in 1945 and is now the Vice Chairman of the Committee for the Basic Law of the HKSAR under the Standing Committee of the NPC. He and his wife Wu Liying informed XMU they would endow a building, and XMU received the money just three days later! And the building was named after them: Bao Xin Liying lou.

第7章 献礼到永恒——校友的捐赠

葛先生已经80多岁了,但仍然白天在实验室工作,晚上回家处理其他事情。由于时差的原因,厦大校友总会上午打电话的时候,他那里就已经是晚上或者夜里了。不过他从来都很乐意接听。葛先生的夫人说:"夜里的电话都是厦大的!"

葛先生有一个独特的、保留了很多年的习惯。他每次一回来,当天或第二天一大早,一定要来到萨本栋校长的墓前坐一会儿,静静地回忆自己生命中那一段难以忘怀的时光、母校那段艰苦卓绝的历史和带领大家走过战时那段艰难岁月的先师萨本栋——他一生一世的老师和校长……在离开之前,摘几朵墓前生长的黄色小花,凝重地把它们戴在胸前……这早已成为他每次来必做的一项工作——看望他永远崇敬和怀念的老校长,在心里再和他说说话,或者可能在向他汇报自己新近在学术上和生活中又取得了哪些成绩、克服了哪些困难,就像从前那样……然后他离开,胸前黄色小花在阳光下一闪一闪的、伴着眼中的泪光;他心怀谦卑,却又骄傲无比……

> "回到这里来学习,
> 学习我们的中国!"
> ——关于黄保欣

香港校友黄保欣1945年从厦大毕业,现任全国人大常委会香港基本法委员会副主任。在他和夫人吴丽英告知母校他们将捐资建楼后,第三天学校就收到了他们的汇款!这座楼命名为"保欣丽英楼"。

Huang and Wu, his future wife, were in the same class in Changting. Even some of the security passwords he uses now have come from his student number in Changting. According to his brother, Mr. Huang Ruixin, a retired XMU professor, when he accompanied his brother and family to revisit Changting, Huang Baoxin couldn't stop crying. "He sees Changting as his parents", and told his children who were born in other counties that they should never forget China, their country, no matter where they go. He has eight grandchildren and most of them are studying at Harvard or Stanford, but "My desire is that one day they will return to XMU to study Chinese culture," he said.

A list of all XMU benefactors would be endless. Alumni have organized XMU associations throughout China, as well as in Thailand, the Philippines, Hong Kong, North America, and other places around the globe. When they return to XMU and see students seeking materials in the library, they donate thousands of library books. When they see students washing clothes by hand, they donate for laundry rooms and washing machines. When they see students carrying water bottles and rushing about to get water, they donate money for water dispensers to be placed outside classrooms. When they see students lined up to use the computer, they donated hundreds of new computers. Every year they return to celebrate the university's birthday, and get together and chat as though they were young students once again. Being back at the mother university rejuvenates them. Some of them run businesses around the world, flying several times a day. Some do research or teach over ten hours a day. Some are ranking government officials and have important duties to attend to. But the moment they catch sight of campus, embrace old friends and greet former professors, their minds return to the "good old times" and the travails of yesteryear.

People have asked why alumni donations are higher at XMU than other universities around China, and they will find the answer in the faces of these returnees. Our predecessors' willingness and diligence in their devotion to education, starting with our founding father Tan Kah Kee, has inspired generations and will continue to do so for generations to come. Our alumni, who are the most caring, giving and loving children of our mother university, with unshakable faith, collective efforts, extraordinarily beautiful minds and essential goodness of people, have over the years dedicated themselves to the fulfilling of "Pursue Excellence, Strive for Perfection", and have undoubtedly made her proud, prosperous and prestigious.

第7章 献礼到永恒——校友的捐赠

黄先生和吴女士是长汀时期的同学。即使保欣先生现在用的一些密码还是由当年长汀时的学号得来的呢！据他的弟弟、已经退休的厦大教授黄瑞欣先生回忆说，当瑞欣陪哥哥全家回到长汀旧址的时候，保欣一直泪流满面，"他看长汀像自己的父母一样"。他还告诫他在国外出生长大的孩子们，无论他们走到哪里，永远不能忘记自己的祖国。黄保欣先生有八个孙子，大多数都在哈佛、斯坦福读书，"但我的愿望是，有朝一日他们能回到厦大来，学习中国传统文化。"

相信为厦大捐赠过的校友名单是没人能够列出的。校友们在国内各地以及泰国、菲律宾、香港、美洲和世界很多其他国家和地区组织成立了厦大校友会。他们回到学校来，看到学生们在图书馆里查找资料，就捐赠了上万册图书；看到学生们手洗衣服，就捐赠洗衣房和洗衣机；看到学生们提着水瓶急匆匆地去打水，就为教学楼捐赠饮水机；看到学生们在机房外面排队等候上机，就捐赠上千台新电脑……每年校庆期间，校友们从世界各地赶回，欢聚一堂畅谈往事，好像立刻就回到了学生时代——回到母校的怀抱使他们重拾青春岁月。他们中间，有人是全球闻名的实业家、一天飞好几个地方；有人每天从事教学科研十几个小时；有人在政府部门担任关键职务，每天要事缠身……但是只要回到母校，视野中又重现了往日的校园，又见到崇敬的老师，再次拥抱当年亲爱的同学的时候，脑海中就只有那些"金色的年华"和过去那段艰苦的学习生活了。

人们会问，是什么使厦大在校友捐赠这方面在全国的大学中遥遥领先，相信他们会在校友们洋溢着热情和喜悦的脸庞上找到答案的。从陈嘉庚先生开始，先贤们心甘情愿地为教育所付出的努力已经感染了一代又一代厦大人，并将继续激励和鼓舞后来者。我们的校友，这些对母亲最牵挂、体贴和爱戴的孩子们，已经在用他们格外美丽的心灵、永不动摇的信念、善良美好的人格和共同携手付出的努力，实践着"自强不息，止于至善"的校训，并无疑使他们的母亲更加声名远播、骄傲和幸福。

Chapter 8

Xiamen University Today
Strength of the South, Strength of the Nation

XMU's nickname is "Strength of the South" but she's also the "Strength of the Nation" for several reasons.

1) The only university founded by an overseas Chinese, XMU enjoys unparalleled support by Chinese the world over.

2) The only key university in a special economic zone, XMU has made unique contributions to China's modernization and reforms.

3) Strategically located on the Fujian coast facing Taiwan (less than 2km from Jinmen at low tide!), XMU has closer ties with Taiwan than any other Chinese university.

4) At the end of 2005, XMU's undergrad program was the first in China to ever get the highest scores in all 19 categories of the national evaluation!

Considering XMU's traditions of academic excellence and innovation, and her unique position politically, geographically and economically, it's no wonder the State is giving her special support under both the 211 Project[①] and the 985 Project.[②] But what makes XMU unique is the people—the staff, students and alumni who are making a name for XMU not just throughout China but also across the globe.

---

① "211 Project": a national key development project of the 9th Five Year Plan, this program implemented in 1995 aims at producing 100 top universities for the 21st century.
② "985 Project": the central government's program for developing a number of world-class universities

第8章

今日厦大

——南方之强,民族之强

厦门大学有"南方之强"的美称,但同时也应被视作"民族之强",原因如下:

(1)作为唯一一所由华侨建立的大学,厦门大学享受无与伦比的旅居世界各地华人的支持。

(2)作为唯一一所位于经济特区的重点大学,厦门大学为中国的现代化建设和改革做出了特殊的贡献。

(3)战略性的地理位置——位于福建沿海,面向台湾(低潮时距离金门不到2公里!)。厦门大学与台湾有着比中国其他任何一所大学都更为密切的联系。

(4)就在2005年的11月,厦门大学在教育部本科教学评估中19项指标都拿了A,在全国尚属首次。

厦大的学术成就和勇于创新的传统,及其在政治、地理和经济上的特殊地位,使国家在"211工程"[①]和"985工程"[②]上都给予了她特殊的支持。然而,真正成就了厦大之独一无二的,是她的人才——教职员工、学生以及校友,是他们让"厦门大学"的名字声震四海、响彻全球!

---

① "211工程":第九个五年计划的全国重点发展项目,从1995年起开始实施,旨在重点建设21世纪一百所左右的大学。

② "985工程":中央政府旨在创建世界一流大学的项目。

85 Years of Quality Staff XMU's staff of almost 5,000 includes over 2,000 full-time faculty and professional researchers. Over 50 academicians of the Chinese Academy of Sciences (CAS) and the Chinese Academy of Engineering (CAE) have studied or worked at XMU.

XMU teachers have earned numerous national awards. Sixteen under age 45 have obtained the state's "Science Grant for National Outstanding Youth". Eight have received the "Education Ministry Award for Excellent Young University Teacher". Eight have been listed in the "One-hundred plus One-thousand plus Ten-thousand Talent Project". Sixteen have been trained in the Ministry of Education's training program, "Leading Figure for the New Century". Eighteen have been listed in the Ministry of Education's assistance program, "Outstanding Figures of the New Century." One has been honored as "National Distinguished University Teacher".

XMU has distinguished professorships in eight subjects supported by the "State Yangtze Scholar Award Program" and in four subjects supported by Fujian Province's "Minjiang Scholar Award Program."

85 Years of Quality Students Since 1921, XMU has had over 120,000 graduates. The 31,000 full-time on-campus students today include over 19,000 undergraduates, almost 11,000 master students, and about 1800 doctoral students.

XMU's graduates have made a name for themselves and our school. XMU students won three gold medals for three consecutive years in China Undergraduate Challenge Cup for Business Plan Competition, and landed the unique Special Prize in China Undergraduate Contest for Mathematical Modeling in 2003. Not surprisingly, XMU grads have no problem landing jobs! In 2004, XMU's employment rate was 98.1% for graduates and 97.4% for undergraduates —one of the highest in the nation.

Award Winning Academic Programs & Facilities With what is widely regarded as China's most beautiful campus, XMU has some of the nation's best living, teaching, and support facilities. At present, the university has 3 campuses which cover a total area of about over 1315 acre. Xiamen campus, located in the southern part of Xiamen Island, has an area of 411.84 acre, Zhangzhou campus has an area of 423 acre, and Jimei campus has an area of 494 acre.

XMU has RMB 1.5 billion in fixed assets and RMB 579 million in instruments and equipment, as well as several research centers ranked #1 in the nation. The over 80 research institutions include 2 State Key Laboratories, 2 State Specialty Laboratories, 3 Education Ministry Key Laboratories, 1 Fujian Provincial Key Laboratory, 1 Fujian Provincial Research Center, and 5 State Key Research Bases in Humanities and Social Sciences.

第8章 今日厦大——南方之强，民族之强

85年不变的优秀教职人员

厦门大学近5000的教职人员中，包括了2000多名的专任教师和专业研究者。而曾在厦门大学学习或者工作过的两院院士也达50多人。

厦大教师获得国家级奖励情况喜人。45岁以下中青年教师中有16人获国家杰出青年科学基金，8人获得教育部高校优秀青年教师，8人被列入国家百千万人才工程，16人被列入教育部跨世纪人才培养计划，18人被列入教育部新世纪优秀人才支持计划，1人获得教育部高校教学名师奖。

厦门大学的8个学科设立"长江学者"特聘教授岗位，4个学科设立"闽江学者"特聘教授岗位。

85年不变的优秀学生

自1921年建校以来，厦门大学已经培养了超过120000名学生。现有在校学生31000余人，其中本科生约19000人，硕士生近11000人，博士生约1800人。

厦大的毕业生为自己也为学校赢得了荣誉。厦大学生曾连续三年在"挑战杯"中国大学生创业计划大赛中拿了金奖，在2003年的全国大学生数学建模竞赛中获得唯一一个特等奖。因此厦门大学毕业生就业形势极佳也就不足为奇啦！2004年研究生就业率达93.1%，本科生就业率达97.4%，在全国名列前茅。

先进的教学科研设备和公共服务体系

厦大校园被公认为中国最美丽的校园之一，有着一流的生活设施和教学科研设备和公共服务体系。目前学校占地8000多亩，其中位于厦门岛南端的校本部占地近2505亩，漳州校区占地2572亩，集美校区占地3004亩。

厦门大学拥有固定资产总值近15亿元，仪器设备总值5.7亿多元，以及多个全国一流的研究中心。学校设有80多个研究机构，其中2个国家重点实验室、一个国家专业实验室、3个教育部重点实验室、还拥有5个教育部文科重点研究基地。

XMU also boasts one of China's most advanced high-speed information networks (hard to believe that I only made one phone call my entire first year at XMU—and could not get through!).

The 20 schools, 45 departments, and numerous key research institutes offer undergrad, graduate and postgraduate programs in everything from management and economics to humanities, social sciences, natural science, engineering and technology, art education, and medical science. XMU has thirteen "national key disciplines" and 5 subjects (Chemistry, Biology, Life Science & Technology, Economics and History) have been designated as "national educational centers for talents".

An International School XMU is truly an international institute, enjoying close ties and academic exchanges with almost 100 foreign institutes. XMU also has an unparalleled number of links with Taiwan, including ties with 24 Taiwan universities and colleges, 63 research institutes and 34 media outlets. XMU also has over 1600 international students on campus, as well as 6,000 overseas correspondence students, because XMU pioneered distance education in the 1950s, as well as education for foreigners in China.

Lifelong Learning Last but definitely not least, especially with our aging population, XMU is a leader in emphasizing lifelong education, and has a College of Continuing Education and Vocational Education, including:

1) Adult Education
2) Professional Technical Education
3) Internet Education

XMU has so much to offer that I'm thinking of going back to school myself. Maybe I can finally learn Chinese!

Mass Education Movement Poster (1920s)
"Illiteracy is like blindness"

第8章 今日厦大——南方之强，民族之强

厦门大学拥有全国先进的校园高速信息网络（难以置信的是，在我来到厦大的第一年里只打过一个国际长途电话,总是打不通!）

学校设有20多学院、研究院，包括45个系和一批研究机构，成为一所包括管理科学、人文科学、社会科学、自然科学、工程和技术科学、艺术教育科学、医学科学等学科门类相当齐全的培养本科生、研究生和博士生的综合性大学。厦门大学拥有13个国家级重点学科和5个国家基础科学人才培养基地（化学，生物学，生命技术科学，经济学，历史学）。

一所国际化的大学——厦门大学是一所真正意义上的国际化的大学，现与约100所海外研究机构保持着紧密的联系和学术交流。厦门大学与台湾高校的密切联系也是其他国内大学所望尘莫及的。她与台湾24所高校、63所研究机构和34家新闻媒体建立联系。另外厦大在上世纪50年代就开始了远程教育，也是留学生教育的先行者，现有外国留学生1600多人，海外函授生约6000人。

终身学习　厦门大学还特别注重终身学习，拥有继续教育与职业教育学院，包括：

（1）成人教育

（2）职业技术教育

（3）网络教育

在厦大可以学到这么多东西，我都想再回到学校当学生了！也许，我真的有一天可以学会汉语！

Chapter 9
Tour XMU!

104 XMU Sites at a Glance!

1. XMU Hospital (厦大医院)
2. Ocean Research (国家海洋三所)
3. West Villages (新旧西村)
4. West Gate (西校门)
5. "Book-Bird" Fountain (喷泉)
6. Travel Ctr. (厦大票务中心)
7. Postal Center (邮局代办点, 即 "厦大信箱")
8. Mingpei Gym (明培体育馆)
9. Swimming Pool (王清明游泳馆)
10. Nangying Bldg. (囊萤楼)
11. Tong'an Bldg. (同安楼)
12. Qunxian Bldg. (群贤楼)
13. Foundation Stone (奠基石)
14. Tan Kah Kee Statue (陈嘉庚像)
15. Jimei Bldg. (集美楼)
16. Yingxue Bldg. (映雪楼)
17. Luxun Memorial(鲁迅纪念馆)
18. Xiaxian Sports Field(下弦场)
19. XMU Press(厦大出版社)
20. Lu Xun Statue (鲁迅像)
21. Sa Bendong's Tomb(萨本栋墓)
22. English & Chinese Corners (英语角, 中文角)
23. Anthropology Museum (人类博物馆)
24. Chengyi Bldg. (成义楼) (Zoology Museum 动物标本馆)
25. Nan'an Bldg. (南安楼)
26. Jiannan Auditorium (建南大礼堂)
27. Nan'guang Bldg. (南光楼)
28. Chengzhi Bldg. (成智楼)
29. Shangxian Field – Soccer Field (上弦场)
30. Oceanography Bldg. (海洋楼)
31. Baicheng Gate (白城校门)
32. Baicheng Produce Market (白城菜市场)
33. Huli Hill Fort (胡里山炮台)
34. Seaside Cafeteria (海滨食堂)
35. New Area Dorms #1& #2 (新区一、二宿舍)
36. Law College (法学院)
37. Art College (艺术学院)
38. Lotus Lake (芙蓉湖)
39. School Motto by the Lake (校训大石)
40. Island Sculpture (胡边雕塑)
41. "Century Cultivating People" Stone ("百年树人"石)
42. Foreign Lang. Dept. (外文学院)
43. Boxue Bldg. #2 (博学二)
44-47. Jiageng Bldgs.(嘉庚楼群)
48. Jianwen Bldg. (建文楼)
49. Yifu Bldg.(逸夫楼)
50. Keli Bldg. (克立楼)
51. Red Brick Bldg, circa 1954(红砖楼)
52. Yellow Cottage (大学路 10 号)
53. Furong #3 (芙蓉 3 号)
54. XMU Library (图书馆)
55. Lin Yutang Memorial (林语堂纪念馆)

第9章 带你游厦大

DISCOVER Xiamen University

56. Furong Dorms 1-4（芙蓉1—4）
57. Students' Center（自钦楼）
58. Sanjia Cun Square（三家村学生广场）
59. Chemistry Dept. Cafeteria（化学食堂，即南光食堂）
60. OEC Bldg.(蔡清洁楼)
61. Lianxing Bldg.（联兴楼）
62. All-Weather Basketball（风雨球场）
63. Journalism Dept.（新闻系楼）
64. Physics Dept.（物理系楼）
65. Furong #5（芙蓉5）
66. Furong #6，10 & 12（芙蓉6，10，12）
67. Furong #11（芙蓉11）
68. Dongbian Community（东边社）
69. Furong Cafeteria（芙蓉餐厅）
70. Shijing (Stone Well) Cafeteria（石井食堂）
71. Furong Bldg. #7 and #8（芙蓉7，8）
72. Shijing Gate（石井大门）
73. Furong # 9 & Shijing # 1 to 6（芙蓉9，石井1—6）
74. Furong #13（芙蓉13）
75. Lingyun Area（凌云区）
76. XMU Reservoir, "Lovers' Lake"（厦大水库,别名"情人湖"）
77. Jiannan Mineral Water Factory（建南矿泉水厂）
78. Jingxian Area Teachers Housing（敬贤区）
79. Koxinga Statue（郑成功雕像）
80. Student's Bomb Shelter（学生防空洞）
81. Foreign Teachers Guesthouse（专家楼）
82. Nano Science & Tech. Ctr., Analysis & Testing Ctr. MEMS,（电镜实验室,分析测试中心,纳米科技中心．环境科学,机电工程系）.
83. #3 Da'nan Rd（大南路3号）
84. #5 Da'nan Rd（大南路5号）
85. Guoguang Area（国光区）
86. Teacher's Bomb Shelter（教师防空洞）
87. Campus Security（派出所）
88. Lingfeng Area（凌峰区）
89. Sino-U.S. Pavilion（中美亭子）
90. Nursery, XMUTV（厦大幼儿园,厦大有线电视台办公室）
91. XMU Archives & Historical Research Ctr.（厦大档案馆）
92. Da'nan Rd #7（大南路7号）
93. Biomedical Center（生物医药中心）
94. Jijin Bldg.（基金楼）
95. Taiwan Research Institute（台湾研究院）
96. Chemistry Bldg.（化学楼）
97. Yixuan Bldg. MEMS Ctr.（亦玄馆,萨本栋微机电研究中心）
98. Economics College and WISE（经济学院和王亚南经济研究院）
99. Southern XMU Gate（南校门,也叫旧校门）
100. Bus Depot（公共汽车站）
101. XMU Street（厦大一条街）
102. Post Office（邮电局）
103. Bank of China（中国银行）
104. Nanputuo Temple（南普陀寺）

Note: This tour is arranged "roughly" in order of places you'll encounter starting from just outside the XMU gate by the fountain.
Enjoy our XMU!

Just Off Campus

1. XMU Hospital and Medical Center. The hospital is on the corner near the Island Ring Road onramp. The independent XMU Medical Ctr. is 100m up University Road towards town.

2. National Ocean Research Bureau Located off campus across from the hospital.

3. Old & New West Village Just outside the West Gate, this was professor's housing. The area now has a park, shopping area, and tiny Yanwu Pond, which a few centuries ago flowed to the sea.

Entering Campus

4. West Gate Also called the "New Gate", this modern granite structure was funded by our famous alumni, Mr. Zhang Zhilu from Taiwan, and finished in 1993. The characters for "Xiamen University" at the top are in the handwriting style of famous author Lu Xun (XMU has used his calligraphic style ever since Liberation in 1949).

5. Zhonglinmei Square This square was completed in March, 1994, with funds from seven brothers, including Zhong Baoyu of Hong Kong, in memory of their mother, Mrs. Zhong Linmei.

Book or Bird? I long wondered if the fountain, designed by XMU's own Li Weisi was supposed to be an open book or a flying bird, and it turns out it is both! The "Bird Book" fountain symbolizes "knowledge and faith flying into the future."

第9章 带你游厦大

请注意! 我们的旅行将从厦门大学喷泉边上那个校门外面开始,大致按照你将看到的景点顺序行进。祝旅途愉快!

校园周边

1. **厦大医院与厦大医学院** 厦大医院位于通向环岛路上坡处的拐角。而独立于厦门大学的厦大医学院则在大学路朝市区方向 100 米处。
2. **国家海洋三局** 位于校外厦大医院对面。
3. **新旧西村** 就在学校西门外,这是学校老师们的住宅群。这里建有公园、购物区,几百年前与大海相连的演武池也在此地。

走进校园

4. **西校门** 也就是新校门,这座现代的花岗岩建筑是由来自台湾的名誉校友张子露先生捐资兴建并于 1993 年竣工的。而校门上方"厦门大学"几个字则是鲁迅先生的手迹(厦门大学自 1949 年解放以来就沿用他的书法风格)。
5. **钟林美广场** 该广场建成于 1994 年 3 月,是由香港的钟宝玉七姐弟捐建的,以此纪念他们的母亲钟林美女士。

是书还是鸟? 李维祀设计的雕塑,既是书也是鸟!这个鸟书喷泉象征着"飞向未来的知识和信念"。

Flying into the Future (Bird-Book)

6. XMU Travel Center Just right of the gate (when facing it). Great service, prices, and convenience; we buy all domestic and international air tickets here. (Tell them I sent you; maybe I'll get a cut on my next ticket).

7. XMU Postal Center. To the right of the Travel Center, they're open 7 days a week rain or shine—except during lunch. And you don't get better service than this. Letters addressed to "Bill Brown, Xiamen University" have still made it to my mailbox. They take their work seriously, and often waylay me when I check my mail to have me decipher scrawled addresses from abroad (but they're good; if they can't figure it out I generally can't either). Thanks for 18 years of keeping those cards and letters coming!

8. Mingpei Gym Our first formal gym, it was funded by famous alumni Mr. She Mingpei, of the Philippines, and the national education ministry.

9. Wang Qingming Pool This two-storey pool is behind the gym, facing XMU Publishing House.

Wang Qingming Pool

第9章 带你游厦大

6. **厦大票务中心** 面向西校门的右手边——这里有优质的服务、低廉的价格和便捷的方式。我们飞国内国外的机票都是在这儿买的。（去的时候，告诉他们是我介绍你去的，说不定他们下次会给我打个折）。

7. **厦大信箱（邮局代办点）** 位于票务中心的右侧，无论风和日丽还是狂风暴雨，他们坚持一周7天上班——当然，除了午饭时间。你无法找到哪里有比这里更好的服务了。例如，就算你的信封上只写着"厦门大学 潘维廉 收"，仍然会被准确无误地投到我的邮箱里去的。他们做事十分认真，经常在我来取信的时候把我截住，让我破解那些字迹潦草的外国来信上的地址（但他们做得很棒，如果他们都看不懂，一般情况下，我也没什么头绪）。感谢他们18年来让我的信件和明信片及时到达！

7 Days a Week—Rain or Shine!

8. **明培体育馆** 这是我们学校第一座正式的体育馆，由菲律宾著名校友佘明培先生及国家教育部投资建成。

9. **王清明游泳馆** 走过明培体育馆就是了，正对着厦门大学出版社。

Mingpei Gym

The Qunxian Complex

Mr. Tan Kah Kee himself lay the cornerstone of XMU's first buildings, the Qunxian Complex. The 5 buildings are connected by corridors and said to be arranged like Chinese character for "one"—which seems no big deal to me since that character is just a straight line (一). Their names (starting from the gate) are Nangying (1923), Tong'an (1921), Qunxian (1921), Jimei (1921), and Yingxue (1923).

10. Nangying Bldg. (Sack of Fireflies) and **Yingxue Bldg.** (Reflected Snow), were both built in 1923 and so christened to encourage students to emulate their ancestors' and work and study hard. I could not see the connection, but Ms. Pan of ICE explained. In the old days, poor scholars who could not afford candles collected fireflies in a sack and studied by their feeble light, or studied by the pale moonlight reflected off the snow.

Nangying was the office of Fujan's first Communist Party Group, later the office for XMU Journal, and is now the Internet College.

> **Luo Yangcai—Representative of Revolutionary Spirit**
> Luo Yangcai was admitted to the Foundation Education of XMU in Dec.1924, was transferred to the Education Department, and joined the Party in Nov. 1925. Luo, with Luo Qiutian and Li Juemin, founded XMU branch of the Party in Feb. 1926. This was Fujian Province's first branch of the Party, and Luo Yangcai was the branch Secretary. Luo was arrested by the Kuomintang in April, 1927, and killed in June in Fuzhou. Luo was an outstanding leader of student movements, and his revolutionary spirit will be passed on throughout the generations.

11. Tong'an Bldg. Named after the county of Mr. Tan's home village of Jimei. A mere 1,000 years ago (yesterday by Chinese' standards), Xiamen was also part of Tong'an, but today the roles have reversed. Tong'an is now part of Xiamen, and given Xiamen's prosperity, probably glad of it. This building had chemistry department offices from the very beginning, and the first floor is classrooms.

群贤楼群

厦大成立以来第一座楼群,由陈嘉庚先生亲自奠基。这五座楼通过走廊连接,呈"一"字形排列。这五座楼的名字依次是(从校门数起):"囊萤"(1923)、"同安"(1921)、"群贤"(1921)、"集美"(1921)、"映雪"(1923)。

10. **囊萤楼与映雪楼**,都建于1923,名称出自古语"胤,博学多通,家贫不常得油,夏夜以练囊盛数十萤火虫以照书";和"孙康,性敏好学,家贫无油,于冬月尝映雪读书"。以此命名,旨在鼓励学生们效仿先辈,努力工作和学习。囊萤楼曾经是福建省第一个党支部的办公室,尔后又成为《厦门大学学报》的办公室,现在是网络教育学院所在地。

罗扬才——革命精神的代表

罗扬才于1924年12月被厦门大学预科录取,而后转到教育系,并于1925年11月加入中国共产党。1926年2月与罗秋天、李觉民共同创立了厦门大学党支部。这是福建省第一个党支部,罗扬才任支部书记。罗扬才于1927年4月被国民党逮捕,6月在福州就义。罗扬才是杰出的学生运动领导者,他的革命精神将代代相传!

---

11. **同安楼** 以陈嘉庚先生的故乡——集美所在的同安县命名。大约1000年前(相对于中国的历史来讲也就是"昨天"),厦门也是同安的一部分,但现在这和关系却颠倒过来了——同安现隶属于厦门,不过考虑到厦门的欣欣向荣,它大概也心甘情愿现在这样吧。从一开始化学系的办公室就设在这里,第一层作教室用。

— 111 —

12. Qunxian Bldg. The main building (behind the statue) derives its name from the first 2 characters of the famous Jin Dynasty calligrapher Xizhi's line, "all talents converge here, whether young or old". Tan named it thus in the hopes that talent would indeed converge upon XMU. Other people wanted to name some buildings after Tan Kah Kee or his brother, Jingxian, but the humble millionaire forbade it. The 5 new lakeside buildings were named after Tan—after he was no longer around to protest.

The characters "qunxian" were written by then XMU President, Prof. Lin Wenqing (our 2nd president). XMU's best-preserved historic building, the tiered-classrooms could seat 400 students. The 5-building complex is now a provincial-level protected site.

Qunxian was the President's office and School of Graduate Students until the president moved to the new lakeside Song'en Tower. Qunxian is now the XMU Alumni Association office and in 2005 became the Tan Kah Kee Memorial Hall.

13. Foundation Stone XMU's most important historic marker is the plaque on the wall near the ground (behind the statue). It was covered with cement in the Cultural Revolution because it referenced the Kuomintang.

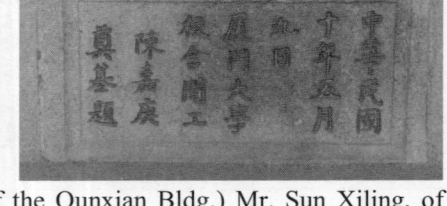

14. Tan Kah Kee Statue (in front of the Qunxian Bldg.) Mr. Sun Xiling, of XMU, designed this bronze statue from a photo taken of Mr. Tan in the 1950s after his return to Xiamen from Singapore. It was erected in 1983 on the 110th anniversary of Mr. Tan's birth.

15. Jimei Bldg. Formerly the Chinese college, now has first floor classrooms and a 2nd floor Lu Xun Memorial Hall. Jimei Bldg. #2 is the literature and history library and reading room.

16. Yinxue Bldg. (Reflect Snow) has first floor classrooms and the upper floor used to be the Software College.

12. **群贤楼** 即陈嘉庚像后的主楼，得名于晋朝著名书法家王羲之的"群贤毕至，少长云集"前二字。陈嘉庚先生以此命名正是希望贤才群集厦大。曾经有人提议以陈嘉庚先生或其弟陈敬贤的名字命名，但是这位谦逊的百万富翁怎么也不允许一座楼以他的名字命名（芙蓉湖边新建的那5座教学楼命名为"嘉庚楼群"，那是在他过世之后，再没法反对了）。

"群贤"二字由当时的校长林文庆教授（厦大第二任校长）亲笔提写。这是厦大迄今为止保存得最完好的历史建筑，这一整排的教室可容纳400名学生。这五座楼群现在是省级保护遗址。

在搬迁到芙蓉湖边的颂恩楼之前，校长办公室和研究生院就在群贤楼。群贤楼现在是厦门大学校友总会所在地，并于2005年成为陈嘉庚纪念堂。

13. **基石** 厦大最具重大意义的标志，靠着地面镶嵌在墙的下部（陈嘉庚像后面），曾在"文革"期间因碑文中提到国民党而被人用水泥覆盖。

14. **陈嘉庚像**（群贤楼群前面） 这尊青铜像是由厦门大学的校友孙锡麟先生根据20世纪50年代陈嘉庚先生从新加坡回到厦大时拍的一张照片设计的。铜像于1983年陈嘉庚先生诞辰110周年时建成。

15. **集美楼** 以前曾经是中文系，现在一楼作教室用，二楼为鲁迅纪念馆。而集美二则为图书馆文史分馆。

16. **映雪楼** 同样地，一楼也作教室用，而二楼曾经是软件学院。

17. Lu Xun Memorial This memorial was opened in October, 1952, in honor of the Father of Modern Chinese Literature, who was a professor in XMU's Chinese department from Sep. 4th 1926 to Jan. 15th, 1927. It was opened in Lu Xun's former living quarters on Jimei Bldg.'s 2nd floor, and later expanded. The memorial has mementos and works of Lu Xun from his time in XMU. Read Prof. Zheng Qiwu's "Two Memorials" for more information.

The name of the first room was inscribed by Song Qinglin, the wife of Sun Yat-sen. When the memorial was enlarged in 1976 it was decided to use the calligraphy of Guo Moruo (1892-1978), famous modern Chinese poet and former president of the Chinese Academy of Sciences.

Guo Morou

During the Cultural Revolution, Guo Moruo worked carefully behind the scenes to preserve traditional culture and values.

18. Xiaxian Sports Ground This modern synthetic track field was the foreigner's horse race track a century ago, and 350 years ago Koxinga drilled his troops here. The area has basketball, volleyball and tennis courts, outdoor exercise facilities, and croquet for retirees.

19. XMU Press is behind the sports field.

20. Lu Xun Statue   XMU's Mr. Li Weisi, who designed the "Bird Book Fountain", also designed the Lu Xun statue.

21. President Sa Bendong & Wife's Tomb President while XMU was in Changting; the tomb is up the hill past Lu Xun's statue.

22. English & Chinese Corners Here's the perfect place to pick up a little English—or Chinese (thanks to Robin's Chinese Corner).

17. **鲁迅纪念馆** 该纪念馆成立于 1952 年 11 月，旨在纪念中国现代文学之父——鲁迅先生。他曾经于 1926 年 9 月 4 日至 1927 年 1 月 15 日在厦门大学中文系执教。纪念馆最初设在鲁迅先生集美二二楼的寓所，而后扩建。纪念馆内收藏有鲁迅先生在厦大期间的纪念物及作品。（参见郑启五老师的《林语堂纪念堂和鲁迅纪念馆》一文。）

纪念馆第一陈列室的名字是由孙中山先生夫人宋庆龄题写的。而馆名则是在 1976 年扩建时使用了中国现代著名诗人、第一任中科院院长郭沫若先生（1892—1978 年）的手书。

在"文化大革命"期间，郭沫若曾经暗地里努力保护这个传统文化遗产。

18. **下弦场** 这里 350 年前曾经是明朝爱国将领郑成功操练大军的地方，一百年前曾是外国殖民者的跑马场，现在已成为人工田径场。这里还拥有篮球场、排球场、网球场、门球等各种户外运动设施。

19. **厦大出版社** 就在运动场后方。

20. **鲁迅像** 仍然出自"鸟书"的设计者李维祀之手。

21. **萨本栋校长夫妻墓** 萨本栋教授是厦大在长汀时期的校长，其夫妇的墓就在鲁迅像后面的坡上。

22. **英语角，中文角** 鲁迅像广场现在是每周英语角和中文角的所在地！这可真是个学习中文和英语的好地方啊！（中文角可是费菲的小发明！）

English Corner *and* Chinese Corner

It is ironic that for many years, Lu Xun, the "Father of Modern Chinese Literature" and former XMU teacher, has been forced to endure throngs of people surrounding him at night practicing English!

The Tuesday and Friday night English Corners, held from about 9 PM until whenever the last few straggle off into the night, are the best place for Chinese and foreigners to meet because they are attended regularly by both Overseas Education College foreigners and XMU foreign teachers. Some diehard foreign teachers even manage two English Corners on Friday nights. They hit the Zhangzhou campus across the bay at 7 PM, and then take the ferry back to catch another batch of English learners besieging the statue of Lu Xun.

No one knows anymore who started this English Corner because it has become a self-organized activity, taking on a life of its own. You can expect to meet all kinds of people there, from students and teachers to business people, doctors, lawyers—virtually anyone wanting to improve their English. But as of November 27th, 2004, our illustrious Lu Xun is finally able to see and hear the language he loved being used by Chinese and foreigners alike because my friends and I organized as one of the Putonghua ("Standard Chinese," or Mandarin) Art Association activities a Chinese Corner for foreigners. The Chinese Corner is every Sunday evening from 7 PM until as late as you want to stay.

We think Mr. Lu Xun, who once taught at XMU, must be happy to see this marriage of Chinese and Western languages taking place right around him.

Deutsches Eck German Corner is at the Lianxing Bldg. in the Nanguang Area, Thursday evenings from 7:30-9PM. Info at: german_corner@yahoo.com

英语角和中文角

要"中国现代文学之父"、曾在厦门大学中文系当过教授的鲁迅先生长年累月地忍受着人群围着自己"叽里呱啦"地讲英语到深夜,真的是有点为难他老人家。

于每周周二和周五晚上进行的英语角,从晚上9点开始,直至深夜,最后一撮人才纷纷散去。这是中国人和外国人相识的好地方,因为很多海外教育学院的学生和厦大的外教都会来参加。一些"硬汉"老外还在周五晚上"赶场"似的参加两个地方的英语角:他们漂洋过海地去参加在漳州校区7点开始的英语角,然后乘船回来,匆匆忙忙地奔向包围在鲁迅像身边的另一群英语爱好者。

已经没有人知道英语角的来历了,它早已成为一个自发的活动,无须组织而独立存在了。这里你能见到各种各样的人,有学生、教师、商人、医生、律师……差不多各界想提高英语口语的人都会聚在这里!而在2005年11月27日,我们伟大的鲁迅先生终于见到并听到外国人和中国人一样开口讲他最爱的语言——汉语了,因为我和我的朋友们为老外们搞了个"中文角",作为我们"普通话艺术协会"的活动之一。中文角于每周日晚上7点开始,至于结束嘛,想呆多久都没问题啦!

我想,鲁迅先生离开厦大多年后,终于看到我们的汉语和西方的语言就这样在自己身边"联姻"了,一定挺高兴的吧。

德语角! 有人要参加吗?每周四晚7:30—9:00在南光区的联兴楼举行。联系方式为:german_corner@yahoo.com

23. China's First Anthropology Museum Boxue Bldg. #1 Lu Xun, "Father of Modern Chinese Literature," was also in a sense the "father" of our Anthropology Museum, which was the first in New China. In the Fall of 1926, Lu Xun held an exhibition of cultural relics at XMU and set up a Cultural Exhibition Center in the School of Chinese Studies. Lu Xun did not stick around long, but he'd gotten the ball rolling, and in 1934, Professor Lin Huixiang created a Director's Office for the Anthropology Museum, Xiamen, and after 1949 he donated all of his cultural relics and books to the university.

In 1952, the National Education Ministry authorized XMU to establish an anthropology museum, which was opened to the public in 1953 for the purposes of anthropological research, teaching and social education. The center has performed research on the New Stone Age era of S.E. China (mainly Fujian and Taiwan) and S.E. Asian, Chinese and foreign maritime transportation in Quanzhou (start of the Maritime Silk Route), ancient kilns (Dehua was one of China's key ancient porcelain centers), and ancient Chinese exports. The Center has also studied the relationships between the ancient Yue, She, Gaoshan, and S.E. nationalities.

The center has a corridor of steles, 32 exhibition rooms, 4,575 ancient and modern exhibits, and over 7,110 books or journals. The 3 main divisions are: Hall of Genesis, Evolution of Culture, and Hall of National Relics from Home and Abroad.

The Hall of Genesis and Evolution of Culture display Stone Age artifacts, ancient currency, porcelain, paintings, weapons, sculptures, calligraphy, etc. The National Relics Hall has cultural relics from China, India, Australia, and South East Asian countries.

The center has published Research on Anthropology, History of the She Nationality, History of Gaoshan Nationality, Zheng Chenggong and Gaoshan Nationality, etc.

The callibraphy above the museum's entrance was written bu Xu Beihong.

23. 博学——中国第一个人类博物馆

"中国现代文学之父"鲁迅先生,从某种意义上来说,也是我们的人类博物馆之父。我们的人类博物馆是在新中国建立的第一所人类学专科博物馆。早在1926年秋天,鲁迅先生在厦大举办了一场考古文物展览会,后在国学院成立文化陈列所。鲁迅先生虽然并没有逗留多久,但是他却让这个"雪球"滚动了起来。1934年,林惠祥教授创建了厦门市人类博物馆筹备处,而且在1949年后,他毕生搜集的文物和图书都捐给了学校。

1952年,经教育部批准,厦门大学人类博物馆正式成立并于1953年对外开放,主要用于科研、教学和社会教育等。该馆陈列了中国(主要集中在台湾和福建)和东南亚在新石器时期的相关研究成果,还有泉州大海船模型(泉州是海上丝绸之路的起点)、古瓷(福建德化曾经是中国三大古瓷都之一)以及中国古代的出口产品。该馆还从事有关古代百越民族、畲族、高山族同东南亚各国关系的研究。

馆内有碑廊、32间陈列室、约4575号(每号1件或数十件不等,)文物以及多于7110多号专用图书。陈列分为人类的起源和发展、文化的起源和发展、中外民族文物三大部分。

人类的起源和发展及文化的起源和发展部分陈列了石器时代的旧石器、古代货币、瓷器、字画、武器、雕塑品、书法作品等等。中外民族文物部分陈列有中国、印度、澳大利亚及东南亚各国的民族文物。

该馆还出版了有关人类学、畲族历史学、高山族历史学及郑成功等方面的一系列研究刊物。馆名由著名画家徐悲鸿题写。

China's 1st Anthropology Museum

Jiannan Auditorium Complex

The largest university auditorium in China even today, this is XMU's most photogenic building, perched upon the hill "overlooking the sea like a tiger" (in Prof. Zheng Qiwu's picturesque parlance).   Mr. Tan chose this location so they would be folks' first site as they sailed into harbor.

The 5-building complex, built between 1952 and 1954, was funded by Mr. Tan's son-in-law, Lee Kong Chian. Since 1995, the "Lee Foundation of Singapore" has maintained the buildings in accordance with Li's will.   Their names, from left to right (facing them from the sea), are: Chenyi, Nan'an, Jiannan, Nanguang, and Chengzhi.

24. Chengyi Bldg. ("Become Righteous"). Wetlands & Environmental Research Center. The stone says "Strength of the South". Visit their **Zoology Museum**

25. Nan'an Bldg. (Lee Kong Chian's hometown of Furong was in Nan'an county, just north of Xiamen). It is now the Life Sciences Center.

26. Jiannan Auditorium

27. Nan'guang Bldg. ("Light of the South") Originally the Accounting Department, now the Architectural Research Center.

28. Chengzhi Bldg. ("Become Wise"), formerly the Electrical Engineering Department, the small pavilion in front is a Municipal-level protected relic.

29. Shangxian Field – the soccer field in front of the Chengzhi Complex.

30. Oceanography Building This building is just outside the campus, across the road from the Chengyi Bldg.

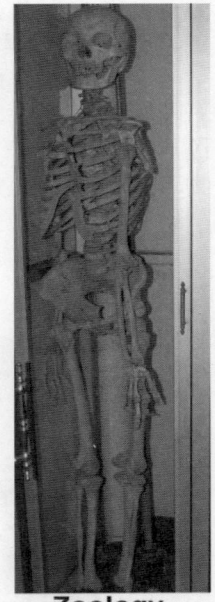

Zoology Museum
(Skeleton Crew?)

建 南 楼 群

迄今为止，建南大礼堂一直是国内高校最大的礼堂，也是厦大最上镜的建筑物，站在山上"猛虎般俯视大海"（出自郑启五老师的妙语）。陈嘉庚先生之所以将其选址于此，是因为他希望当人们驶入港口时，第一眼看到的就是它。

这个五栋楼群是 1952 到 1954 年间由陈嘉庚的女婿李光前捐资兴建的。"新加坡李氏基金会"遵照他的遗愿，从 1995 年开始陆续捐资对楼群进行翻修。这些楼的名字，背向大海的方向、从左到右分别是：成义楼、南安楼、建南大礼堂、南光楼、成智楼。

24. **成义楼** 是湿地与生态工程研究中心所在地。楼前有块大石，大石上写着"南方之强"。参观一下这里的动物标本馆吧。

25. **南安楼**（李光前先生的故乡南安县芙蓉乡位于厦门北面的南安县）现在是生命科学学院。

26. **建南大礼堂**

27. **南光楼** 原来是会计系所在地，现为建筑与土木工程学院。

28. **成智楼** 原为电子工程系。楼前的小亭子为市级保护遗址。

29. **上弦场** 就是在成智楼前的那个足球场。

30. **海洋楼** 在校外，成义楼的马路对面。

Towards the East Part of Campus

31. Baicheng Gate Also called "Beach Gate" because it faces the sea; named after the ancient city wall once here.

32. Baicheng Produce Market This market is most lively in the morning, and sells veggies, fruits, meats, doufu, etc.

33. Huli Hill Fort—China's Doorstep (From Amoy Magic) This famous tourist spot, on the coast just off campus, has a marvelous stone collection and the world's largest cannon! (in Guiness World Records) Huli Fort boasts the World of Exotic Stones (3,850 exotic stones with 'natural pictures on them, including the Emperor Qianlong's Pet Rock), and an exhibition of ancient armaments. The 455 weapons include guns, swords, and cannons, including a 12th century cannon reputed to be the world's oldest. But its real claim to fame is the world's largest cannon. (Guinness lists a cannon in Moscow, but we're working on changing that!). The German-made Krupp coastal defense gun, installed by some big shot back in 1896, weighs 60 tons, is 13.96 meters long, and cost 60,000 taels of silver.

34. Seaside Cafeteria A two floor cafeteria mainly for students living in the east area of campus.

35. New Area Dorms #1 and #2 Girls in Bldg. #1 get a sea view; boys in Bldg. #2 get a view of the hills (and the girls?).

36. Law College This modern complex also has some simulated courtrooms, and a UN Depository Library.

37. Art College

从校园东区开去

31. **白城大门** 也叫"海滩之门",因为它面朝着大海。它是以曾经耸立在那里的旧城墙命名的。

32. **白城菜市场** 清晨是这里最热闹的时候。蔬菜、水果、肉类、豆制品……应有尽有。

33. **湖里山炮台——中国的门阶**(《魅力厦门》摘录)

这个著名的景点离学校很近,那里有奇石的收藏和世界上最大的一门炮(吉尼斯世界纪录)。

这座古要塞里还有一个世界奇石馆和一个古代世界兵器展览馆。世界奇石馆陈列着 3850 种带有天然花纹的奇石,其中包括乾隆皇帝的收藏。兵器馆里陈列的 455 种兵器包括了枪、剑和火炮,其中一门制于十二世纪的火炮号称是世界上最古老的大炮。不过,这里最有名的还是世界上最大的一门炮。(吉尼斯世界纪录里收入的是莫斯科的一门大炮,我们正准备改写这一记录)这门铸造于 1896 年的德国克虏伯岸炮重达 60 吨,长 13.96 米,耗费了白银 6 万两。

34. **海滨食堂** 这是个两层的餐厅,主要为住在学校东区的学生服务。

35. **新区一二宿舍** 住在 1 号楼的女生可以观赏美丽的海景,而住在 2 号楼的男生看到的则是山(还有美女?)。

36. **法学院** 这幢现代化的建筑里有模拟法庭以及一个联合国托存图书馆。

37. **艺术学院**

Lotus Lake Area

38. Furong (Lotus) Lake. This lake was created in 1982 on a former vegetable patch. It was so named not because it was planted in lotus but because of the surrounding Lotus Dorms.

39. School Motto by the Lake Facing the Song'en Tower, this row of eight round stones bear the 8 characters for the school motto: ("Pursue Excellence, Strive for Perfection").

40. Island Sculpture This is of Tan Kah Kee and Students

41. "Century Cultivating People" Stone An upright volcanic stone with 4 characters, Bainian Shuren, "100 Years Cultivate People."

42. Foreign Languages Department By the above stone..

43. Boxue Bldg. #2 Just past the Foreign Languages Department, one of XMU's main lecture facilities with tiered classrooms that accommodate almost 200 people.

芙 蓉 湖 区

38. **芙蓉湖** 建于 1982 年，所在地原为一片菜园。此湖并不是因为它建于芙蓉地上而得名，而是因为环绕在湖四周的芙蓉宿舍区而得名。

39. **湖边的校训** 在湖边面向颂恩楼的那一侧耸立着八块圆形巨石，上刻校训"自强不息，止于至善"。

40. **湖边雕塑** 刻画的是陈嘉庚和学生们在一起。

41. **"百年树人"** 矗立于湖边的一块大石，刻有"百年树人"四字。

42. **外文学院** 就在"百年树人"石旁边。

43. **博学二报告厅** 走过外语教学部就是了。博学二报告厅是厦大主要的报告厅之一，可容纳 200 人。

Jiageng [Kah Kee] Buildings

Mr. Ding Zhengzeng and Mrs. Cai Yueshi, an alumni couple from Thailand, funded the main building, which is said to be 21 floors high to represent the 21st Century. The flanking 4 7-storey buildings were built with overseas Chinese' donations. Zhong Mingxuan Lou was funded by Hong Kong and Singapore Overseas Chinese Zhong Jianghai and his brother. Zuying Lou was financed by the Philippines overseas Chinese Mr. Hong Wenbing. Chengfeng Lou was built by the descendents of Singapore, Malaya overseas Chinese Mr. Li Chengfeng. Baoxin Liying Lou was sponsored by Hong kong Alumni Mr. Huang Baoxin and his wife Mrs. Wu Liying.

The buildings cover 49,000 m2 and cost RMB 115 million, of which RMB 40.6 million was from donations.

Management College

44. Jiageng #1 and #2 Management College.

45. Song'en Tower (Jiageng #3) "Song'en" means "Commend grace/favor"

46. Jiageng #4 has physics laboratories.

47. Jiageng #5 is for the Modern Technology Education Center.

48. Jianwen Building (Workers' Union) This 7-storey 5,000m^2 building was funded by the couple that built the 21-storey main building, Mrs Cai Yueshi and Mr. Ding Zhengzeng. It was named in memory of Mrs. Cai's father, Mr. Cai Jianwen The first 3 stories are used for teachers activities and the 4th through 7th stories are guest rooms (the most inexpensive of the three buildings on that intersection and, in my opinion, the nicest; we've had many guests stay there). (Read more about Mrs. Cai in the "Giving" chapter).

49. Yifu Building, or "Xiamen University International Academic Exchange Center," was named after the man who funded part of its construction, the famous Hong Kong businessman Sir Shao Yifu, of the "Shao Brothers." Construction on the 7-storey building began on Dec. 1989 and was finished in April 1991.

嘉庚楼群

主楼由泰国校友丁政曾和蔡悦诗伉俪捐资建成,楼高 21 层,象征着 21 世纪。两侧的四幢楼则分别是:香港、新加坡华侨钟江海兄弟捐建的钟铭选楼;菲律宾华侨洪文炳先生捐建的祖营楼;新加坡、马来西亚华侨李成枫先生后裔捐建的成枫楼;香港校友黄保欣、吴丽英伉俪捐建的保欣丽英楼。

楼群占地 49000 平方米,总耗资 11500 万人民币。其中 4006 万来自捐赠。

44. **嘉庚1号、2号楼**　为管理学院。
45. **颂恩楼(嘉庚3号楼)**
46. **嘉庚4号楼**　设有物理实验室。
47. **嘉庚5号楼**　主要是现代教育技术中心的办公地点。
48. **建文楼(工会)**　这座高 7 层、占地 5000 平方米的建筑是由嘉庚主楼的捐建者丁政曾、蔡悦诗伉俪捐资建成的,因纪念蔡女士的先父蔡建文而得名。底下三层用作教职工活动中心,四至七层则作为客房,其所在交叉路口处三座楼中,这是住宿最便宜的,我觉得也是最好的。我们曾带许多客人到那里住宿(关于蔡女士的更多内容参见第七章)。
49. **逸夫楼(厦门大学国际学术交流中心)**　以捐赠者香港著名富商"邵氏兄弟"之一的邵逸夫先生的名字命名。这幢 7 层楼高的建筑于 1989 年 12 月奠基并于 1991 年 4 月竣工。

Photo by Mr. Pan Wanhua

Fine Yifu Dining! With every kind of cuisine imaginable in Xiamen, Sue and I prefer eating right on campus the Yifu Restaurant. The food's great, prices are reasonable, and the English menu has all standard "American Chinese dishes," as well as delightful local specialties, unusual soups with flaky French pastry crusts, and delectable North China dumplings (jiaozi).And try an awesome shampoo and head massage at the Beauty Salon (very reasonable, too)..

Some Fine Cookin', Folks!

Yifu has fine accommodations too! Yifu, Keli and Jianwen Buildings all have reasonably priced accommodations, with Yifu being the upper end and Jianwen the lower—but we actually prefer Jianwen.

50. Keli Bldg. The famous HK financier Mr. Huang Keli, donated part of the funds for this 7-story building, which was remodeled the end of 2005. It has guest rooms, lecture halls, a nice coffee shop, and a very small but well-stocked supermarket.

51. The red brick building to the right of Keli Bldg. was built in 1954 for 50,000 RMB. I was told the balconies were built so girl students could sit outside and read while combing their hair.

52. Yellow Cottage, #10 University Rd Just behind Yifu Bldg., facing Keli Bldg., this European-style cottage is my favorite. Prof. Zheng Qiwu 's family lived here during the "Intellectual Spring" (1950-57), but in 1957 academics entered the winter. His father fell from favor, was branded a rightist, and they moved to a humbler abode—Guoguang Bldg. 3 #17. (Uncle Beard lived in Guoguang #3 as well).

53. Furong #3 Female PhD housing. Just to the left of the Yellow Cottage, Furong #3 (with #1 and #2) was built by Lee Kong Chian about 1952-1955. In 1958 white paper was taped to all of Furong #3's windows to keep them from shattering during bomb blasts. XMU was the only campus in China where students were forced to study with "Pens in one hand and guns in the other!"

第9章 带你游厦大

美味餐饮尽在逸夫楼！ 尽管厦门各式餐饮应有尽有，我和妻子更喜欢在校内的逸夫楼餐厅用餐。这里的菜太好吃了，价格也合理，而且他们还有英文菜单。他们有全套的标准美国人爱吃的"中国菜"，还有令人赏心悦目的地方特色小吃、味道独特的法式酥脆薄饼汤，美味的中国北方饺子。来到这里，你不妨尝试在美发沙龙享受一下洗发和头部按摩（价格也同样合理哦！）。

逸夫楼的住宿也很不错！ 逸夫楼、克立楼和建文楼的住宿价格都很合理，其中逸夫楼价格最高、建文楼最低——事实上，我们更喜欢建文楼。

Yifu--Home Away From Home

50. 克立楼 部分资金是由著名的香港金融家黄克立先生捐赠的。这幢高7层，该楼曾于2005年底重新装修过。内设客房、报告厅、一家很优雅的咖啡厅，还有一家虽小却备货齐全的超市。

51. 克立楼右侧的那幢红砖绿瓦屋建于1954年，总耗资5万人民币。有人告诉我们，修建那个阳台的原因是为了女生可以坐在屋外梳头发的同时看报。

52. "黄色小别墅" （大学路10号） 就在逸夫楼后，面对克立楼，这种欧式风格的小别墅是我的最爱。郑启五老师的家曾在这里住过一段时间——"知识分子的春天"时期（1950—1957年），但在1957年知识分子却进入了寒冷的冬天。他的父亲被扣成"右派"，他们也就搬到了一个简陋的住所——国光三号楼17号。（大胡子伯伯也住过国光三号楼哦！）

Hansel and Gretel?

53. 芙蓉三 女博士的住所，就在"黄色小别墅"的左侧。芙蓉三（连同芙蓉一、二）于1952—1955年间由李光前建成。1958年间，芙蓉三所有的窗户都被用白纸糊上以免在炸弹爆炸时被震落。厦门大学是国内唯一一所学生不得不"一手执笔，一手拿枪"的大学！

54. XMU Library I used to be so frustrated with the library's short hours that I went half a decade without darkening its doors, and started my own library at home. But now the XMU library is open 7 days a week from 8 AM to 10 PM, and they have 3,750,000 books—about 3,745,000 more than I have at home (and I'll never catch up because they're spending 1 million Yuan each year adding 50,000 volumes annually; if I bought that many books my wife would kill me).

The library was founded in 1921 and moved to the present site in 1987. The building was expanded to 22,000m^2 in 2001 and 2002 and now has half a million foreign language books, over 10,000 periodicals in Chinese and over 12,000 in foreign languages.

The digital library system was started in 2000 and offers 24 hour interlibrary loans, database mirror-site services, over 100 major online databases, digital archives and libraries, over 18,000 electronic periodicals in Chinese and foreign languages, and searches. Website: http://210.34.4.20/english/

55. Lin Yutang Memorial On library's 3rd floor. See Prof. Zheng Qiwu's article, "Two Memorials".

56. Furong (Lotus) Dormitories 1 thru 4 These dorms were built by Mr. Lee Kong Chian in the 1950s. Furong #1 & #2 Male Dorms Furong #3 Female PhD Dormitory Furong #4 Grad Students' Dormitory

57. Students' Activity Center (Ziqin Lou) This was called Three Home Village (Sanjia Cun). In 1992, Mr. Xu Ziqin from the Philippines funded the Ziqin Bldg. The 3-storey 2,300m^2 main building has a Karaoke, dance hall, exhibition hall, etc. It has offices for the university students' union, and editors of two magazines, "XMU Youth" and "XMU Warp & Woof. " Parties and activities are held on the 2/F Furong Hall.

第9章 带你游厦大

DISCOVER Xiamen University

54. 厦门大学图书馆 我过去常常抱怨图书馆的开放时间太短了,好几年都没去,于是在自己家里开了个图书馆。但厦门大学图书馆现在一周7天都开放,从早上的8点到晚上10点并且馆藏375万册图书——大概比我家图书馆的藏书多出374.5万册(而且我永远也赶不上了,因为他们每年还投入100万元以增加5万册新书。如果我也购置这么多的书,我夫人会杀了我的!)

图书馆建于1921,年并于1987年迁至现在的馆址,又于2001到2002年间扩建到

2.2万平方米,现有50万册外文图书,1万多种中文期刊及12000多种外文期刊。

数字图书馆系统于2000年正式启动,提供24小时馆际互借,数据库镜像服务,100多种在线数据库、数字化档案室及图书馆,18000多种中、外文电子期刊及搜索。

可通过此网址访问英文版: http://210.34.4.20/english/

55. 林语堂纪念室 就在图书馆三楼。参见《林语堂纪念室和鲁迅纪念室》一文。

56. 芙蓉一至四 这些宿舍楼都是由李光前先生在20世纪50年代兴资建成的,芙一、二为男生宿舍,芙三为女博士研究生宿舍,芙四为硕士研究生宿舍。

57. 学生活动中心(自钦楼) 这里又叫做三家村。在1992年,菲律宾校友

许自钦先生出资建立了自钦楼。校学生会及《厦大青年》、《厦大经纬》的办公室也设在这里。很多学生活动则在二楼的芙零厅举办。

58. Sanjia Cun Square A lively intersection with news bulletin boards and a job information center.

59. Nan'guang Cafeteria. I read it is called a "boys cafeteria because portions are large but not particularly tasty!"

60. Overseas Education College It's hard to believe the OEC has such nice accommodations nowadays! When I came in 1988, we had to hole up in the building off campus that now has the KFC. Now, with over 1200 foreign students, there are many choices. The 10-storey Cai Qingjie Building, opened in 1993, was funded by Mr. Cai Qingjie, from the Philippines. Many foreigners enjoy the 2/F Mingyuan Café.

OEC's Cai Qingjie Bldg.

61. Lianxing Bldg. Adjacent to the OEC, this is for the architecture department. Students used to cram for exams here because it was one of the few places with lights all night. Visit the Thursday evening German Corner, 7:30-9PM. For info, e-mail: german_corner@yahoo.com

A Smart Tip for Finals!

The main campus' electricity is cut off sharply at midnight every night except Friday and Saturday, but if the workaholic Chen Jingrun (see Maths College chapter) was still around, he would be grateful that XMU now has one classroom that is open all night for students!

During the last two weeks of each semester, one building (usually Boxue Lou) is open around the clock for students to prepare for finals. It is quite a scene. Students headed home after a full day in the classrooms come across friends who have just showered, brushed their teeth, and are ready for another session of study. And here's a *valuable tip*: stock up on coffee well before exam time arrives, because if you wait too long you'll find the campus grocery store shelves are bare of coffee. It has all been "robbed" by the diligent "never-sleepers"!

62. All-Weather Basketball Court Adjacent to Nanguang Buildings numbers 6 and 7; this also has a badminton court.

第9章　带你游厦大

58. **三家村学生广场**　有新闻公告栏和就业信息中心。

59. **南光食堂**　听说它有个外号叫"男生食堂",因为那里的分量大但却不那么可口!

60. **海外教育学院**　真是难以想象,海外教育学院现在有这么好的住宿条件!我1988年刚来的时候,还得"窝"在校外现

在肯得基的那个地方。现在,对于这1200名海外留学生来说,他们的选择可多了。开放于1993年的10层高的蔡清洁楼由菲律宾校友蔡清洁先生捐资兴建。很多外国人都喜欢去2楼的咖啡厅就餐。

61. **联兴楼**　就在海外教育学院的旁边,供建筑系使用。学生们经常考前在这里"临阵磨枪",因为这里有学校里为数不多的通宵自习室。了解一下有关每周四晚上7:30—9:00在这里进行的德语角吧,可以联系:e-mail: german_corner@yahoo.com

期末考试小贴士

　　学校除周五、周六外,每天晚上都实行熄灯制度,12点整熄灯。但是,如果"工作狂"陈景润(参见"数学科学学院"一章)还在的话,他一定会因为学校有个通宵教室而狂喜不已的!

　　每逢期末的最后两周,学校都会开放一幢通宵教学楼(通常是博学楼)以备学生们准备期末考试。这场面可值得一看啊:在教室里泡了一整天准备"回家"的学生们通常会在回去的路上碰见刚刚洗了澡、刷完牙,准备开始打"下半场"的同学……这里秘传你一个十分有用的小贴士:在每次期末来临前,先储存好足量的咖啡,期末到来的时候,你会发现超市里的咖啡架子基本上没什么东西剩下了——咖啡早被勤奋刻苦彻夜不眠的家伙们洗劫一空啦!

62. **风雨球场**　就在南光六、南光七附近,这里还有一个羽毛球场。

63. Journalism Department These two buildings have offices, classrooms, small library, a broadcast center—and a great sea view.

64. Physics Department, also called **Nanguang #3**

65. Furong #5 Formerly a computer science male dorm. The killer 1999 Typhoon Dan ripped off the roof. It was renovated and became XMU's first student apartment building; 4 students to a room.

Gulangyu's Koxinga Statue & Typhoons
From "Discover Gulangyu"

Professor Shi Yi, from Beijing's Central Fine Arts College, spent 3 ½ years researching and building her 16.2 meter, 1,617 ton masterpiece, which consists of 625 blocks of granite. Locals claim the statue protects Xiamen from typhoons but after the disastrous storm of October, 1999① wreaked havoc on our beautiful island, I asked a friend, "Where was Koxinga when we needed him?"

"Koxinga was laid off," he replied. "Tough times, you know."

66. Furong #6 , 10 & 12 Formerly male dorms.

67. Furong #11 Holds a special place in students' hearts! It was the only co-ed dorm on campus, with boys on floors one to four and girls sequestered on the top floor. Boys were driven out of Eden in 2000, but they still hang around the gates with high hopes. (Read about dating strategies in "Changting Tales").

---

① Typhoon Dan, the 14th of the season, was Xiamen's worst in 46 years. It landed October 9th; I spent 4 hours chopping trees to get out of our apartment.

63. **新闻系** 这两座建筑内设有办公室、教室、小型图书馆、新闻中心——还有美丽的海景喔！

64. **物理系**，也就是甬光三。

65. **芙蓉五** 以前是计算机科学学院的男生宿舍。1999 年的一场台风①就像杀手一样把他们的屋顶都给掀翻了！后来经过重修成了厦大第一幢四人一间的学生公寓。

鼓浪屿郑成功塑像与台风

这座高达 16.2 米，重达 1.617 吨的花岗岩塑像（在鼓浪屿）由 625 块花岗岩组成。来自北京中央美术学院的时宜教授经过长达三年半的时间进行调研并完成了她的杰作。当地的居民感激地说它可以保护厦门风平浪静。在 1999 年 10 月台风肆虐我们美丽的厦门岛之后，我问一个朋友，"当我们需要他的时候，郑成功到哪里去了？"

"郑成功'下岗'了，你知道世道艰难，"他诙谐地说。

（摘自《魅力鼓浪屿》）

66. **芙蓉六、十、十二** 以前是男生宿舍。

67. **芙蓉十一** 它在学生们的心中可有特别的地位喔！它曾经是学校里唯一的男女生混住的宿舍楼，男生住在一至四层、五至顶层由女生居住。男生们在 2000 年被逐出了伊甸园，但他们仍然徘徊在楼下"垂涎三尺"。（参见《长汀轶事》）

---

① 台风 Dan，是 1999 年第 14 号台风，是厦门 46 年一见的强台风，对厦门造成重创。它于 10 月 9 日登陆厦门，我花了 4 小时砍掉大树，从公寓逃出。

68. Dongbian Community Used to be a small fishing village, with popular food stalls and a fun little fisherman's cinema.

69. Furong Cafeteria Site of former Physics Cafeteria, Art Cafeteria, and specialty cafeteria, they were combined into one three-storey Furong Cafeteria, with quality (and price) rising from 1st floor to third.

70. Shijing (Stone Well) Cafeteria Often called a "girls' cafeteria because of tasty food but tiny portions.

71. Furong Bldg. #7 and #8 Both scheduled to become girls' dorms.

72. Shijing Gate The girls' dorm gate (Heaven's Gate?); scene of passionate partings every evening.

73. Furong # 9 and Shijing # 1, 2, 3, 4, 5, and 6 Girls' Dorms.

74. Furong #13 Grad Student Dorm

75. Lingyun Area Dorms for grad and PhD students (hike the hills behind to reach the Xiamen Botanical Garden, or visit the beautifully landscaped reservoir area).

Gate to Girls' Dorm

76. XMU Reservoir "Lovers' Lake"

77. Jiannan Mineral Water Factory This school-run factory provides drinking water for classrooms and other uses. (In early years, our water was so dark it resembled coffee; even hospitals tied clean socks on the faucets to strain it!)

78. Jingxian Teachers Housing

79. Koxinga Statue In front of a house built in 1963 is a statue of Koxinga (1624-1662) on a horse. Koxinga ousted the Dutch from Taiwan in 1662, and promptly died of what one historian called "overwork." (Let it be a lesson to all of us).

Koxinga was a genuine "made in Japan" Chinese hero, because he was born in Japan of a Chinese father and Japanese mother. And I actually "met" the great man! I played the last Dutch governor of Taiwan, Frederic Coyett, in a TV series, and after surrendering to Koxinga he and I had Chinese fast food.

第9章 带你游厦大

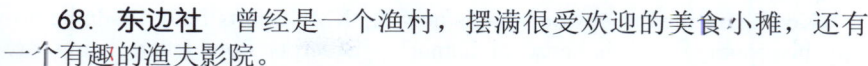

68. **东边社** 曾经是一个渔村，摆满很受欢迎的美食小摊，还有一个有趣的渔夫影院。

69. **芙蓉餐厅** 曾经是物理系餐厅、美术系餐厅和特色小吃餐厅的所在地，后来三家餐厅被合并为现在三层楼的芙蓉餐厅。从下往上，餐饮质量逐级递增，价格也逐级攀升。

70. **石井餐厅** 通常被称作"女生食堂"。这里的食物量虽小，却很美味！

71. **芙蓉七、芙蓉八** 都被设计为女生宿舍。

72. **石井大门** 通向女生宿舍区的大门。每天晚上你都可以看到情侣们缠绵的惜别场景。

73. **芙蓉九和石井一至六女生宿舍区**

74. **芙蓉十三，研究生宿舍**

75. **凌云区** 硕士和博士公寓区（后面有一条山路可通向厦门万石植物园，也可以通向风景秀丽的水库）。

76. **厦大水库，别名'情人湖'**

77. **建南矿泉水厂** 这个由学校经营的工厂主要向教学楼及其他单位供应饮用水。（头些年，我们的用水黑得像咖啡，即使医院也得把布系在水龙头上过滤！）

78. **敬贤区**

79. **郑成功雕像** 在一所建于1963年的古屋前树立着一尊郑成功骑马的雕像。郑成功（1624—1662）在1662年从荷兰人手里收复台湾后不久就去世了，一位历史学家的说法是"操劳过度"。（我们可得从他身上吸取教训呀！）。

郑成功是个真正的"日本制造"的中国民族英雄，因为他生于日本，父亲为中国人，母亲为日本人。我还曾经"见过"他呢！我在一部电视剧中出演荷兰驻台湾的最后一任总督，向他"投降"之后，我们还共进了中式快餐！

Bill (left) as Governor Frederic Coyett

Koxinga drilled troops on what is now the XMU sports field. I admire not only his courage but his sense of humor! Excerpts from letters below are adapted from *Discover Gulangyu* 《魅力鼓浪屿》摘录.

Excerpts from *Discover Gulangyu*

Koxinga Warned the Dutch: "On land you saw how the pride of Captain Pedel was so much humbled that he with his men, who are as foolish as himself, could not even bear the look of my men; and how, on the mere sight of my warriors, they threw down their arms and willingly awaited their well-deserved punishment with outstretched necks. Are these not sufficient proofs of your incompetency and inability to resist my forces?"

…"You Hollanders are conceited and senseless people; you will make yourselves unworthy of the mercy which I now offer; you will subject yourselves to the highest punishment by proudly opposing the great force I have brought with the mere handful of men which I am told you have in your Castle; you will obstinately persevere in this.

"Do you not wish to be wiser? Let your losses at least teach you, that your power here cannot be compared to a thousandth part of mine…If I wish to set my forces to work, then I am able to move Heaven and Earth; wherever I go, I am destined to win. Therefore take warning, and think the matter well over."

Governor Coyett described Koxinga's formidable troops: "The archers formed Koxinga's best troops, and much depended on them, for even at a distance they contrived to handle their weapons with so great skill, that they very nearly eclipsed the riflemen.

"Every tenth man of them is a leader, who takes charge of and presses his men on to force themselves into the ranks of the enemy. With bent heads and their bodies hidden behind the shields, they try to break through the opposing ranks with such fury and dauntless courage, *as if each one had still a spare body left at home.* They continually press onwards, notwithstanding many are shot down; not stopping to consider, but ever rushing forward like mad dogs, not even looking round to see whether they are followed by their comrades or not."

Koxinga's view on Taiwan's relation to mainland China: "Hitherto this island [Taiwan] had always belonged to China, and the Dutch had doubtless been permitted to live there, seeing that the Chinese did not require it for themselves; but requiring it now, it was only fair that Dutch strangers, who came from far regions, should give way to the masters of the island.…"

郑成功曾在如今已是厦大的田径场的地方操练大军。我不仅敬佩其勇气,还有他的幽默感!下面是《魅力鼓浪屿》的一则摘录。

郑成功再次要求荷兰人投降 "你看,在陆地上骄傲的贝德尔上尉是多么的卑微。他和他的军队一样的蠢,甚至不敢正视我的军队,而且,我的军队无须动刀,只须用咄咄逼人的目光,就能让他们放下武器,伸出脖子,等待罪有应得的惩罚。这些难道还不足以证明你们无能又无法与我抗衡吗?"

"……你们荷兰人既自负又迟钝,你们不配同情。如果你们以仅有的少数人(我被告之你们的城堡人数已经不多)愚顽抵抗,你们将会遭到最严厉的惩罚。还要顽固抵抗吗,不想放聪明点吗?至少让失败教训你们,你们所有的力量加起来还不及我千分之一……如果我的军队进攻,他们将无坚不摧;不管进攻哪里,一定大胜而归。因此,听听我的忠告,仔细掂量一下吧!"

揆一眼中的郑成功军队 "弓箭手是郑成功最精良的军队,而且是他的主要依靠力量。因为即使在很远的距离,他们也能以娴熟的技术操使武器,这使得我们的步枪手黯然失色。"

"每10个人中,就有一个队长,队长掌管队伍并促使他的队伍向前,迫使他们向敌人的队伍进逼。他们低着头,把身体藏在盾牌里,以激烈和不屈的勇气,向对方进攻,像是家里还有一副多余的躯体似的。他们不断地向前进逼,尽管很多人被击毙,他们想都不想,仍然像疯狗一样向前冲,也不向四周看看有没有同伴跟上。"

郑成功关于台湾和大陆关系的论述 "然台湾者,早为中国人所经营,中国之土地也……今余既来索,则地当归我。荷兰人毫无疑问只是被允许居住而已。荷兰人,来自遥远地区的外国人,只有把她交还给她的主人,才是理所应当……"

(摘自《魅力鼓浪屿》)

80. Student's Bomb Shelter (behind the house with the Koxinga Statue). Students dug this shelter between 1954-1956, and dug it even deeper in the 1970s. On Aug. 23, 1958, bombs blanketed Xiamen but only 3 hit XMU. A popular student slogan was "Pen in one hand, gun in the other!" Another was "American imperialists must withdraw from Taiwan!"

81. Foreign Teachers' Guesthouse Our family lived here from 1989-1990 in a room next to Nanputuo Temple. I was told the monks banged gongs and drums all night to drive away demons. Whether true or not, it sure did a number on us foreign devils.

82. Electron Microscope Lab Behind Guesthouse: the XMU Nano Science & Technology Center, and Analysis & Testing Center. The buildings right behind are the Environmental Science Building, the Dept. of Mechanical & Electrical Engineering and the MEMS lab.

83. #3 Da'nan Rd Across from the Foreign Teacher's Guesthouse, was built in the 1930s by an Overseas Chinese from the Philippines, Mr. Yang Bojing. The present occupant is his grandson, Yang Mingyi—the only one on XMU with a better beard than Uncle Beard's! (Prof. Ji Yuhua).

84. #5 Da'nan Rd Historic Overseas Chinese home predating XMU. Note the rock garden and pool. These granite homes were built by hardy Hui'an women using nothing but simple mallets and chisels. (I've often wondered what the men were doing).

85. Guoguang Area Teachers Housing. These three rows of red brick buildings were built by Lee Kong Chian, Tan Kah Kee's son-in-law, in 1955 (at this time he also built Furong #1,2,3; Fengting #1,2,3; and the granite Jiannan Auditorium 5-building complex).

86. Teacher's Bomb Shelter Up the road from Foreign Teacher's Guesthouse; now hidden by a new white building.

Guo Guang

87. Campus Security This is the white building at the top of the road leading uphill from Keli Bldg.

88. Lingfeng Area Teacher's hillside housing behind Campus Security.

80. **学生的防空洞** （就在郑成功雕像的那座房子背后）由学生们挖于 1954—1956 年间，并于 70 年代在原有基础上挖深。1958 年 8 月 23 日，在两岸炮战中，厦门遭到从金门发出的数千枚炮弹的轰炸，所幸仅有 3 枚落到厦大。当时学生中流行的口号是："一手执笔，一手拿枪！"，还有一句是："美帝国主义必须从台湾撤离！"

XMU Beach in the 1950s

81. **专家楼** 紧挨着南普陀寺，我家从 1989—1990 年曾安在这里。有人告诉我说，和尚们整夜整夜地敲钟是为了要驱走妖魔鬼怪。不管是不是真的，当时确实把我们这群"洋鬼子"折腾得够呛啊！

82. **电镜实验室** 位于专家楼后面。分析测试中心和纳米科技中心都设在这里。其正后方的那幢楼是环境科学学院，紧接其后的是机电工程系和 MEMS 实验室。

83. **大南路 3 号** 位于专家楼马路对面，于上世纪 30 年代由菲律宾华侨杨伯京先生建造。现在杨老先生的孙子杨明宜先生居住在此。杨明宜先生可是现在在厦大内唯一一个胡子比大胡子伯伯（纪玉华教授）还多的人！

84. **大南路 5 号** 历史上曾经是一家华侨的住所，是比厦大本身还古老的建筑。注意看里面的假山和水池！那可是勤劳的惠安女只用简易的锤子和凿子雕刻出来的！（惠安的男人都干嘛呢？）

85. **国光区教师公寓** 这三排红墙建筑是由陈嘉庚先生的女婿李光前于 1955 年兴资建成的（在这期间，他还兴建了芙蓉一、二、三号楼、丰庭一、二、三号楼以及花岗岩建筑建南楼群）。

86. **教师的防空洞** 就在去往专家楼的上坡路段

87. **厦大派出所** 从克立楼往山上走到这条直路的尽头，坡顶上的那幢白色建筑就是派出所了。

88. **凌峰区** 在派出所后山上的一片教师宿舍区。

89. Sino-U.S. Pavilion I made this Chinese pavilion in our garden with tile-covered concrete water pipes for the pillars, and green tile for the roof. It was XMU's first (and only) Sino-US joint venture pavilion.

90. Children's Nursery XMU Cable TV office in back。 XMU's oldest building, it predates XMU. It was built around 1900-1910 by an Overseas Chinese family. XMU bought it and the Sun family moved to the cute yellow European cottage behind Yifu Lou

91. XMU Archives & Historical Research Ctr. Just below the Nursery at Da'nan Rd #3. Built about 1930, this was commandeered by Japanese in the 1940s, then used by the XMU President, and later as Red Guards headquarters during the Cultural Revolution. The gate is Art Deco①, a style popular in the 20s and 30s and common on Gulangyu. (Read more in "Discover Gulangyu")

Art Deco Gate

92. Da'nan Rd #7 An Overseas Chinese' home built around 1904 or 1905; it once had a beautiful walled garden.

93. Biomedical Center Behind Song'en Tower (check out their beautiful little roof garden).

94. Jijin Bldg. Has language laboratories and registration center for English Grade, GRE and TOEFL exams.

95. Taiwan Research Institute

96. Chemistry Bldg.

97. Yixian Bldg. Sah Bendong MEMS Research Center

98. Economics College The management college was here for my first decade in XMU. The statue in front is Prof. Wang Yanan (next page).

---

① Art Deco originated in the 20s, inspired by discovery of King Tut's tomb, with highly stylized Egyptian motifs. Art deco employed clean, streamlined designs with such elements as cubic forms, zigzags, and ziggurats (from "Discover Gulangyu")

第9章 带你游厦大

89. **中美亭子** 我在自家的花园里造了这座亭子,用混凝土水管作亭子的柱子并在表面贴上瓷砖,并用绿色的瓦片盖了亭子的屋顶。这可是厦门大学第一座(也是唯一一座)中美合资的亭子哦。

Sino-U.S. Pavilion!

90. **幼儿园托儿部** 后面是厦大有线电视台办公室。比厦大建得更早,是厦大校园内最古老的建筑了。由一个华侨家庭建于1900——1910年间。厦大后来买下了它,而孙家也就搬到了逸夫楼后面的大学路10号的"欧式黄色小别墅"。

91. **厦大档案馆** 就在托儿所下面的大南路3号,建于1930年左右,曾经在20世纪40年代被日本人霸占过,后来一度作为厦大校长办公室,又在"文革"期间用作"红卫兵"总部。它的大门是经过艺术装饰①的,采用在20世纪二三十年代十分流行的一种风格,在鼓浪屿上的建筑中很常见。(详见《魅力鼓浪屿》)

92. **大南路7号** 建于1904或1905年,以前是一个华侨家庭的住所。曾经设有一个十分漂亮的有围墙的花园。

93. **生物医药中心** 在颂恩楼后面(有美丽的"空中花园"!)

94. **基金楼** 内设语音教室和英语等级考试、GRE、托福考点。

95. **台湾研究院**
96. **化学楼**
97. **亦玄馆** 萨本栋微机电研究中心。

Roof Garden

98. **经济学院** 以前的管理学院也在这个地方。门前的那尊雕像就是王亚南教授(见下页)。

---

① 艺术装饰:起源于19世纪20年代,灵感源自埃及法老图坦卡门陵墓的发现,该陵墓具有典型的埃及特色。艺术装饰善于运用简练新型式设计,多采纳立体、Z字形、神塔式等元素。(摘自《魅力鼓浪屿》)

Wang Yanan
Spirit of Devotion to Science

Wang Yanan was born in 1901 and devoted his entire life to teaching and doing research on Marxian political economics and supporting student movements.

At the beginning of 1949, Wang had to stay in Hong Kong to survive the so called "darkness before the dawn". According to his friend Tao Dayong, who lived downstairs and worked nights, Wang arose well before dawn every day to study and write. So before Tao was ready for bed early each morning, the light in Wang's room was already on.

Another example of Wang's hard work was his discipline in learning foreign languages. There were times during the war when his entire school had no rice to eat. Wang went with some of his students to the government in Hunan Province to ask for rice, and even while staying in the hotel there, Wang arose early every morning to read German aloud.

During the Cultural Revolution, when Wang was forced to stay home and write self-criticisms, he never missed a single day of studying French. Within only a few months he was able to read the French version of Chairman Mao books, and he happily wrote to his daughter, "I'm able to understand another language now, meaning I've got one more crutch to help me with translation work in the future."

In order to devote more time to work, Wang set up a rule for himself: "No theater except on Sunday." He never broke his rule, even when he was in Shanghai and his favorite ballet group came to perform for two days. Wang was very excited about seeing the performance, but did not because none of the performances were on Sunday. While he was ill in the hospital, he wrote to the Party, "If one stops working even for one day, what's the pointing of living?"

王亚南——科学献身精神

王亚南,生于1901年,毕生从事教育工作、马克思政治经济学研究,并支持学生运动。

1949年初,被称为"黎明前的黑暗"的那段时间里,王亚南被迫避居香港,但仍不放松学习和写作。当时住在他楼下的陶大镛回忆说:"我习惯于'开夜车',而王亚南一向在黎明前奋笔。每当我刚躺下去,楼上的灯光已亮,他早就伏在案头了。"

从王亚南学习外语时的自律也可以看出其学习之努力。据他的学生回忆说,有一次因为没米吃,他带领几个学生到当时的湖南政府要米,尽管是短期出差,住在宾馆,仍然每天天不亮就起来念德语。

甚至在那"史无前例"的动乱年代,王亚南被勒令在家里写"交代材料"的时候,仍然抓紧时间学习法语。经过几个月的刻苦自学,就能看懂法文版的毛主席著作了。他高兴地写信给女儿说:"我又掌握了一门外语,以后的翻译又多了一根拐杖……"。

Wang Yanan
(Photo Courtesy of W.I.S.E.)

为了把更多的时间用于工作,王亚南给自己制定了一条规则:非星期天不看影剧。他从未违反过这条规则,即使是在上海,当时他喜爱的芭蕾舞团来沪演出,时间只有两天。他当时非常兴奋,但是却没有去观看,因为这两天都不是星期天。有一次他生病住院,厦大党委做出决定要他休息,他写信给党委说:"一个人如果整天在那里不做一点工作,生活还有什么意思?"(参考《王亚南治学之路》)

99. Southern Gate (or "Old Gate")
100. Bus Terminal
We had only about 3 main bus routes when we arrived in 1988; now we have well over 100! From the XMU Gate you can go easily, quickly and cheaply to anywhere in Xiamen—or China, for that matter. (Buy long distance bus tickets in the small office at the gate).

The bus stop used to be small and congested but they doubled its size (and tripled the buses, I think). But our modern buses are clean and quiet (many run on clean LPG), and most have TVs. They used to be a pain, but nowadays my wife and I sometimes hop on one at random just for fun, to see where we end up.

XMU Gate, 1957 (Mr Bai Hua)

101. XMU Lane
This bustling little street is what really gives the vicinity a "college town" flavor. We had our very first meal in China at Lin Duck House, and it's my favorite (clean, tasty food, inexpensive, English menu). Also try the vegetarian restaurants, or Relax Café. Dozens of small shops sell everything from books and trinkets to clothing, shoes and sports equipment.

102. Post Office
Open 7 days a week, all day, rain or shine.

103. Bank of China

104. Nanputuo Monastery
Nanputuo Temple, right outside the #1 Bus terminus and Xiada's old gate, sprawls across the Five Old Man Mountains like a Chinese miniature landscape on steroids. The complex's original structures were built over 1,000 years ago, during the Tang Dynasty.

Buddha's Bugs (Qing Dynasty Tale, from "Amoy Magic") A Buddhist monk vowed to offer his blood to feed other living things, but after mosquitoes had bitten him for hours the itching got to him and he began swatting them with abandon.

"What happened to your vow?" asked a bystander.

The monk sighed. "Some of them have started coming back for seconds."

第9章 带你游厦大

99. **南校门**，也叫旧校门。

100. **公共汽车站** 当我们在1988年到厦大的时候，全厦门只有3条公交车的主要线路，现在却有100多条！在厦大校门前往厦门的任何一个地方都很方便、快捷，票价也很便宜。——当然，也可以满中国地跑！（因为你可以在校门旁边的票务代办点买到长途汽车票。）

原来公共汽车站很小、很拥挤。现在已是过去的两倍大（我猜想，他们的公共汽车数量也同时扩大到三倍了吧？）。但这些现代化的公共汽车却十分清洁、安静（很多都使用液化石油气体），大多数车上都有线电视。以前，乘坐公共汽车可是件痛苦的事，但现在我和妻子有时候随便跳上一辆，只为消遣——还为了看看它到底把我们载哪儿去。

101. **厦大一条街** 正是这条街，厦大周围才有了"大学城"的味道。我们家来到中国的第一餐是在林家鸭庄吃的，而且它是我最喜欢去的餐馆（这里的食物卫生、美味、便宜，还有英文菜单！）。偶尔也可以试试素菜馆或者"美丽时光"咖啡…还有各种各样的小店：书籍、饰品、衣服、鞋子、运动品等等。

102. **邮电局** 一周营业7天，无论晴、雨，全天候服务。

103. **中国银行**

南普陀寺，（《魅力厦门》摘录） "就在厦大老校门外1路公共汽车终点站旁边。整个寺院在五老峰的山麓上横向铺开，就像是地理缩微模型里的中国城。南普陀始建于1000多年前的唐朝。"

Nanputuo Temple (686 A.D.)

清代民间故事——佛虫 一个和尚发誓要用自己身上的血喂养其它的生灵。在任由蚊虫叮咬了好几个小时之后，他终于瘙痒难耐开始拍打起来。

"你不是发过誓吗？"一个旁观者问道。

和尚叹了口气，说："蚊子也不守信用，过一会儿就飞回来一趟。"

Lu Xun & Lin Yutang Memorial Halls
by Zheng Qiwu
(a rough translation)

At a symposium held in the Taiwan Institute in Xiamen University, 12 scholars from Foguang University, Taiwan (including its president, Gong Pengcheng) and I had a very good exchange of views about two giants who taught in the 1920s: Lin Yutang and Lu Xun. After the symposium, we visited two important memorials: the Lin Yutang memorial and the Lu Xun memorial. It was then that I realized that the two literary giants had contributed a lot to XMU, to the Mainland and to Taiwan as well.

Lu Xun Memorial Two things most interested me in this hall: an essay and a love postcard. While he was in XMU, Lu Xun completed many famous works of literature, including the elegant essay: *From Courtyard to Private Study*. This essay is well known in China and was chosen for Chinese middle school textbooks. It is one of my favorite essays and I have read it so many times that I can recite it. Another thing that greatly interested me was a postcard Lu Xun mailed to his lover, Xu Guangping, in Guangzhou hundreds of miles away. This was the first time I saw this postcard, though I should have seen it during my previous visits. Was it the latest addition? Maybe it had been there all along but I had never noticed it?

On the postcard were two plain half-penny stamps with "sail" pictures. The stamps were issued by the post-office of the Kuomintang government, the then dominant Chinese government. I could not tell when it was mailed from Xiamen because the card was face up and the date was on the back of the card. To my knowledge, it should have been mailed about 1926. Lu Xun wrote on the postcard in ink with a Chinese brush. Lu Xun's handwriting was beautiful so this postcard is not only a relic left by a famous literary giant but also a precious work of calligraphy. The sender's address on the postcard was Xiamen University, Fujian Province.

The calligraphy on Xiamen University's seal must be Lu Xun's because it is almost identical with that on the postcard. I compared the two for quite a time and could find no difference.

I told the Taiwanese scholars about my discovery of the similarity between the handwriting on our current Xiamen University seal and that of the 1926 Lu Xun postcard. They were very amazed and excited, and immediately photographed the postcard.

林语堂纪念室和鲁迅纪念馆

郑启五

在厦门大学台湾研究院主办的一次研讨会上,我与台湾佛光大学校长龚鹏程一行 12 人在厦门大学台湾研究所举行座谈,谈得十分投机,事后我陪同台湾师友们参观校园里的鲁迅纪念馆、林语堂纪念室,不料漫步在这两个鼻子底下的展览中我竟有所新得:旧物旧照的闪回现身说法,拂去了多少历史缤纷的落尘!

鲁迅在厦大时著作很多,特别是那精美的《从百草园到三味书屋》,为中国百姓家喻户晓,也是我的最爱,爱之深,能背下来。纪念馆在介绍先生的《两地书》时,出现了一枚鲁迅当年从厦门大学寄给广州许广平的明信片,嘿,是新增的史料,还是自己过去走马观花的忽略?

明信片贴两枚民国的"帆船"面值半分的普通邮票,盖的厦门日戳时间不太清晰,总是 1926 年的吧。因为展示的是明信片的正面,故主要内容不详,但作为邮品,视野足矣!鲁迅的毛笔墨迹娟秀可人,使明信片本身不但是文人文物,而且是书法珍品,特别是那落款"福建厦门大学鲁迅寄"几个字。如今我们校徽上的"厦门大学"四个字就是取自鲁迅的手书,不知是否就是取自这枚明信片上的。我看了半天,几乎毫无二致,只是明信片上的为竖行书写罢了。

我把现场的"重大发现"告诉了台湾的同人,他们也兴致勃勃,把明信片的风采拍摄了下来。

林语堂与鲁迅 夫妇合影

Lin Yutang Memorial Hall This hall's two most unusual and precious objects are a desk and a Lin Yutang stamp. Lin Yutang taught longer in XMU than Lu Xun. He was also the director of the art college and a secretary of the Chinese college, as well as a professor of the foreign language department. Lin is the one who recommended that Lu Xun come teach in XMU. The Lin Yutang Memorial is on the third floor of the XMU Library.

Most eye-catching is the old desk, its edge worn completely smooth. It was at that desk that Mr. Lin completed many excellent essays. Lin Yutang also mentored his nephew, Lin Yijin, who became a famous English-Chinese translator. Lin Yijin translated several famous American novels, including *Farewell to Arms* and *All Quiet on the Western Front*.

I took an undergraduate course from Lin Yujin when he was director of XMU's foreign language department. Lin Yujin's daughter, Lin Mengru, was my classmate in Shuangshi middle school, and she gave us a tour of the Memorial. Taiwan also has a Lin Yutang memorial, which the government authorized Foguang University to manage. So the 12 guests from Foguang University visited the Xiamen Lin Yutang memorial in high spirits and carefully examined every object on display. We drew special attention to a stamp in honor of Lin Yutang. That stamp was issued by the Taiwan post-office on Lin Yutang's 100th birthday (October 10, 1995). Coincidentally, the XMU Lin Yutang Memorial was set up on the very same day. The stamp bears an image of Lin, smiling slightly. Many mainland literature anthologies list Mr. Lin among the Taiwan writers, but many Taiwan literati regard him as a mainland writer. Is Mr. Lin a mainland writer or a Taiwan writer? I am afraid we would need to ask Mr. Lin himself. I prefer to think Lin Yutang belongs to both sides of the Taiwan Strait, to both Mainland China and Taiwan. (Read more about Lin Yutang in the Humanities Chapter)

Lin Yutang's Desk

林语堂在厦门大学任教的时间比鲁迅久,当年他是厦门大学文学院的主任兼国学院的秘书,也是外文系的教授。鲁迅就是经由他的荐请来厦大的。纪念室设在厦门大学图书馆的一隅,其中的书桌是先生当年在上海时的旧物,多少名篇佳作就是在那上面成就的。林语堂的侄子林疑今是著名的翻译家(《永别了,武器》、《西线无战事》等多部英美巨著的译者),是厦大外文系的老系主任、我的大学本科时的恩师。林语堂的侄孙女、林疑今教授的女儿林梦如是我双十中学"老三届"的同学,临时约请她担任纪念室的讲解。因为台湾有关当局把台湾的林语堂纪念馆划归佛光大学管辖,因此台湾学人对林语堂纪念室参观得更加认真与细致,我也细致了起来。参观中发现了一枚"林语堂"纪念邮票的首日封,那是台湾邮政为林语堂百年诞辰时发行的,而我们厦门大学的"林语堂纪念室"也是在先生百年诞辰时设立的。邮票上的先生风度翩翩,含笑微微。林老先生在笑什么,大陆不少文选把先生列为台湾作家,而台湾不少读者又把先生视为大陆作家,台胞乎,闽胞乎,这恐怕连先生自己都分不清楚!我想,语堂师其实是血脉相连的海峡两岸共同的先生。(有关林语堂的更多内容参见"人文学院"一章)

林语堂与鲁迅、孙伏园等在厦大后山合影
Lin Yutang and Lu Xun at XMU

Supplement   Lu Xun—"Father of Modern Chinese Literature"
(from "Amoy Magic—Guide to Xiamen")

The statue beside XMU's Anthropology Museum is of Lu Xun (1881-1936), author of "True Story of Ah Q" and other modern classics.   Lu Xun (a pen name for Zhou Shuren, 周树人) broke 5,018① years of literary tradition with his first story, "Madman's Diary," because he wrote in the language of the people—which is worlds apart from the hallowed written language that scholars had perfected over the centuries.

For over 2,000 years, any scholar worth his salt mastered the classics of Confucius and Laozi, and then wrote brilliant essays about the brilliant essays written by his forebears. The writing was stylistic and terse, and totally unlike oral Chinese, which like oral English is a living language, changing constantly. So Lu Xun decided to write like people talk.   It was a bold move—akin to Westerners' translation of the Bible from dead Latin into common English. Fortunately, unlike Tyndale and Bible translators, Lu Xun wasn't burned alive at the stake—but he did make a lot of enemies.

Lu Xun taught in XMU the last few months of 1926, but he disliked the professors' constant bickering and politicking (common on any campus, in China or elsewhere!).   He wrote curt essays like "How to Write?" (怎么写?).   And having said his piece, and having disturbed what little peace the place had, he packed his bags and moved to Guangzhou in January, '27.

In "Old Tales Retold," Lu Xun wrote,"In some places the narrative is based on passages in old books, elsewhere I gave free reign to my imagination. And having less respect for the ancients than for my contemporaries, I have not always been able to avoid facetiousness."

You can pick up Lu Xun's works in Xiamen bookstores or even download some from the internet.

---

① I was told China has 5,000 years of history but that was 18 years ago.

鲁迅——"中国现代文学之父"

——摘自《魅力厦门》

厦门大学人类博物馆旁有一座鲁迅雕像。鲁迅（1881－1936）原名周树人，写下了《阿Q正传》等现代文学经典。他的第一篇小说《狂人日记》打破了中国5018年①的文学传统，因为这篇小说是用白话文——人民的语言写成的。这与千百年来文人墨客不断推敲雕凿的文言文简直有着天壤之别。

两千多年以来，每个合格的文人都要熟读孔子、老子等先贤的经典，然后就前辈们写出的美文再写出一篇篇华美的文章。这种文章体裁严谨语言精炼，跟中国人的日常口语完全不同。其实汉语口语跟英语口语一样，都是活生生的、不断演变着的。鲁迅下定决心，要用人们说话的方式来写文章。就像当年西方人把圣经从艰涩难懂的拉丁文翻译成通俗的英文一样，这无疑是个大胆的举动。幸运的是，鲁迅跟廷代尔和那些圣经译者不同，并没有被绑在木柱上遭受火刑的命运——不过他还是树敌不少。

1926年的最后几个月，鲁迅来到厦门大学任教。他对教授们无休止的攻击和争吵感到厌恶。鲁迅就此写了一篇短文《怎么写》。该说的话已经说了，生活中的那一点点平静也被打破了，1927年1月，鲁迅收拾行囊去了广州。

在《故事新编》中，鲁迅写道：

"叙事有时也有一点旧书上的根据，有时不过是信口开河。而且因为自己的对于古人，不及对于今人的诚敬，所以仍不免有时有油滑之处。"

你可以在厦门的书店找到鲁迅的著作，甚至还可以从网上下载！

---

① 一位厦大的教授告诉我中国有五千年的历史，但是那是18年前。

Chapter 10

XMU — An International University

News Flash! "In September last year, XMU had the great honor of welcoming His Excellency Prime Minister Abdullah Ahmad Badawi. Following the great initiative proposed by His Excellency to set up a Malay Studies Program in XMU, XMU stressed its full commitment to this proposal." Common Talk, Xiamen Daily, Nov. 17, 2004

Pioneer in Education for Foreigners—Both on and off Campus

In this Internet Age, many schools across the globe are offering quality online degrees, but XMU pioneered distance education in 1956—decades before the rest of the world. Over the past 50 years, XMU has taught over 30,000 overseas correspondence students from over 100 countries and regions.

We also pioneered on-campus education for foreigners in China, and now have over 1,600 resident students from over 50 countries and regions studying everything from Minnan Dialect to Acupuncture.

Exchange & Cooperative Programs

XMU has over 100 sister universities and close ties with over 80 higher education institutes in the U.S., Canada, the U.K., New Zealand, Australia, Japan, the Netherlands, Singapore, France, Belgium, Italy, Russia, Malaysia, Indonesia, Korea, Thailand, the Philippines, and Israel, as well as Hong Kong, Taiwan and Macao. Cooperative foreign institutes include South Korea's Inha Univ., France's LeHavre Univ., the United States' Univ. of Rhode Island and Univ. of Washington, Australia's RMIT (Royal Melbourne Institute of Technology), and Israel's Haifa Univ.

Over 100 XMU scholars go abroad each year through faculty exchange programs with such institutes as the Univ. of Illinois and Calvin College in the USA, the Univ. of Amsterdam in Holland, Soka Univ. in Japan, Ateneo de Univ. de Manila in the Philippines, and Inha Univ. in Korea.

第10章

厦门大学——一所国际性的大学

快讯！ "去年九月，厦门大学荣幸地迎来了马来西亚首相阿卜杜拉·巴达维的访问。阁下提出了一项极有意义的提议：在厦门大学成立马来西亚研究院。厦大全力以赴地将这一提议落到实处。"

《厦门日报·双语周刊》2004年11月17日

留学生教育的先行者——校园内外

在当今网络时代，许多学校都开设优质的网上远程教育课程。但厦门大学却是这方面真正的先行者，早在1956年就已经拥有远程教育的课程，领先世界数十年之久。在过去50年里，参加厦门大学函授课程的学生超过30000人，分别来自100多个不同的国家和地区。

厦门大学的留学生教育也领先于中国其他很多大学。现在学校有来自50多个国家超过1600名留学生在这里学习各种学科，从闽南语到针灸，应有尽有。

China Studies Program (U.S.)

交流合作项目 厦门大学有100多所兄弟院校，并与美国、加拿大、英国、新西兰、澳大利亚、日本、荷兰、新加坡、法国、比利时、意大利、俄罗斯、马来西亚、印度尼西亚、韩国、泰国、菲律宾、以色列，以及香港、台湾和澳门的80多所高等院校有着紧密联系。其中保持合作关系的外国院校包括：韩国的仁荷大学，法国的勒阿弗尔大学，美国的罗德岛大学和华盛顿大学，澳大利亚的墨尔本皇家工业学院，以及以色列的海法大学等。

厦门大学每年有100多名学者通过教职员工交换项目到下列大学进行学者访问：美国的伊利诺斯大学和加尔文大学，荷兰的阿姆斯特丹大学，日本的创价大学，菲律宾的马尼拉安德雷尔大学，以及韩国的仁荷大学等。

Our numerous joint programs with foreign institutes include an environmental program with the Univ. of San Francisco, and an innovative media arts program with the U.K.'s Univ. of Luton. Students complete two years in XMU, one year in Luton, and receive two bachelor degrees, one from each university (and can stay another year in Luton to complete a masters in media arts). XMU is also exploring further projects with Curtin Technology Univ. in Australia, Oxford Brooks Univ., Sussex Univ., and Newcastle Univ. upon Tyon in the U.K., and Saint Mary's Univ. in Canada.

We are not only sending our students all over the world but bringing the world's students to XMU with innovative programs.

The World Comes to XMU Since the 1980s XMU has invited over 3000 foreign scholars to teach, lecture, or engage in research. Our foreign experts teach undergrad and grad courses in English, Russian, Japanese culture and language, Japanese history, history of modern and classical foreign literature, literary criticism of American and British literature, Western culture, management, economics, etc.—the list grows each semester. We've even had Michael Dell lecture a couple of times, and granted him the title of Honorary Professor (not bad for a man who never finished college).

On XMU one often encounters groups of foreign college students and teenagers participating in the numerous cross-cultural activities hosted by our campus. For example:

The Xavier China Experience (XCE) held at XMU each semester offers junior high students from the Philippines a six-week crash course in Chinese language and culture. 280 students participated in 2004.

Website: http://xce05.xs.edu.ph/

The China Studies Program (CSP), hosted by the Overseas Education College (OEC), is sponsored by the Council for Christian Colleges and Universities in Washington, D.C., and has students from colleges throughout the U.S. (CSP is introduced later in this chapter).

Website: http://csp.bestsemester.com

The 4th Cross-Straits University Students' "South Fujian Culture Study" Summer Camp was hosted by XMU in the summer of 2005. Sixty students from eight Taiwanese universities spent nine days studying South Fujian culture through classroom activities and on-site tours to places of historical and cultural interest.[1]

---

[1] Common Talk, *Xiamen Daily*, July 13, 2005

第10章 厦门大学——一所国际性的大学
DISCOVER Xiamen University

在与众多的海外高校的合作项目中,有与旧金山大学的环境项目,与英国鲁顿大学的富有开创性的传媒艺术项目。学生在厦门大学学习两年,再在鲁顿大学学习一年,就可毕业,并拥有由这两所大学分别颁发的学士学位。之后可继续在鲁顿大学深造一年,取得传媒艺术的硕士学位。厦门大学也在与澳大利亚的柯廷技术大学,英国的牛津布鲁克斯大学、萨塞克斯大学、纽卡斯尔大学,加拿大的圣玛丽大学积极探讨更多的合作方式。

我们不仅将学生送往世界各地,也以充满创意的专业吸引着世界各地的学生前来深造。

厦大喜迎八方来客

从1980年开始,厦门大学共邀请了3000多名学者前来教学、开讲座、做研究。 我们的外籍专家为本科生和研究生开设了英语、俄语、日本文化和语言、日本历史、现代和古典外国文学史、美英文学批评、西方文化、管理、经济等等课程,且每学期都有新的课程增加。厦大甚至还邀请过戴尔电脑的总裁迈克·戴尔先生做过几次讲座,并授予他荣誉教授的称号。(这对于这个大学未毕业的人来说够可以的啦!)

在厦大,经常会看到成群的外国留学生参加各种各样由学校主办的跨文化活动。例如:

光启学校中国—厦门学习之旅 每学期都会在厦大举办。参加者都是来自菲律宾的初中生,他们在厦大度过六周时光,学习中国的语言及文化。2004年有280名学生参加了这一活动。

网址: http://xce05.xs.edu.ph/

"美华"项目(CPS) 是由海外教育学院主办,由华盛顿美国基督教大学联盟赞助的一项活动。每年都有来自美国各地学院的学生参加。(这一项目将在随后作详细介绍)

网址: http://csp.bestsemester.com

第四届海峡两岸大学生闽南文化研习夏令营 这项活动于2005年夏天在厦门大学举行。来自台湾8所大学的60名学生在这里度过了九天,通过课堂活动和实地考察历史文化胜地了解了闽南文化。[①]

---

① 引自《厦门日报·双语周刊》2005年7月13日。

Popular Host of International Conferences With our beautiful seaside campus and mild climate, XMU is a popular venue for conferences. In fact, since 1995 we've hosted over 100 key international and regional academic conferences, such as the STATPHYS 19 and ISE 46 conventions.

国际会议的主办之地 厦门大学拥有美丽的海景和温和怡人的气候，这些都让它成为召开大型会议的首选之地。事实上，自从 1995 年以来，厦大共举办了 100 多场国际或地区性的学术会议，例如，第 19 届纯物理和应用物理国际联合会统计物理学研讨会以及第 46 届国际电化学协会研讨会等。

A Sample Year of XMU International[①] Conferences
(March 2004-March 2005)
我校举办国际[①]学术会议一览表, 2004 年 3 月—2005 年 3 月

1. 2004　2nd Intl. Society of Electrochemistry 第二届中国际电化学会春季会议
   （Chemistry and Chemical Engineering College 化学化工学院）
2. 2004　China and S.E. Asia Challenges, Opportunities and the Reconstruction of S.E. Asian Chinese Ethnic Capital　中国和东南亚之间华人资本的流动
   （Center for S.E. Asian Studies 南洋研究院）
3. 2004　Symposium on the Suffix of the Noun, a Comparative-study Plan on the Dialects of the Southeast of China.中国东南部方言比较研究计划之名词词尾国际研讨会 （School of Humanities 人文学院）
4. 2004　Seminar on Cambridge Phenomenon of Science　大学科技园之剑桥现象高级研讨班
5. 2004　Tenth Annual Conference of Assoc. of Chinese Social History and the Intl. Conference on Ritual, Custom, and Social Order
   第十届中国社会史学会年会暨"礼仪、习俗与社会秩序"国际学术研讨会
   （School of Humanities 人文学院）
6. 2004　Intl. Symposium on Economy Globalization and China Economy Development　经济全球化与中国经济发展国际研讨会（School of Economics 经济学院）
7. 2004　The Second Seminar on the Development of Cross-strait Chemistry, Biology and Biotechnology and Medicine　第二届海峡化学生物学与生技、医药发展研讨会

---

① Includes Taiwan, HK and Macao Regions 包括港澳台地区

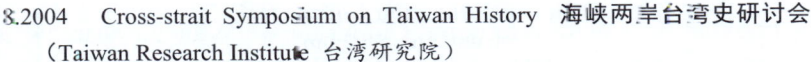

8.2004　Cross-strait Symposium on Taiwan History　海峡两岸台湾史研讨会（Taiwan Research Institute　台湾研究院）

9.2004　Academic Symposium on History and Culture of Hakka，客家历史文化学术研讨会（School of Humanities　人文学院）

10.2004　Cross-strait Symposium on Rent Taxation　海峡两岸租税学术研讨会（School of Economics　经济学院）

11.2004　China and S.E. Asia Challenges, opportunities and the reconstruction of S.E. Asian Chinese ethnic capital　东南亚华人资本在中国与东南亚的流动（Center for S.E.Asian Studies　南洋研究院）

12.2004　2nd Intl. Conference on Environmental Concerns 第二届关于环境问题的国际会议（College of Oceanography and Environmental Science　海洋与环境学院）

13.2004　4th Intl. Symposium on Accounting & Finance　第四届会计与财务问题国际研讨会（School of Mgmt.　管理学院）

14.2004　Sino-French Symposium for Advanced Chemistry and its Applications 中法先进化学与应用学术研讨会（Chemistry & Chemical Engineering College　化学化工学院）

15.2004　The First Annual China Finance Conference　首届中国金融学年会（School of Economics　经济学院）

16.2004　International Economic Law and China in Its Economic Transition　国际经济法与经济转型期的中国（School of Law　法学院）

17.2004　International Symposium on Baiyue Culture 百越文化国际学术研讨会（School of Humanities　人文学院）

18.2004　International Symposium on Comparative Study of China and Japan 中日比较研究国际学术研讨会（School of Foreign Languages and OEC　外文学院和海外教育学院）

19.2004　Intl. Symposium on Hakka Dialect　客家方言国际学术研讨会（School of Humanities　人文学院）

20. 2005　1st Cross-strait Symposium on Russian Language Teaching and Research　首届"海峡两岸俄语教学与研究学术讨论会"（School of Foreign Languages　外文学院）

21.2005　Recent Developments in the Law of the Sea and China "海洋法的新发展与中国"国际学术会议（School of Law　法学院）

Overseas Education College (OEC)
www.xmuoec.com

One of China's oldest institutions offering programs to overseas students, the Overseas Correspondence College was founded in 1956 and in 1991 renamed the Overseas Education College. The OEC is one of the few institutes designated by the State Council's Office of Overseas Chinese Affairs to support neighboring countries with Chinese courses.

OEC is responsible for foreign students in all XMU departments, but also oversees Chinese language training for on-campus and correspondence students, and administers the annual HSK (Chinese Proficiency Test). OEC offers Bachelors and Masters in a variety of courses, including Chinese language and culture and business Chinese, as well as PhDs in art studies in collaboration with the Department of Chinese Language and Culture in the College of Humanities. OEC also offers students, free of charge, cultural courses such as Chinese Folk Dancing and Martial Arts.

OEC offers 3 forms of accommodation. The towering Cai Qingjie Bldg. is but a 3 minute walk to either classrooms or the beach, and offers hotel-style facilities and service. Each room has a telephone, air conditioner, cable TV and hi-speed internet access (utilities are charged separately). Rooms in the Nanguang #5 building are about half the cost of the Qingjie Building. The third option is off-campus housing.

Foundation College of Xiamen University (FCXM)

FCXM has one goal: prepare Chinese students to go abroad! FXCM is a joint program started in April 2005 with the China Scholarship Council. They emphasize improving education quality and promoting international cultural and academic exchange, and faculty members are either foreigners or Chinese with overseas experience. The bilingual curriculum not only meets international standards but also individual students' needs by providing a tailor-made study plan that even includes help in choosing overseas colleges or applying for visas.

FCXM Guarantee! Students passing the entry level requirements can enter one of dozens of cooperative universities in the U.K., Ireland, France, Canada or the U.S.A. And if they fail to make it abroad, they can pursue undergraduate or graduate studies in a cooperative Chinese university.

Regardless of where they end up, they live in style while at FCXM. FCXM is temporarily on the beautiful Zhangzhou campus, and dorms are equipped with computers, phones, air conditioners, washing machines, etc.

海外教育学院

（www.xmuoec.com）

海外函授教育学院成立于1956年，是中国最早开展对外教育的机构之一。在1991年它更名为海外教育学院，成为国务院侨办支持周边国家的少数几个重点单位之一。

海外教育学院主管全校各系的外国留学生，以及所有通过函授方式或在校接受汉语培训的学生。同时还主持每年的汉语水平考试。学院开设有一系列授予学士和硕士学位的授权点，包括汉语及中国文化、商务汉语，以及与人文学院的中文系联合授予文艺专业博士学位。学院还免费为学生开设其他文化课程，诸如中国民间舞蹈和武术等。

OEC's Cai Qingjie Bldg.

海外教育学院提供三种住宿方式。高踞山顶的蔡清洁楼距离教室和海边都只有三分钟的路程，提供宾馆式的住宿条件和服务。每间房都有电话、空调、有线电视以及高速网络（如果使用电话需要另外缴费）。南光5号楼的费用是蔡清洁楼的一半。第三种方式则是选择在校外居住。

厦门大学留学预科学院

厦门大学留学预科学院的宗旨是为中国学生出国留学深造做好准备工作。学院由国家留学基金管理委员会与厦门大学合作设立。学院注重提高教育质量，促进国际文化和学术交流。教职员工都是外籍教师和具有海外留学背景的中国教师。开设的双语教学课程不仅仅达到国际标准，根据学生具体情况而设置的教学计划也满足了个别学生的具体需求，甚至包括帮助学生选择海外的学校或申请签证。

学院的承诺！ 通过入学考试的学生可以进入与学院合作的、英国、爱尔兰、法国、加拿大或美国的大学。如果不能出国，学生可以在与之合作的中国大学里继续攻读学士或硕士学位。

不论怎样，在学院期间的生活可是现代化得很。学院现设在美丽的漳州校区，寝室里都配备电脑、电话、空调、洗衣机等。

China Studies Program

"The Chinese will tell you that the future does not escape the past. Risk your present reality. Come explore China's past and help shape her future." CSP website

Chinese are learning about the world but the world still has a lot to learn about China, so I'm forever urging foreigners to visit China to teach, study, do business, or even just tour. For years, I envisioned an XMU short-term crash program to "orient" foreign students in everything from Chinese history and culture to politics, language, and canine cuisine. So imagine my surprise when in March, 2000, OEC phoned to say "China Studies Program" (CSP) was considering XMU as a base.

I met with Dr. Richard Gathro, Executive Vice President for the Council for Christian Colleges and Universities (CCCU), and Yili Lundelius, wife of CSP's Director, Dr. Jay Lundelius. Over dinner I painted a portrait (unbiased, of course) of life in idyllic Xiamen. They must have liked what they saw and heard because CSP began classes at XMU that Fall and for six years now CSP has been XMU's primary source of American students. Dr. Lundelius said he appreciates XMU's professional management and support, but he's even now signing a new contract with XMU, and he noted that many Chinese universities have fine campuses and programs. In other words, there's competition out there. So let's hope OEC keeps the quality up, because it would be a loss for both XMU and CSP if they relocated.

25% Return While CSP students all must apply through CCCU, not all come from Christian campuses. Students have hailed from Univ. of Virginia, James Madison, Cornell, etc. But more interesting than where students are *from* is where they *go* after CSP. Fully 25% return to China to study at the OEC, to teach, to work in community development projects, or to do business. One student returned to work for Coca-cola in Shanghai and then started his own business. About 10% of CSP students serve in the Peace Corp, from Mongolia, to Morocco, Uganda, Egypt, etc.

Dr. Jay said, "CSP helps students become much more aware of international issues, especially in China. It's good for American students to get to know China and for Chinese to get to know Americans. Most American students are apprehensive when they come because they don't know much about China, but they come, they make friends, and when they leave they are gung ho about China—and many come back."

第 10 章 厦门大学——一所国际性的大学

"美华"项目(CSP)

"中国人会告诉你过去其实与今天一脉相承。来中国吧,来探索她伟大的过去,一起创造她美好的未来。"——CSP 网站

中国人在不断地了解世界,而世界还需要更好地了解中国。因此,我一直试图让更多的外国人来中国,要么教学、读书、做生意,要么哪怕就来看一看。这么多年来,我一直希望厦门大学能够给外国学生提供一种短期培训教程,让他们在短时间内对中国从历史、文化、政治、语言到可口的中国菜都有一个大致的了解。所以,2000年,当海外教育学院打电话说"美华(CSP)"正考虑来厦大时,我别提多高兴了。

于是,我与"美国基督教大学联盟"副主席 Richard Gathro 博士、CSP 负责人 Jay Lundelius 博士的夫人 Yili Lundelius 女士见了面。晚饭时,我简要介绍了生活在厦门这个田园般美丽城市的情况(当然,是十分"客观"的——我都是拣好听的说)。他们当时一定是被我的介绍迷住了,因为当年秋天,CPS 就"落户"厦大了,在随后的 6 年里,这个项目成了厦大美国学生的主要来源。Lundelius 教授说,他非常欣赏厦大专业化的管理,并感激其对项目的大力支持,还正在与厦大签订新的项目合同。但他也意识到,中国拥有众多优秀的学校和项目,因此竞争依然激烈。让我们共同期望厦大海外教育学院能够继续不断改进和完善自己,不要让这个项目移师别处,那样的话,对厦大、对 CSP 都将是个巨大的损失。

25%的人回到中国 所有想加入此项目的学生都必须向"美国基督教大学联盟"提出申请,但并不一定必须来自基督教大学。学生来自很多不同大学,有弗吉尼亚大学、詹姆斯麦迪逊大学、康奈尔大学等等,但更有意思的是他们完成学习后的去向——足足有 25%的学生再次回到中国来,或读书、或教书、或做生意、或帮助社区的发展。有一个学生回到中国后,在上海的可口可乐公司工作并随后开创了自己的公司。大约 10%的 CSP 学生加入了在蒙古、摩洛哥、乌干达和埃及等地的和平团。

Jay 博士说:"这个项目帮助外国学生了解世界,特别是中国。让美国学生了解中国,也让中国人更好地了解美国,确实是件非常有意义的事。大多数美国学生刚来的时候都有点担心,因为他们对中国了解太少,但来到这里后,交了无数的中国朋友,对中国产生了热情——甚至最后回到中国来。"

6% Joint Venture CSP has not only acted as matchmaker for Chinese and American cultures but also been a matchmaker for at least three couples who married each other after completing the programs! A Romanian student from Iowa's Dordt College joined CSP and married a Greenville College student he met in Xiamen. Another couple met in Xi'an, married, and are in the Peace Corp in Romania. The article at this chapter's end is by Andy and Annie, who not only married after meeting at XMU but returned to work here. The way I figure it, about 6% of CSP students end up marrying each other, so if you want a spouse, sign up!

On Nov. 10, 2005, the U.S. Senate passed resolution 308 making 2006 the "Year of Study Abroad" to promote global education, globally literate citizenry, global peace, and global trade. Let's hope the CSP stays at XMU so we can get our share of those American students—and so 6% of those may have hope of getting married! Here's a tale of two CSP students who did tie the knot....

How Andy met Annie at Xiada
by Andy and Annie Platt

Andy 'n Annie *before* Marriage (Fall, 2002)

I guess that technically Annie and I first met in Los Angeles Airport, but we only muttered a muffled "Hi" to each other, so for all practical purposes we actually met here in Xiamen as students in the CCCU's China Studies Program, so that is what we tell most people.

And it would be a really cool story to tell you that it was love at first sight and that Xiamen served as a very exotic backdrop for a budding romance, destined to entwine the hearts of these two young students in eternal amour, but the truth is hardly so clean cut as that, though actually far more interesting.

I could start with our first genuine words to each other being my insulting her, but I will spare you the gory details. We began as model students, gleaning as much as we could comprehend from the wealth of information our professors gave us daily about this wondrous ancient nation so far from home. Much that we learned here was evidenced or came in handy later, like the hospitality of our friends in Xi'an and Xiamen, or the issues of face that so affected our later work environment.

第10章 厦门大学——一所国际性的大学

6%的学生喜结良缘

CSP 不仅仅使中美文化"联姻",还充当了至少三对学生的"月下老儿",他们相识在 CSP,后来就双双走到一起了!一个来自 Iowa's Dordt 学院的罗马尼亚学生在 CSP 学习期间,认识了一个来自 Greenvile 学院的学生,两人后来就结了婚;另一对学生相识于西安,结婚后一起去了罗马尼亚的和平团。下面是由 Andy 和 Annie 写的一篇文章,他们在厦大相识、在美国结婚,又一起回到厦大来工作。我算了一下,大约有 6%的 CSP 学生最后走到一起。所以,如果你正处在为自己"另一半"的寻寻觅觅中,赶紧报名加入我们这个项目吧!

2005 年 11 月 10 日,美国参议院通过了 308 号议案,确立 2006 年为"海外学习年",以此来让国人了解世界,促进世界教育、世界和平和世界贸易。让我们共同期望 CSP 继续在厦大开展,这样我们才能有机会吸引更多的美国学生——也才能有其中 6% 的喜结良缘!

下面就是这对被"中国结"系在了一起的 CSP 学生的浪漫故事:

两个美国学生的厦大情缘

Andy Platt 和 Annie Platt

严格点儿说,我和 Annie 初次见面其实是在洛杉矶机场,但那时只是含糊地说了个"嗨"。作为"美华(CSP)"的学生,我们的相识实际上是在厦门。后来对朋友们我们也是这样讲的。

说起来本应是个传奇的爱情故事:两个年轻的学生在美丽的厦大校园相遇,一见钟情,逐渐萌芽的爱让彼此心意相通,越走越近。但事实却不是那样简单。当然,要有趣得多。

我本可以从我们第一次向对方吐露"真言"开始讲起——那一次是我对她出言不恭,但我还是不赘述那些"血腥"的细节了吧。我俩可都是模范学生,天天都在埋头苦

Annie and Andy Today

读,如饥似渴地消化教授们所传授的关于中国——这个离家如此遥远的神秘国度的一切。我们那时候所学到的关于中国的知识日后都得到了证实,并且是非常实用的。比如西安和厦门朋友的热情好客,以及对我们后来的工作环境产生影响的所谓的"面子问题"等。

The class load was so heavy that Annie and I had little to do with each other early on in the semester, but towards the end, when the load had lightened somewhat, she and I and another guy who remains my best friend to this day were spending a lot of quality conversational time together, mostly along the Bai Cheng beach area, or in the stairwells of Nanguang #5 where we lived.

Then I did the unforgivable. Pressed with the fact that the end of the semester was looming and in a month or so we would genially go our separate ways, I decided that this incredibly good friendship warranted some degree of preservation and I sought this in the only binding way I could think of, a relationship. Thanksgiving day, 2002, after we had finished our lovely dinner of duck and cranberry sauce, I walked her back to campus in the midst of a downpour, while pouring my heart out to her. Her reaction was less than what I hoped for. To make it short (very short, because we discussed this for many hours over the course of at least two days), she refused me.

All's well that ends well, though. We left Xiamen a few weeks later, having mended what we could, and fortune would have it that our universities were within a few hours drive of each other. That spring I bought a cell phone and logged over 10,000 miles (and made a long drive to her home in Spokane, WA). By graduation we were a couple. By Christmas we were engaged, and we married on Feb. 29, 2004 (I tried to find the most unique date possible).

Because of our previous experiences at XMU, we knew China could be a wonderful place to work, so we moved to Xi'an to teach English, and when offered a position teaching history with our alma mater, so to speak (the CCCU and Xia Da), we couldn't refuse. So here we are, back in Xiamen, where we frequently walk past the point where I was rejected, and I think in irony of whose hand now bears my ring.

Note: for more insights on how XMU students get girls, read the chapter "Changting Tales!"

第10章　厦门大学——一所国际性的大学

开始的时候，学习任务比较重，安妮和我没什么来往。到了学期的后半段，课业轻松一点儿了，安妮、我和另一个至今仍是我最好的朋友的男生，在一起聊天的机会多了起来。我们经常在白城的沙滩，或是在当时居住的南光5号楼的楼道里开怀畅谈。

接下来我做了一件不可原谅的事：想到再过一个多月学期就要结束、我们就要各奔东西了，这段美妙的友谊值得珍藏，而我却决定以另一种方式——我对Annie的爱恋将变其为永恒。2002年的感恩节那天，我们在一起享用了美味的烤鸭和小红莓酱大餐，尔后，我在倾盆大雨中的校园，向她倾吐了自己的心。她的反应不像我所希望的那样……简单点儿说（这里说得是够简单的，因为事实上我们就这件事在接下去的两天里讨论了好几小时），她拒绝了我。

但故事的结局总算令人欣慰。几星期后我们离开了厦门，而此时也已经为打破两人之间的僵局尽了力。命运注定我们彼此的学校距离只有几个小时的车程。那年春天我买了手机，远隔千山万里打电话给她（我还长途驱车到她的家乡华盛顿州的斯彼坎市去看她）。毕业时，我们已经是一对情人，圣诞节时，我们已经订了婚，2004年2月29日，我们举行了婚礼。（选择这个日子，是因为我想让我们的结婚之日尽量地与众不同。）

由于之前在厦大的经历，我们知道，中国将是工作和生活的天堂，于是我们来到西安，教授英语。之后接到母校的邀请(可以这么说，美国基督教大学联盟和厦大都是我们的母校)请我们回去教授历史课程，我们怎能不欣然从命呢？直到现在，我们还经常经过当初她将我拒绝的那个地方，每每此时，我都会狡黠地想，当年那个倔强女生的手上现在正戴着我的戒指呢！

补充：想要更多地了解厦大学生是如何追女生的，请看第四章《长汀轶事》

Chapter 11

"It's News To Me" XMU Media

"Hot News, Hot Reporters" XMU News Center

Since its founding in 1997, XMU News Center has captured our university's life and growth from interviewing, photographing and writing to editing and broadcasting. Even as I prepared to interview Ms. Lou Hongying, Director of the News Center, she claimed proudly, "This is a real treasure land because students who have worked here are terrific!"

The following is what a student reporter remembered about one of his experiences: "In March, 2003, a few other student reporters at our news center and I went to cover The First Xiamen International Marathon. And I think we did great that day. We were so thrilled by the spectacular scene that kept us busy that day. When we were done and ready to leave, my friend caught sight of the Honorary President of the Chinese Olympics Committee, Mr. He Zhenliang, standing not far away from us. What an opportunity! We raced toward him without thinking. We navigated our way through swarms of reporters from various media and eventually reached him and interviewed him! We even asked him to share what he felt about our University!" There was a remarkable number of reporters from all over the world but it was our student reporters who got the scoop. Well done! Our student reporters seized the spotlight of the Marathon media coverage and even made their way on to Fujian TV!

第11章

厦大主要媒体

校新闻中心——新闻人才的摇篮

厦门大学新闻中心成立于1997年。每周一期的新闻,从采访、拍摄、撰稿、到后期制作,它用"影像"记录着厦大的今天。在我采访新闻中心主任楼红英老师的时候,她自豪地说:"这可是块宝地哦,从这里锻炼出来的学生记者可都是很棒的!"

这里是一位学生记者对一次外出采访的回忆:"2003年3月,我和另外几位学生记者去报道厦门第一届国际马拉松。那天,我们几个表现得别提有多出色了,壮观的场面让我们激动不已也忙个不停。报道结束,正当我们快要离开的时候,一位同学眼尖,突然看见当时任中国奥委会名誉主席的何振梁先生就在不远处,多好的机会啊!我们没有多想就追了过去,穿过那些层层簇拥的媒体记者,最终采访到了何先生,而且还请他谈了对我们厦门大学的深刻感受呢!"当时在场那么多来自世界各地的专业记者,偏偏我们的学生记者拿到了"独家新闻",干得好!记得那回我们这些惹眼的学生记者还被当成了马拉松比赛中的一大亮点在福建电视台上秀了一把。

Lou Hongying (center)

Their work experience in the news center helps develop students who initially know very little about media work into sophisticated, brave, talented and hard-working journalists. Some of them have gone on to work for important programs on CCTV, such as "Legal Report," "Topics in Focus," etc. Some have become journalism majors of Tsinghua University, and even those whose major had nothing to do with journalism shifted their career to the media… The news center focuses its camera on university events, but stories about how it cultivates intellectuals via "camera work" are endless.

"Bitter Sweet Editing" XMU Newspaper

From the initial "New XMU" to the current "XMU Paper", XMU's paper has kept us informed for the entire 85 years.

I found the editor-in-chief, Mr. Lu Minghui, in the very back cubicle of the Paper office, head submerged beneath a pile of paperwork. When I told him I wanted to interview him about his work, he ducked his head beneath those piles again—an editor's instinct, I thought. But then I realized he  was just looking for a piece of paper he fished out of another pile. This is what he showed me—a paper undergoing the editing process (see photo). Lu said a paper being edited until it was completely unrecognizable was not uncommon. But this one was a classic from a day that he and Ms. Zheng were editing it with an axe until they wanted to kill themselves. It was so painful that he wrote a poem saying "Beauty with an axe." Lu kept this piece because it was so representative of his work. When we read the final product, we would never imagine the sweat and even "pain" of editing—and the unique ways that editors have fun even during this drudgery.

第11章　厦大主要媒体

就是这些学生记者,从最初对媒体知识了解甚少,到在新闻中心培养下锻炼成为细心、有勇气、聪明能干的优秀新闻人才。后来他们有人去了央视的《今日说法》、《焦点访谈》等重档栏目,有人考上了清华大学新闻专业的研究生,还有的非新闻专业学生干脆彻底地把职业取向转移到了新闻媒体上……新闻中心把她的镜头对准记录学校重要事件和活动,但到底有多少镜头外的故事恐怕在这里是写也写不完的啦!

厦大校报——苦乐相伴编编编

从最初的名字《新厦大》到如今的《厦门大学报》,校报陪伴厦大整整走过了风风雨雨85年。

在校报办公室的最后一个小格子里,我总算找到了正在埋头工作的主编卢明辉老师。也许是一个新闻编辑多年来形成的职业习惯,他听说我采访的来意后,连身子都没有转过来,就又把头埋回到一大叠的稿子和报纸中去了。随后就翻出一堆的报纸给我看——哈,原来他是去找实物啦!这就是他紧接着展示给我的杰作——一张被划拉得面目全非的某期校报某版大样(见图)。卢主编说,像这样的情况很多,那天他和版面编辑郑莉"挥斧"砍稿子砍得直要吐血,极少写诗的他不禁在上面题诗曰:"美女竞挥斧……"这期这个版很有代表性,所以卢主编特意留了下来。是啊,大家每周拿到校报读得津津有味也好,扫一眼也罢,又有几人知道编辑们改稿子的辛苦甚至"痛苦",还有他们的"苦中作乐"呢?

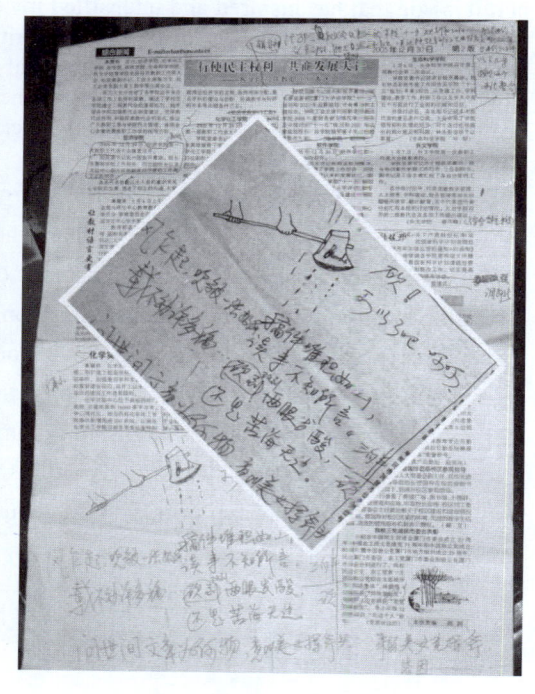

One way editors make boring work fun is to add "voiceovers." Lu pointed to a front-page photo of two leaders talking while leaving a conference. He said the one on the left was saying, "Hey man, what are we gonna have for lunch today?' and the other one responded, "Well... I think it's gonna be "chicken feet burgers" and "rice cream."

Though lighthearted, they are very careful with their work, and some of their articles become very influential, such as "Broad and Selfless," which is about Huang Wenying of XMU's Department of Foreign Language and Culture. Written by Chen Fulang, former editor-in-chief of XMU Press, it was reprinted on the entire front page of "Guangming Daily". XMU Paper has also helped cultivate and inspire generations. Pro. Zheng Qiwu, who has published many works, recalls that when he was young the XMU Paper asked him to write something; it was his first letter of that kind. He excitedly wrote, "The university paper, it is you that has inspired and intensified my desire to write!"

Lu also told me that besides observing, writing, editing, typesetting, proofreading, printing and publishing, they also had numerous meetings to discuss work plans, paid author's remuneration, etc. The paper is in charge of the News Press Department too, which entails annual checkups, meetings, reviews..."well, lots of things!"

"Painful but Joyful" XMU Broadcasting Station (XMBS)

XMUBS has two studios, one on Zhangzhou campus on the first floor of Building #5, and the other on the main campus on the third floor of Jiannan auditorium. They both cover news, music, fashion, sports etc, and have new programs each and every day. One would love working there. I certainly did during my two years' stay at Zhangzhou campus where I joined the Chinese broadcasting team and later started an English program. There have been far more reasons than I could ever possibly write down in such a short piece. But the most inspiring is how much time, energy and talents my colleagues devote to their work.

第11章 厦大主要媒体

不过，编辑们会在工作枯燥的时候偷偷地给自己找些乐趣的。例如，给新闻照片加画外音！卢主编翻出一张校报，某版刊登了一幅照片：照片上是两位领导正边走边交谈，他指着照片悄悄问我："你能从照片中看出他们在说什么吗？"我摇摇头。"我们校报的编辑们就能！这就是他们加的画外音：左边那个正在说'老弟，咱们今儿中午吃什么啊？'，右边这位答'这个嘛…估计是清蒸八宝猪，要不就是红烧狮子头'……"

搞笑归搞笑，编辑们一本正经工作的时候可了不得啊。发表在校报上的很多文章影响很大，比如厦大出版社总编辑、作家陈福郎在校报当编辑时采写的介绍厦大外文系黄文鹰教授事迹的《心底无私天地宽》一文就被《光明日报》头版以整版篇幅全文刊登！校报培养和激励了一代又一代人，已经有众多著作出版和发表的作家郑启五老师回忆起大学时收到校报编辑发来的自己的人生第一张约稿函，激动地写到："啊，校报，是你激发和强化了我一生的写作欲求！"

卢主编告诉我，校报除了"采、写、编、排、校、印、发"这诸多环节的工作，还有开不完的会来讨论工作拟定计划，还有编制稿费表、发稿费，新闻出版部门还管着校报呢，一会儿通知要年检，一会儿要开会，哈哈，好多事，烦着呢……

校广播电台——"痛，并快乐着"

厦大的广播电台在两个校区分别有工作室，一个设在漳州校区嘉三的一楼，另一个设在本部建南大会堂的三楼。两边都制作新闻、音乐、时尚、体育等节目，每天都是新的。你肯定会爱上那儿的工作的！在漳州校区的那两年，我先加入了电台的中文广播组，后来又去开设了一个英语节目。爱上电台有很多的原因，多得举不完。而那里的同学们所付出的时间、精力和显示出的才智给我带来的感动和启发应该是其中最主要的一点。

I remember vividly the first time I "made my voice heard". Back then we produced our programs on the main campus under the guidance of senior broadcasters. They were so helpful and patient that the first time I broadcasted they almost showed me how to read every single character! And so with their help we recorded that program again and again until 2:00am and they let me stay in one of their dorms because it was too late to go back to Zhangzhou. The next morning I got up at 6:00 and went back to the studio to check on them. I was so surprised to find that our editors were still editing the program we worked on that night. They never even left the room! And that very morning at 8:30, they were going to take their final exams!

Slowly I found out that my colleagues spent many a night in the same way. As I recall those many marathon nights when my colleagues worked till dawn just to make sure that when people crossed campus they could catch the latest news, enjoy a good piece of music or hear a moving story, I'm not surprised at all when Mr. Ma Jinlong the director of XMB, told me that this year more than 400 students of Zhangzhou campus alone applied to join XMBS. Of course, it's not possible for all of them to "make their voice heard" through the speakers, but like everyone else who walks about our campus, they will certainly appreciate the diverse color and infinite enjoyment that XMBS brings to them.

第11章 厦大主要媒体

第一次录制节目的情形依然历历在目。那时候，我们录节目要到本部去，在学长们的指导下进行。本部的"老播"都非常地敬业与耐心，几乎到了手把手教我每一个汉字发音的地步。由他们作指导，我们一次又一次地重录，一直到夜里两点。而由于太迟回不去漳州了，他们让我就住在一位学姐的宿舍了。第二天早上，我6点钟起了床，来工作室看看情况如何。可没有想到的是，编辑们居然还呆在那里为昨天晚上录的节目作后期！原来他们根本一整夜都没有离开那个房间啊！而那天早上的八点半，就是他们的期末考试……

渐渐地我发现，那样的晚上只是无数中的一个而已。想起电台的同学们通宵达旦地工作，就是希望人们行走于校园的时候，能听到最新的新闻、最美的音乐、最感人的故事。基于这一点，当电台负责人马进龙老师告诉我，今年光漳州校区电台纳新就有超过400人报名的时候，我一点儿都不感到惊讶。当然，要想这400多人都实现自己的播音梦不太可能，但是可以肯定的是，他们，就像所有其他行走于校园中的人们一样，无疑地会被厦大电台所包含的多彩的节目、所传递的无限的欢愉所深深感染……

Robin Interviewing a Foreign Teacher

Chapter 12

XMU Activities & Sports

New Student Welcome
About mid September a flock of new students descends on XMU with parents and sometimes even the whole family. They commandeer every restaurant and hotel near campus. And XMU has one grand practice seen on no other Chinese campus. All freshman and sophomores start out at Zhangzhou campus across the bay, so ferries and buses shuttle students, families, and luggage for two days from morning till midnight.

Uniformed student volunteers stand ready to help newcomers at not only both campuses but also at the dock, the train station, the airport and the long-distance bus station. I would say that during these two days Xiamen's entire public transportation system is commandeered by XMU students.

Newcomers are picked up at the airport, train station or bus station, escorted to the main campus, helped to register, and then sent on another bus along our beautiful island ringroad to a ferry for a fascinating sea crossing to the beautiful Zhangzhou campus. What a trip. It's new, exciting, and students are helped every step of the way!

Once on Zhangzhou campus, students are given yet another warm welcome, and an *orient*ation to their new university life. Banners and little colored flags everywhere on each campus and along the road read, "Welcome to XMU, your new home!"

You probably know they moved quite a large population to build the Three Gorges? Well, we've got a small population movement right here.

第12章 欢迎来到厦门大学！

DISCOVER Xiamen University

第*12*章
欢迎来到厦门大学！

两次"迎新"

大约每年的九月中旬，是新生报到的日子。每到这时候，新生和随其而来的家人（有时候是整个家族）几乎"占领"了学校附近所有的饭店、宾馆。而且，厦门大学有一个在其他大学罕见的奇观：跨海迎新！由于全部大一、大二学生生活在彼岸的漳州校区，新生报到的那两天，满载着学生、家人以及行李的船只、汽车，不断往返于两地之间，从一大清早一直到半夜，景象蔚为壮观。

Sino-U.S. Basketball Game

穿着统一服装，戴着工作证的志愿者们，不仅遍布两个校区，还坚守在码头、火车站、机场以及长途汽车客运站，随时准备迎接到来的新生。可以毫不夸张地说，那两天，厦门的整个公共交通系统是厦大学生的天下。

从机场、火车站、汽车站接到新生后，志愿者们会把他们引领到本部，然后帮助其注册，再将他们送上"迎新专列"，"专列"汽车沿环岛路驶向轮渡，学生再从轮渡乘船到美丽的漳州校区。这跨海之旅让人如痴如醉，奇特而迷人，一切都是崭新的，整个过程中，处处有人关心、随时受人帮助。

踏上了漳州校区，还有一个热烈的欢迎仪式等着他们呢！横幅、彩旗遍布校园的每个角落，一路上，处处可见的标语上写着"欢迎来到厦门大学——你们的新家"！

你大概知道为了建三峡工程需要大规模移民吧？那么，我们这里可是有个小型的"移民工程"啊！完成了在漳州校区两年的学业后，升入大三的学生要搬回本部，正如那些离开家园的三峡移民一样，学生们离开漳州校区时的心情也是复杂的：带着对两年"故土"的眷恋，怀揣满心的期待和兴奋，迫不及待地盼望在一个全新的环境里开始别样的生活。就我所知，中国甚至全世界还没有哪个大学的学生有这样的经历——"跨海搬家"，新的起点！

After their second year on Zhangzhou Campus the entire Junior class migrates to Xiamen Island's main campus. And like the folks moving at Three Gorges, they leave with pleasant memories of their home, and at the same time are eager for a fresh new start in a completely new environment, with minds filled with anticipation and hearts full of excitement. As far as I know, students in no other university in China have such an experience—a brand new start across the sea!

"Talent Scout"— Ms. Xu Shanna
Youth League Committee Secretary

The young lady in the photo is Roberta, an Italian student at XMU Overseas Education College. Her dancing talent was discovered by our "talent scout", Ms. Xu Shanna, secretary of the Youth League Committee.

During the 2005 newcomers' reception, as the Ziqin Bldg. area was crowded with busy teachers and students, an exotically beautiful young lady walked in and looked around. She caught a student's attention, who asked her if she needed help. She was looking for the "art association," so he led her to Secretary Xu's office. Although Xu had her hands full at the moment, her lengthy experience in student activities, and intuition, led her to suspect this girl might be a rarely gifted performer .So she put her work aside and asked Roberta to perform a short dance right there in the office.   Later it turned out that Roberta's dance was ''the most popular performance" at the "graduates reception" gala, where she was called "the exotic beauty who descended to earth from heaven!" And not long after that her dance was selected to represent overseas students at the "Reception Gala for Teaching Appraisal", where she wowed the evaluating experts with the versatility of XMU's overseas students.

第12章 欢迎来到厦门大学!

"星探"书记徐姗娜

照片上的女孩叫做董罗蓓,来自意大利,现在在厦大海外教育学院就读。说到她是如何能够登台演出的,我们不得不提到"相马"的"伯乐"——校团委书记徐姗娜。

2005年迎新期间,自钦楼里里外外都是老师学生们忙碌的身影。这时候,一个美丽的外国姑娘走了进来,她东瞧瞧西看看,学生会的一位学生见状便过去询问是否需要帮忙。她回答说她想找"艺术团"。于是这位同学把她带到徐书记办公室。正在忙碌的徐书记见到这个气质极佳的女孩子后,多年从事学生文艺工作的经验马上告诉她,这很有可能是一个不可多得的艺术人才!于是她停下手里的工作,请罗蓓姑娘就在现场表演一小段舞蹈……后来罗蓓的舞蹈成了"研究生迎新晚会"上最受欢迎的节目,被称为"异国的美女从天而降";紧接着又作为迎接教育部本科教学评估晚会上留学生的代表节目,向评估专家组展示了厦大留学生的风采!

Every time Secretary Xu passes students on campus, her intuitive radar and sharp insights help her not to miss any potential talent, and sometimes she even walks right up and questions them straightforwardly...Xu has directed numerous activities for the arts, including XMU's annual anniversary gala for the past ten years. Every time before a gala is put on, she arranges dinner for workers and performers, but it often happens that only after midnight does she remember that she herself has not eaten. Xu gives students confidence and consideration, and her "scouting" skills have given more students opportunities to develop well rounded talents, and thanks to her outstanding "director" work the university has been able to have great achievements in student activities.

Sports at XMU
By Hong Mujin

When you think of sports, people usually think of traditional events like track, jumping, basketball, soccer, etc., and no doubt you'll come across these while strolling about our beautiful campus. But nonetheless, we also have some fresh and new sports catching on.

Mr. Hong Mujin

Golf Golf is an exotic sport for us. G=green, for lawns; O=oxygen, for fresh air; L=light, for sunshine; F=friendships we have made through the sport. Golf is a noble, even mystic, sport. Many businessmen have taken to it for entertainment, exercise—and getting business done. Many college students are itching to try it too, but don't often have a chance—so XMU to the rescue!

第12章 欢迎来到厦门大学!
DISCOVER Xiamen University

徐书记每次在校园里行走,与学生擦肩而过时,直觉和敏锐的洞察力都会告诉她不要错过眼前的贤才,她有时甚至直接走过去将学生拦住询问一番……徐书记策划组织了无数文艺活动,仅校庆晚会就已经制作指导十几台了。每次晚会前,她会为演出和工作的学生安排好晚餐,可是自己忙到深夜才想起又忘了吃饭……她对学生给予信心和关怀,也正是有了一个杰出和"慧眼识英才"的"星探"兼"总导演",才有了校园文化"精品"的打造,也才有了更多学生锻炼和展示自己的平台!

厦大的趣味运动
洪木进

人们一提起运动,自然就会想到跑步、跳远、篮球、足球等一些传统的项目。当然,置身于美丽的厦门大学,你随处可以见到这些运动项目。而一些新鲜、有趣的运动也正在吸引着你的眼球。

高尔夫

高尔夫,是一个舶来品,其英文名称 Golf。Golf 这个单词中,G 代表 Green,意即绿色的草地;O 代表 Oxygen,即新鲜的空气;L 代表 Light,明媚阳光之意;F 代表 Friendship,即通过运动建立友谊。在中国,高尔夫球是一项贵族运动,它的贵族色彩同时为它增添了神秘的色彩。许多商务人士把它作为消遣,而商务活动也在这过程中完成了,同时,通过该运动可以健身强体。很多大学生对它有着浓厚的兴趣,跃跃欲试,但又没有机会接触它。厦大便对他们伸出了援助之手。

To satisfy students' curiosity, broaden their social contacts, and improve their communication skills, XMU's physical education program has set up a course in golf (a "golf course"?). Though it is an elective, many students choose it and pursue it with vigor.

"I prefer the recreational atmosphere and quiet life style that golf links can provide," said international trade student Ted Anderson when he explained why he chose the course.

"I chose it because it is a noble and mysterious sport," said a Korean exchange student.

"It is very novel and it will help me make social contacts, so I chose it," said a philosophy major.

Whatever their goals, they all take golf seriously and make great efforts to master it. Breathing fresh air, bathing in sunshine, they all feel relaxed and refreshed after a round of golf. In a word, golf has given much pleasure to our campus.

Dragon Dancing Dragon dances used to be common during Chinese festivals, but as China modernizes this tradition seems to be fading away. But once again, XMU to the rescue! To save this important part of our heritage, XMU's Physical Education program now includes Dragon Dancing.

"It is fun," one student told me, "but it also gives us a taste of our motherland's traditional culture. We attend each class with a sense of mission, and enjoy the program."

第12章 欢迎来到厦门大学!

为了满足同学们的好奇心,让在校的学生早点接触社会,提高交际能力同时锻炼身体,厦大校长朱崇实极力推崇这项运动。在学校的支持下,高尔夫球运动进入了体育课程。

这是一门选修课,但同学们的积极性不亚于专业课。

"本人比较喜欢休闲安静的环境,而高尔夫球场就给人这种安静的心情,给人这个氛围。"03级国际经济专业的田林庆幸自己选上了这门课。

一位韩国交流生如实说:它是一项贵族运动,带有神秘色彩,所以我选择它。

"高尔夫球是非常新颖的活动,而且将来在社交场合会很有用,而且我喜欢新奇的运动,所以我选择高尔夫。"一个哲学系的同学这样认为。

尽管同学们目的不尽一样,但他们都努力地学习着。他们在绿色草地上用心地学着挥杆,呼吸着新鲜的空气,享受着明媚的阳光,享受着运动的乐趣,其乐融融。

厦大把贵族运动"平民化",让学生感受着运动的快感。

舞龙舞狮

这是一个中国传统的活动,早期的中国人每逢喜事,都要举办此活动。但随着中国的现代化进程,这个传统活动也正在被慢慢地淡忘了。

为了弘扬传统文化,丰富同学们的业余生活,厦大开设了"舞龙舞狮"这个体育课程。

"我们在感受中国传统运动的同时也享受着运动的乐趣。我们带着一种使命感去上好每一节课。我们运动着,我们快乐着。"一个同学告诉我。

Wilderness Survival Can't cope with the challenges of our environment? No problem! XMU's "Wilderness Survival" teaches how to face up to difficulties you encounter in hiking—or in life!.

To enrich course contents, XMU organized a training course on the small island of Anjing, were students trained in directional cross-country hiking and rowing. They also learned about tents, desalinization of water, fishing, archery, making fires and cooking. Every group did a good job expressing their own creativity and team spirit, overcoming the restrictions of their limited tools, and proving their will power.

They also organized am evening bonfire, did some team games, and let the students share their own insights and revelations. Students said they had learned a lot and changed their own attitudes about themselves. They discovered new-found potential and a new space within their soul. In a word, they had learned more than just what was covered in class.

Directional Cross-country The new sport of directional cross-country racing has become fashionable all over the world, and it is also flourishing right here at XMU, which has always been a trend setter in China. XMU organized the first cliff scramble in Fujian Province, which provided a combination of both racing and training for teachers and students alike. They enjoyed themselves while at the same time challenging their limitations.

野外生存

如果你身处恶劣的环境,如何面对呢?厦大在全国高校中率先开设了"野外生存"课,教同学们如何面对野外环境。

为了丰富课程教学内容,提高学生的素质,老师还组织了同学们进行一次海岛野外训练。

他们来到距厦门 100 公里的一个小岛——安井岛。在那里,他们进行了环岛定向越野、扎皮筏艇救生、简易帐篷建造、海水淡化、捕鱼钓鱼、接绳过涧、制作弓箭、无锅生火做饭等训练科目。各组队员充分地发挥了创造力和团队协作精神,克服了工具的限制和意志的考验,都出色地完成了各项训练科目。

晚上,教师们还组织了篝火晚会,做了有教育意义的团队游戏,让同学们在乐趣中受到启示,得到锻炼。

同学们纷纷表示,经过了野外生存的学习和实践,自己的素质得到了很大的提高,不再固执己见,还发现了自己心灵新的空间和自己从未意识到的潜力,得到了从书本上学不到的东西。他们运动并快乐着!

定向越野

定向越野运动作为一项集合了体能和智慧的新兴运动早已风靡全球,在我国也充满着蓬勃的生机,而一向走在时代前沿的厦门大学已经举办了两次越野大赛。

为了让这项活动顺利地进行,厦大还建了福建省第一个攀缘壁,为广大师生提供了一个集比赛和训练为一体的场所。

同学们通过该运动,挑战着自己,挑战着极限,七享受着运动的乐趣!

Mountain Climbing   Climbing is an outdoor activity that requires strong will and a team spirit. "Constantly strive to become stronger" is the motto of each XMU student, and unwilling to be left behind, XMU students established Fujian's first Climbing Association—the XMU Climbing Association.

In 2002, they climbed the eternally snow clad 6,206m Qizi Peak. From the south the mountain seems rounded, while from the north the mountain seems almost a vertical drop-off. In 2003, they climbed the 6,100m Tangla'angqu mountain, and in 2004 climbed it again.

On August 15th, 2005, the team successfully ascended Tibet's Sangdankangsang Peak.

They are a courageous group, full of courage, energy, and charm. They enjoy the truth of nature and the truth of life—and they pass on their vitality to the entire campus.

Exercise and be happy! And may all of our charming Xiamen University take pleasure in sport!

登山运动

登山运动是一项户外运动。它要求登山者要具备很强的意志力和团队精神。

以"自强不息"为校训的厦大学生不甘为人后,他们组建福建省第一家登山协会:厦门大学登山协会。

2002年,厦大学生登上了启孜峰。这个山峰海拔6206米,终年积雪,从南面看上去整个山体浑圆,但北面却陡峭如刀劈一般。

2003年,他们再上新高,攀登唐拉昂曲峰,登至海拔6100米。

2004年,他们继续攀登唐拉昂曲峰。

2005年8月15日,他们成功登上位于西藏自治区境内海拔6590米的桑丹康桑峰顶。

他们不畏艰险,勇于攀登。他们在付出努力的同时也收获了喜悦和快感。

传统运动在校园里焕发着新活力,新鲜运动也在校园里散发着它的魅力。

我运动,我快乐!魅力厦大,快乐运动!

"Xiamen International Marathon" Fun and Funny!

XMU students have been a large part of the "Xiamen International Marathon", which has been held every March since 2003—and XMU students have had outstanding results! 184 XMU students finished the entire race within the given time in 2003. In 2004, 430 finished—accounting for 1/3 of the total number of qualifiers, and 386 finished in 2005. One student said, "Running a marathon is a lot of fun!" And here are a few tales to show shy.

The Physical Exam Marathon participants are required to take a physical exam before entering. One female student remembers waiting for the exam. A good many other people were also waiting in line, excited and thrilled—until a nurse came out and said they would be charged for the physical exam. "Within a minute," the girl said, "half of the people in line were gone!" A little while later, another nurse came out and announced that the examinees would have to take off all their clothes to be examined, "This time, within a second, the other half were gone!"

"Come on! Come on, Amoisonic!" Marathon participant are usually given a T-shirt as a souvenir and to wear during the race. A student told of his experience wearing a T-shirt with the words "Amoisonic"(the electronics company that sponsored the marathon that year) emblazoned on the back. After running a few miles he was exhausted and started to walk. The excited spectators lining both sides of the route shouted for him to keep running, but what what they shouted was, "Amoisonic, come on! Come on, Amoisonic!" They thought Amoisonic was his name! He had a good laugh and started running again.

Mr. Amoi?

第12章 欢迎来到厦门大学!

厦门国际马拉松——有趣又好玩儿

从 2003 年以来,在每年三月举办的厦门国际马拉松赛中,厦大学生总是其中一个很大的组成部分,并且有非常不错的表现。;2003 年在规定时间内跑完全程的有 184 人;2004 年 430 人,占那次比赛跑完全程总人数的三分之一;2005 年,有 386 人在规定时间内跑完全程。一位学生说,"跑马拉松真是乐趣无穷啊!"从以下的故事中你就知道为什么了。

体检 参加马拉松必须经过体检,一位女生说起那天等待体检的情形,搞笑得很:很多人在排队等着体检,显得很兴奋——直到一个护士出来说体检是要收费的。"一分钟内",她说,"一半人都跑掉了!"又过了一会儿,又有一个护士出来说体检的时候必须脱光衣服,"这回啊,不到半秒钟,另一半儿也跑光了!"

"厦新,加油!" 组委会通常会给参赛者每人发一件 T 恤衫,比赛时可以穿,同时也作为留念。一位学生讲起他和他的背后印着醒目"厦新"(赞助当年马拉松的公司之一)字样的 T 恤衫的经历。跑了几公里后,他已筋疲力尽,就停下来走一会儿,赛道两旁兴奋的观众们拼命给他加油助威,但是你知道他们喊的是什么吗?他们声嘶力竭地喊着"厦新,加油!加油,厦新!"原来他们把"厦新"当成他的名字了!这位同学真是哭笑不得,于是又迈开大步跑了起来……

1 of 99 Marathon Sculptures on Island Ring Road

Chapter 13

Taiwan Research Institute

News Flash! "The 4th Cross-Straits University Students' "South Fujian Culture Study" Summer Camp has opened at XMU. Sixty students from eight Taiwanese universities will study South Fujian culture for nine days through lectures, social customs investigations, folk opera attendance, and visits to places of historical interest."
Common Talk, Xiamen Daily, July 13, 2005

    A leaflet from a mainland propaganda balloon that landed on our Air Force base in Taiwan is what piqued my interest in Chinese history and culture, and started me on a decade-long journey that ended up here at XMU. Fortunately, cross-Straits exchanges are no longer limited to propaganda balloons, thanks in part to XMU's Taiwan Research Institute (TWRI). China's first academic institution specializing in Taiwan studies, TWRI was founded in 1980—just two years after I left Taiwan.

    For a quarter of a century TWRI's goal has been to "understand Taiwan historically, comprehensively and truthfully to improve cross-Strait academics and serve the reunification course of China". TWRI's 43 faculty members include 19 professors who research five key areas of Taiwan: Politics, Economy, History, Literature, and Cross-Straits Relations.

    Centre for References and Information TWRI offers excellent facilities for its researchers and masters and doctoral students. The Center for References and Information has a collection of 25,000 Taiwan published books, 13,000 bound volumes of Taiwan newspapers and journals, and a 300G-disk collection of "China Times," a Taiwan newspaper. TWRI has subscriptions to 230 different newspapers and magazines published in Taiwan, Hong Kong and overseas, and has a high-speed intranet, a database for research in Taiwan and an indexing system for full texts.

第 13 章　台湾研究所

第13章

台湾研究院

快讯！ 第四届海峡两岸大学生"闽南文化研习"夏令营活动在厦门大学拉开帷幕。来自台湾的8所大学的60名大学生将用9天的时间通过听讲座、调查社会习俗、观看民间戏曲和游览名胜古迹来学习闽南文化。

《厦门日报·双语周刊》2005 年 7 月 13 日

　　在台湾空军基地时，一个宣传气球上散落下来的传单，激起了我对中国历史和文化的兴趣。因为这种兴趣，我对其进行了 10 年之久的探求，我也因此来到了厦门大学。在这里，因为有厦门大学的台湾研究院（原台湾研究所），海峡两岸的交流不再局限于气球传单。厦门大学台湾研究院，是中国的第一个专门从事台湾研究的学术机构，成立于 1980 年，也就是我离开台湾后的第二年。

　　25 年来，台湾研究院的宗旨一直是"历史地、全面地、实事求是地认识台湾，促进海峡两岸学术交流，为祖国统一大业服务"。台湾研究院有 43 位工作人员，其中 19 位教授专门从事以下 5 个方面的研究：台湾的政治、经济、历史、文学和海峡两岸关系。

　　文献信息中心　台湾研究院为研究人员、硕士研究生和博士研究生提供良好的设备。该中心藏有 25000 册台版图书，13000 册台湾报刊资料合订本，其中台湾《中国时报》光盘数据库的数据量达 300G 以上。台湾研究院订了 230 种台湾、香港和海外出版的报纸和杂志，并拥有一个高速的院内局域网，该网络是研究台湾的数据库，也是各种文献的索引系统。

"Taiwan Research Anthology," the first of its kind on the mainland, was started in 1983 and is considered the premier journal in the areas of not only Taiwan but also Hong Kong and Macao studies.

By the end of 2003, TWRI's staff had published 122 monographs, books, collections of dissertations and reference materials; and over 1800 academic papers. Since 1988, those books and papers have gained 103 Excellent Social Scientific Awards from the state, Ministry of Education, and the Fujian Provincial and Xiamen Municipal governments.

Practical Exchanges TWRI's focus is practical as well as theoretical, and it has engaged in numerous research projects for the Taiwan Affairs departments at all levels of government. In 2002 and 2003, TWRI was visited by 489 scholars, experts and prominent figures from Taiwan, as well as 8 Hong Kong scholars and 63 foreign journalists and scholars. In that same year, 32 TWRI researchers went abroad in academic exchange programs. Between 2000 and 2003, TWRI held 13 academic seminars or symposia, 12 of which enjoyed the participation of scholars from both sides of the Taiwan Strait.

TWRI has extensive academic and cultural exchanges and cooperation with institutes in Taiwan, Hong Kong, Macao and foreign countries, including: the Graduate Institute of National Development of Taiwan University; Sun Yat-sen Graduate Institute of Social Science, Research Center for International Relations of Taiwan Chengchi University, the Graduate Institute for Mainland China Studies of Chinese Culture University, the Graduate Institute for Mainland China Studies of Tamkang University, the Graduate Institute of Political Science, Sun Yat-sen Institute of Interdisciplinary Studies, Institute for Mainland China studies of Taiwan Sun Yat-sen University, the Department of Policy and Public Administration of Chi Nan University, the Graduate School of Chinese Studies of Yunlin University of Science & Technology, the Political Department of Taiwan Soochow University, the Department of Politics and Public Administration of the University of Hong Kong, the Institute for East Asia Studies of Singapore; the Asia-Pacific Center For Security Studies of the USA; Soka University of Japan, etc.

So Why Xiamen? Xiamen is the perfect location for TWRI because of our exceptionally tight ties with Taiwan (3/4 of Taiwanese are from South Fujian). By the end of 2004, Taiwan was Xiamen's largest investor, with 2,284 investment projects with a contractual investment of 4.282 billion USD (accounting for about 6% of all Taiwan investment in the mainland).

第13章 台湾研究所

《台湾研究集刊》是大陆第一家同类杂志,创办于1983年,被海内外学术界誉为不仅在台湾而且在港、澳研究领域都具有重大影响的权威刊物。

截止到2003年底,全院共出版有关台湾研究的专著、论文集、资料集等122部,发表学术论文1800多篇。1988年以来,这些著作、论文荣获国家级、省级及厦门市级优秀科研成果奖103项。

实践交流 台湾研究院的重点是理论与实践相结合,参与各级政府关于台湾事务的多项研究项目。仅2002—2003年,台湾研究院就接待来自台湾的专家、学者及知名人士489人次,香港学者8人次,外国专家学者、记者及学者63人次。同一时段,该院赴境外进行学术交流的也有32人次。2000年到2003年四年间,台湾研究院举办了13次学术研讨会,其中,海峡两岸学者共同参加的12次。

厦门大学台湾研究院和台湾、香港、澳门以及国外的研究机构保持广泛的学术、文化交流与合作。这些学术机构包括:台湾大学国家发展研究所,台湾政治大学中山人文与社会科学研究所,台湾中国文化大学大陆研究所,台湾淡江大学大陆研究所,台湾中山大学政治学研究所,中山学术研究所、大陆研究所,台湾暨南国际大学公共行政与政策学系,台湾云林科技大学汉学资料整理研究所,台湾东吴大学政治系,香港大学政治与公共行政学系,新加坡东亚研究所,美国亚太安全研究中心,日本创价大学等等。

为什么选择厦门? 厦门是设立台湾研究院最理想的地方,因为她与台湾有着最紧密的联系(四分之三的台湾人来自闽南)。到2004年年底,台湾仍是厦门的最大投资者,在2284个投资项目中合同投资资金为42.82亿(占台湾在大陆总投资的6%)。

As famous Taiwan businessman Wu Jingzhong said, "People here speak the same language as in Taiwan. That makes me feel like at home."[①] Wu had difficulties in early years because his suppliers were in Taiwan, but he persuaded all of them to move to Xiamen. Now that his complete production chain is in a Xiamen industrial park, Xiamen exports over 120 million sunglasses yearly, replacing Taiwan as the world's largest manufacturer of sunglasses.

Retiring in Xiamen Not only have many major Taiwan firms made Xiamen their base, but many Taiwanese are retiring here as well! Since 2001, when direct ferry service opened between Jinmen and Xiamen, people from Jinmen alone have bought over 3,000 apartments in Xiamen (about 1 Xiamen apartment for every 17 Jinmen residents). It's not surprising; at low tide Xiamen and Jinmen are only 1800 meters apart, and many Jinmen residents have relatives here in Xiamen.

Sixty percent of the residents of Wujiang Diamond Plaza are from Jinmen, and the developer, Jinmen native Chen Jingwu, said, "In my opinion, so many Jinmen people buy houses in Xiamen mainly because they have strong identification with their motherland."[②]

As it is written, "For where your treasure is, there your heart will be also." It looks to me like Xiamen, and Xiamen University, are capturing Taiwan's heart as well as its treasure!

Contact Information Phone: 218-6415 Fax: (0592)218-3538
E-mail:twri@jingxian.xmu.edu.cn
Website:http://twri.xmu.edu.cn

---

① China International Business, Feb. 01, 2006
② China Daily, "Calling Home Across the Straits," by Li Dapeng, March 22, 2005

第13章 台湾研究所

台湾著名商人吴进忠说，"厦门和台湾同说一种方言，我在厦门有宾至如归的感觉。" 吴先生在厦门头几年经商困难，因为他的供货商在台湾。他劝说那些配套商都搬到厦门来。现在他的产业链在厦门的工业园区，目前，厦门每年出口太阳镜 1.2 亿副，已经超过台湾，成为世界上最大的太阳镜生产基地。

退休在厦门 不仅许多台湾大公司扎根厦门，而且许多台湾居民也要在厦门安度晚年。自从 2001 年厦门和金门开始民间客运直航以来，单单从金门来的台湾人，就在厦门购置了 3000 多套住房（大约每 17 个金门人在厦门就购有一套住房）。这并不奇怪，因为金门和厦门在海水落潮时相隔仅仅 1.8 公里，而且许多金门居民在厦门都有亲属。

浯江钻石广场楼盘 60%的住户是金门人，浯江钻石广场的开发商之一、地道的金门人陈经武先生说："我认为，这么多金门人在厦门购置住房，主要缘于他们对祖国强烈的认同感。"

有句话说："你的财富在哪里，你的心也就在哪里。"在我看来，厦门和厦门大学正在同时赢得台湾的两者——财富和心！

联系方法

厦门大学台湾研究院
邮编：361005
电话：218-6415 218-3192 218-5374
传真：(0592)218-3538
电子邮件:twri@jingxian.xmu.edu.cn
网站:http://twri.xmu.edu.cn

Interview with Prof. Chen Kongli
Taiwan Research Institute

In 1992, as Director of XMU Taiwan Research Institute and president of XMU Alumni Association, Professor Chen set foot on the "Jade Island" for the first time.

He said that from as early as the triumph of the war with Japan, about 500 XMU graduates crossed from Fujian to Taiwan between 1945 and 1949 to help with construction and development. These people soon played a key role in many of Taiwan's industries. At the same time, many Taiwan students came to study on the Mainland; over ten of them chose XMU. Li Keshi, an XMU alumnus from Taiwan, recalled in his article "After returning to Alma Mater from Taiwan", "I remembered that Taiwan enrolled 126 government-sent students that year [summer, 1948] to study at their own expense in 17 state-run Mainland universities. Over 600 people applied to go. "Most of them were young people with great aspirations," Pro. Chen added. Among them was Zhang Kehui, the current vice chairman of the Chinese People's Political Consultative Conference, who was also one of Prof. Chen's classmates when they both entered XMU in 1948.

Taiwan students who stayed here made great achievements in their fields of study and contributed tremendously to the Mainland, while XMU graduates in Taiwan made outstanding achievements as well. For example, He Yici, a graduate of XMU's Dept. of Mechanical and Electrical Engineering, helped found Taiwan Xinzhu Industrial Park, "the Silicon Valley of Taiwan."

Prof. Chen recalled the sincere remarks of an XMU alumnus in Taiwan, "All these years, we XMU alumni have been working diligently and living honestly ever since we settled in Taiwan, which should make our Alma Mater proud"

第13章 台湾研究所

访台湾研究院陈孔立教授

1992年,时任厦大台湾研究所所长、校友总会会长的的陈孔立教授第一次登上了宝岛台湾。

他说,早在抗日战争胜利时,从1945年到1949年将近五年的时间里,大约500名厦大毕业生从厦门到台湾,帮助台湾建设和发展。后来这些人在台湾的各行各业都担当了非常重要的角色。同一时期,台湾学生也来大陆读书,有几十人来到了厦大。 厦大台湾校友李克世在《从台湾来到母校后》一文中回忆道:"忆起那年(1948年夏),在台湾招收赴大陆17所国立大学的公派自费生126人,竟有600多人报名。""这些年轻人很多都很有抱负",陈教授说。现任全国政协副主席的张克辉就是当时台湾来厦大的学生之一,也是1948年入学的陈孔立教授同届的同学。

这些留下来的台湾同学学有所成,为大陆做出了不少的贡献;去台湾的厦大校友也有杰出的业绩。陈教授回忆了来自厦大台湾校友会的真诚话语:"几十年来我们在台湾的校友都能够勤勤恳恳做事、老老实实做人,这是可以告慰母校的。"何宜慈,当年厦大机电系的毕业生,就是有"台湾的硅谷"之称的台湾新竹工业园区的创始人之一。

Although Pro. Chen first set foot on the Jade Island in 1992, he had tried to visit in Jan. 1988, and failed. As a scholar of Taiwan, he was invited to attend the "Seminar on Taiwan History". But after he arrived in Hong Kong he was told that only those who had stayed in HK for at least 5 years were qualified for a visa to Taiwan. He had no choice but to give up, but the paper he had composed was read during the conference, and a Taiwan newspaper published an article entitled, "Chen Kongli--Article arrived, but Not the Person ··· Initial Communication of Taiwan Strait Academic Field."

In August, some Taiwan scholars planned to organize themselves into a group to visit XMU, but Taiwan authorities ordered them to drop the attempt. The group finally received permission to visit Xiamen, but only after writing in the application that they were "not a group." And so on August 2nd, with the cooperation of the XMU Taiwan Research Institute, the first seminar attended by both Mainland and Taiwan scholars was finally convened.

Prof. Chen said that from day one, XMU Taiwan Research Institute has played an important role in cross-strait communication. As early as 1979, more than ten XMU teachers had been studying Taiwan's history and one professor had already started studying its economy. So given Xiamen's unique location and close ties with Taiwan, the central government set up a Taiwan Research Institute in XMU

The institute has four major duties: academic study; enrolling graduates and doctoral students; composing research reports as references for high level departments' decision-making; and all-encompassing exchanges with Taiwan.

Postscript

Nowadays, Taiwan Research Institution holds frequent cross-Straits exchanges in many fields. Their friendships, and frank and sincere exchange of ideas with each other, have greatly promoted mutual understanding between Taiwan and the Mainland . We truly owe a great debt of gratitude to Prof. Chen and the Taiwan Research Institute for the great contributions they have made to overall Taiwan studies and cross-strait communications.

第 13 章　台湾研究所

关于赴台交流，陈教授的经历不应该从 1992 年开始，而应该从 1988 年 1 月的第一次"试图抵台"说起。当时作为研究台湾的学者，他应邀准备去参加"台湾史研讨会"。可是到了香港之后却被告知说"要在香港居住 5 年以上才能办理去台湾的手续"！于是只好作罢。但他所撰写的论文已经在会上宣读，台湾报纸刊登题为《陈孔立文到人不到——台湾学术首开交流》的文章。

当年 8 月，台湾一些学者打算组团前来厦大，可是受到台湾当局的阻挠。团内成员只好在"简介"中的"名字"一栏里把团的名字填为"不是团"，最后终于成功地来到了厦门。8 月 2 日，他们与厦大的台湾研究所合作。海峡两岸学者的第一次研讨会终于召开了。

陈教授说，厦大的台湾研究院在两岸交流中有着重要的地位，而它的历史也可以追溯到 1979 年。当时厦大已经有十几位老师正在研究台湾历史，一位教授开始研究台湾的经济，加上厦门独特的地理位置和与台湾众多方面的紧密联系，于是国家决定在厦大成立台湾研究所，后改名为"台湾研究院"。

他们的主要工作有四项：学术交流，招收硕士、博士研究生，撰写调研报告供上级机关决策参考，与台湾及海外各方面的交流。

现在，台湾研究院经常与台湾各界进行交流，他们交了许多朋友，彼此各抒己见，坦诚相待，增进了两岸同胞间的相互理解。我们真的应该感谢陈教授和他所在的厦门大学台湾研究院在台湾研究和两岸交流这方面做出的巨大贡献。

XMU Campus Life of Taiwan Students Chen Anqi and Zhong Yuanlang

By Lou Hongying

Recently, more and more students from Taiwan have chosen to pursue their studies in Mainland China. The communication and assimilation have gained irreversible momentum. Over recent years, Xiamen University has become the most popular university among Taiwan students. XMU began to enroll students from Taiwan as early as the late 1980s. XMU now has 128 students from Taiwan, including 39 doctoral candidates and 15 master's degree candidates.

It is said that Taiwan students at XMU have very diverse backgrounds. Some came to the Mainland after graduating from high school and enrolled in XMU via preparatory education or an entrance examination. Some came to the Mainland with their parents at an early age and were admitted by the university after receiving their primary and high school education here. Some had already accumulated some working experience and they chose to continue their study in the Mainland to fulfill their career dreams.

Chen Anqi: A Taiwan Girl Who Sometimes Skips Lessons

Chen Anqi, a girl from Zhanghua County, Taiwan, came to the Mainland with her parents, who are in business. She's now a senior economics major in XMU. She said Xiamen is similar to Taiwan in many ways, such as dialect, customs, and climate, so life here is not alien to her.

As for skipping lessons, Anqi chuckled and argued that in every university students sometimes play truant. She gave some persuasive reasons (though not actually applying them to herself). "It is because of the way the teachers give lectures," Anqi said. She said she was not satisfied with some teachers' lecture methods, such as just repeating what the books say, and giving rigid homework assignments, paying no attention to students' attitudes towards their tasks and the quality of their work. They only care whether you hand it in on time. "Nowadays, the internet is highly developed and some students just copy papers and essays from it. Then, they hand in their "homework" to teachers and actually learn nothing," Anqi said.

However, Anqi also praised some excellent teachers. "Mr. He Xinming, who teaches us Marketing Management, is lively and creative when he lectures to us. Furthermore, his opinions are always persuasive. He designs and prepares different lectures for students of different majors. What's more, the cases he cites are fresh, practical, and keep abreast of the times. If there were more and more teachers like him, I believe there would be less and less students skipping lessons."

台生陈安琪和钟源郎在厦大的求学生活

楼红英

来大陆高校求学的台湾学生近年越来越多,两岸的交流与融合成为势不可挡的潮流。厦门大学是近年来台湾学生最看好的高等学府。厦大从上个世纪80年代后期就开始接收台湾学生,现在已有在读台湾学生128人,其中有39名博士生、15名硕士生。

据了解,来大陆的台湾学生经历各有不同,有的是高中毕业后来到大陆,或通过预科或通过直接考试进入大学;有的是从小跟随父母来大陆,在大陆接受了小学、中学教育后而考入大学;还有的是已经有过工作经验,通过对自己人生的规划选择来大陆继续求学深造。

陈安琪:一个会逃课的台湾女学生

来自台湾彰化县的陈安琪,从小学三年级就跟随做生意的父母来大陆,现在是厦大经济学专业的大四学生,她说在厦门无论语言、习俗、气候等方面都与台湾很相近,对这里的环境没有陌生感。

说起逃课,安琪咯咯地笑了。辩解说,大学生都有过逃课的经历。她剖析原因,尽管没在自身找原因,但也找到一点有说服力的。"这跟老师的讲课方式有很大关系呀。"安琪对一些教师的授课方式以及要求表达了不满,比如有的老师喜欢照本宣科,而且要求完成作业的方式也很死板,没有重视学生完成这件事情的态度和质量,只要按时交上来就可以了。"现在网络很发达,学生为了应付,经常把网上的内容剪辑粘贴一下了事,而没有学生自己的东西。"安琪说。

不过,安琪也很客观地表扬了另一些优秀的教师。"比如,有一位教授市场营销学的何新明老师,他讲课风格很活泼、有新意、观点很有说服力。而且他对不同专业的班级都有针对性,给出的案例都很新,很有实效性、时代感。如果学校里这样的老师多,逃课率肯定会下降。"

Zhong Yuanlang: Oldest Master's Degree Candidate in Taiwan Research Institute

Zhong Yuanlang, born in Taoyuan, Taiwan, in 1964, is the oldest master's degree candidate in XMU's Taiwan Research Institute. Before studying in the Mainland, he worked as a journalist in Taiwan and then for the government. When asked why he chose XMU to further his study, he answered frankly, "It is too cold in North China for Taiwanese and it is too expensive in Shanghai. Nevertheless, in Xiamen, I can hear the Minnan Dialect easily and eat similar food to what I had in Taiwan. What's more important is the experts and researchers in XMU's Taiwan Research Institute are the top ones in China!"

Mr. Zhong, with a strong Minnan accent, emphasized that his mandarin was "fluent". Before coming to the Mainland, he thought that the people in the Mainland all spoke mandarin, which is pleasant to hear but hard to learn. Until he arrived, he did not know that the Mainland has numerous dialects and that natives do not speak perfect mandarin. He pointed out that there were some different usages of the same words in Taiwan and the Mainland. He took jinzhang (紧张) for instance. In Taiwan, jinzhang means nervous, while in the Mainland it has a broader meaning. For example, it can be used to describe a situation of short supply. The slight differences in customs also used to make Zhong nervous. He talked about the custom of "Jiaoweifan (a bowl of rice at someone's feet)". In Taiwan, when relatives hold a memorial ceremony for the deceased, they place a bowl of rice at their feet with three stick of incense inserted. Once, Zhong ate with his classmates, and a classmate stuck his chopsticks into his bowl when his cell phone rang. That is taboo in Taiwan, and Zhong felt very uneasy. However, he gradually got accustomed to it and now does not care that much. "Communication makes better understanding!" Zhong exclaimed.

"The General Public in Taiwan Happy To See Sound Development of the Cross-strait Relations."

Although the Mainland and Taiwan Island are geologically separated by just a narrow strait the estrangement between them cannot be erased within a short period, but they undoubtedly identify themselves as people of Pan-China. As for Cross-strait relations, Zhong believes they will develop positively. "The general public in Taiwan are happy to see the sound develop of cross-Strait relations. And this is an irreversible trend in the Mainland's reform and opening-up." Zhong also said that the Taiwan authorities' present obstructions are just temporary. No matter what state the Cross-strait relations are in, even during opposition, the non-official communications between the Mainland and Taiwan will definitely not be suspended.

Anqi, whose family motto is "Be concerned but not involved in politics," said, "Economically, Taiwan's high-tech and agricultural products can make good use of the Mainland' great market. Earning money is good for both sides. The Mainland people can get access to Taiwan agricultural products while Taiwan farmers can make profits. A peaceful and stable situation is the key to bringing happiness to the people across the Strait.

钟源郎：台湾研究院最年长的硕研

钟源郎，1964年出生于台湾桃园县，现是厦大台湾研究院在读最年长的硕士研究生。来大陆求学前，他曾在台湾当过记者，也在政府部门工作过。之所以选择厦大，钟源郎心直口快地说，北方太冷，上海的高校又太贵，不像在厦门，话是乡音闽南话，台湾叫得上名字的菜这里都有。更重要的是，厦大台研院的专家学者在台湾研究方面是非常尖端的。

一口闽南腔的钟源郎强调，自己的普通话"很流利"。没来大陆前，以为大陆讲普通话都是"京片子"，好听却难学，而到了大陆后，才知道这里有不少地方方言，大陆老百姓普通话说得并不怎么好。钟源郎说，台湾和大陆有些用词上会有些不同，比如"紧张"，在台湾常用来表示情绪紧张，而在大陆"用途广泛"，还可以指车票等市场行情的"紧张"。因为两岸习俗的一些小差异也曾让钟源郎感到有点"紧张"。钟源郎讲起了台湾"脚尾饭"的习俗，就是家属祭奠去世的亲人，在脚边放置一碗白米饭，上面插三炷香。有几次，钟源郎和同学一起吃饭，同学遇到电话响就随手把筷子往饭上一插，而这在台湾却是忌讳，坐在饭桌上的钟源郎当时有些不适，后来"习惯了"也就不太当回事了。"多交流才能更好地沟通理解。"钟源郎深有感触地说。

"台湾百姓乐见两岸关系良性发展"

大陆台湾一水之隔，尽管历史造成两岸隔阂无法在短时间内消除，而对大中华的民族认同却是毫无疑问的。谈到两岸关系时，钟源郎认为，两岸关系一定会往正面的方向发展，"台湾百姓乐见两岸关系良性发展，而且这种发展趋势是不可逆的。就像大陆的改革开放是不可逆转的大方向。"钟源郎还说，目前，台湾的执政当局阻挠也只能是一时的现象，无论两岸之间是什么样的状态哪怕是敌对的状况，而两岸交往民间的对话是绝对不会中断的。

抱着家训"关心政治但不要沾染政治"安琪也说，从经济方面讲，台湾的高科技产业和农产品到大陆找市场，有钱大家赚没有什么不好。大陆人能吃到台湾农产品，台湾农民也能得到经济利益。要想两岸的老百姓都能过上好日子，和平稳定当然是最重要的了。

4 Generations of XMU Taiwan Family!
(1921-2006)

Note: We are honored that Prof. Peng from Taiwan wrote this article especially for this book. His family has had 4 generations of XMU graduates, dating from 1921! Unfortunately, it arrived too late to translate, so we include only an abridged Chinese version.

彭家四代厦大情

厦门大学成立85年以来，桃李满天下，其中不乏缘结数代，渊源深长者。今年82岁高龄的台湾彰化师范大学教授彭驾骍先生，就是出自这样一个家庭。彭家四代人与厦大之情谊，用彭驾骍先生的话说，"应如鹭江深且长"。

Family Visit to XMU

彭驾骍先生祖上与陈嘉庚先生及厦门大学的缘分，可以上溯到其曾伯祖父信谊公。他于28岁时中光绪十四年（1888年）进士，35岁时出任惠安知县，与陈嘉庚先生之尊翁陈杞柏公时相来往，后调任广东梅县，41岁任泉州知府，又与陈家结为姻亲。彭驾骍先生之曾祖父信书公，清光绪十七年（1891年）举人，曾应聘鹭江书院教席达十年之久。厦大创校时，彭驾骍先生的祖父义潋公奉其遗命，将所藏经史子集六七万册，悉数捐赠厦大图书馆。据彭驾骍先生回忆，他在厦大读书时，尚亲见赠书专柜。

信谊、信书两公与厦门大学之情谊，应属彭家第一代。

第二代与厦大关系最深者，首推彭驾骍的二伯公彭义安先生。义安先生早岁追随陈嘉庚先生之胞弟陈启贤先生经商，其后自行创业义记商行，专营木材布帛并代理陈启贤先生部分之商务。陈嘉庚兴学厦大时，多有捐输之义举，曾屡获厦大首任邓萃英校长及接任之林文庆校长表扬。彭驾骍幼年参拜宗祠时，曾亲见奖状以及义安公与陈嘉庚、陈启贤昆仲的合影。

与厦大情谊至深之彭家第三代，计有彭驾骍的叔叔彭传珍、叔彭传晨和彭传津。

第13章 台湾研究所

　　1921年陈嘉庚创办厦门大学，彭传珍即以优异成绩考入预备正科，翌年入大学部首届师范部，享有全公费待遇，学费、膳费、宿舍费均免。因其成绩名列全班之冠，制服、书籍费亦获全部补助。附带可以一提的是，彭传珍还担任校篮球队队长。1926年参加厦大首届毕业典礼，同时毕业之各系学生仅35名。大学毕业后，先后为福建省政府教育厅督学、福建龙岩县立中学校长（1929）、福建福州职业学校校长（1931）、福建师范专科学校校长（1946）、国立海疆专科学校校长（1948）、国立编译馆编纂兼任台湾师范大学工业教育系及台北工业专科学校教授（1950年后）等职。

　　1935年，彭传珍前往美国哥伦比亚大学教育研究所进修，主攻学校行政与总务管理，并取得教育硕士学位。1937年至1946年间，彭传珍先后在萨本栋、汪德耀校长领导下，任校长室秘书（兼办总务）、总务长等职，同时在教育学系讲授心理学与测验统计。其间厦大迁校至长汀，以及光复后回迁，传珍先生之辛劳，自不难想见。

　　彭驾骍的七叔彭传晨，曾于1941年来厦门大学就读一年，后辗转前往四川，在重庆大学完成学业。十二叔彭传津，1942年考入厦门大学土木系，1946年毕业，曾任职于国民政府水资源委员会、福州技术学校等。

　　彭驾骍先生属于第四代。彭先生原名家燊，后经其先祖改名为"驾骍"，取孔子所云"犁牛之子骍且角"之意。1944年报考厦门大学历史学系，名列5人中之第三，恰好占全公费生之末（当时学校规定每系新生前一半者，始克享有全公费待遇）。彭驾骍至今还说，"此一制度惠我良多也"，不忘恩情。彭先生于1948年6月取得文学士资格，参加了厦大第23届毕业典礼。后来，数度负笈海外，回国后仍坚持教育岗位，诲人无数。

　　第四代中还有驾骍先生的弟弟彭步连，1950年入厦门大学工学院电机系，1953年提前毕业。曾在北京工业学院（今北京理工大学）等任教，讲授电机学、控制电机、电力拖动等课程。

　　"鹭江深且长，彭家四代厦大情更长。"彭驾骍先生一家四代的厦大情缘，正是陈嘉庚先生和厦门大学传承文化、造福桑梓、振兴中华、遗泽后世的绝好象征！

（王依民根据彭驾骍先生提供的文章编写）

Some Taiwan XMU Alumni(1926-1948)
部分在台厦大校友（1926-1948）

陳泗孫
1926
教育

薛人仰
1931
教育

黃福藩
1934
(1955～75﹜

徐　瑛
教育

林禎祥
1933
教育

鄒亨觀
1935
教育

林秀欒
1931
教育

林　慎
1934
社會

李廣相
1936
教育

林雪英
1935
數學

王貞宏
1936
數學

葉　英
1938
政治經濟

葉世稀
1935
歷史

洪福增
1936
法律

沈祖穆
1939
商

第13章 台湾研究所

王添泉
1939
中文

沈祖馨
1939
化學

林玉存
1939
商

鄺雄謀
1939
教育

王華錟
1940
商

陳爲綱
1940
化學

李瑞成
1940
中文

曾翼程
1940
語文

劉晉燈
1940
數理

陳安祺
1941
經濟

陳南陽
1941
數理

陳揚綏
1941
化學

吳國樑
1942
教育

黃其欣
1941 土木

方舜華
1945 政治

廖建安
1948
法律

鄺拱光
1948
土木

盧志純
1948
法律

— 207 —

章家粢
1945
土木

徐承泰
1945
機電

徐得位
1945
機電

張子德
1945 化學

周惠慈
1946 生物

梁星坦
1945
經濟

陳樹勛
1945
機電

程詩濤
1945
經濟

蘇永清
1945
機電

王兆奎
1946
教育

鄧鴻興
1945
銀行

朱立瑞
1946
經濟

吳厚沂 [81]
1946 教育
陳梅卿 [95]
1946 會計

李星輝
1946
化學

過鮑生
1948
航工

黃海
1948
機電

傅友岩
1948
政治

第13章　台灣研究所

陳耀南
1946
政治

楊肇鳳
1946
機電

黃　揚
1946
機電

劉木水
1946
經濟

鍾隆津
1946
經濟

劉詩華
1946
機電

薛小生
1946
機電

魏綏群
1946
經濟

王之槐
1947
土木

王萬青
1947
機電

朱希曾
1947
機電

沙熾光
1947
教育

林茂棣
1947
土木

陳昌釗
1947
機電

官兆璋
1947
機電

林思賢
1948
銀行

劉文華
1949
教育

盧淑恬
1949
外文

— 209 —

Chapter 14

Research School of S.E. Asian Studies
Center for S.E. Asian Studies
Xiamen University

(This introduction is courtesy of the Research School)

New China's earliest research institution on S.E. Asian and Overseas Chinese studies began in 1956 as XMU's Research Institute of Nanyang. The institute's focus is research on S.E. Asian politics, economics, history, and issues concerning overseas Chinese.

The Institute made great achievements during the initial decade, especially in research on overseas Chinese in S. E. Asia, and field studies and interviews with overseas Chinese have yielded one of the best collections of materials available on overseas Chinese investment in the mainland and Chinese contract workers in S. E. Asia.

The Institute was closed during the "Cultural Revolution" and re-opened in 1972. In 1996 the institute was re-organized into a research school as the staff increased and research fields expanded.

In addition to library, administrative office and translation department, the Research School has four institutes: Institute for Studies of Politics and Economy, Institute of Overseas Chinese Studies, Center for History of China's International Relations, and Center of Chinese Literature.

The library has what is generally considered China's best collection on S.E. Asia and Overseas Chinese affairs, with 45,000 books, 10,000 monographs on special subjects, 20,000 bound periodicals, 25,000 bound newspapers, and subscriptions to 120 foreign periodicals and newspapers. The library has published "A Combined Bibliography of the Books on Issues of Overseas and Ethnic Chinese in Fujian," and four "Title Indexes to the Papers on S.E. Asian Studies and Overseas Chinese."

第14章
东南亚研究中心暨南洋研究院

厦门大学南洋研究院（原"南洋研究所"）成立于 1956 年，长期以来，致力于东南亚政治、经济、历史以及华侨华人问题的研究。

在研究所创立的最初十余年间，研究重点为东南亚华侨华人，对华侨投资国内企业史、东南亚契约华工以及归国华侨等研究课题进行了广泛而又细致的田野调查、资料搜集和访谈工作，取得了丰硕的研究成果。

"文革"期间，研究所曾一度关闭，直到 1972 年才恢复。1996 年，研究所进行体制改革与学科调整，扩大规模，更名为南洋研究院。

研究院设图书馆、办公室和编译室以及四个专题研究机构：东南亚政治经济研究室，东南亚华侨华人研究室，东南亚国际关系研究室，东南亚华文文学研究中心。

图书馆收藏了丰富的有关东南亚研究领域的图书资料，包括 45000 册中外文图书、10000 余种专题研究报告、20000 余份期刊和 25000 份的报纸，长期订购有 120 余种的国外报刊，是国内公认最好的东南亚研究和华侨华人研究资料中心之一。此外，还出版了一部福建省馆藏华侨华人书目、四部有关东南亚及华侨华人问题研究的论文资料索引。

The School publishes two quarterly journals: "STUDIES OF SOUTHEAST ASIAN AFFAIRS" and "SOUTHEAST ASIAN STUDIES (A QUARTERLY JOURNAL OF TRANSLATIONS)." Since 1972 the former has carried articles by researchers in and beyond the School, while the latter, published since 1957, carries translated foreign theses and systematic materials on S.E. Asia, Asian-Pacific economies, the economies of developing countries and overseas Chinese affairs.

XMU Center for Southeast Asian Studies. To further focus and improve research on S.E. Asian issues, the research school, in cooperation with other Institutes, established the Center in early 2000. This center was jointly sponsored by both XMU and the office for Overseas Chinese Affairs of State Council, PRC. Examined and ratified by Ministry of Education, in Sept. 2000 the Center became one of the hundred National Key institutes for humanities and social science.

Director of Center: Prof. Zhuang Guotu
Vice-director of Center: Prof. Liao Shaolian.
Contact: Tel & Fax: 86 592 2186414
Email: xianan@jingxian.xmu.edu.cn

第14章 东南亚研究中心暨南洋研究院

研究院编辑出版国内外发行的学术刊物有：《南洋问题研究》、《南洋资料译丛》。前者于1972年开始出版发行，刊载由院内外研究人员撰写的学术研究论文；后者创刊于1957年，刊载国外有关东南亚、亚太经济、发展中国家经济以及华侨华人问题的论著与系列资料。

厦门大学东南亚研究中心为了强化研究重点和提高对东南亚问题的研究水准，研究院结合校内其他相关研究机构，于2000年初成立了该中心。该中心由厦门大学与国务院侨务办公室共建，经教育部考核验收后，于2000年9月被正式批准成立为国家教育部百所人文社会科学重点研究基地之一。

现任中心主任庄国土教授，副主任廖少廉教授。

联系方式：电话、传真：2186414
电子邮件：xianan@jingxian.xmu.edu.cn

S.E. Asian Studies Reading Room

Chapter 15

School of Economics

China's 1st Ph.D.s in Accounting, Finance and Auditing!"

XMU's largest school and one of the best in China, the School of Economics (SE) was founded in 1923 as the Department of Economics and became the School of Economics in 1982. SE has 12 undergrad, 26 masters and 25 secondary doctoral programs.

Key departments and institutes include:
Department of Economics
Department of Planning & Statistics
Department of Public Finance
Department of Finance
Department of International Economics and Trade
Institute of Economics

To date, the Economics College has 4 national key subjects: accounting, finance, banking, political economics. The economics and theoretical economics are national 1st level doctoral programs.

The SE's economics and management library has over 200,000 volumes. The school also has an experimental teaching lab, finance and banking information system simulations lab, statistical analysis and investigation lab, electronic commerce lab, multi-media lab for network marketing, etc.

The SE has extensive academic exchange and cooperation programs with institutions in the U.S., Europe, Australia, Singapore and Japan, as well as with Hong Kong, Macao and Taiwan.

The Economics Department set up a "Cornell Office" to coordinate ties with Cornell (a sister university since 1987). The office' work was interrupted but has now re-opened within the Wang Ya'nan Institute of Economic Research (see next chapter).

Contact Information: Tel: 218-2027 Fax 218-6340
Email: xmujjxy@xmu.edu.cn
Website: http://se.xmu.edu.cn

第15章

经 济 学 院

经济学院是厦门大学最大的学院，也是国内同类最好的学院之一。它渊源于1923年成立的经济系，并于1982年建立成为经济学院。现设有12个本科专业、26个硕士学位授权点和25个二级学科博士学位授权点。

主要的系别和研究所包括：

经济学系	计划与统计系	财政系
金融系	国际经济与贸易系	经济研究所

目前，学院拥有统计学、财政学、金融学、政治经济学四个国家重点学科，应用经济学和理论经济学2个一级学科博士学位授权点。

经济学院图书分馆馆藏图书20多万册；学院设有教学实验中心、财政金融信息系统模拟实验室、统计调查分析实验室、国家经济基础人才培养基地多媒体教学实验室、电子商务与网络营销多媒体实验室等。

经济学院积极开拓和发展对外学术交流与合作，与美国、欧洲、澳大利亚、新加坡和日本，以及港、澳、台地区的高校建立了各种形式的学术交流。

为了加强同康奈尔大学的联系（该校自1987年来就是我校的姊妹院校），经济学系成立了厦门大学康奈尔合作中心，该办公室的工作曾中断过，但现已恢复并归属于王亚南经济研究院。

Administrative Leadership and Management
The Solid Foundation for Academic Research
An Interview of Prof. Zhang Xingguo, Party Secretary of SE

Only a solid administrative foundation makes academic progress possible, and that requires solid leadership. An inspiring example is Prof. Zhang Xingguo, Party Secretary of the School of Economics (SE). During the interview Prof. Zhang said there are 4 keys to his management philosophy at SE: decisions, hiring, authorizations, and innovations. Zhang especially emphasized "mind" and "spirit". He said the main reason the SE has become one of China's "Top Five" economics schools has been because of its "Yanan Spirit", which has been passed down through the generations. The essence of this spirit is, "face difficulties and conquer them."

As if running a school isn't enough responsibility already, Prof. Zhang also gives classes and pursues research in his field of statistics. Zhang can manage so much so well because of an excellent habit: he jots down whatever thoughts and ideas pop into his head, and later organizes and prioritizes his ideas into systematic theories which he then puts into practice—an intelligent way to keep up with many different responsibilities at the same time. During our interview I noticed Zhang fish a small piece of paper out of his pocket. He referred to it as he spoke about his ideas and management techniques in a very clear, energetic and well organized manner. This habit explains how he can cope so successfully with so much work and stress.

行政领导与管理：学术科研的坚固基石
——访经济学院党委书记张兴国

只有拥有坚实的行政管理基础，才能谈得上学术科研的进步，而坚实的行政管理基础需要坚强的领导——这是经济学院党委书记张兴国副教授留给我们的启示。接受采访时，张书记谈到他从事经院管理的四个核心词："决策、用人、授权、创新"。他特别强调了"思维"和"精神"的作用，他说，经院之所以能够跻身于全国经济学科综合实力前5名，很大程度上是因为对"亚南精神"的传承，一代又一代的经院人传承着这种"勇于面对困难并最终战胜困难"的思想精髓。

张书记不仅与院办公室诸位领导承担着管理整个学院的责任，而且还从事统计学的教学和科研工作。张书记能够同时出色地完成这么多工作，大概与他良好的习惯分不开的：把自己随时想到的想法记录下来，有空再酝酿、梳理这些想法，形成系统的思路并运用到实践中——这是同时应对多项工作的一个聪明的方法！比如，在采访张书记期间，我注意到一个小细节：他从口袋里掏出一张小纸张，随即讲出一些他的管理理念和方法，他讲的时候条理非常清晰，逻辑非常严密。当然，这也可以从某种程度上解释为什么他能够自如应对工作及其带来的压力了。

In spite of his success, Zhang is very humble because he realizes that he has much yet to learn. Not long ago he organized a tour to some well-known universities in America with other professors, and one small incident made him ponder. While using a computer at a university library in Boston, he was surprised to find a photo from a very recent XMU annual sports meeting that had just been placed on the SE website. He clicked on the photo and within half a second it filled the entire screen. "In the age of the internet, everything we do is observed ", he said. "It was quite impressive! Though a small incident, it reflected how much more we need to improve ourselves, in everything. We certainly have a long way to go."

Zhang then emphasized the "5 Awareness" needed for running any institute or bureau:

1) Awareness of Opportunity
2) Awareness of Development
3) Awareness of Overall Situation
4) Awareness of Responsibility
5) Awareness of Hardship

We feel honored to have leaders like Zhang Xingguo, for it is their consistent endeavors that insure our university's institutes, at all levels, continue to progress towards perfection.

Luo Yucong (material provided by Prof. Luo). Professor Luo has 57 years of teaching experience. His research interests are classic monographs of Marxist economics and modern reality. His academic achievements include three monographs on Engels Studies, two corpuses composed of theoretical papers, and two jointly edited books. His main academic perspectives are as follows: the materialistic viewpoint of history is the guide to scientific research. With the evolvement of economic and class structures, developed countries and developing countries are moving forward towards modern socialism.

尽管如此，张书记仍很谦逊，因为他觉得还有很多东西要向人家学习。前不久，他组织院里的一些教授到美国几所世界知名的大学参观访问，其中发生的一件小事，对他的触动非常大。他在波士顿一所大学的图书馆里使用电脑，却非常意外地发现：电脑里有一张最近刚被厦大经院放到网页上的运动会照片。于是他点击了一下，不到半秒钟，照片就弹出来，占据了整个屏幕！"在网络时代，我们的一举一动，都在人家的眼皮底下了！"，他说，"这件事给我的印象非常深，虽然只是件小事，但它从某种侧面反映了我们各方面的工作有待改进，还有许多路要走。"

张书记强调了任何管理都需要的"五个意识"：

（1）机遇意识，（2）发展意识，（3）大局意识，（4）责任意识，（5）忧患意识。

我们对身边拥有如张兴国书记这样的领导感到荣幸，因为，正是在他们的不懈努力下，我校各级机构的运作机制才不断得到完善和发展。

罗郁聪

罗郁聪教授执教 57 年。他的研究领域是马克思主义经济学经典著作与现代实践。他的学术成就包括 2 本理论性文集、3 本恩格斯理论专著和 2 本与他人联合主编的书。他的主要研究方向是：辩证唯物史观指导科学研究。他的理论观点是随着社会历史的发展，当代资本主义发达国家和发展中国家不同程度地以各种形式趋向社会主义。

附：罗郁聪教授著作：

2 本理论性文集：《现代社会主义论——社会主义建设道路之中国特色》、《现代社会主义论——两种类型社会主义建设道路的探索》；

3 本恩格斯理论研究专著：《恩格斯经济思想研究》、《恩格斯与〈资本论〉》、《〈反杜林论〉研究》（与苏振富教授合写）；

2 本与蒋绍进教授联合主编的关于《资本论》研究和解释的书：《〈王亚南文集〉第二卷——〈资本论〉研究》、《〈资本论〉选读讲座》。

Chapter 16

Wang Yanan Institute for Studies in Economics (WISE)
(This section provided by WISE)

In 2005, the XMU "985 Project II", "Macroeconomic Analysis and Prediction" Philosophy and Social Science Innovation Base officially started, and the Wang Yanan Institute for Studies in Economics of XMU was founded. WISE was set up as an innovation base. Fulfilling tasks and goals of the innovation base will be WISE's-objectives for the next three years, laying a solid foundation for its long term development.

WISE is seeking to become a top-ranking modern economics research institute of China and the Asia-Pacific Region in a short period of time while adhering to international standards. WISE will try to fulfill the following goals:

    Publishing papers in top economics journals in China and abroad;
    Cultivating outstanding economists who can well represent WISE;
    Becoming an influential international economic exchange center in the Asia-Pacific region;
    …Making XMU's economics study in fields such as econometrics, banking, macroeconomics, political economics, etc. the top in China and influential abroad.
    ….Become a think tank for national and local economic development.

WISE has invited Pro. Wang Luolin, a well-known economist and a former vice president of the Chinese Academy of Social Science (CASS), as its honorary director, and the Professor of the Economics Dept. of Cornell University, "Yangtze Scholar" of the Ministry of Education, Prof. Hong Yongmiao, as it director. They have also invited the following professors as academic counselors: Zou Zhizhuang, the honorary professor of economics dept. of Princeton University; Clive Granger, honorary professor of economics dept. of the University of California at San Diego and the "Nobel Prize for Economics" winner in 2003; Jerry Hausman, professor of economics dept. of MIT and Clark Award winner; Xiao Zheng, professor of economics dept. of the Southern California University and editor-in-chief of the top-notch journal, *Journal of Econometrics*; Lawrence Klein, honorary professor of economics dept. of Pennsylvania University and Economic Nobel Prize winner in 1980, and so on.

第16章 王亚南经济研究院

2005年,厦门大学"935工程"(Ⅱ)——"宏观经济分析与预测"哲学社会科学创新基地建设项目正式启动,厦门大学王亚南经济研究院正式成立。研究院是在创新基地的基础上启动和发展起来的。圆满完成创新基地所提出的各项任务,是研究院今后三年的阶段性目标,这也将为研究院的长期发展奠定坚实的基础。

王亚南经济研究院力争在不太长的时间内成为亚太地区和中国一流的、与国际接轨的现代经济学研究机构,将致力于:

◆在国际顶尖和一流经济学期刊上积极发表论文;

◆在国内顶尖和一流经济学期刊上积极发表论文;

◆培养一批一流精干的中青年经济学家,塑造WISE品牌;

◆成为亚太地区一个有影响的经济学国际交流中心;

◆使厦门大学经济学科在一些主要领域,即计量经济学、金融学、宏观经济学、政治经济学等研究在国内处于顶尖地位,在国外有一定的影响;

◆成为国家和地方社会经济发展重要的"智囊团"和"思想库"。

研究院已聘请著名经济学家、原中国社会科学院常务副院长王洛林教授担任名誉院长,康奈尔大学经济学系教授、教育部"长江学者"讲座教授洪永淼担任院长,同时聘请的学术顾问有:普林斯顿大学经济学系荣誉教授邹至庄,加州大学圣地亚哥校区经济学系荣誉教授、2003年诺贝尔经济学奖获得者克莱夫·格兰杰,麻省理工学院经济学系教授、美国经济学会克拉克奖获得者杰瑞·豪斯曼,南加州大学经济学系教授、经济学国际一流期刊《经济学资源数据库》主编萧政,宾州大学经济学系荣誉教授、1980年经济学诺贝尔奖获得者劳伦斯·克雷恩等。

WISE has several academic units, including Cornell-XMU Exchange Center, Center for Econometric Research, Center for Financial Research, Center for Labor Economic Research, Macro Economic Research Center, Center for Statistical Research, and Center for Political Economics Research Institute. The Macro Economic Research Center is a key Research Base of Humanities and Social Sciences of the Ministry of Education. WISE will set up further research centers when it's capable of doing so. WISE is at the same level as other schools of XMU, and has 50 faculty members.

Contact Information:
   Phone: 218-7878 218-0855
   Fax: 218-7708
      Email: wise@xmu.edu.cn Website: www.wise.xmu.edu.cn

第 16 章　王亚南经济研究院

目前研究院拥有康奈尔合作中心、计量经济学研究中心、金融经济学研究中心、劳动经济学研究中心、宏观经济研究中心和统计科学研究中心、政治经济学研究中心等学术单位，其中宏观经济研究中心是教育部人文社会科学重点研究基地。研究院在条件成熟时将建立其他研究中心。

王亚南经济研究院与厦门大学其他学院属同一级别，拥有 50 个研究人员的编制。

联系方式

电话：218-7878　218-0355
传真：218-7708
电子邮件：wise@xmu.edu.cn
网址：www.wise.xmu.edu.cn

W.I.S.E. Guys...and W.I.S.E. Girls too!

Hong Yongmiao, President
Wang Yanan Institute for Studies in Economics
(W.I.S.E.)

"Hong Yongmiao, associate professor of economics, is an expert on the economy of China. Professor Hong has been the inspiration for Cornell's partnership with Xiamen University promoting faculty and graduate student exchange in economics and related fields. In August 2005 Xiamen University's President Zhu Chongshi visited Cornell to reaffirm their commitment to the Cornell-Xiada relationship."
Cornell University Press Release, 2005

(This chapter provided by W.I.S.E; thanks!)

It's been 20 years since Hong Yongmiao rode a bike across XMU campus, and now he is here again as Dean of the Wang Yanan Institute for Studies in Economics. It seems there is an invisible thread

Coffee Economics!

connecting him and the university across time and space. When Prof. Hong recalls his life on campus, a special feeling arises in his heart. At that time, he used to discuss with his classmates the world situation and politics and they were always red faced because of different opinions. They made bets and the one who lost would go to buy baozi (Chinese filled-buns) in Qinye Dining Hall. The Baozi were delicious but he would end up penniless by the end of every month. Now while working at XMU, he sometimes asks his secretary to buy him meals from the dining hall to recall the old days.

From Xiamen to Beijing, from San Diego to Ithaca, Prof. Hong has had a lot of opportunities. He shares his life experience with others: in the face of interest and opportunities, people's minds and life experience are filled with changes and leaps.

第 16 章 王亚南经济研究院

洪 永 淼
——王亚南经济研究院院长

"洪永淼,经济学教授,中国经济专家。洪教授开启厦门大学与康奈尔大学的伙伴关系,促进了教师和研究生在经济学和相关领域的交流。2005年8月,厦门大学校长朱崇实参观访问了康奈尔大学,并重申了康奈尔大学——厦门大学的伙伴关系。" (2005年康奈尔大学新闻稿)

从学生时代骑自行车穿过大半个校园,到今天重返母校担任新成立的王亚南经济研究院院长,时光一晃就是 20 年。然而,仿佛有一根无形的线,穿越时空,维系着学子对母校的牵挂——这是刈不断的血脉,割不断的情缘。当日理万机的洪永淼教授回想当年的校园生活,心中总会情不自禁地涌起一种别样的感觉。那时,他常常与同学们谈论世界形势、国家大事,并为不同的"政见"而争得面红耳赤。跟人家打赌,输掉了就被罚去勤业食堂买小笼包。食堂的小笼包味道很好,只是每到月底,他就会发现兜里的饭菜票已经所剩无几。现在,他在厦大工作,偶尔还会让秘书给他带食堂的饭菜,这也可以说是温"故"而知"新"吧。

从厦门到北京,从圣地亚哥到伊萨卡,在这 20 年中,洪教授的人生际遇发生了很大的改变。他坦言自己的人生感受:在机遇和兴趣面前,人的思维和经历常常充满变幻和跳跃。

After getting his doctor's degree in economics in California University, San Diego, he taught at Cornell University and was granted tenure. At the invitation from Party Secretary General Haojie Wang and President Chongshi Zhu, he returned to XMU and planned the establishment of W.I.S.E. He said he did this because he admires the two leaders' verve and vision, and also because he loves the university. He hopes eagerly to contribute to turning XMU into a world-class university.

Professor Hong is clear-minded and creative. He applied his physics study approach to economic studies. He is now applying the spectrum analysis method to depict periodical changes in economic cycles and financial markets. He is good at adopting economic rules in his teaching methodology and teaching pattern. For example, he divides a four-hour class into two two-hour classes according to the "diminishing return" theory in economics. In this way, the information of each class increases, and students are fresh-minded each time. As a result, students can digest and master more knowledge.

This talent of incorporation not only distinguishes him in field study, but also has helped him to construct his own teaching concept after years of overseas study and teaching experience. He talks about his study in California University San Diego in particular. The Department was established in 1964. By 2003, two people had won the Nobel Prize for economics and the department was listed in the top 10 US universities for economics in only 40 years' time. The outstanding performance of the economic department is closely related to its theory — "only do the best". Hong said vision is the key to development of a department, or even of a university, and he hopes to finish his mission with the guidance of this concept.

Prof. Hong put forward his own ideas for running the department. First of all, adopt the mechanism of being in line with both the international and China's situation, vigorously promote communication with foreign universities, "invite people in and send people out", and work hard to promote the influence of XMU's economic studies both at home and abroad. Second, with the most competitive salaries in China, recruit a school of young economic scholars from both home and abroad to fully enhance the XMU's level of economic study.

第16章 王亚南经济研究院

1993年,他拿到美国加州大学圣地亚哥校区经济学博士学位后,就一直在康奈尔大学任教并获得终身教职。在校党委书记王豪杰、校长朱崇实的力邀之下,他慨然应允,回母校担当筹建王亚南经济研究院的重任。他说,他之所以这么做,一是因为他钦佩两位学校主要领导的气魄和理念,二是因为深深的母校情结。他迫切地希望能为厦大赶超世界一流大学贡献自己的一份力量。

洪教授头脑清晰,善于创新。他将物理学的方法应用于经济学研究,他目前所从事的一个研究,就是将物理学的频谱分析方法推广到经济学中,用来刻画经济周期和金融市场中的周期性变动规律;同时他也善于把经济学规律引申到教学方法和授课模式上去。例如,他根据经济学里的"报酬递减"规律,将一次四个课时的课分成两次,每次按两课时来上。通过这种方式,教授们每次的授课量相应增多了,同时学生们每次上课头脑会更清楚,从而可以消化和吸收更多的知识。

这种触类旁通的禀赋不但使他在专业研究领域上成绩斐然,也让他在经历了多年的海外学习和教学工作后,形成了自己的办学理念。他特别谈及自己在加州大学圣地亚哥校区经济系学习时的感受,这个1964年成立的系,至2003年时已有两人拿到诺贝尔经济学奖,40年内便进入美国大学经济学科前10名。该校经济系之所以取得如此骄人的成绩,是与他们那种"不是最好的不做"的理念密不可分的。他说,作为支撑一个学院乃至整个学校发展的灵魂,理念是最重要的东西,他也希望能以此为指导,来完成自己的使命。

针对研究院的构建,他提出了自己的一套办学思路:首先,实行与国际接轨并且和中国实际相结合的新机制,积极开展对外交流,"请进来,走出去",努力扩大厦门大学经济学科在国内外的影响力;其次,还以在中国境内最有竞争力的待遇,从海内外招聘一批受过现代经济学系统训练的青年经济学者,全面提高厦大经济学研究水平;第三,率先在厦大对硕博研究生培养制度进行改革,用更加科学和先进的方式培养一代新人。

Chapter 17

School of Management

News Flash! First group of MPAcc students enrolled at XMU
"A group of 150 students of the program of Master of Professional Accounting (MPAcc) who came from the financial and accounting industries recently began their studies for the program which is jointly offered by Xiamen University and Xiamen National Accounting Institute. Xiamen University is among 21 pilot institutions selected by the Office of Academic Degrees Committee of the State Council and the Ministry of Education out of the 150-plus universities which had applied for offering this new program. "
Common Talk, Xiamen Daily, March 29, 2005

Our School of Management (SM) was ranked #3 in China in 2003—which may explain our mushrooming enrolment. We now have 230 doctoral students, 1860 master students, over 1800 undergraduates, and 17 fellows in post-doctoral programs.

SM has departments for accounting, business administration, management science, and tourism management, as well as centers for MPAcc, MBA and EMBA Education, Logistics, and Project Management Education. The four institutes include Accounting, Management Science, Human Resources, and Finance Management.

SM offers 7 undergraduate programs, 5 masters programs, a doctoral program and a post-doctoral program in the fields of accounting, business management, corporate finance, technological economics and management, and tourism management. Four professional graduate programs are in MBA, EMBA, M.P.Acc, and Logistics and Project Management.

The *Real* Boss!

第17章 管理学院

快讯！　首批 MPAcc 研究生在厦入学

"150 名财务、会计等相关行业从业者昨日走进高校课堂攻读硕士，这些由厦大和厦门国家会计学院联合培养的学生，是中国首批会计硕士专业学位（MPAcc）学员。国务院学位办和教育部在 150 多所申请高校中选取了 21 所作为首批试点院校，厦大是试点院校之一"

《厦门日报·双语周刊》2005 年 3 月 29 日

厦门大学管理学院在 2003 年排名位列第 3，这或许可以解释为什么会有那么多学生选择厦大管理学院。学院现有 230 名博士研究生，1860 名硕士研究生以及超过 1800 人的本科生，还有 17 个博士后。

管理学院由会计系、企业管理系、管理科学系、旅游管理系以及 MPAcc 教育中心、MBA 教育中心、EMBA 教育中心、物流管理与项目管理工程硕士教育中心组成。管理学院还包含四个研究所，分别为会计研究所、现代管理科学研究所、人力资源研究所和公司财务研究所。

管理学院目前在会计学、企业管理、财务管理、技术经济与管理、旅游管理等领域开设了 7 个本科专业，5 个教科类硕士学位授权点，1 个博士学位授权点，1 个博士后流动站以及 MBA、EMBA、MPAcc、物流管理与项目管理工程硕士等 4 个专业硕士学位授权点。

The large staff includes three of China's top authorities in accounting: Professors Xuying Yu, Shuipeng Wu, and Jiashu Ge. Professor Wu Shinong is Vice Chairman of the National Supervisory Committee for MBA Education.

Since the period of the Tenth Five-Year Plan, SM faculty members have published over 1100 academic papers and nearly 100 monographs, won over 30 research awards, and undertaken over 70 research projects at provincial, ministerial or national level. The School now has an in-place research fund of RMB 11 million.

SM has long-term collaborative relations with many overseas universities, including Cornell University and Washington University in the U.S., the University of Newcastle in the U.K., and St. Mary's University in Canada. Top scholars from home and abroad are adjunct professors at SM, and give lectures for both students and faculty.

Contact Information   Tel: 21-82873 Fax: 218-7289
Email: xdmba@jingxiang.xmu.edu.cn
Website: http://sm.xmu.edu.cn

Professor Ge Jiashu
Living Legend in China's Accounting

Professor Ge received his Bachelors of Commerce from XMU in July, 1945, and has been teaching and researching ever since. He has been the chief editor of six university-level social and science textbooks, four of which won first prize, and published over 130 articles in Accounting Research and other national journals, as well as two in international journals. Professor Ge's many awards include several by the Ministry of Education.

Professor Ge has passed a bright torch, mentoring 43 PhDs in economics and management, and one in post-doctoral research. His protégés include the first accounting PhD in China trained by Chinese, Taiwan Province's first PhDs in auditing and accounting, and China's first female PhD in accounting. (I wonder if she could help my wife balance our budget?)

第 17 章 管理学院

管理学院拥有一支高素质、优秀的师资队伍，包括中国会计学的三大专家：余绪缨教授、吴水澎教授、葛家澍教授。还有吴世农教授，他是全国工商管理硕士（MBA）教育指导委员会副主任。

自从第十个五年计划开始，管理学院的教师已经相继发表了 1100 多篇的学术论文，提出了近 100 项的专题，获得了 30 多项奖励，承担了 70 多个国家级、部级、省级的科研课题。学院现有立项的研究基金将近 1100 万元。

管理学院与海外的许多大学都有长期的合作联系，包括美国的康奈尔大学、华盛顿大学，英国的纽卡斯尔大学，加拿大的圣玛丽大学。学院拥有多名客座教授，来自多所国内外顶尖大学，经常给学院师生开讲座。

联系方式

电话：218-2873　传真：218-7289
电子邮件：xdmba@jingxiang.xmu.edu.cn
网址：http://sm.xmu.edu.cn

葛家澍教授——中国会计学的传奇人物

葛家澍教授 1945 年 7 月获厦门大学会计系商学学士学位，毕业后留校开始了教学与研究的生涯。他是 6 本大学用社科类教科书的主编，其中的 4 本教材获得一等奖。他在国内外会计学期刊发表了 130 多篇论文。葛教授获得了许多荣誉，包括教育部所授予的荣誉。

葛教授在教学上也取得了辉煌的成绩，他是一名杰出的教师，至今培养了 43 名博士，1 名博士后，并且创造了许多第一，包括：我国自己培养的第一位会计学博士、第一位审计方向博士、第一位我国台湾籍的会计学博士、第一位会计学女博士。

（我想知道他是否愿意帮我太太平衡我们家的预算？）

Ancient Tales of Business Conquest

(Adapted from "Amoy Magic"). Those who think Chinese are new at business better think again. These ancient tales prove otherwise!

Limited Partnership (Ming Dynasty Tale) Two brothers planted wheat together and at harvest time discussed how to share the yield. The older brother said, "I'll take the top half and you take the lower."
"But all the wheat's on the top!" said the younger brother.
"If you think it's unfair, next year I take the bottom half and you take the top!" The younger brother agreed, and the next year they planted potatoes.

If the Shoe Fits Share It (Ming Dynasty Tale) Two brothers saved enough money to buy one pair of shoes, which they shared. The older wore them from morning till night. The younger, to get his share of the benefit, waited till his elder brother went to bed, put on the shoes, and walked all over the countryside until dawn. When the shoes were worn out, the elder brother asked, "Want to buy another pair of shoes?"
"No, thanks. I need to get some sleep."
Moral: If someone says, "We're like brothers," hide your wallet!

Don't Wine① **About it** (Ming Dynasty Tale) Two men decided to make wine together. One said, "You supply the rice and I'll supply the water."
The second said, "If I provide all the rice, how do we divide the results?"
"I will be absolutely fair. When the wine is ready, we get back what we put in. I'll take the liquid and you keep the rest."

On "Caveat Emptor" (Buyer Beware)
Mosquito Amulet (Ming Dynasty Tale) A man bought an amulet to ward off mosquitoes but when it didn't work he returned to the vendor. The vendor said, "You have to use it in the proper place for it to work!"
"And where is that?"
"Under a mosquito net!"

---

① Wine about it: a play on 'whine' about it (whine = complain).

第17章 管理学院

古代商业故事

（摘自《魅力厦门》）

假如你认为中国人在生意场上是新手的话，那么请三思，因为下面这些古代故事可以证明事实正好相反。

明朝故事——有限合伙 两兄弟一起种小麦。到了收成的时候，他们讨论如何分配收益。

大哥说："我拿上面一半，下面的一半归你。"

弟弟说："可所有的麦穗全在上面！"

"好吧，如果你觉得这样做不公平，那明年我要底下部分，你拿上面的！"

弟弟表示同意。第二年，他们种的是马铃薯。

明朝故事——兄弟合穿一双鞋 两兄弟攒够钱买了一双鞋子轮流穿。大哥从早穿到晚，弟弟为了得到他应分享的好处，必须等到大哥上床睡觉，他才得以穿上鞋子，到乡间四处走，一直走到黎明。鞋子很快就穿破了。

大哥问道，"再买一双鞋子，如何？"

弟弟回答说，"不用了，谢谢。我想去睡觉。"

这两则故事的寓意是，假如有人对你说"我们亲如兄弟"，那么赶快把你的钱包藏好！

明朝故事——别发牢骚！ 两个人决定一起酿酒。一个说："你提供大米，我提供水。"

第二个说："我提供大米，那酒怎样分呢？"

"绝对公平。酒酿好后，我们取回各自投入的东西。我只拿回液体，其余的全都归你。"

（关于"货经售出，概不退换"）

明朝故事——驱蚊护身符 某人买了一个护身符来驱走蚊子，可是护身符不起作用。于是，他就回来找商家。

商家说："你必须把它用在合适的地方才能起作用！"

"什么地方？"

"蚊帐内！"

Chapter 18

MBA & EMBA Education Center

News Flash! XMU EMBA #4 on Popularity List
最受欢迎 EMBA 厦大排第四
"Xiamen University's EMBA (Executive Master of Business Administration) Program ranks 4th on the recently published list among China's top 10 EMBA programs of 2005..."
Common Talk, Xiamen Daily, Nov. 16, 2005

20 Years of MBA! [1]

It is no surprise that XMU has emphasized business education ever since its establishment in 1921. After all, our university's founder, Mr. Tan Kah Kee, the "Henry Ford of Asia," was himself a consummate businessman and entrepreneur. But over the decades our program has evolved from basic business education, finance, and economics into one of China's most strategic centers for modern business administration education.

Prof. Weng Junyi at HBS

Back in 1983, after agreements between the Chinese and Canadian governments and authorization by the Chinese Ministry of Education, XMU began cooperation with Canada's Dalhousie Univ. and St. Mary's Univ. and sent selected lecturers to study in Canada. But our actual MBA education started in 1986. From 1987 to 1991, in cooperation with Dalhousie and St. Mary's, our MBA Center recruited and educated more than 120 MBAs. In 1991, the National Commission of Degrees designated XMU as one of the first 9 universities and colleges to have (postgraduate) MBA students (XMU actually awarded the first MBA degree in China).

---

[1] This chapter written with the invaluable assistance of: 陈玲、吴慧芸、程林、李鸿艺、钟孟博、刘钢炳、庄慧颖

第18章 MBA 和 EMBA 教育中心

第18章
MBA 和 EMBA 教育中心

快讯！最受欢迎 EMBA 厦大排第四 "在最近公布的 2005 年中国最受欢迎的 EMBA 的十所院校中，厦大 EMBA 名列第四。"
《厦门日报·双语周刊》2005年11月16日

20年的MBA教育历史

厦门大学自 1921 年建校起就开始商学教育，并给予重视。毕竟，我们的校主——陈嘉庚先生，本身是一名成功的华侨商人及企业家，被誉为"亚洲的亨利·福特"。近十几年厦大的商学教育经历了从商学、财经和经济学到中国目前最完善的现代工商管理教育的转变。

在中国教育部的授权下，按照中国—加拿大两国政府签署的中—加管理教育交流协议，厦门大学在 1983 年与加拿大达尔豪西大学和圣玛丽大学建立了合作关系，选派了大量教师赴加拿大学习。而厦门大学的 MBA 教育实际上始于 1986 年。厦门大学 MBA 教育中心在 1987—1991 年期间，与加拿大达尔豪西大学和圣玛丽大学联合招收和培养了 120 多名 MBA。1991 年经国务院学位委员会和国家教委批生，厦门大学成为我国首批培养 MBA 研究生的 9 所院校之一（厦门大学是全国首批招收和培养 MBA 研究生的院校之一）。

> **Chen Guang**, Sino-Canada MBA 1990 Graduate   General Manager of Credit Lyonnais, Xiamen Branch
> "The best and most impressive part of the MBA program during my MBA time in XMU was its comprehensive management knowledge & training and the integrated English language environment."

As of this writing, over 1300 MBAs have graduated from the MBA Center and over 1700 students are now in the MBA program, which is one of China's most important bases for MBA education.

Outstanding Staff   MBA Center's staff of 23 full-time teachers, most of whom are Ph.D.s, including famous professors from universities in China and abroad, and top managers from outstanding Chinese and foreign companies. Many of the MBA teachers have long participated in municipal and provincial strategic planning, and have great administrative experience and knowledge as consultants or independent directors of famous companies.

The MBA Center provides quality courses and lectures by retaining many outstanding lecturers and entrepreneurs in special fields from home and abroad. The Center has close cooperative relationships with Dalhousie, St. Mary's and McGill universities in Canada, Cornell and Oregon Univ. in the U.S., Ulster Univ. in the UK, Singapore National Univ., and famous management colleges in Hong Kong SAR and Taiwan Province.

Long History, Wide Alumni Network.   80 years' of business education and 20 years' of MBA education have enabled XMU to accumulate rich experience and establish a wide network of alumni, with alumni associations and MBA unions in such cities as Beijing, Shanghai and Shenzhen. Our alumni are throughout the nation in such fields as banking, securities business, insurance, trade, IT, consulting and manufacturing.

International Cooperative Relationship   Our School of Management has international cooperative relationships with Dalhousie, Saint Mary's and McGill universities in Canada, Oregon Univ. in the U.S., Ulster Univ. in the U.K., Singapore National Univ., and famous management colleges in Hong Kong and Taiwan, etc.

第18章 MBA和EMBA教育中心

> **陈光**：1990年中一加MBA毕业，法国里昂信贷银行厦门分行行长。"我在厦门大学MBA项目就读期间最美好的和印象最深的回忆，是其全面的管理知识和训练体系，及与英文环境的完美结合。"

目前，厦门大学MBA教育中心已经培养MBA 1300多名，在读MBA学员1700多人，是我国MBA培养的重要基地之一。

杰出的团队 MBA教育中心的师资由中心专职教师、各大学知名教授、聘请的国外教授、知名企业高层管理者组成。中心拥有一批熟悉国内外MBA教育动态的高素质师资队伍，现有MBA专职教师23名，主要由留学归国的学者、外国专家组成，其中教授8人（包括教授生导师3人），副教授10人，绝大部分拥有博士学位。许多教师长期参与政府的经济发展战略规划，担任国内一些知名企业的管理顾问或独立董事，具有丰富的管理咨询经验。

为了保证提供优质的课程教育，MBA教育中心在国内外聘请了一批优秀的专业课教师和在实际部门工作的企业管理专家授课。MBA教育中心与国外著名商学院保持着密切联系及良好的合作关系，如加拿大的达尔豪西大学、圣玛丽大学、麦吉尔大学，美国的康奈尔大学、俄勒冈大学，英国的阿尔斯特大学，新加坡国立大学，以及香港、台湾地区的其他知名的商学院。

悠久的历史，宽广的校友网络 厦门大学拥有80年的商科教育、20年的MBA教育历史，积累了丰富的管理教育经验，形成宽广的校友网络，目前已在北京、上海、深圳等大城市成立了MBA校友会和MBA联合会，校友广泛分布于全国各地的银行、证券、保险、贸易、IT、咨询服务和制造业。

国际联系 厦门大学管理学院与加拿大的达尔豪西大学、圣玛丽大学、麦吉尔大学，美国的康奈尔大学、俄勒冈大学，英国的阿尔斯特大学，新加坡国立大学，以及香港、台湾地区的其他知名的商学院建立了良好的合作关系。

> **Zuo Min,** MBA 2000 Graduate   Director, Senior Vice-President and Chief Financial Officer of Fuyao Glass Industry Group Co., Ltd. Chairman of Postgraduates' Union of Xiamen University (1997-1999)
> "I guide my work with the knowledge, skills and ideas learned in my MBA courses and improve myself in practice, thus my team contributes to the ongoing prosperity of my company."

A Leader in Finance and Economics XMU leads the nation in finance and economics. About 1/3 of China's doctoral degrees in accounting come from XMU (our accounting is #1 in the nation). About 1/3 of our MBA alumni are engaged in finance and investment management. Hundreds of graduates have become the CFO of large enterprises, thus XMU's nickname of "CFO's Huangpu Military School".

Cultivate capability centered on management practice   Our MBA Center refined traditional MBA courses, introduced courses requiring strong practical skills, and developed professional competence training modules for managers and series of course modules to cultivate management practices. Xiamen University has established an MBA "management practice platform" through organizing challenging management contests among international enterprises, as well as with university students.

The Man with the Money!

"5 Cs for 1 L"   Twenty years of experience help us develop quality business leaders with international perspectives to cope with the great opportunities and challenges of unprecedented growth, accession to WTO, and internationalization. Our creative education model is called, "5 Cs for 1 L". This model emphasizes developing student's competitive capability, self-confidence, esprit de corps, creativity and creditability through class work, thesis writing and defense, and practical management experience. This unique educational model enables students to face the global challenges faced by business leaders in the 21st Century.

第18章 MBA和EMBA教育中心

左敏：MBA2000级毕业生，福耀玻璃股份有限公司董事/高级副总裁/CFO，厦门大学研究生联合会主席（1997—1999）。"我用MBA课程中学习到的知识、技能和观点来指导我的工作，并在实践中提升自我，这样我的整个团队都能为我所在的公司的持续繁荣贡献力量。"

财经学科优势突出 厦门大学拥有全国一流的财经学科群体，会计学名列全国第一。培养了全国近1/3的会计学博士，MBA校友中有将近1/3从事财务和投资管理类工作，近百名成为了大企业的财务总监，被誉为"CFO的黄埔军校"。

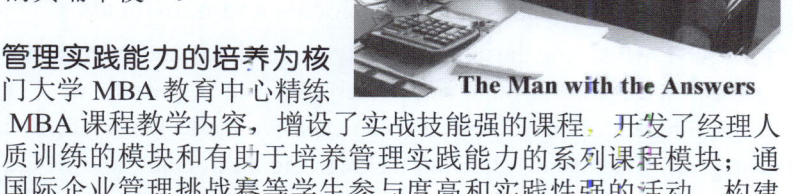

The Man with the Answers

以管理实践能力的培养为核心 厦门大学MBA教育中心精练了传统MBA课程教学内容，增设了实战技能强的课程，开发了经理人职业素质训练的模块和有助于培养管理实践能力的系列课程模块；通过组织国际企业管理挑战赛等学生参与度高和实践性强的活动，构建了MBA"管理实践能力平台"。

"5Cs +1L" 20年丰富的MBA教育经验帮助厦大MBA培养具备国际视野的商业领导，以应对全球化及加入WTO所带来的空前的机遇与挑战。厦大MBA教育创建了"5Cs+1L"的教育模式，即在课堂教学和论文撰写、答辩过程中始终贯穿培养学生的"竞争能力、自信心、合作精神、创造性、诚信"，使之通过管理实践，成长为能够迎接21世纪挑战的"企业领导者"，形成了颇具特色的教育风格。

The Man with no Answers and no Money!

> **Guo Zeli,** MBA '97 Graduate   General Manager of Xiamen Overseas Chinese Electronics Co., Ltd.   "Xiamen University's MBA program is the second stepping stone in my life."

State-of-the-Art Facilities   The 8000m^2 Center has over 1500 graduates and over 1100 undergraduates.   The modern, business-like environment includes advanced international standard teaching and research facilities, with case-study rooms, group-discussion rooms, role-playing classrooms, computer labs connected with internet, case-teaching research labs, a Dow-Jones global financial information system lab, accounting labs, a management process lab and a long-distance education lab.   (Read Lijin's view of our technological changes at the end of this chapter)

EMBA   The highly flexible Executive MBA (EMBA) program allows students to study either full-time or part-time in evening or weekend classes set up for locals and non-locals.

Our EMBA program targets highly professional and ethical senior management in large or medium-sized enterprises and organizations.   The 18-24 month program offers students a comprehensive mastery of modern enterprise management theory and decision making, and an in-depth knowledge of both domestic and foreign commercial enterprise.   EMBA students acquire the strategic and management skills and knowledge required for modern enterprises to participate in domestic and international economic, social and technical arenas.

EMBA faculty come from internationally acclaimed schools and universities such as Harvard Business School, University of Chicago, INSEAD, Singapore National University, etc, as well as famous management consulting companies and XMU.   The interactive teaching and learning style is augmented by highly qualified executives and alumni who are invited to share ideas with students.

Contact: Phone: 218-0968   Fax: 218-7907
E-mail: emba@xmu.edu.cn
Website: http://sm.xmu.edu.cn/emba

第18章 MBA 和 EMBA 教育中心

> 郭则理：MBA 1997级毕业生，厦华股份有限公司董事长
> "厦门大学 MBA 课程的学习是我人生的第二块基石。"

艺术的教育设施 中心现在是超过 1500 名毕业生及 1100 多名在学学员的家。8000 平方米的 MBA 教育中心拥有先进的营养设施，为 MBA 学生提供现代化、完善的、公司体验式的学习环境。设有符合国际标准的案例教学研究实验室、团队讨论室、情景模拟教室、计算机实验室、道.琼斯全球财经信息系统实验室、会计实验室、管理过程实验室和远程教学实验室。（请阅读本章末李劲描述的技术支持的变化！）

EMBA

"高级经理工商管理硕士"的英文缩写。学员每月利用一个周末集中四天学习（周五至次周一）。

EMBA 研究生教育项目旨在培养具有高度政治素养、责任心和职业道德的大中型企业的高层管理者。他们通过 18~24 个月系统的课程学习，全面掌握现代企业管理理论和决策方法，深入了解国内外企业的商业模式，具备在复杂的国内外经济、社会和技术环境下制定企业发展战略、进行企业日常经营管理决策、领导企业参与国内外竞争的能力和知识。

EMBA 的师资来自全球领先的学术机构，如哈佛商学院、法国 INSEAD、新加坡国立大学等，以及知名的管理咨询公司及厦门大学。为了强化实践知识的掌握，同时还安排有来自大型跨国公司的顾问、经理人和高层领导人及校友与学员分享商业智慧。

联系方式：
地址：厦门大学管理学院 EMBA 教育中心（361005）
电话：218-0968　传真：218-7907
电子邮件：emba@xmu.edu.cn
网址：http://sm.xmu.edu.cn/emba

Great Changes in Management College Technology
by Li Jin

Before 1998, the MBA Center had only six "286" desktop computers in a tiny office less than 20m². All teachers and teacher's secretaries had to share these six computers, so because of limited hard drive space, the computer always had notes stuck on it saying, "Please do not delete XX files..."

In 1999, the MBA Center moved in Jiageng Building #1. We now have a Synthesized Cable system with over 460 net ports and 100 mb/s access to the Campus Intranet. The Center has also established a Teleconferencing Education System and 2 MBA special case study rooms. Moreover, students have 110 computers in 3 computer labs. To ensure convenience in teaching and scientific research, each teacher has been assigned a notebook computer for their personal office.

In 2005, the MBA Center, School of Management renovated JiaGeng Building #2, which now has over 250 computers for students. The two buildings combined have over 1000 network ports, and wireless internet service to allow students with laptops to access online resources. School of Management also provides education internet and Telecom public internet connections and has many high performance web servers. The system offers web services, a IPVOD video system, a teaching and research arrangement system, and IBM's Workplace, which coordinates research teamwork. Other software includes ERP (Enterprise Resource Planning) software for teaching, such as SAP R3, SAP Business One, Yongyou, Jindie and Xinzhongda. There is also an LED multimedia display system and simultaneous interpretation system. All of the above provide both teachers and students with a modern, professional teaching, learning and office environment.

第18章 MBA 和 EMBA 教育中心

管理学院教学设备的巨变

李 劲

1998年前,厦门大学 MBA 教育中心有6台286台式计算机,机房设在一个不到20平方米的办公室内。所有的老师和教学秘书挤在一起共用这6台PC。由于硬盘太小,文件经常会被别人删除,大家经常要在桌上写张字条提醒别人:"请不要删除××目录的文件!"

1999年,MBA 中心入驻嘉庚一号楼,在嘉庚一号楼实施综合布线,为学生们提供460多个网络接口,100M 带宽的校园网交换到桌面。建设了远程教育主讲系统,建设了两个 MBA 专用案例室,拥有3间计算机实验室,110台学生用计算机。每位教师都有了自己的个人办公室并配备了笔记本电脑,方便地进行教学和科研活动。

2005年,MBA 中心所在的管理学院进行嘉庚二号楼改造项目,管理学院目前拥有250多台学生用计算机,学院拥有1000多个有线网络接口,并在嘉庚1号和2号教学大楼实施无线网络覆盖,方便学生使用笔记本电脑上网。学院为师生们提供教育网和电信公众网两种互联网出口,拥有多台高性能服务器,提供 WEB 服务、IPVOD 视频点播系统、教学科研管理系统和 IBM WORKPLACE 科研团队协作平台,拥有 SAP R3、SAP Business One、用友、金碟、新中大等多套大型 ERP 教学软件,还建设了 LED 多媒体显示系统和同声传译系统,为广大师生提供了现代化、公司化的教学办公环境。

XMU MBA in Alumni's Eyes

Huang Zirong, 1998~2000: Master of Business Administration (MBA), studied in XMU MBA Center
Present: Executive Director, Vice General Manager, Xiamen International Port Co., Ltd. General Manager, Senior Engineer, Xiamen Port (Group) Haitian Container Terminal Co., Ltd. Member of Academic Degrees Committee, MBA Center, school of Management, Xiamen University

Experiences in XMU Whenever I think of MBA life in XMU, what I most recall is how we classmates enthusiastically and intently discussed cases with each other after class in the hallways of Boxue and Nanqiang buildings.

My most unforgettable event during my time at XMU was probably the first time I lectured as a visiting professor to MBA senior students about Container Terminals. I was so excited to finally have the opportunity to stand on the platform to share my years' of management experience before an audience of MBA students, whom many call "God's favorite one" and "Management Elites". But even though I'd a great deal of material by myself and made a richly illustrated PPT, and even practiced it repeatedly to control the time, I was still so nervous because I was afraid that my lecture was not specific enough, and I was also afraid the audience would not be satisfied with the content I had prepared. I felt fearful, and trembled as if I were skating on very thin ice.

Over two years of study at XMU not only brought me the accumulation and improvement of knowledge but also gave me the platform to communicate with classmates of vastly different backgrounds and positions. Such communication can stimulate consistent innovation and timely collection of information. To date, some classmates have started up their own consulting company, and established a fast and convenient information network for all classmates to communicate with and learn from each other.

As a visiting professor in XMU, what impresses me most is my own deficiency of knowledge. When I prepare lessons, I often demand of myself that I acquire a great deal of knowledge. This arouses my desire for ever higher and newer knowledge and enables me to endeavor to continue to live and learn in the future.

第18章 MBA和EMBA教育中心

校友眼中的厦大MBA中心

黄子榕：1998年至2000年在厦门大学管理学院学习，并获MBA硕士学位，现为厦门国际港务股份有限公司执行董事、副总经理，兼厦门港务集团海天集装箱有限公司总经理、高级工程师，同时获聘为厦门大学MBA中心答辩委员会委员。

在厦大的经历

每当想起厦门大学MBA，想到最多的是当年在课间休息时，博学二和南强二教学楼的走道上同学们热烈的交流，和在案例分析时大家面红耳赤地辩论的情形。

在厦大期间，最难忘的应该是第一次作为客座教授给MBA中心即将毕业的同学作关于集装箱港口讲座时的兴奋与紧张的心情。兴奋的是自己终于能够有机会上台授课，介绍自己多年的管理经验，而且授课的对象是一群被誉为"天之骄子"和"管理精英"的MBA学生；紧张的是虽然课前自己收集材料并制作图文并茂的POWERPOINT，还进行模拟演讲，力求把握好时间，但还是既担心讲得不透彻，又担心授课内容无法满足同学的要求。当时的心情，真是如履薄冰，忐忑不安！

两年多的厦大MBA求学经历，给我带来的不仅仅是知识的积累和提高，更多的是从此有了一个与各种专业背景和各种岗位的同学之间相互交流的平台，这种交流所激发出来的是观念上的不断更新和信息的及时捕捉。目前，已有同学建立了自己的咨询公司，为同学们建立一个互通有无、相互学习、快速便捷的网络信息平台！

在厦大担任兼职教授，最大的体会是感到自己知识的不足，实际上在备课的过程中，往往也要求自己必须具备多方面知识。因此在授课的同时，也唤醒了自己对更高更新知识了解与掌握的渴望，让我在今后的工作历程中永葆学无止境之心境！

— 245 —

Qiu Xiaowen MBA Part-time professor   On Xiamen Division, State Administration of Foreign Exchange   Professor Qiu remembers XMU's MBA program for its flexible modular courses, knowledgeable teachers, and communication among different MBA students and teachers during case studies, which enabled each one to share their knowledge and experiences in their own areas of expertise.   Qiu thinks that all of these elements of his MBA courses enabled him to expand his vision in Economics and Management.

Professor Qiu's most unforgettable moments include obtaining his XMU MBA Degree in 1996, and gaining his senior engineer certificate. After that Qiu was hired by the People's Bank of China as a senior engineer and this began his new and rewarding management career.

Yang Jinchang, MBA   Vice General Manager of Fujian Shipping company, Advanced economist

1. When I looked back on my MBA studies at XMU, I remember my class mates proud, happy and confident expression when I gave the speech representing the whole class at commencement. I registered in the MBA Spring Class in 1997, which was XMU's first MBA Spring class. Most of my classmates were mid-level and high level managers from large and medium-size enterprises. We were all relatively older, and occupied with work. It was not easy for us to pass XMU's entrance examination, not to mention gaining a degree after three years of study. It was no wonder that our whole class was so proud.

2. During our study on campus, one teacher's family had great difficulty. I was monitor of the class, and everyone in the class was worried when I told them I had just learned that the teacher's spouse was seriously ill. Everyone in our class came forward to help the teacher with manpower or material resources. It was unforgettable for me. They offered many suggestions.   To avoid causing any trouble or embarrassment, we gave our help (money, etc.) to the teacher through the class committee. This would not only help the teacher with material resources but also give the teacher great comfort.

3. I received two things from my studies in XMU that I consider most valuable. One was the good teacher-student relations and the profound friendships between students. These are a legacy for life. The other was the learning, which gives us a great command of knowledge and of life.

4. As a part-time professor of XMU, I feel both constrained and driven. I feel constrained because I am not able to research related subjects as I am too busily engaged in daily work and social activities. But at the same time I feel driven because I learn so much from my part-time job, and so I force myself to learn even more.

第18章 MBA和EMBA教育中心

丘筱文：厦大 MBA 中心兼职教授。现任职国家外汇管理局厦门市分局

对厦门大学 MBA 的体会 灵活整合的模块课程设置和知识渊博的授课导师，案例教学中来自于不同学科、不同工作岗位的莘莘学子之间以及学生和导师之间的知识、经验的碰撞与整合，迅速开拓了他在经济和管理方面的视野。

最难忘的一件事 1996年硕士研究生毕业获得 MBA 学位、并获得了高级工程师资格同时被聘为中国人民银行的高级工程师专业职务，开始了丰富多彩的管理生涯。

杨锦昌：工商管理硕士、高级经济师，现任福建省厦门轮船总公司副总经理

1. 回忆起在厦大的 MBA 的学习经历，印象最深的是学位授予仪式上我作为代表发言的情景。当时在台上看到下面的同学们的表情充满了兴奋、自信和自豪。我是厦大 1997 级 MBA 春季班的学生，当时大部分同学是大、中型企业的中高层管理人员。他们年龄偏大，工作非常忙，能够通过联考被厦大录取已不容易，又经过 3 年的学习圆满完成了学业，难怪大家毕业时是那样自豪。

2. 还有一次，我当时作为班长，得知一位 MBA 老师的爱人得了重病，便将此事告诉大家。同学们听了都很着急，便出资出力帮助老师摆脱困境。当时的情形真是令人难忘啊，他们积极提出解决办法，又怕给老师添乱，便通过班委将捐款和暖人心的话语转给这位老师，这些都给这位老师帮上了很大的忙。

3. 厦大 MBA 的学习经历使我受益匪浅，而其中有两样东西最值得永久珍藏：一是那深厚的师生之情和同学之谊；二是掌握的相关知识，通过这些知识改进了理念、提高了境界。

4. 担任厦大 MBA 的兼职教授，最大的体会是压力和动力。由于平时忙于工作和应酬，很难较系统地研究相关学科知识，对这项兼职工作感到有压力。但正由于担当此任，迫使自己抽出时间来学习，从中获益。

Chapter 19

College of Foreign Languages and Cultures (CFLC)

News Flash! "Recently, the School of Foreign Languages and Literature, XMU, received the fund from EU-China Small Projects Facility Program.[①] Prof. Feng Shounong, Prof. Wu Jianping and several other professors from School of Foreign Languages and Literature had applied for the fund with the "EU and Fujian: 21st Century Cross-Cultural Identification and Interaction" project and received the €94,000 fund."

XMU Office of International Cooperation and Exchange (ICE)

One of XMU's oldest institutes, CFLC was founded in 1923 as a department and is now a college. CFLC consists of the Department of Japanese Language, Department of European Languages and Literatures, and the College English Department. Affiliates include the Research Institute of Foreign Languages and Literatures, the Research Center of Japanese Language Education, the Center for Bilingual Lexicography and Bilingual & Bicultural Studies, and 4 centers for foreign language testing and training.

The college offers bachelors, masters and a Ph.D. program, and with 20 foreign experts, CFLC is one of XMU's most active institutes in academic exchanges and international cooperation. CFLC has undergraduate and graduate exchange programs with universities in Britain, France, Japan, Russia and other countries, with part of the study completed at XMU and part abroad.

CFLC Contact Information   Tel: 218-6380
Email: cflc@xmu.edu.cn   Website: http//cflc.xmu.edu.cn

[①] EU-China Small Projects Facility Program is a cooperation and exchange program between China and the EU with the purpose of introducing EU culture and enhancing Sino-EU exchange.

第19章

外 文 学 院

> **快讯!** 近日,厦大外文学院收到了来自"欧盟—中国小项目便捷基金项目"[①]资助。据悉,外文学院的冯寿农,吴建平等多位教授申报的研究项目是"欧盟与福建:面向21世纪的跨文化认同与互君",此次资助基金达94000欧元。
>
> 厦门大学国际合作与交流处

厦大外文学院是厦门大学历史最悠久的院系之一,其前身是创立于1923年的外文系。目前外文学院由英语语言文学系、日语语言文学系、欧洲语言文学系和外语教学部组成,并设有外国语言文学研究所、日本语教育研究中心、双语词典与双语语言文化研究中心等研究单位以及4个各类外语考试、培训中心。

厦大外文学院可授予学士、硕士学位,并拥有一个博士点。常年聘请20多位外国专家,在对外学术交流与合作方面是厦大最为活跃的院系之一。与此同时,外文学院与英、法、日、俄等国的多所大学开展了本科、研究生的合作项目,学生可在厦大和国外共同完成学业。

联系方式:
电话: 2186380
电子信箱: cflc@xmu.edu.cn
网址: http://cflc.xmu.edu.cn

[①] 中国——欧盟小项目便捷式基金项目是欧盟与中国合作交流项目,旨在介绍欧盟文化,加强中欧交流。

XMU's Uncle Beard

My very first friend at XMU was the famous "Uncle Beard", Prof. Ji Yuhua of the English Department, and former Dean of the Foreign Language Department in the Tan Kah Kee College. On campus or even across China, Ji is better known as Uncle Beard or Grandpa Beard, as he has, under these names, written and published over 40 books (with tapes/VCDs). Eight of his books contained his 61 episode cartoon series The Three Little Pigs, which was broadcast on CCTV and dozens of local TV channels and well received by millions of Chinese children. Of course when I met him in September, 1988, he wasn't famous yet, but it seemed to me that if there were any justice in the world, Ji was destined for greatness, for I had never met a more dedicated teacher or student (what great teacher is not a great student as well?).

Ji's English was practically perfect, even though he met few foreigners and had never been abroad. Many Chinese lament, "I don't have an English environment," but Ji created his own environment. Whether studying, cooking, doing dishes, sweeping, or caring for his darling daughter Clara, he was either listening to English radio or cassettes or reciting.

Little Clara, not surprisingly, also spoke perfect English because Ji spoke to her only in English (figuring she'd pick up Chinese easily enough on her own).

Ji's experiences as a father and experiments with teaching English to children led him to develop his innovative "Sandwich Story Methodology" (SSM), which has been lauded by language experts throughout the world as a way to learn a second language without suffering the pains and miseries most of us experience learning a foreign tongue. They are certainly the most user-friendly foreign language texts I have ever read, and in 2002 China's Ministry of Education Audio-Visual Press listed SSM as one of the most famous English language teaching methods in China.

第19章 外文学院

厦门大学的"大胡子伯伯"

我在厦大的第一个朋友就是大名鼎鼎的"大胡子伯伯"。他叫纪玉华,是英文系的教授,原嘉庚学院外文系主任。在厦大,甚至在全国,人们更熟悉的是他的笔名:"大胡子伯伯"或"大胡子爷爷",他以这些笔名编写出版了40多种书(含音带/光碟),其中8种包含了创作的61集"三只小猪"卡通连续剧,该作品已在中央电视台和数十家地方电视台热播,深受中国儿童的喜爱。当然了,在1988年9月我刚认识他时,他还是个默默无闻的教书匠,但我当时就觉得,只要世上有公理,此人必成大业,因为我从未见过像他那样执著的老师(也可以说是学生吧,因为世上的名师都是身兼二职——同时又是孜孜不倦的学生)。

虽然他当时并未见过几个外国人,也从未出过国,但是他的英语却棒得不得了。许多中国人哀叹自己没有英语环境,而他却能自创环境,不管是散步、做饭、洗碗、扫地、还是照看女儿克拉拉,他不是在听英语广播或磁带,就是在背诵英语课文。所以他的女儿也顺理成章地说一口地道的英语(他的思路是:甭为女儿学汉语操心,她会自然而然轻松学会的)。

纪玉华做父亲的经验和他教儿童学英语的实验,让他发明了颇有创意的"三文治故事教学法",该方法已获得国内外语言教育专家的好评。它是一种专为那些想学外语但又不堪其苦的人而设计的方法。刚开始学外语时,我们大多数人都尝尽了苦头,而"三文治故事"则是我读到的最友好的外语课文。他的"三文治故事教学法"在2002年被教育部电化教育音像出版社列为中国当代著名英语教学法。

On Sept. 27, 2004, Ji shared on CCTV 9's 30 minute show, "Dialogue," how he developed SSM after experimenting with dozens of approaches for teaching English to Chinese children. SSM takes advantage of children's innate love for stories by sandwiching chunks of English words and sentences within Chinese. English words, phrases, and entire sentences are grasped naturally as the percentage of English content increases gradually. Consider the classic Three Little Pigs, which Ji renamed, "The three little pigs want to live independently." I enclose at the end of this chapter a reverse version broadcast on TV to help foreigners learn Chinese!

Though aimed primarily at children, SSM has been found to be ideal for adults as well, and Ji has given me many of his delightful children's books (perhaps thinking they're more my level than the college texts that other adults use). The 61 cartoons about 3 little Beijing pigs were narrated, recorded, and mixed with background music, all by Uncle Beard himself.

Apart from admiring his multi-talents, I also appreciate Ji's sense of humor about more adult topics. In a series of lectures in Willamette University (Oct.2004), University of Findlay, Rowan University and West Chester University (Jan-Mar., 2005) in the USA, he spoke on "Colors of Collars: Economic/educational reforms and business opportunities in China" and "Modes of Thinking and Intercultural Communication: Insights from Chinese Stories." I think we could use Uncle Beard in our MBA Center!

Ji has done more than any other person over my 18 years in China to help me understand not just China's language but her people and culture. He once performed a comic dialogue with me on campus, and in 1996 he traveled around the UK as a comedian entertaining Chinese students there. He even went so far as to translate some Peking opera pieces into English and then sang them to me!

Thank you, Uncle Beard, for 18 years of friendship.

第19章 外文学院

2004年9月27日CCTV9播出30分钟的"对话"节目，专访纪玉华，了解他通过对其他英语教学法进行多次实验后首创"三文治故事教学法"的过程。该方法充分利用儿童爱听故事的天性，把英语单词、词组和句子镶嵌在汉语故事中，把英语的比例逐步提高，直到孩子们能听懂完全用英语编写的故事。传统的三只小猪故事被他重新命名为"三只小猪要独立生活"。我将该故事的英文版，即电视上播出的翻版，附在本章后面，以帮助老外学习汉语之用。

虽然"三文治故事教学法"最初是为儿童设计的，现在发现它对成人学习外语也很有效。他送给我不少他编写的儿童书，设计精美，赏心悦目。（或许他觉得这些书比成年人所使用的大学课本更适合我的现有水平。）61集关于三只小猪的卡通剧，从朗读录音到背景音乐编排合成，都是大胡子伯伯一个人完成的。

除了钦佩他在儿童教育方面的多才多艺，我还特别欣赏他谈论有关成年人话题的幽默感。2004—2005年，他在美国的威拉姆特大学、芬德利大学、罗文大学和西彻斯特大学做了一系列的讲座，其中有《领子的颜色：谈中国的经济和教育改革与商机》和《思维方式与跨文化交际：中国故事中的启示》。我想，我们的MBA中心可以启用大胡子伯伯这样的人才。

在过去的18年中，纪玉华是对我学习中国语言和了解中国风俗及文化给予帮助最多的人。他曾经与我在校园同台表演过相声。1996年他在英国巡回演出，用他的相声给留英的中国学生带去欢笑。他甚至还将京剧选段译成英语唱给我听。

大胡子伯伯，谢谢你，为我们18年的友谊！

The Three Little Pigs Want to Live Independently

Long ago there was a *zhu ma ma* (momma pig). She had three *xiao zhu* (little pigs). The three *xiao zhu* were quite different in character. The first *xiao zhu* was very lazy and careless. He never did his job properly and was scared of working hard. The second *xiao zhu* was not as lazy as the first *xiaozhu*, but he certainly did not enjoy working hard. When he got tired, he hated doing his job properly. The third *xiao zhu* was never lazy. He was careful, hardworking and responsible.

One morning, the sun shone brightly in the blue sky. The three *xiao zhu* were having breakfast. The first *xiao zhu* said, "Living with *mama* (mommy) is nice except *wo* (I) have little freedom. *Ma ma* often asks *wo* (me) to clean the *fang zi* (house). Every time *wo* (I) clean the *fang zi* (house), *wo* get so tired. Oh, how *wo* wish to go out to live independently, without *ma ma* supervising *wo* (me)."

The second *xiao zhu* said, "Wo agree with you. Imagine how much more freedom we will enjoy if we go out to build our own *fang zi* and live independently." The third *xiao zhu* said, "*Ma ma* has been taking good care of us for so long and she is very tired. Now that we are big boys, we should go out to build our own *fang zi* and live independently." With that the three *xiao zhu* came to *zhu ma ma* and the first *xiao zhu* said, "Ma ma, wo am a big boy now. *Wo yao* (I want to) go out to build a *fang zi*. *Wo yao* (I want to) live independently." The second *xiao zhu* said, "*Ma ma, Wo* am a big boy now. *Wo yao* go out to build a *fang zi*. *Wo yao* live independently." The third *xiao zhu* said, "*Ma ma, wo* am a big boy now. *Wo yao* go out to build a *fang zi*. *Wo yao* live independently."

Zhu ma ma was very happy to hear that. She said, "My dears, you are big boys now. It's time you lived on your own, but be careful. There is a big wolf in the wood. He *yao* eat you. Make sure your *fang zi* are strong enough." The first *xiao zhu* said, "Don't worry, *ma ma*. We won't be caught by the big wolf."

Zhu ma ma said, "Do you know the big wolf has two younger brothers? They also *yao* eat you." The second *xiao zhu* said, "I know the big wolf has two younger brothers. *Wo* hear they are very silly. *Wo* am not afraid of them." The third *xiao zhu* said, "Don't worry, *ma ma*. We will sure live a peaceful independent life. Bye-bye, *ma ma*." *Zhu ma ma* said, "Bye-bye. Come back to see your *ma ma* often, OK?"

So, the three *xiao zhu* left their *fang zi*. They *yao* go out to build their own *fang zi* and live independently.

第19章 外文学院

三只小猪渴望独立生活

从前,有一只 Mummy Pig,她养了三只 little pigs。这三只 little pigs 性格都不一样:第一只 little pig 非常懒惰,做事不认真,什么事儿只要能偷懒就偷懒,能省事儿就省事儿,他呀,就怕累着自己。第二只 little pig 做事还算认真,一般不敢偷懒,但有时他也怕吃苦,累了的时候,他也是能省事儿就省事儿。第三只 little pig 做事最认真,最能吃苦,从不偷懒。

一天早上,外面风和日丽,晴空万里。三只 little pigs 边吃早饭边聊天。第一只 little pig 说:"跟 Mummy 住在一起好是好,就是不太自由。Mummy 经常让我们打扫 house,每次打扫 house 我都累得腰酸背痛。嗨,要是能出去独立生活,没有 Mummy 管着该有多好啊。"

第二只 little pig 说:"是啊,I 同意你的看法。要是出去自己盖一座 house,独立生活该有多自由啊。"第三只 little pig 说:"Mummy 照顾我们弟兄三个,日夜操劳,实在太辛苦了。如今我们都长大了,该出去自己盖一座 house,独立生活,自己照顾自己。"说完,三只 little pigs 就来到 Mummy Pig 跟前,第一只 little pig 说:"Mummy,我现在长大了,I want to 出去盖一座 house, I want to 独立生活。"第二只 little pig 说:"Mummy,我现在长大了,I want to 出去盖一座 house, I want to 独立生活。"第三只 little pig 说:"Mummy,我现在长大了,I want to 出去盖一座 house, I want to 独立生活。"

Mummy Pig 听到这话高兴极了,她说:"孩子们,你们的确长大了,是该出去独立生活了。盖 house 可要盖结实点儿,树林里有一只大灰狼,他做梦都 want to 吃掉你们,你们可要多加小心哪。"第一只 little pig 说:"Mummy,您放心吧,我们不会让大灰狼抓住的。"

Mummy Pig 接着说:"你们知道吗?大灰狼还有两个弟弟,他们也同样 want to 吃掉你们。"第二只 little pig 说:"我知道大灰狼有两个弟弟,I 听说他们都很愚蠢,I 才不怕他们呢!"第三只 little pig 接着说:"Mummy,您就别操心了,我们一定会平平安安地独立生活的。Bye-bye, Mummy。"Mummy Pig 赶紧说:"Bye-bye,有空常回来看看 Mummy。"

就这样,三只 little pigs 离开了他们熟悉的 house,他们 want to 出去自己盖 house,过独立的生活。

SFLC 80th Anniversary Address
by Joseph Bosco (visiting Professor) April 5, 2003

It is with great pride and great humility that I stand before you today, both proud and profoundly humble to be a small part of this great department, and this great university....We are gathered here today to celebrate the 80th anniversary of the College of Foreign Languages and Cultures of XMU. 80 years—in the expanse of Chinese history those 4 score years are but rain drops in the river of time. But what an incredible 8 decades they were. They encompassed nothing short of a latter day miracle: The magnitude of the dramatic turnaround of China has no equal in the history of modern statehood. I and my wife are often asked: "Why did you come to China?" We have one consistent answer: "We believe that China will define, and uniquely influence the 21st Century as she assumes her rightful place in the vanguard of the world's greatest nations. We want to be a small part of that process, to witness it, perhaps even to chronicle it."

...Now, on a more personal note, I must tell you of my students. Never in my long career as a journalist, author and teacher, have I known brighter, more motivated, more diligent young people than my students here at XMU. It is with a sense of joy and wonder that I enter my classrooms every day—joy and humble wonder that I am fortunate enough, honored enough, to be allowed to teach them what little I know about a language and a culture that I love so deeply, and am actually paid to share. I must also say something about the kindness of these same young people. From the first moment I entered a classroom last August, I was warmly welcomed and respected—without qualification, without conditions, even though they knew how much I had to learn about how to teach them. In truth, of these eight months I can say that my students have taught me more than I have taught them. But soon I learned that wasn't unique to my students, or even XMU, it was the same with the Xiamenese people...Now, as a representative of my colleagues, the other Foreign Language professors, I wish to express our sincere gratitude to XMU, the College of Foreign Languages and Cultures, and particularly to Vice President Deng Li Ping, Dean of the college, Lian Shu Neng, and Dean of the college and dean of the English Department, Yang Xinzhang. Thank you; and congratulations on *our* 80th anniversary".

第19章 外文学院

厦大外文学院（原外文系）成立80周年庆典上的讲话

约瑟夫·鲍斯科

（厦门大学外文学院客座教授）

2003年4月5日

今天，我满怀自豪和谦恭站在你们面前。作为这个出色的学院以及这所伟大学府的渺小一员，我感到了自身的微不足道，同时又感到无比骄傲……我们相聚在此共同庆祝厦门大学外文学院八十华诞。过去这80载，也许只是古老中国悠久历史长河中的浪花一束，但却是令人惊叹和难以置信的80载，它见证了一个当代奇迹的诞生：中国社会的巨变在现代国家的历史上是前所未有的。有人问我和我的妻子："你们为什么来到中国？"我们的答案始终如一："因为我们坚信：中国将会对整个21世纪产生不可替代的决定性的影响，因为中国找到了其正确的位置，并将逐渐成长为走在世界前列的强国。我们要成为这一进程的参与者、见证者，甚至记录者。

从个人来说，接下来我得谈一下我的学生。在漫长的职业生涯中，我先后做过记者、作家、老师，但厦大的学生是我所遇到的最聪明、最积极进取、最勤奋的年轻人。我每天满怀欣喜地走进课堂，欣喜并惊叹自己是如此幸运、又如此荣幸有这个机会与他们分享我所钟爱的语言和西方文化，而获此殊荣之外，居然还被给予物质报酬。与此同时，他们的友好善良也给我留下深刻的印象，去年八月，我第一次踏进教室，就受到了热烈的欢迎，而当时我还缺乏教学经验，也没有任何背景，而且他们也知道我的教学技能还有很多要改进的地方。事实上，这八个月以来，我从他们身上学到的远比我所教给他们的多得多。不过，不久后我就发现，不只是我的学生，也不只是厦大，厦门这个城市的人们也都是如此……今天，我谨代表所有外教，向厦门大学，向外文学院，向邓力平副校长、连淑能院长和英文系杨信彰主任，表示我们衷心的感谢，并为学院的80岁生日送上我们最诚挚的祝福！

Chapter 20

Research Center for Higher Education Development

You can't get any higher in higher education research than XMU because it started here! China's very first Research Center for Higher Education Development (RCHED), was founded here in May 1978 by the Father of Higher Education Research, our own Professor Pan Maoyuan (a 1945 graduate of XMU).

Our RCHED was the first authorized to grant Masters (1981) and PhDs in higher education (1986), and Pan Maoyuan was China's first tutor for this doctorate. The RCHED was also first in China to produce monographs on higher education research.

In 1988, China designated RCHED as a unique national key unit in the key discipline of Higher Education Research. In 2000, the RCHED was designated a key liberal arts research base. Thanks to Pan's pioneering efforts, China now has over 700 institutes of higher education science, and it is China's only national key discipline on higher education science under the "211 Project." Prof. Liu Haifeng directs the independent RCHED, which has 3 Divisions:

Research Division of Higher Education Theory and Policy
Research Division of Curriculum and Pedagogy in Higher Education Institutions
Division of Higher Education Testing Research

Professor Brian Tam (U.S. U.K.)

第20章
高等教育发展研究中心

要想在高等教育研究领域取得"高等"的成就，就请来厦门大学吧。因为这里，正是高等教育研究的发源地。中国高等教育研究之父——潘懋元教授（1945年毕业于厦大）于1978年5月在厦大创立了厦门大学高等教育发展研究中心，始开中国高等教育研究之先河。

高教中心在1981年第一个被批准授予高等教育硕士学位，随后又在1986年第一个被批准授予高等教育博士学位，同时也是中国第一个出版高等教育研究专著的机构，潘懋元教授是中国第一位高等教育博士生导师。

1988年，国家确定厦门大学高等教育发展研究中心为高等教育研究领域的唯一国家级重点单位。2000年，高等教育发展研究中心被批准为教育部人文社科重点研究基地之一。由于潘懋元教授富有开创性的不懈努力，如今中国已有超过700家高等教育研究机构，并且高等教育研究还成为中国"211工程"中唯一一个高等教育科学的国家级重点学科。

刘海峰教授现任厦大教育研究院院长。作为一个独立研究机构，高教中心下设三个部门：

高等教育理论和改革研究部
高校课程设置和教学法研究部
高等教育测试研究部

The RCHED Reference Room has over 10,000 books in Chinese, over 5,000 foreign language books, about 800 different journals and newspapers in Chinese, and dozens of different journals and newspapers in foreign languages. RCHED also produces 3 of its own journals:
"*Higher Education Journal*" (quarterly electronic edition)
"*Higher Education*" (jointly with People's University Information Center
"*Research on International Higher Education*"

RCHED has hosted numerous academic conferences, including:

"Inaugural Meeting of Chinese Higher Education Research Committee and the First Academic Seminar"
"First Comparative Higher Education Seminar in China"
"First Conference on History of Higher Education"
"Conference on Taiwan Higher Education"
"Conference on the Discipline Development of Higher Education"
"Conference on Developing College Students' Abilities"
"Conference on Counseling Psychology"
"National conference on Postgraduates Work of Higher Education"
"Conference on Private Higher Education in Asia and Pacific Area"
"Conference on Sino-US Higher Educational Financing"
"Conference on University Education across the Taiwan Straits"
"National Conference of Presidents from Non-government-run Universities"
"Equity & Efficiency: International Conference on Higher Education in the 21st Century"

Pan Maoyuan—Father of China's Higher Education Research

On August 4th, 1920, a year before Tan Kah Kee created XMU, China's Father of Higher Education Research was born into a family of almost no education. Pan Maoyuan's father had attended primary school, and his mother had no education, but they believed education and culture was the key to escaping poverty. Pan's father made rice cakes and sold them in the street to finance their sons' education, and Pan's older brother grew up to become a primary school teacher and even published a book of poems. Though he died at only 21, he deeply influenced his little brother Maoyuan. Maoyuan was an avid reader and often set aside the pittance his father gave him for lunch to buy books.

第20章 高等教育发展研究中心

高教中心资料室拥有 10000 多册中文图书，5000 余册外文图书，800 种中文报纸期刊以及几十种外文报纸期刊。并拥有三种自己的期刊：

《高等教育期刊》（基地电子版季刊）
《高等教育》（人大复印报刊资料）
《国际高等教育研究》

曾举办的学术会议包括："中国高等教育研究会成立大会暨首届学术研讨会"，"首届中国比较高等教育研讨会"，"首届高等教育史会议"，"台湾高等教育会议"，"高等教育学科发展学术讨论会"，"大学生能力培养讨论会"，"咨询心理学术研讨会"，"全国高等教育研究生工作会议"，"亚太地区私立高等教育研讨会"，"中美高等教育财政研讨会"，"海峡两岸大学教育会议"，"国家民办高校校长论坛"以及"公平与效率：21世纪高等教育国际学术研讨会"。

潘懋元——中国高等教育研究之父

1920年8月4日，也就是陈嘉庚先生创办厦门大学的前一年，中国高等教育研究之父——潘懋元出生在一个几乎毫无教育背景的家庭。潘懋元的父亲仅念过小学，母亲没有上过一天学。但没有文化的父母都深知：教育和文化是改变贫穷的唯一出路。父亲靠在街上卖米糕来供自己的几个儿子上学；而潘懋元的哥哥，长大后成了一所小学的老师，甚至还出了一本诗集。尽管这位哥哥在21岁的时候就去世了，可他却深深地影响了幼年的潘懋元。潘懋元从小就是一个如饥似渴热爱读书的人，常常将父亲给他买午饭的零钱省下来去买书。

1945: Pan Maoyuan
B.E. from Changting XMU

Pan's father had no money for him to go beyond primary school, but one of his short stories so impressed the headmaster of the secondary school where his brother taught that he was allowed to attend school for half the fee. His short story was published in a newspaper, which helped supplement the small amount his father could pay. When he was 12 published a story in the *Shantou People's Daily*, but many of his stories were rejected, which was hard for him to take.

Pan's high school headmaster was strict but caring. He told Pan that children from rich families did not have to worry about grades because they could go into the family business, but poor students had to work hard.

When Pan was 15 his older brother took ill so he returned to his hometown to care for him and began his teaching career with a post in the primary school. He worked hard at his job, spending much time on preparation, but after 15 minutes of teaching he'd said all he had to say and didn't know what to do next. Students threw things when his back was turned, and that's when it dawned upon him that there must be a more practical methodology for teaching!

Pan entered school again and supported himself by teaching in an evening school and writing short stories, but the Japanese invaded Shantou in 1937 and Pan moved inland to teach, do propaganda work, and train civilians to resist the Japanese. During those years the Kuomintang and the Communist propaganda cooperated, but as the KMT became more corrupt Pan engaged in propaganda against them, and was warned to flee for his own safety.

XMU had just moved to Changting, which was relatively close, so Pan and his friends walked for a week to get there for exams. Unfortunately, Pan disliked math, knew little about sciences, and failed the entrance exam. Fortunately, just at that time Fujian province started a two-year teacher training program that provided, free of charge, everything from tuition and room and board to meals and clothes. Pan entered, and while there he reviewed textbooks, and in 1941 again took the XMU entrance exam, and this time succeeded.

During his second year Pan started teaching part time in primary school and high school, and in his fourth year became the director of education administration in a local high school. He tried to link university theory with practice, but the theories were mainly from America, and did not fit the Chinese situation.

第20章 高等教育发展研究中心

到了念中学的时候，父亲已经没有钱继续供他读书。但是他写的一篇小故事却深深地打动了哥哥曾经执教的那所中学的校长。这位校长看中潘懋元的才气，免了他一半的学费，使他得以继续完成学业。这篇小故事后来在报纸上发表了，他将所得的稿费和他父亲给的一点零钱凑在一起，交了中学的学费。在12岁那年，《汕头人民日报》也发表了他写的一篇小故事。但是其他很多作品却被退了回来，这让他感到难以接受。

潘懋元的高中老师是一个既严厉又慈爱的人。他说，富家的孩子不用担心自己的学习成绩，因为他们的家里都是做生意的，不用念书，也能找到事做；但穷人家的孩子为了生存，却必须加倍努力。

在潘懋元15岁那年，他的哥哥生了重病，所以他不得不回到家乡来照料哥哥，同时也在家乡的小学谋得了一份教职。他工作相当努力，花了大量时间备课，但准备的内容15分钟就讲完了。不知道接下来该干嘛。他转过去写板书时，孩子们就朝他扔东西。正是在那个时候，他想到：一定要有更为切实可行教学方法！

潘懋元再一次回到了学校继续学习，并靠在夜校教书和写短篇小说来支持自己的学业。1937年日本侵略汕头，他转移到了内地继续执教，开展宣传工作，同时训练平民以抵抗日本的入侵。那一时期国民党和共产党建立了统一战线，但随着国民党越来越腐败，潘懋元开始转向了反对国民党的宣传活动，这就使得他不得不为了自己的安全再次转移。

厦门大学那时已暂时把校址迁移到了距离潘懋元所在地很近的长汀。于是他和朋友一起步行了一周去那里参加考试。可惜，由于不喜欢数学，理科方面知识欠缺，他没能通过入学考试。此时，福建省启动了一个两年的教师培训计划，并且学费食宿全免。他参加了这个培训计划，并开始全面复习，在1941年再次参加厦门大学入学考试，获得成功。

大学二年级，潘懋元开始在小学和高中兼职教学；大四的时候他已经成为当地一所高中的教务长。他尝试将在大学里学到的理论和实际结合起来，但这些理论多来自于美国，并不适用于中国的具体情况。

In 1945, Pan graduated from XMU, which returned to Xiamen in 1946. Xiamen was the KMT's last hold on the mainland before it fled to Taiwan on October 17th, leaving behind a force on Jinmen. But Mao saw the KMT occupation of Jinmen as a military advantage because it would deplete their military strength. Indeed, American intelligence thought the same, and urged Chiang Kai Shek to abandon Jinmen. That the Communists could have easily retaken Jinmen is obvious from their experience with Hainan Island, from which they easily drove KMT occupation forces. [Happily, Jinmen is now a part of Xiamen for all practical purposes. We have daily ferries between the two islands, and one in 17 Jinmen families has an apartment in Xiamen!]

When XMU's Department of Education moved to Fuzhou, Pan was supposed to go with it, but he stayed behind—fortunately for us and the rest of China. Pan had to abandon his research of Chinese education history, but this redirected him towards researching education itself. Pan was not only an education researcher but also a university administrator, so he quite naturally focused on researching higher education. Shouldering both administrative and teaching duties was a burden, but this experience helped him formulate his pioneering philosophy of higher education.

In 1978, while vice president of XMU, Pan created the Institute of Higher Education Research, which focused on resolving concrete problems. In 1984, Pan edited "Higher Education," which sold over 50,000 copies and was made compulsory reading for teacher trainees. Deng Xiaoping's promotion of science and education as forces for economic development were part of his philosophy behind the Four Modernizations. Of these four, science and technology were key. Deng emphasized setting up key universities to develop talent, encourage more students to study abroad to promote internationalization and introduce more talent from abroad, and increase the number of university students. The RCHED has of course played a strategic role in putting Deng's theories into practice.

2003: Visiting Professor, Wanli College, Zhejiang Province

In Norway, on November 30, 2005, the publication ceremony was held for the English version of "Pan Maoyuan—a Founding Father of Chinese Higher Education Research," written by Arild Tjeldvoll and published by the Norwegian University of Science and Technology.

第20章 高等教育发展研究中心

潘懋元 1945 年从厦大毕业。厦大也在 1946 年将校址迁回厦门。厦门是国民党在大陆的最后一个据点。国民党于 10 月 17 日逃往台湾，在金门留下了残余武装。 毛泽东认为国民党对金门的武装占领对共产党来说其实是一个军事优势，因为这样可以将敌方的军事力量消耗殆尽。 事实上，美国情报方面也是这样认为的，于是敦促蒋介石尽快放弃金门。 因为据以往的经验来看，共产党曾经成功地将国民党从海南岛赶了出去，那么就有可能再次不费吹灰之力地将其驱逐出金门。 （很高兴看到的是，现在金门实际上已经成为厦门的一部分。每天都有渡轮往返于两岸，在金门，17 个家庭中就有 1 个在厦门拥有房产。）

厦门大学教育系在五十年代初搬到了福州，潘懋元本来也应该一同前去的，但他却留了下来——这不能不说对我们乃至整个中国都是一件值得庆幸的事。他将研究兴趣从中国教育史逐渐转向教育实践。并且由于在大学行政制度方面也做了许多研究工作，他的研究课题很自然地就转到了高等教育研究方面。 行政和教学这两个担子同时落在了他的肩上。但这一段经历却极大地帮助潘懋元逐渐形成对于高等教育问题的前卫理解。

1978 年，作为厦门大学当时的副校长，潘懋元创立了高等教育研究所，其主旨在于解决教学中遇到的实际问题。1984 年，潘懋元教授的著作《高等教育》国内第一本高等教育专著和教材。这一著作销量超过 50000 本，已成为教师培训的必读书。 中国改革开放的总设计师邓小平极力倡导科教兴国。在四个现代化当中，科技是关键。 邓小平强调建立一流大学来培养优秀人才，鼓励更多的学生出国留学以促进国际化，引进更多的国外人才，增加大学生人数等等。 在将他的理论付诸实践方面，高等教育发展研究中心无疑发挥了关键性的作用。

2005 年 11 月 30 日，在挪威举行了《潘懋元——位中国高等教育研究的创始人》（英文版）一书的首发式，这本书的作者是阿里·谢沃，由挪威科技大学出版。

Chapter 21

School of Math Sciences

Beautiful Minds An Oscar-winning movie depicted Nobel Laureate John Nash as a "beautiful mind", but XMU's School of Mathematical Sciences (SMS), founded in 1923, has had more than its share of beautiful minds, including the world-renowned Chen Jingrun, Lin Qun and Xie Xide (all introduced at the end of this chapter).

SMS offers undergrad and grad programs in pure and applied mathematics, computational mathematics, probability and mathematical statistics, and operations research and control sciences.

SMS' advanced facilities include a computational science laboratory with state-of-the-art SGI Octane work stations and hundreds of PCs available to "all faculty members and graduate students" (so do undergrads still use pencil and paper?).

The Institute of Mathematics publishes *"The Journal of Mathematical Studies,"* and members regularly participate in domestic and international conferences—though I've not the slightest idea what those conferences are about. Zhang Fuji, for instance, wrote about *"K-resonance of open-end carbon nanotubes"* and *"regular hexagonal tessellation of a cylinder."* Was that in Chinese, English or what?

Contact Information
School of Mathematical Sciences
Tel: (592)258-0777 (592)258-0668
Fax: (592)218-3209
Email: mathky@xmu.edu.cn

第21章

数学科学学院

荣获奥斯卡奖的影片《美丽心灵》讲述了诺贝尔奖获得者约翰·福布斯·纳什的故事,但厦门大学建于1922年的数学科学学院拥有更多的"美丽心灵",包括举世闻名的陈景润、林群和射希德(本章将介绍这三位)。

学院为本科生和研究生开设了基础数学、应用数学、计算数学、概率和数理统计、运筹学等多个专业。

学院拥有先进的教学设施,包括 SGI Octane 图形工作站和几百台电脑,可供学院的所有教员和研究生使用(这么说,本科生还在用笔和纸计算吗?)

数学研究所还出版了学术期刊《数学研究》,其成员定期参加国内和国际研讨会——尽管我一点都不懂这些研讨会究竟在研究什么。比如,张福基发表了《K-resonance of open-end carbon nanotubes》和《Regular hexagonal tessellation of a cylinder》。这是中文?英文?还是什么?

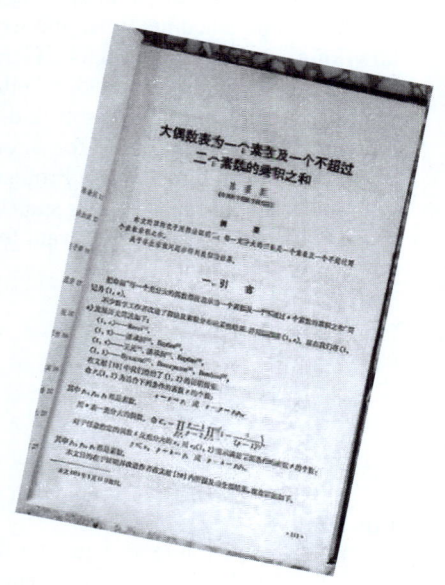

联系方式

电话:258-0777 258-0668

传真:218-3209

电子邮箱:mathky@xmu.edu.cn

SMS's Beautiful Minds

Chen Jingrun   One of the most popular books of the 1980s was the Goldbach Conjecture① about the life of XMU mathematician Chen Jingrun (陈景润). A 1953 graduate of XMU and researcher at the Chinese Academy of Science's Institute of Mathematics, Chen was the planet's leading mathematician in the study of the Goldbach Conjecture"哥德巴赫猜想"中的(1+2), and his conclusions are now called Chen's Theorem (陈氏定理). But though Chen was a wiz at solving math, he was not so hot at teaching it.

Chen became a middle school math teacher after graduating from college, but a year later XMU's president rescued him (and Chen's students) by making him an XMU teaching assistant and putting him over the teacher's reading room, where he could pursue research in peace and quiet.

Chen lived in Qinyezhai Room 106, a tiny $7m^2$ room, where he worked day and night. One night the guards saw a tiny gleam of light in one window of an otherwise darkened building. They were suspicious because a teacher would have turned the light on, but when they knocked on the door, a befuddled Chen, rudely roused from his world of math, answered the door. He had made a large black cloth cover for his lamp and buried his head beneath it so he could work late into the night without disturbing others—or being disturbed.

Chen cherished his time, and would often refuse to open the door no matter how long visitors banged upon it. He disbound his books so he would always have portions on hand to read, whether he was walking about campus or hiding in an air shelter during a bomb raid. Yet in spite of his fixation with math, he must have found some time for a social life, because I read that a Chinese student's father told him, "When Professor Chen was in his 40s he could still land a wife in her 20s because he was such a famous mathematician."

It just proves that if you want to "be fruitful and multiply"② you should become a mathematician.

---

① On June 7th, 1742, Goldbach proposed to mathematician Euler the following hypothesis:
  (a) Every even integer n greater than two is the sum of two primes.
② Be fruitful and "multiply": have children, Genesis 1:28

第 21 章 数学科学学院

数学科学学院的"美丽心灵"

陈景润 1978 年徐迟的著名报告文学《哥德巴赫猜想》介绍了杰出的数学家陈景润。①。陈景润于 1953 年毕业于厦门大学数学系,后调到中科院数学研究所。他在对"哥德巴赫猜想"的研究上取得了辉煌的成就,他的结论被称为"陈氏定理"。陈景润虽然在数学研究方面是个天才,但在教学方面却不是块"料"。

从厦大毕业以后,陈景润被分配到一所中学教书。一年之后,厦大当时的校长王亚南"解救"了他(恐怕也解救了他的学生吧),把他安排回到数学系当助教,负责管理系里的教师阅览室,也让他有个比较安静的环境作研究。

陈景润当时住在"勤业斋"106 室,这是一个 7 平方米的小房间,他在那里夜以继日地工作。一天深夜,巡逻的人看到一个窗子透出微弱的灯光。便觉得纳闷儿,如果是老师在开夜车,为什么不把灯开亮?于是他们去敲门,陈景润从他的数学世界中被吵醒,满脸疑惑地开了门。原来,他为了深夜工作,做了一个很大的黑灯罩,把灯光遮起来,埋头在里面工作,这样就不会打扰别人——也不会被人打扰了。

陈景润惜时如命,专心致力于研究工作,经常让访客吃"闭门羹"。他经常把书撕成一页一页带在身上,这样就可以随时随地读书,无论是走在校园里,还是空袭时躲在防空洞里。尽管陈景润如此痴迷于数学,但他肯定还是为社交安排了一些时间,因为一本书中说一个学生的父亲告诉他:"陈景润 40 多岁的时候,仍然娶到了 20 多岁的媳妇。"

---

① 公元 1742 年 6 月 7 日哥德巴赫(Goldbach)写信给当时的大数学家欧拉(Euler),提出了以下的猜想:
(a) 任何一个 ≥6 之偶数,都可以表示成两个奇质数之和。

In 1956 it was lights out every night at 10:00 PM—except in the toilet. So every night at 10 PM, like clockwork, Chen showed up with pen and paper, and all hours of the night people found him seated on the floor, back to the wall, calculating away. In the morning, when everyone else headed for breakfast, Chen headed back to his room for another day's work.

In the 1960s, another illustrious XMU mathematician, Dr. Lin Qun (introduced later in this chapter) asked Chen Jingrun how he could sleep so little and have so much energy when Dr. Lin himself suffered from insomnia. Dr. Chen thought carefully, and replied, "Insomnia means you don't need to sleep, so you should get up and work."

In the 1980s the two mathematicians shared a Xiamen hotel room and when Dr. Chen went to bed at 11:00 PM, Dr. Lin thought Dr. Chen was finally taking better care of his health. But at 2 AM Chen whispered, "Is it okay with you if I turn on the lights now and get some work done?"

Chen's lifestyle did take a toll on his health. After every marathon bout with a math problem he ended up in a hospital But as soon as he was discharged he went at it again, round the clock and year-round. In winter, when the ink in his pen froze, he grabbed a pencil, bundled up in every stitch of clothing that he owned, huddled close to a 100 watt light bulb for warmth, and pressed on with his work.

Since he never left his room except to eat or drink water people were naturally curious about what was inside his inner sanctum. Years later they found it had nothing but a wooden bed, a small desk, dozens of pill bottles, and bags full of the sheets of paper on which Chen did his calculations.

Chen had a philosophy similar to Edison, who said, "Genius is 99% perspiration and 1% inspiration." Chen said, "There's no secret to math; it's just like climbing a mountain. Ten paths may reach the peak but most people try only one or two, fail, and quit. But I try every path until I find the one that reaches the peak."

Chen reached the first of many peaks when he sent a math paper to the preeminent mathematician Hua Luogeng. On Hua's recommendation Chen was transferred to the Chinese Academy of Science's (CAS) Mathematics Research Institute in 1957, but he appears to have remained humble in spite of his celebrated successes. When he attended XMU's 60th birthday in April, 1981, he took the "hard sleeper" even though he didn't have to pay for the ticket himself. When asked why, he said, "China is still not wealthy and soft sleepers are expensive."

第21章 数学科学学院

1956年，陈景润住的房间规定每晚10点熄灯——厕所除外。所以一到每天晚上10点钟，陈景润都会出现在楼道公共厕所，背靠墙壁，席地而坐，手拿一张纸、一支笔，接着卫生间的灯光算题，整夜，去卫生间的人们都会看到他。直到天光大亮，楼道里所有人都起床吃早饭了，陈景润才摇摇晃晃地走回到自己房间，继续工作。

上世纪60年代，厦门大学另一位著名数学家林群教授（本章随后介绍）曾问陈景润为什么他能睡那么少，而自己则常失眠，就怕缺觉，睡得比他多却精力没他足，陈景润想了想，然后认真地回答说："失眠就是说明不缺觉，应该起床工作。"

80年代，这两位数学家一起去厦门出差，住在宾馆。晚上11点，陈景润就睡觉了，林群很奇怪，陈景润也开始保养身体了？没想到，凌晨2点，陈景润摇醒他，问："我要是现在开灯工作，不会影响你吧？"

陈景润的生活方式搞垮了他的身体。每次长时间地研究数学问题，待他解决了一道难题，他也该住院去了。一出院，就又开始新一轮的马拉松回合，整年昼夜不停地工作。冬天，墨水结冰了，他就抓支笔，把所有的衣服全穿上，把整个身体围在棉被套里，只装了一只100瓦的灯泡取暖。

除了吃饭和喝水，陈景润从不离开自己的房间。人们很好奇，房间里究竟有什么东西。数年后，人们进了他的房间，发现一张木床、一张小桌子、一堆药瓶和几袋草稿纸，仅此而已。

对于成功，陈景润与爱迪生有着相同的理解——天才等于99%的汗水加1%的灵感。他说："数学没有什么秘密，就是要拼命，就像爬山，如果有十条路，一般人爬一条或两条通不到顶，可能就算了，而我是要爬遍的，从而找到一条能到达峰顶的路。"

当陈景润把他的数学论文寄给著名数学家华罗庚时，自己已经开始了爬上数学高峰的跋涉。经华罗庚推荐，陈景润1957年转到了中国科学院数学研究所。尽管他取得了巨大的成功，但他还是一如既往的谦虚、严谨。1981年，为了参加厦门大学建校60周年校庆，他乘坐火车硬卧赶回厦门，当人们问他为什么不按规定坐软卧，他回答说，"国家还困难，硬卧会便宜些。"

Chen lectured in England in the 1970s, and when the university president offered him a princely salary to stay, he declined, saying he was a member of the National People's Congress and needed to get home to his work. The Chinese back home must have been quite relieved because the Xinhua Press announced proudly, "Chen Jingrun has returned!"

Chen labored right up until the end. He refused to let nurses give injections in his right hand so he could keep working, and even in the hospital he mentored a graduate student and three doctoral candidates.

When Japan published the book "100 Challenging Math Problems," they mentioned two Chinese mathematicians. One was Zu Chongzhi, who discovered the value of "π", and in 462 calculated the year within an accuracy of 50 seconds. The other mathematician was Chen Jingrun. But personally, I think they should have also included Dr. Lin Qun.

Dr. Lin Qun—Beautiful Mind *and* Beautiful Sense of Humor

Dr. Lin Qun, who complained to Chen Jingrun about insomnia, is yet another of XMU's beautiful mathematical minds. He graduated from XMU in 1956 and is a member of both the CAS and the Academy of Sciences for the Developing World (TWAS).

Insomnia not withstanding, or perhaps because of it, Dr. Lin has certainly been working. He received the CAS 1st Prize in Natural Sciences in 1989, and in 2001 was awarded Bolzano Honorary Medal of Merit in the Mathematical Sciences from Academy of Sciences of the Czech Republic.

Painless Calculus? Dr. Lin not only has a beautiful mind but a beautiful sense of humor to match it. He wrote, for example, "Painless Calculus: Proofs are Limited to one Line." Personally, I need only one line to prove that calculus is never painless, but had Dr. Lin been my professor it may have been both painless and fun.

Dr. Lin also wrote, "Free Calculus—a Liberation from Proofs":

"Free calculus preaches a tactic: "replace a theorem to be a definition" and so liberates from proof. Such a theorem is a sustaining platform of calculus (including the fundamental formula, Taylor formula and the properties of a differential function), but itself needs a long proof (spent even two chapters about real numbers and continuous functions). While the definition (replacing the theorem) is also a sustainable platform of the same calculus:

a suitable definition ≅ a theorem.

70 年代，陈景润到英国讲学时，一个大学校长想重金聘请，他毫不犹豫地回答说，他得回中国去，他是全国人大代表，应该回去。新华社为此专门发表文章，向全国人民报告："陈景润回国了！"这回国人大可放心了。

陈景润长期住院，始终不辍工作。他要用右手写字，因此不让护士在右手上打针。他甚至在医院里还在培养一个硕士生和三个博士生。

日本出版了一本《100 个最有挑战性的数学问题》，书中只提到两个中国人。一个是祖冲之，他计算出了圆周率的值，并于公元 462 年将一年的时间精确到 50 秒；另一个便是陈景润。其实，还有一个人应该被提及，那就是林群，请看下文：

林群博士——充满幽默感的"美丽心灵"

曾向陈景润抱怨失眠的林群博士，是厦门大学的又一颗"美丽心灵"。他 1956 年毕业于厦大，后成为中科院院士和第三世界科学院院士。

尽管"失眠"（见"陈景润"一文），林群博士一直兢兢业业地工作着——或者正因为失眠？他于 1989 年荣获中国科学院自然科学奖一等奖，于 2001 年荣获捷克科学院"数学科学成就荣誉奖章"。

无痛微积分？ 林博士还是位幽默的教授。比如，他写道，"无痛苦的微积分：证明只限于一条线。"对我来说，只需要一条线来证明微积分学绝不是无痛苦的，但如果他是我的老师，微积分将是无痛苦的和充满趣味的。

林博士还写道：

自由微积分——从证明中解放出来

自由微积分支持一个策略："用定义代替定理"，由此从证明中解放出来。这种定理为微积分提供了可持续的平台（包括基本公式，泰勒公式和可导函数的性质），但它本身需要一个很长的证明过程（甚至要先花两章来解释实数和连续函数）。而定义（用来代替定理的定义）也可为同一个微积分提供了可持续的平台：

即一个恰当的定义≅一个定理

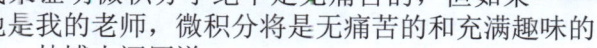

但它本身却不需要证明就可以让人接受并得到相同的微积分，而且节省了两章，这是多经济的方法啊（简直就是免费的午餐）！

"But itself is accepted without proof and so wins the same calculus but saves two chapters, what an economical approach (even a free dinner)!"

Free dinner? Now *that* I can understand!

Prof. Lin Qun is evidently in no hurry to retire. I *pre*tired just reading his demanding schedule, and I'm decades younger. In March 2006, Prof. Lin is chairing the Symposium on Mathematics Education Reform in Beijing, and in July, 2006, Beijing will host the International Workshop on Scientific Computing in honor of Dr. Lin Qun's 70th birthday.

Happy 70th birthday, Dr. Lin! And thanks for making math less painful.

Madame Xie Xide—Selfless Service

Madame Xie Xide (1921-2000) graduated from XMU's Department of Mathematics and Physics in 1946, and obtained her doctorate from the Massachusetts Institute of Technology, where she became known as "Hilda." She returned to China in 1952, founded Fudan University's Modern Physics Institute, and in 1983 became Fudan's President.

In 1980 she was elected as a Committee Member of the Mathematics and Physics Department of the Chinese Academy of Sciences, and an Academician of the Third World Academy of Sciences in 1988.

When U.S. President Reagan visited Fudan in 1984 he said he hoped his visit would be remembered as the day when "America and China accepted the challenge to strengthen the ties that bind us, to strive for a more just and secure peace in the world." Madame Xie then set out to help make that hope a reality. A year after Reagan's visit, she created the USAID-funded "Center for American Studies." The center is now one of Asia's leading authorities on U.S. foreign policy, arms control and nuclear nonproliferation.

Madame Xie served as an advisor after retiring in 1988 and was one of very few women in those years to be elected to the Communist Central Committee. After her death, the March 7, 2000 issue of The New York Times noted that "Madame Xie taught us the meaning of selflessness."

第21章 数学科学学院

但它本身是不需要证明就可以被接受的并获得同样的微积分，但省了两章，这是多经济的方法啊（简直就是免费的午餐）！

"免费的午餐"？这个我倒是听得明白！

林群教授显然并不急于退休。光看他的日程安排我就想提前退休，尽管我比他年轻几十岁。2006年3月，林教授将主持在北京召开的数学教育改革研讨会；2006年7月，科学计算国际研讨会暨林群院士70诞辰学术研讨会将在北京召开。

生日快乐，林教授！我们还要感谢您使数学变得不那么令人痛苦。

谢希德女士——无私的服务

谢希德女士(1921—2000)，于1946年毕业于厦门大学数理系，并在麻省理工学院获博士学位。在那里，同学们都称她为"Hilda"。1952年，谢希德回到中国，创立了复旦大学现代物理研究所，并于1983年就任复旦校长。

1980年，谢希德被选为中国科学院学部委员(即中科院院士)，1988年，她当选为第三世界科学院院士。

美国总统里根1984年访问复旦大学时说，他希望他的来访"能够成为美中两国迎接挑战，加强团结的纽带，希望两国共同为创造一个更公正和平的世界而努力"。谢希德女士是努力把这个期望变为现实的人之一。一年后，在美国国际开发署的资助下，谢希德建立了复旦大学美国研究中心。该中心目前已成为亚洲研究美国外交政策、军队控制和防止核扩散的主要机构。

谢希德1988年退休后，以顾问的身份继续工作，她也是当时中共中央委员会为数不多的女性委员之一。在她去世后，2000年3月7日出版的《纽约时报》写到："是谢女士教会了我们什么叫做'无私'。"

Chapter 22

School of Physics and Mechanical & Electrical Engineering (PMEE)

News Flash! "Xiamen Jiansong Electronics Co. Ltd. has recently kicked off construction of a new plant on a 50,000m^2 site in the Torch Hi-tech Development Zone...the company has inked an agreement with Xiamen University to develop automobile satellite navigation technologies..."
Common Talk, Xiamen Daily, March 3, 2004.
(I wonder if this could navigate my wife's car *away* from Xiamen's new shopping centers?)

When XMU President Sa Ben Dong founded the Department of Mechanical and Electrical Engineering, it had but 9 students, but by 1944 there were 202 students. For many years this was XMU's largest department, and attracted not only the most students but the best teachers.

Today, the School of Physics and Mechanical & Electrical Engineering (PMEE), established July 1999, includes the physics department, the medical and electrical engineering department, as well as the Pen-Tung Sah Micro-Electro-Mechanical Systems Research Center. Half of the large academic staff have doctorates, and the school offers 6 undergraduate majors and several masters and doctoral programs. PMEE has close links with universities and research institutes in many countries and regions, including the U.S., Europe, Australia, Singapore, Japan and Taiwan.

The "Small-seeing" Eye
Peng-Tung Sah MEMS Research Ctr.

Famous graduates include such members of the CAS as Ai Xing, Zhang Qixian, Ming Guirong and Jue Duanlin.

第22章

物理与机电工程学院

快讯！ "厦门建松电器有限公司新厂于日前开工，新厂位于火炬高技术产业园内，占地约 5 万平方米。同时，公司还与厦门大学签订了旨在开发汽车卫星导航设备的相关协议……

《厦门日报·双语周刊》2004 年 3 月 3 日

（这个能不能把我夫人的车从厦门的购物中心给引走啊！）

　　机电工程系是由厦门大学前校长萨本栋教授亲手创办起来的，创立时只有9名学生，到1944年，学生人数已增至 202 人，曾连续多年为厦大第一大系，吸引了无数优秀的教师和学生。

　　组建于 1999 年 7 月的物理与机电工程学院，包括物理系、机电工程系和萨本栋微机电研究中心。师资力量雄厚，在职教师中，一半以上获得博士学位。学院现有 6 个本科专业，多个硕士、博士学位授权点。并同美国、欧洲、澳大利亚、新加坡、日本和台湾等许多国家和地区的高校和研究机构建立了广泛的联系和合作关系。

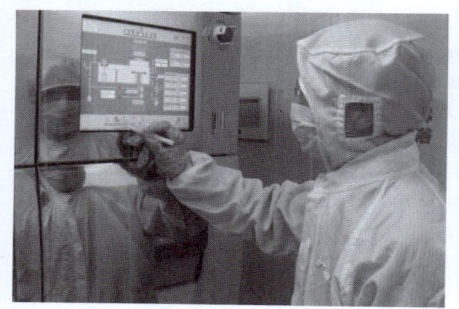

　　办学成绩斐然，不少毕业生成为享誉世界的英才，中国两院院士艾兴、张启先、刘桂荣、阙端麟，就是其中的佼佼者。

Dr. Hu Guoqing

There's forever a pile of shoes outside my neighbor Dr. Hu Guoqing's (胡国清) door. He and his wife entertain students so often I wondered if he ever got any work done, but it turns out he is one of the most productive young professors on campus. This expert in electromechanical engineering (MEMS) and a few other fields has published over 100 papers for international and domestic journals and conferences, written two books, and received 4 Chinese patents for his inventions.

After receiving his Ph.D. from Sichuan University in 1993 and serving as their associate professor, he was a visiting professor in the U.S. at Case Western Reserve University from 2000 to 2001 and a visiting professor at the Chinese University of Hong Kong in 2003. He became an XMU professor in 2001 and has been Deputy Director of the Dept. of Mechanical and Electrical Engineering and Vice Dean of the School of Physical, Mechanical & Electrical Engineering. During his brief career he has already completed over 30 projects for such groups as the Natural Science Foundation of China, Post-doctoral Foundation of China, Key Foundation of Fujian Province, and the Natural Science Foundation of Fujian Province, as well as International Co-operation Projects, Hong Kong Co-operation Projects and various corporate co-operative projects.

(I wonder if this electro-mechanical genius can fix our 13-year-old van Toy Ota?)

Dr. Wen H. Ko

I was impressed with my neighbor's 4 inventions, but Dr. Wen H. Ko has 21 patents, as well as 317 publications in everything from implant electronics to micro-sensors and biomedical instrumentation. Of course, Dr. Ko graduated from XMU before Hu Guoqing was even born!

Currently a professor emeritus of EE of Case Western Reserve University in Ohio, and with XMU's Pen-Tung Sah MEMS Research Center, Dr. Ko received his B.S.E.E. from XMU in 1946, and his M.S. and Ph.D. in E.E. from Case Institute of Technology, Cleveland, Ohio, USA, in 1956 and 1959, respectively.

第22章 物理与机电工程学院

胡国清博士

胡国清教授是我的邻居，他和妻子很喜欢请学生到家中做客，所以他家门口总能见到一堆鞋。我以为这可能会影响他的工作，但胡国清教授这位年轻的机电工程、微机电系统及其他相关领域的专家，取得的科研成果却颇丰，先后在国内外重要学术

刊物和会议上发表论文100多篇，出版学术专著2部，获得4项发明专利。

1993年，胡国清教授在四川取得博士学位，并留校担任助教，2000年到2001年，任美国凯斯西储大学客座教授，2003年任香港中文大学客座教授，2001年任厦门大学机电工程系副系主任，物理与机电工程学院副院长。工作经历虽不长，但硕果累累，已为众多机构完成项目30多个。这些机构包括国家自然科学基金委员会，国家博士后研究基金委员会，福建省科技重点项目基金委员会，福建省自然科学基金委员会，以及国际合作项目，香港合作项目等多种合作项目。

(真想知道这位机电方面的天才能否帮我修好已用了13年之久的丰田车！)

葛文勋博士

胡国清教授的4项发明让我印象深刻，但葛文勋教授取得的成就更让我佩服，共有21项专利，发表论文317篇。论文涉及面广泛，有植入电子学、微传感器及生物医学检测仪器等领域。当然，当葛文勋博士从厦大毕业的时候，我的邻居胡教授还没有出生呢！

葛文勋教授1946年取得厦门大学电机工程系获学士学位，后又分别在1956年和1959年在美国俄亥俄州克里夫兰的凯斯理工学院获得硕士、博士学位。现在是美国俄亥俄州凯斯西储大学电机工程学荣誉退休教授，并一直致力发展厦门大学萨本栋微机电研究中心的工作。

Dr. Ko is on the editorial board of Sensors and Actuator, Micro-system Technologies, Telemetry and Patient Monitoring, and Medical Progress Through Technology. He was chairman of the int'l steering committee on solid state sensors and actuators conferences from 1983 to 1987 and chairman of the int'l steering committee on chemical sensor meetings from 1991 to 1993.

Dr. Ko received the Career Achievement Award in the Transducer 97 conference in Chicago, USA. Since 1992 he's been president of the Transducer Research Foundation that sponsored the Hilton Head Workshops on Sensors and Actuators in America.

Cradle of Chinese Aviation! PMEE has one of only 4 aeronautical engineering schools in China, which is appropriate enough because XMU helped pioneer modern Chinese aeronautics!

"Save the nation through aviation!" was Sun Yat-sen's rallying cry after Japan's attacks. So Chinese in the Philippines founded an "aviation commission", and since most were from South Fujian, they chose Xiamen for their school and airfield. In August, 1928, they started China's 1st private aviation school, Xiamen Wutong Aviation School, on the northeast coast of Xiamen in Wutong (near our new bridge). They started with 100 students, including 11 from abroad, and recruited teachers from Denmark. Unfortunately, 86 students were expelled and the school closed for lack of funding, but XMU later had an aeronautics department from 1944 until 1951 (it merged with Tsinghua University in 1952).

XMU Training Plane (Boeing 747)

XMU's aeronautics dept. was started while the university was in Changting, which had a large American airbase. Some say it was China's most important aviation school at the time because of the great contributions of graduates such as Chen Yijian, who was the chief designer of China's fighter-bomber, the FC-1.

Contact
Tel: 218-4577 Fax: 218-9426
Email: phys@xmu.edu.cn
Website:http://pmee.xmu.edu.cn

第22章 物理与机电工程学院

葛文勋教授在"传感器和传动器"、"微系统技术"、"遥测技术与患者监测"以及"技术推动医学进步"编委会工作。1983年到1987年,葛教授任国际固态传感器与传动器学术会议的指导委员会主席,他还担任过1991年到1993年国际化学传感器会议的指导委员会主席。

1997年在美国芝加哥的"'97国际换能器学术会议"上,葛文勋教授被授予职业成就奖。葛教授是换能器研究基金会董事长,该基金会从1992年开始资助研究传感器与传动器的希尔顿顶级专题讨论会。

中国航天业的摇篮!

厦门大学的航空工程系创办时是当时全国仅有的四所本科航空学系之一,这里培养了许多中国航天业的名人志士。

日本侵华后,旅菲华侨遵循孙中山"航空救国"的遗训,组织了航空委员会。因为他们大多来自闽南,就把学校和空军基地建在了厦门。1928年8月,中国最早的民办航空学校成立了,即厦门五通民用航空学校,校址位于厦门东北海岸的五通(在新桥附近)。创办时有100名学生,其中有11名国外学生,并从丹麦招收老师。遗憾的是,后来有86名学生离开,学校也因为资金短缺而停办。但不久厦大于1944年组建了航空工程系(1952年并入清华大学)。

厦大航空系是抗战时期内迁长汀办学时创建的,当时在那里有个很大的美国空军基地。因其毕业生的杰出表现,例如,被誉为"飞豹飞机之父"的中国工程院院士陈一坚教授就毕业于厦大航空工程系,所以厦大被认为是当时中国最重要的航空学校。

Zeng Cuo'an Airport

联系方式
电话:2184577
传真:2189426
电子邮件:phys@xmu.edu.cn
网址:http://pmee.xmu.edu.cn

Chapter 23

College of Chemistry & Chemical Engineering (CCCE)

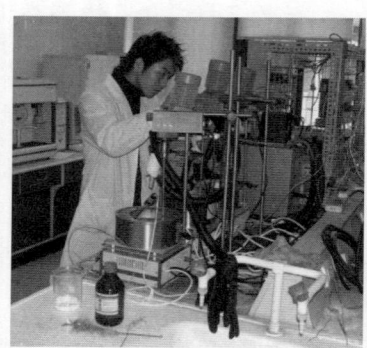

XMU has been pioneering chemistry in China since day one (or at least day two). The Department of Chemistry was founded in 1922 and in 1991 became the College of Chemistry and Chemical Engineering. Its luminaries have included such scientists as Lu Jiaxi (1915-2001).

Lu Jiaxi, a Xiamen-native who graduated from our chemistry department in 1934, obtained a doctorate from London University in 1939, and did postdoctoral research at the California Institute of Technology. Lu returned to XMU in 1945 when it relocated from Changting to Xiamen and helped make the chemistry department a world-class institute. Lu was president of the CAS from 1981 to 1987.

By the way, Fang Yi, CAS president before Lu, was also from Xiamen—so two of the four former CAS presidents were Xiamenese!

"Beautiful Minds" of CCCE

第23章 化学化工学院

厦大化学化工学院从成立的第一天起（至少从第二天起吧），就引领着中国化学的发展。厦门大学化学系成立于1922年，并于1991年成立化学化工学院。学院培养出一批杰出的化学人才，其中包括著名的化学家卢嘉锡（1915—2001）。

卢嘉锡

卢嘉锡，厦门人，1934年毕业于厦大化学系，1939年获伦敦大学博士学位，之后他在加州理工学院从事博士后研究。1945年厦大从长汀迁回厦门，卢嘉锡回到厦大，并帮助厦大化学系成为世界级的研究基地。1981至1987年，卢嘉锡担任中国科学院院长。

顺便提一句，卢嘉锡的前任、中科院院长方毅也是厦门人，因此在四任前中科院院长中，厦门人就占了两席！

Prof. Ye Yiwen and Bruker Smart APEX

Top 50   It is no wonder that CCCE is one of China's premier training grounds for young chemists. They have giants' shoulders to stand upon—and top-quality programs to attract and motivate them. For example, each year the top 50 undergrads of the 1000-student body join a special "honors" class to receive more advanced and intensive education. Almost 70% of these go on to graduate work, and CCCE's alumni are studying and working in prestigious institutions all over the planet.

The Department of Chemistry is home to an NSFC-supported Center for Excellence of Education in Chemistry and offers Bachelors, Masters, PhDs, and postdoctoral fellowships. The "State Key Laboratory for Physical Chemistry of Solid Surfaces"(LPCSS) was ranked first in the nation in 1999 in a national appraisal, and the youth research group was one of the first two "Pioneering Research Groups" in chemistry in China.   The Ministry of Education's Research Laboratory Analytical Science for Materials and Life Chemistry (KLAS) is the only key laboratory in analytical sciences in all of China! (15 of the 17 staff have studied abroad).

The CCCE's Division Library, in a building next to the college, has over 170 international and 220 domestic journals.

The large faculty includes a member of the Chinese Academy of Engineering (Zhang Litong) and eight (yes, eight!) Academicians of the CAS:: Tsai Khirui, Tian Zhaowu, Zhang Qian'er, Wan Huilin, Huang Benli, Zhao Yufen, Zheng Lansun and Tian Zhongqun (who was admitted in 2005). Ten of the younger professors have received the "National Distinguished Young Investigator" awards.

第 23 章　化学化工学院

50 强

毫无疑问，厦门大学化学化工学院是国内培养青年化学工作者最重要的基地之一。这里的学生有幸站在科学巨人的肩膀上——许多一流的课题吸引并激励着他们在科学的道路上不断前进。例如，（化学系）每年从 1000 多名学生中选出 50 个优秀本科生组成"基地班"，接受更高强度的训练。据说"基地班"里 70％的本科毕业继续攻读硕士学位。化学化工学院校友的足迹更是遍布全球重要研究机构。

化学系是国家自然基金委员会支持的国家级化学人才培养基地，同时也是学士、硕士、博士学位授权点和博士后科研流动站。其所辖的"固体表面物理化学国家重点实验室"（LPCSS）在 1999 年的国家评估中名列全国第一。该实验室的青年研究团体是中国化学学科首批两个"创新研究群体"之一。该系的"现代分析科学教育部重点实验室"前身是"厦门大学材料和生命过程分析科学国家教委实验室"，时为全国分析学科惟一的教育部重点实验室（该实验室的 17 名研究人员中，有 15 人有留学经历）。

化学化工学院拥有自己的专属图书馆，毗邻学院大楼，收藏有 170 余种外文期刊和 220 种中文专业期刊。

学院的师资队伍雄厚，包括一位中国工程院院士（张立同）和八位（是的，有八位之多）中科院院士：蔡启瑞，田昭武，张乾二，万惠霖，黄本立，赵玉芬，郑兰荪，田中群(2005 年当选)。学院还有十位年轻教授获得了"国家杰出青年科学基金"。

李兆雄 教授
Zhao-Xiong XIE

叶艺文 高级工程师
Yi-Wen YE

张庆红 副教授
Qing-Hong ZHANG

伊晓东 博士
Xiao-Dong YI

徐昕 教授
Xin XU

周剑章 博士
Jian-Zhang ZHOU

周朝晖 教授
Zhao-Hui ZHOU

卓向东 高级工程师
Xiang-Dong ZHUO

Photos Courtesy of CCCE

杨勇 教授
Yong YANG

张鸿斌 教授
Hong-Bin ZHANG

王敏 办公室副主任
Min WANG
Head of Admin Office

俞剑敏 硕士, 工程师
Jian-Min YU
Engineer

吴剑鸣 硕士, 工程师
Jian-Ming WU
Engineer

CCCE's two key departments are the Dept. of Chemical & Biochemical Engineering and the Dept. of Materials Science & Engineering (which has seven labs, including two undergrad labs for Polymer Chemistry and Polymer Physics).

CCCE is also a key player in XMU's Center for Nano-Science and Technology, which has an interdisciplinary team with over 50 faculty members from chemistry, materials science and engineering, physics, electrical engineering and biosciences.

Laser Plasma Source Time-of-Flight Mass Spectrometer (homemade!)

International Ties CCCE has such cooperative programs as the XMU-Hong Kong Baptist University Joint Laboratory on Chinese Medicine.

CCCE has also organized or hosted numerous international academic conferences, including:

1985: International Conference of Photo-catalysis, Electro-catalysis and Bio-mimetic Catalysis

1987: Third China-Japan-America Conference of Catalysis

1994: China-Japan Conference of Theoretical Chemistry,

1995: 46th Annual ISE Conference (hosted by LPCSS, it had over 800 participants from 50 countries).

1999: Fifth Asian Conference on Analytical Sciences

2000: International Symposium on Raman Spectroscopy

2004: ISE Spring Conference of ISE[1] on "Electrochemistry at Nano-scale" (sponsored & hosted by the LPCSS)

Contact Tel:218-2240/3050 Fax: 218-6400
E-mail: pqhuang@xmu.edu.cn
Website: http://chemistry.xmu.edu.cn

---

[1] ISE: International Society of Electrochemistry

第23章 化学化工学院

化学化工学院的另外两个系分别是化学工程与生物工程系和材料科学与工程系（该系拥有7个实验室，包括两个面向本科生开放的实验室，分别是高分子化学实验室和高分子物理实验室。）

化学化工学院在厦门大学纳米科技中心也发挥关键的作用。该中心拥有一个跨学科的团队，包括来自化学，材料科学工程，物理，电子工程和生物科学领域的50多位科研人员。

国际交流　化学化工学院参与了许多国际合作项目，例如与香港浸会大学共建的厦门大学－香港浸会大学中药研究联合实验室。

化学化工学院曾举办许多国际性学术会议，包括：

1985年：国际光催化、电催化和仿生催化会议；
1987年：第三届中日美催化会议；
1994年：中日理论化学会议；
1995年：46届国际电化学会议（由固体表面物理化学国家重点实验室主办，来自近50个国家和地区的800多位专家到会）；
1999年：第五届亚洲分析科学大会；
2000年：国际表面拉曼光谱座谈会；
2004年：国际电化学学会(ISE)春季会议，主题为"纳米尺度上的电化学"（由固体表面物理化学国家重点实验室承办并主办）；

联系方式

电话：218-2240/3050　传真:218-6400
电子邮件：pqhuang@xmu.edu.cn　网址：http://chemistry.xmu.edu.cn

Electronic Microscope

Chapter 24

School of Life Sciences

News Flash! "Protein found to control tumor growth in certain breast cancers!"
U.S. National Academy of Sciences, Feb. 1, 2006

Our School of Life Sciences (SLS) made the groundbreaking discovery above while performing joint research with the prestigious Scripps Research Institute. SLS's faculty and alumni have helped bring life to millions around the world with innovative discoveries and processes.

In 2003[①], Xiamen University and Beijing Wantai Biological Pharmacy Enterprise received approval from the State Drug Administration for an HIV test that takes 30 minutes, compared with 2 weeks for conventional tests. And in June 2002, Jinhua Chen, a 1982 graduate of XMU, was on the Abbott Laboratories team that was awarded for their innovative process of producing the HIV/AIDS drugs ritonavir and lopinavir.

Zoology Museum

The Biology Department was founded in 1922, became the SLS in November, 1999—and our Life Sciences has been growing like a living organism ever since, with over 100 staff and faculty.

The SLS, in the two granite buildings west of Jian'an Auditorium, has over 10,000m² of teaching and research space, and over 40 million RMB in equipment, but I suspect they're going to grow much larger. The Ministry of Education's "985" program budgeted 100 million RMB for the Department of Biomedical Sciences.

---

① Xinhua News Agency, Feb. 21, 2003.

第24章

生命科学学院

快讯! "发现蛋白质可控制某些乳癌肿瘤生长!"
　　　　美国国家科学院　2006年2月1日

厦门大学生命科学学院在与著名的 Scripps 研究院的合作研究项目中取得了突破性的进展。事实上,生命科学学院的全体人员曾经无数次用他们的新发现造福了世界各地千千万万的人。

2003 年[①],厦门大学与北京万泰生物药业有限公司研制出我国第一个艾滋病毒(HIV)快速诊断试剂通过了国家药品监管局的检验。利用这种艾滋病检测试剂 30 分钟内即可知道检测结果,而传统的艾滋病检测试剂需耗时两周。还有,2002 年 6 月,厦大 1982 届毕业生陈金华所在 Abbott 实验室的小组因研制出抗癌药品洛匹那韦和利托那韦而获嘉奖。

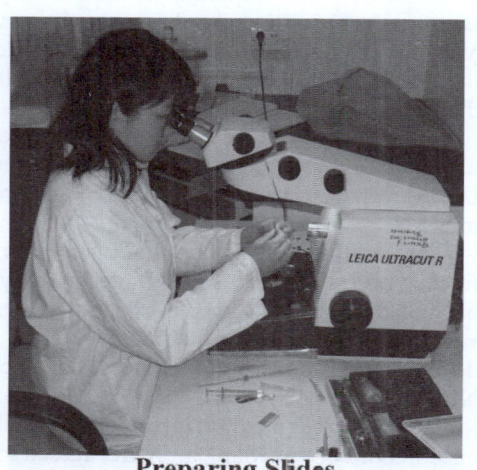

Preparing Slides

厦门大学生命科学学院的前身为 1922 年创建的生物学系,1999 年 11 月正式组建成为厦门大学生命科学学院。如今,在全院 100 多名教职工的辛勤努力下,生命科学学院正不断地发展壮大。

生命科学学院坐落在厦门大学建南大礼堂西侧的两座花岗岩大楼,拥有 1 万多平方米的教学科研用房和 4000 万余元的现代生物学实验仪器设备。教育部"985 工程"已将 1 亿元人民币编入生物医学科学系的预算当中。

---

① 新华社 2003 年 2 月 21 日。

> **News Flash!** On May 5, 1992, the first international environmental protection conference in Xiamen, the "International Conference on Clean Technology," was held at Xiamen University and jointly run by the State Environmental Protection Administration and the Paris Industrial and Environmental Office of UNED. Xiamen became the first Chinese city to introduce the clean technology production concept.
> Common Talk, *Xiamen Daily*, October 9, 2005

The SLS' key departments include Department of Biology, Department of Biochemistry & Biotechnology, the Department of Biomedical Sciences, the Ministry of Education Key Laboratory for Cell Biology & Tumor Cell Engineering, the National Ministry of Education Cell Biology Research Laboratory, and the National Ministry of Education Parasitology Research Laboratory.

The School of Life has close cooperation with many companies and has set up several biotech firms. It also has academic exchanges with colleges in the U.S.A., Japan, Germany, Canada, Singapore, and other Southeast Asian countries.

In October, 2004, the school helped organize the 5th Sino-Singapore Conference on Life Sciences and Biotechnology. In 2000, the National University of Singapore (NUS) signed a trilateral agreement with XMU and Tsinghua University that provided for funding of projects, exchange of staff and graduate students, organization of conferences, and the teaching of Structural Biology by NUS staff at XMU.

NUS also signed an agreement to establish an XMU-NUS Joint Life Science Laboratory in Xiamen. XMU agreed to invest about 5 million RMB in setting up the laboratory, and NUS will appoint six faculty members as PhD supervisors at XMU (the students will also spend six months in Singapore taking NUS graduate courses).

SLS People As elsewhere at XMU, the people make the programs. Here are just a few SLS Talents:

Lin Shengcai (林圣彩), Dean of the SLS, received his B.Sc. from XMU in 1984, a PhD in 1991 from UT Southwestern Medical Center in Dallas, and was a Postdoctoral Fellow at the Howard Hughes Medical Institute, UCSD, from 1991-1995.

Dean Lin Shengcai

第 24 章 生命科学学院

> **快讯！** 1992年5月5日，国家环保局与联合国环境署巴黎工业和环境办公室联合在我市厦门大学召开"清洁工艺国际会议"，这是我市第一次召开环保国际性会议，厦门也成为我国首个引进清洁生产理念的城市。 （《厦门日报·双语周刊》2005年10月9日）

厦门大学生命科学学院下设生物学系、生物化学与生物技术学系、生物医学科学系、细胞生物学与肿瘤细胞工程教育部重点实验室、教育部细胞生物学研究室以及教育部寄生动物学研究室等。

厦门大学生命科学学院与许多企业密切合作，并成立了一些生物科技有限公司，同美国、加拿大、德国和日本、新加坡等东南亚国家的高校开展学术交流。

Life Science Display of... foreigners?

2004年，厦大参与组织了第五届中国新加坡生物科技学术大会。2000年，新加坡国立大学同厦门大学和清华大学签署了一份三边协议，此协议有助于今后更好地开展三校之间的交流活动，如项目拨款、师生交流、会议组织及由新加坡国立大学委派教授在厦大开设结构生物学课程等。

另外，新加坡国立大学与厦门大学达成共建"生命科学联合实验室"的合作协议。根据协议，厦门大学斥资约500万人民币建立实验室。新加坡国立大学将委派6名教授将作为厦门大学的博士生导师。（招收的博士生也将有机会到新加坡国立大学学习半年。）

系友：这些项目的成功离不开许多系友的辛勤和努力。以下是厦门大学生命科学学院的一些杰出系友：

林圣彩：现任生命科学学院院长。1984年毕业于厦门大学生物系。1991年获美国得克萨斯大学西南医学中心生物化学博士。1991—1995年霍华德·休斯医学院博士后。

Madame Professor Tang Chongti. (唐崇惕). One of the school's outstanding scientists, she received her B.S. from XMU in 1954 and has been a professor of biology at XMU since 1986. She became a member of the CAS in 1991, and from 1987-1990 was Director of Parasitology Research Lab and a member of the Committee of Sciences and Technology of State Education Commission of China. She was also a member of the Committee for the 19th International Congress of Zoology. She has won 12 awards in her field, including a Science and Technology Award from the Fujian Provincial government.

Chen Yiyu, who graduated from XMU in 1964, became vice president of the CAS in 1995 and was chair of the International Geosphere and Biosphere Program (IGBP) National Committee of China. Other luminaries have included Peng Lin and Deyao Wang, who was President of XMU from 1945 to 1949 and rebuilt XMU after the War. Prof. Wang was still heading a cell biology lab even into his 90s!

Prof. Lin Peng, a member of the Chinese Academy of Engineering and an XMU graduate in biology, is China's top mangrove scientist, having spent 40 years studying the coastal forests. He has written 23 books, and published over 300 dissertations! One of his many posts has been Executive Director of the China Ecology Institute.

Other CAS members include: Zhongzhang Tang, Peigen Xiao, Xianwen Wu, and Chengkui Tseng.

Contact: Tel: 218-2929 Fax: 218-1015
Email: biology@xmu.edu.cn
Website: http://life.xmu.edu.cn

News Flash! 2nd Prize for HIV Test "More than 80% of in-home HIV testing products are produced using the antigen we developed in 1999," said Jun Zhang, associate professor from the Research Center for Medical Molecular Virology of Fujian Province, XMU. He said this antigen is the crucial element used in an HIV test called 'ELISA' (酶免疫吸附法).

"There were only second-generation tests with lower accuracy available in China before 1999, which were imported from advanced foreign countries. 'The antigen we developed is a great breakthrough in the China HIV testing field. The accuracy rate of the test made with our antigen is up to 99.6% which is close to international advanced levels,' said Mr.Zhang, 'For this achievement we were granted the second prize of the National Science and Technology Progress Award by the Ministry of Science and Technology in 2000.'" Common Talk, *Xiamen Daily*, Dec. 8, 2004

第24章 生命科学学院

唐崇惕：学院杰出科学家之一。1954年获得厦门大学理学学士。1986年至今担任厦门大学生物系教授，1991年成为中科院院士。1987—1990年厦门大学寄生动物研究室主任及国家教育委员会第一届科学技术委员会委员。她还担任第十九届世界动物学大会委员会委员。唐教授在这些领域赢得12项荣誉，其中包括福建省政府颁发的科技奖。

陈宜瑜：1964年毕业于厦门大学。1995年任中国科学院副院长，2004年任国家自然科学基金委员会主任。

汪德耀：于1945—1949年任厦门大学校长，并担负起战后重建厦门大学的重任。汪教授90岁高龄时仍工作在生物细胞实验室。

林鹏：中国工程院院士，厦门大学生物系毕业，中国杰出的红树林研究科学家。从事海岸湿地红树林研究40余年，取得了丰硕的科研成果，出版著作23部，发表论文300多篇，曾任中国生态学会理事。

生命科学学院培养的其他中科院院士有：唐仲璋、肖培根、伍献文、曾呈奎。

联系方式：
电话：218-2929　传真：218-1015
电子邮件：biology@xmu.edu.cn　网址：http://life.xmu.edu.cn

快讯！ 厦门大学福建省医学分子病毒学科研中心张军副教授指出，国内超出80%的艾滋病测试产品是利用厦门大学生命科学学院1999年开发的抗原原料产生的。他还指出，这种抗原原料是一种名为"酶免疫吸附法"的艾滋病检测方法的关键元素。

1999年以前，国内艾滋病检测试剂还停留在第二代试剂的检测水平上，且多从发达国家进口。张指出，我们所开发的抗原原料在国内艾滋病检测领域无疑是一个重大突破。利用我们的抗原原料生产的艾滋病检测试剂对艾滋病的检出率高达99.6%，达到国际先进水平。2000年国家科技部授予该项技术科技进步二等奖。

（《厦门日报·双语周刊》2004年12月8日）

Chapter 25

College of Oceanography & Environmental Science

News Flash! "The first Xiamen University Ocean Festival kicked off on May 28. Over 100 students and teachers explored the western ocean area, the coastline and the present situation of the environmental protection of the islets." Common Talk, Xiamen Daily, June 2, 2004.

XMU, "A Cradle of Chinese Oceanography." XMU was one of the first (if not the first) Chinese university to offer a Ph.D. in oceanography. The Department of Oceanography was founded in 1946, and the present College of Oceanography & Environmental Science (COES) comprises the Dept. of Oceanography, Dept. of Environmental Science and Engineering, and Environmental Science Research Center.

The State Key Laboratory of Marine Environmental Science was founded in 1995, and the Institute of Subtropical Oceanography was set up in 1978. The college also has the XMU Center for Oceans Policy and Law, and the Xiamen International Training Center for Coastal Sustainable Development.

The Institute of Environmental Science (1982) became the Environmental Science Research Center (ESCR) in 1992. The ESCR runs a joint Masters program in Environmental Management with the University of San Francisco. The college also has a departmental level agreement with the Graduate School of Science of Japan's Tohoku University's (Lu Xun studied here as a foreign student!).

The College's six research divisions include Marine Biogeochemistry, Marine Microbial Ecology, Environmental Ecology, Environmental Chemistry, Environmental Planning & Management, and Environmental Engineering.

The college has almost 500 students, including 4 foreign students; about one fourth are masters or doctoral students.

Contact Info: Tel: 218-3064   218-3065   Fax: 218-6397
        E-mail: ocean@jingxian.xmu.edu.cn
        Website: http://ois.xmu.edu.cn

第 25 章 海洋与环境学院

快讯！ "厦门大学第一届海洋节于5月28日拉开帷幕。100多名师生去西部海域考察海岸线以及小岛环境保护的现状。"
（《厦门日报·双语周刊》，2004年6月2日）

厦门大学——"中国海洋学的摇篮"

厦门大学是中国首批能够授予海洋学博士学位的大学（有可能是首个）。海洋学系创立于1946年，如今海洋与环境学院下设海洋学系、环境科学与工程系，以及环境科学研究中心等。

近海海洋环境科学国家教育部重点实验室成立于1995年，而亚热带海洋研究所是1978年组建的。学院还设有厦门大学海洋政策与法律中心以及厦门海岸带可持续发展国际培训中心。

环境科学研究所成立于1982年，1992年更名为环境科学研究中心。该中心与旧金山大学联合培养环境管理专业硕士研究生。同时，学院还与日本东北大学自然科学研究生院有系级合作协议（鲁迅先生曾在这里留学！）。

学院有海洋生物地球化学、海洋微型生物生态学、环境生态学、环境化学、环境规划与管理及环境工程等很多研究方向。

学院有近500名学生，其中有留学生4名，四分之一的学生为硕士研究生或博士研究生。

联系方式：
电话：2183064, 2183065　传真：86-592-2186397
电子邮箱：ocean@jingxian.xmu.edu.cn
网址：http://ois.xmu.edu.cn

XMU Giant in Oceanography—Zeng Chengkui Zeng Chengkui was born in Xiamen, received his B.A. from XMU in 1931, an M.Sc. from Lingnan University Research Institute in 1934, a PhD from the University of Michigan in 1942, and an honorary doctorate from Ohio State University in 1987. Over his career Zeng discovered over 100 new species of alga, two genera, and even an entirely new family. He was elected a member of CAS in 1980 and Academy of Science for Developing World (TWAS) in 1986. In 1991 Zeng became a Permanent Honorable Member of the World Aquiculture Cultivation Academy, and Honorable Dean of the CAS Institute of Oceanography.

Zeng's contributions transcended science. He was active in social and political circles, and deputy to the 2nd to 9th National People's Congress. Zeng died on January 20, 2005, at the age of 96—but OES students, staff and alumni are carrying the torch in XMU and prestigious research institutes around the world, including Woods Hole Oceanographic Institution, Scripps Institute of Oceanography, the International Arctic Research Center, etc.

Prof. He Daren's Fishy Behavior One of Prof. He Daren's 4 books on fish is "Fish Behavior" . I told him that I'd written a similar book, "Organizational Behavior", because people are pretty fishy too sometimes.

I took some oceanography courses myself in college, and fancied myself at least an amateur oceanography enthusiast, but after getting to know Professor He and his wife I realized I knew nothing about fish. For example, one of his papers was on observations of the "sacculus of Tilapia…" Sacculus? All I know about Tilapia is that I like them sautéed, with white wine and lemon sauce.

第25章 海洋与环境学院

厦大海洋学巨人——曾呈奎

曾呈奎出生在厦门，1931年从厦大本科毕业，1934年在岭南大学研究院获得硕士学位。1942年，获得密歇根大学博士学位。1987年又被授予俄亥俄州立大学荣誉博士称号。他一生中发现了100多种新的海藻，2个新的属，以及一个全新的科。1980年他当选为中科院院士，1986年又成为第三世界科学院院士。1991年，曾教授成为世界水产养殖学会终身荣誉会员以及中国科学院海洋研究所名誉所长。

曾先生对社会的贡献不仅限于科学方面。他热心社会政治活动，曾连续数届当选为全国人大代表。他于2005年1月20日去世，享年96岁。然而海洋与环境学院的师生以及校友们正在厦大以及一些享有国际声誉的研究院，如伍兹霍尔海洋学研究所、斯克里普斯海洋学研究所、国际北极研究中心等，继续着前辈未完成的研究。

何大仁教授

何大仁教授的鱼类行为学 何大仁教授一共写了4本有关鱼类学的书，其中一本名为《鱼类行为学》。我对他说，我已写过一本类似的书——《组织行为学》，因为组织行为有时也相当"fishy"。(英文中，"fishy"一词由"鱼"一词而来，有"古怪、可疑"之意)

我自己也选修过一些海洋学课程，自认为算得上一个业余海洋学爱好者，但是当我结识了何教授和他的妻子后，感到对鱼我其实一无所知。他写过一篇观察罗非鱼的文章。罗非鱼？我只知道嫩煎罗非鱼配上白葡萄酒以及柠檬沙司是无比的美味。

100 Years of Service to XMU? I was surprised when Prof. He was awarded for 100 years of Service to Education at XMU. That would make him at least 120-years-old (and XMU is only 85 years old). But it turns out the award was for the combined services of Prof. He, who taught at XMU from 1953 to 1996, his father, who worked at XMU from 1926-1958, his wife Prof. Sophie Jiang, who taught at XMU from 1954 to 1992, and his daughter. Only one other XMU family (Professor Zhengzhong) has received this 100 Year Award. (I've only got 82 years to go!).

Prof. He Daren, like Prof. Zheng Qiwu, has spent his entire life at XMU. He was born here in 1932, graduated from XMU in 1952, and taught fish and stamps until he retired in 1996. But like most of XMU's so-called retirees, Professor He is as busy as ever, researching, lecturing, and writing books and papers—over 60 academic papers on fish, and well over 300 on stamps.

Father of College-level Philatelics! While Prof. He is officially an oceanographer, he is increasingly famous for his stamps—especially his Russian stamp collection, which he began while doing advanced studies at Leningrad University from 1957-1959. Prof. He gave the first college-level philatelic course in China, and over the past 20 years over 2000 students have given their stamp of approval to his stamp course. He proudly told me that universities all over China now have stamp classes, but his was first.

Ms. Jiang, He's wife, has written over 20 papers and received 2nd place in a natural science award. Her expertise was fish embryos and eggs.

In 2004, XMTV celebrated Prof. He and Sophie Jiang's 50th wedding anniversary.

Stamp Exhibit (XMU 80th Anniversary)

第25章 海洋与环境学院

厦大百年贡献? 当我得知何教授获得厦大教育百年贡献奖的时候很惊讶。这么算来他起码也要120岁了(而厦大只有85岁)。后来才得知这个奖是表彰何教授全家对厦大的贡献。何教授从1953年起执教厦大,1996年退休,他的父亲于1926年至1958年在厦大工作,他的妻子江素菲教授也从1954年从事教学工作直到1992年退休,如今他们的女儿也在厦大工作。全厦大还有一个家庭获此殊荣,那就是郑重教授一家。(而我还有82年的漫漫长路要奋斗!)

何大仁教授和郑启五老师一样,所有时光也在厦大校园里度过。他生于1932年,1952年从厦大毕业,教授鱼类学和集邮学,1996年退休。然而,和许多厦大其他的已经"退休"的教师一样,何教授忙碌依旧,做研究、开讲座、出书、写论文,他已经发表了60多篇鱼类学的学术论文以及300多篇关于集邮的文章。

大学里集邮课程之父! 何教授的职业是一名海洋学家,但却因收藏的邮票更加出名。特别是他的前苏联邮票,1957至1959年他在列宁格勒大学进修时就开始收藏了。何教授首次在中国大学里开设了集邮课程。20多年来,2000多名学生上过何教授的集邮课。他骄傲地告诉我现如今中国的大学都开设了集邮课程,而他是带头人啊!

他的妻子江教授也发表论文20余篇,并获省级科技进步二等奖。她主要研究鱼的晶胚和卵。

2004年,厦门电视台曾制作节目纪念何教授和妻子江素菲庆祝结婚50周年。

Chapter 26

XMU Medical College

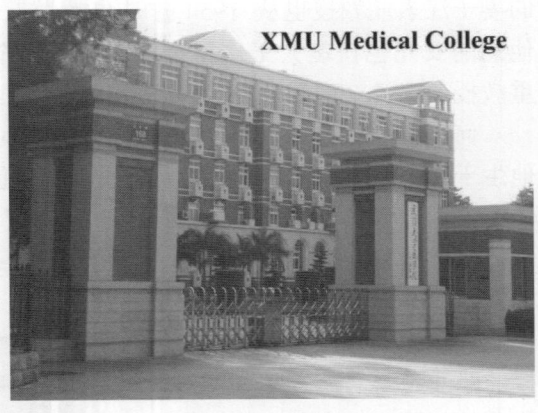

XMU Medical College

News Flash! China First Genetic Hepatitis E Vaccine Dec. 2004, A proprietary genetically engineering hepatitis E vaccine, developed by XMU, was recently approved by the state authorities for I/II clinical trials. The vaccine expects to be the second GE tools preventing hepatitis in the world, following the appearance of hepatitis B vaccine.
China Science & Technology Newsletter, Dec. 20, 2004

XMU Medical College was approved by the National Education Ministry on October 11st 1996, and is a joint program of the Xiamen Municipal Government and XMU. Thanks in part to the generous financial support of many Overseas Chinese, this innovative college has a beautiful new 70,000m^2 campus just west of the XMU Hospital.

The College's 600+ students come from all over the mainland, as well as Hong Kong, Macao, Taiwan, and S.E. Asian countries.

The staff of almost 400 includes two CAS members, as well as two directors of a major laboratory approved by Chinese Health Ministry. Nearly 200 of the teaching staff hold the title of Professor or Associate Professor, and over 38% have doctoral degrees.

The Medical College runs five-year undergraduate courses in Clinical Medicine, Chinese Medicine, and Preventive Medicine, as well as a four-year undergraduate course in Pharmaceutics and a three-year postgraduate course in biomedicine.

 第 26 章　厦门大学医学院

第26章

厦门大学医学院

快讯！中国首次研制成功基因工程戊型肝炎疫苗！

2004 年 12 月，拥有核心自主知识产权的基因工程疫苗——重组戊型肝炎疫苗在厦门大学研制成功了，目前已正式获准进入Ⅰ／Ⅱ期临床试验。该疫苗有望成为继乙肝疫苗之后，世界上第二个基因工程病毒疫苗。

2004年12月20日《中国科学技术通讯（英文版）》

厦门大学医学院于1996年10月11日经国家教育部批准正式成立，是一所由厦门市人民政府和厦门大学联办，得到海外华侨、华人大力资助的学院。这所新兴的学院占地7万多平方米，坐落于厦门大学医院的西侧。

该院的600多名学生来自中国大陆、香港、澳门、台湾以及东南亚一些国家。现有教职工近400人，其中中国科学院院士2人，卫生部重点实验室主任2人，教授、副教授近200人，38%以上的教师具有博士学位。

学院开设了五年制本科临床医学专业、中医学专业以及预防医学专业，四年制本科药学专业及三年制硕士生物医学工程专业。

Departments include: Clinical Medicine Department, Preventive Medical Department, Chinese Medical Department, Pharmaceutical Department, General Medical Department, Biomedical Engineering Research Center, Anticancer Research Center, one affiliated comprehensive hospital, and five teaching hospitals

The College gives students hands-on practical clinical experience with many Xiamen institutions, including: #1 Clinical College of the Medical College, Xiamen Cardiopathy Center, Xiamen First Hospital, Xiamen Traditional Chinese Medicine Hospital, Xiamen Ophthalmology Hospital, Xiamen Stomatology Hospital, Xiamen Xianyue Hospital

Contact Tel: 218-2736 Fax: 218-3069
Email: xmumc@jingxian.xmu.edu.cn
Website: http://rsc.xmu.edu.cn/english/xmu/yixueyuan.htm

Ancient Chinese Doctor Tales! (from "Amoy Magic")

First Things First – A Ming Dynasty Tale (1368-1644) A doctor was detained by the furious relatives of a patient he had killed with the wrong prescription, but he escaped by night and swam across a wide river to reach home. When he saw his son studying medical texts, he said, "Don't be in such a hurry to study medicine. First things first. And first, learn to swim."

Quack[①] Compensation – A Qing Dynasty Tale (1644 -1912) When a quack doctor's treatment killed a family's son, he was forced to give them his own son. He lost his daughter in the same way. One day a man knocked on his door and asked his help. "Who's the patient?" the doctor asked.
"My wife," the man said.
The tearful doctor told his wife, "Sweetheart, I fear someone has taken a fancy to you."

Getting the Boot[②] A Ming Dynasty Tale (1368-1644) A heavily laden woodcutter stumbled into the local doctor on a narrow path. When the doctor drew back his fist to hit him, the woodcutter dropped to his knees and begged, "Please kick me instead."
A bystander asked, "Why would you rather him kick you?"
The terrified woodcutter replied, "Treatment by his hands would be much deadlier than with his feet!"

---

① Quack: fraud (or poorly trained or skilled)
② Getting the boot: getting laid off or fired

第26章 厦门大学医学院

学院下设：临床医学系、预防医学系、中医系、药学系、基础医学部、生物医学研究中心、抗癌研究中心、一所综合性附属医院以及五所教学医院。

该院还与医学院第一临床学院（前身为厦门中山医院）、厦门心脏中心、厦门市第一医院、厦门中医院、厦门眼科中心、厦门口腔医院、厦门市仙岳医院等多家机构合作，为学生提供临床实习机会。

联系方法

电话：218-2736　传真：218-3096
电子邮箱：xmumc@jingxian.xmu.edu.cn
网址：http://rsc.xmu.edu.cn/english/xmu/yixueyuan.htm

有关医生的经典故事
（摘自《魅力厦门》）

明朝故事：分清轻重缓急　一位医生因为误诊，治死了病人。病人的家属怒气冲天，把医生扣押下来。医生夜里逃脱，游过大河回到家里。看到儿子正在学习医书，这位医生说："孩子，先别急着学医。要分清轻重缓急。最要紧的是，要学会游泳！"

清代故事：庸医的赔偿　有位庸医误诊治死了别人家的儿子，只好拿自己的儿子作赔偿。由于同样的原因，这位庸医失去了女儿。有一天，一位男子敲医生的门，请他出诊。"病人是谁？"医生问。

"我妻子。"

医生流着泪对妻子说："亲爱的，恐怕有人喜欢上你了。"

明朝故事：给我一脚　在一条窄路上，一位伐木人身负重荷，撞上了一位当地的大夫。医生挥拳要打他，伐木人惊恐万分，迁忙跪下哀求："你还是踢我一脚好了！"

路人问道："你为什么宁可他踢你呢？"

伐木人回答说："他的手可比他的脚更容易置人于死地！"

Chapter 27

College of Humanities

The College of Humanities has 8 research institutes and offers numerous B.A. programs, as well as 25 M.A. programs and many Ph.D. programs.

The 11 undergraduate B.A. programs include Chinese literature, Chinese language, theatrical literature, history, archaeology, philosophy, etc. The anthropology program was discontinued but I'm told our anthropology museum is still the best in China.

第27章

人 文 学 院

　　人文学院下设 8 个研究机构，数个本科专业、25 个硕士点以及多个博士点。
　　8 个本科专业，包括汉语言文学、汉语言、戏剧影视学、历史学、考古学、哲学等。据说，人类学本科专业已不存在，而厦大的人类博物馆在中国仍然是首屈一指的。

Lin Yutang—an "International"Chinese Writer

Lin Yutang

(Adapted from "Discover Gulangyu") Lin Yutang was schooled on Gulangyu, taught at XMU from 1926-1927, and was the first Chinese author to reach the top of the New York Times bestseller list. Pearl S. Buck had to urge the anxious author to publish his 1935 bestseller "My Country and my People," but Lin went on to do more than any one in his generation to bridge the gulf between East and West.

Born the 7th of a Presbyterian minister's eight children in Longxi (龙溪) on October 10th, 1895, Lin wrote, "One of my earliest memories as a child was that of sliding down the roof of the church."[1] Lin, like his father, read everything he could lay his hands on. An Amoy missionary, Abbe Livingston Warnshuis[2], ardently promoted higher education to develop leaders for the new China he believed was coming, and fueled the family's intellectual fire by sending them books and pamphlets on both Christian

> "However inclined one may be to regard the Chinese as strange, peculiar, fantastic, or impossible, for no other reason than that one has never been fortunate enough to gain their friendly, intimate acquaintance, the reading of Mr. Lin's book will very soon dissipate any notion of uncertainty and assure one of the truth[s] of the Confucian statement, that 'Within the four seas all men are brothers.'"
> "The East Speaks to the West," *The New York Times* review of "My Country and My People" December 8th, 1935

and scientific issues. It was a blessing for young Lin Yutang, but led to tragedy for his second oldest sister and best friend, Mei-Kung.

Lin's father refused to let Mei-Kung attend college because, as Lin wrote, "college education for a girl was a luxury which our family simply could not afford." Denied an education, the bright girl married at age 22, and when Lin left for college she gave him forty cents and said,

"…you are going to college. Don't waste your opportunity. Be a good man, a useful man, and a famous man… That is your sister's wish for you.' Knowing her desire so well, I felt the full force of these simple words. It made me guilty about the whole thing. They burned into my heart with the oppressive weight of a great load, so that I had the feeling I was going to college in her place."[3]

---

[1] "From Pagan to Christian," World Publishing Company, Cleveland, 1959, Page 19).
[2] Warnshui: a Reformed Church of America missionary in Xiamen from 1900—1905
[3] Lin Yutang, "Memoirs of an Octogenarian," Mei Ya Publications, Inc. Taipei, 1975

第 27 章 人文学院

林语堂——一位"国际化"的中国作家
(摘自《魅力鼓浪屿》)

林语堂早年在鼓浪屿上读书,1926 年至 1927 年在厦门大学任教。他是第一个高居《纽约时报》畅销书排行榜首的中国作家。尽管是在赛珍珠的促使下出版了成为 1935 年畅销书的《吾国与吾民》,林语堂为跨越东西方鸿沟所做的贡献,在同辈中还是无人能及。

> 只是因为无缘与中国人成为亲朋好友,外国人往往认为中国人陌生,独特,古怪或是难以忍受。不管这些见解多么顽固,只要读了林先生的书,马上就会消除所有模糊的观念,并相信孔子说的一句话,"四海之内皆兄弟"。
>
> R. Emmet Kennedy 著的 *The East Speaks to the West*,该文作为《吾国与吾民》的书评刊登于 1935 年 12 月 8 日的《纽约时报》第六部分,第 1~2 页。

林语堂 1895 年 10 月 10 日出生在龙溪一个长老会牧师家,是八个孩子中的第七个。林语堂曾写道:"孩提时最早的记忆之一就是从教堂的屋顶上滑下来。"①和父亲一样,林语堂什么书都看。一个在厦门的牧师 Abbe Livingston Warnshuis②,相信新中国将要建立,并为培养领袖人物而热心推动高等教育。他还为孩子们提供有关基督教和科学问题的书和小册子,提高他们的智力。这对于年少的林语堂是件幸事,却造成林语堂的二姐、也是他最好的朋友的悲剧。

Lin Yutang's Family

林语堂曾写道,父亲不让二姐上大学是因为"大学教育对一个女孩来说是奢侈的事,我们家实在负担不起。"这个聪明的女孩上不了学,在 22 岁时结了婚。林语堂离家读大学时,二姐给了他四毛钱,并对他说:"你就要上学了。别浪费这个机会。做个好人,做个有用的人,做个名人……这就是我对你的希望。"我知道她多么渴望读书,因此格外感受到这些话的分量,在心里沉甸甸的,并产生一种负罪感,我觉得自己是在代替二姐上大学。③

---

① 《从异教徒到基督徒》,俄亥俄州 1959 年版,第 19 页。
② Warnshui: 1900 至 1905 年在厦门的一间美国传教士的归正教堂。
③ 林语堂著:《八十自叙》,台北美亚图书公司 1975 年版。

Just a year later, the 7-months pregnant Mei-Kung died of the plague, and a haunted Lin strove to become not only "useful and famous" but also to fight injustice, especially against women.

When Lin was ten, he and his two brothers studied in Amoy at the American Reformed Mission's Yangyuan Elementary School (养元小学) and the Xunyuan School (洵源书院). In 1912, he entered the Theological School of Shanghai's St. John University (上海圣约翰大学). He excelled at athletics, and even participated in the 1916 Far Eastern Olympics in Shanghai, but he was an unorthodox scholar. He often skipped classes, and though he gained a reputation as an avid reader, the books he devoured often had no relation to his classes (he wrote of how he secretly read history books during a civil law class).

Lin gradually came to resent that Western education had denied him his Chinese roots, and as he dove into Chinese studies, he abandoned his Christian faith①. He left the Theological School, though he remained in St. John's until his graduation in 1916, after which he taught at Beijing's prestigious Tsinghua University. He wrote,

"To live in Peking then was to come into contact with authentic Chinese society, to see, as it were, ancient China made manifest….Peking was China, authentic China, with its yellow-roofed palaces and terra-cotta temple walls and its Mongolian camels and nearness to the Great Wall and the Ming tombs."②

Lin longed for the East but never quite let go of the West. He continued teaching Christian Sunday School even while delving into Chinese philosophy. Torn, he wrote in a couplet,
"One mind seeks the learning of ancients and moderns;
Two legs straddle the cultures of East and West."

Lin went to Harvard in 1919 but before graduation left for Europe, where he completed his M.A. and, ironically, a Ph.D. in Chinese studies in the University of Jena in Leipzig, Germany. Lin enjoyed studying abroad, but he had qualms about Westerners' preoccupation with logic and scientific method. In "My Country and My People" he wrote,

---

① In "From Pagan to Christian", which he wrote in 1959 after returning to Christianity, he described this period of his life as a three decade "Grand Detour".
② Ibid. p. 33.

第27章 人文学院

一年之后,怀孕七个月的二姐死于鼠疫。在二姐的影响下,林语堂一直努力奋斗,不仅成为"有用的名人",还与社会不公、特别是针对妇女的不公待遇做斗争。

林语堂10岁时,他和另外两个兄弟一起在厦门美国归正教会办的养元小学和洵源书院读书。1912年,他进入上海圣约翰大学神学院学习。在运动方面他成绩突出,还参加过1916年的上海远东奥林匹克运动会。但他又是个离经叛道的学生,时常逃课,书读得很多,可往往与课业无关(他曾描写在公民法的课上偷看历史书的情形)。

林语堂渐渐厌恶起西式教育,认为让他脱离了中国文化的根本,当他转而投入到中文学习中去后,他又摒弃了基督教的文化根本①。他离开神学院,但仍留在圣约翰大学直到1916年毕业。之后他在北京著名的清华大学任教。他写道:

"那时住在北京,能接触到真正的中国社会,原原本本地看到古国的风貌……黄色琉璃瓦的皇宫,红陶土做的寺庙高墙,蒙古骆驼,附近就是长城和明陵——北京代表了中国,真正的中国!"②

林语堂醉心于东方文化,也不忘西方文化,在钻研中国哲学的同时他继续在基督教礼拜日学校教课,还写下这样一副对联:

"两脚踏东西文化,一心评宇宙文章。"

林语堂1919年去哈佛大学读书,但毕业前又离开去了欧洲。具有讽刺意味的是,他在德国莱比锡的耶那大学取得了硕士和中国语言学博士学位。林语堂喜欢留学生活,但他又质疑西方人凡事注重逻辑和科学方法。他在《吾国与吾民》中这样写道:

From "With Love and Irony" (Lin Yutang)

---

① 在皈依基督教后,1959年林语堂写下《从异教徒到基督徒》,文中他将这段人生描绘成一个30年的"大轮回"。

② 《从异教徒到基督徒》第33页。

"It is easy to see why the Chinese mind cannot develop a scientific method; for the scientific method, besides being analytical, always involves an amount of stupid drudgery, while the Chinese believe in flashes of common sense and insight. And inductive reasoning, carried over to human relationships (in which the Chinese are primarily interested) often results in a form of stupidity not so rare in American universities. There are today doctorate dissertations in the inductive method which would make Bacon turn in his grave. No Chinese could possibly be stupid enough to write a dissertation on ice-cream, and after a series of careful observations, announce the staggering conclusion that 'the primary function of sugar [in the manufacture of ice-cream] is to sweeten it'; or after a methodical study in 'Time and Motion Comparison on Four Methods of Dishwashing' happily perceive that 'stooping and lifting are fatiguing'....
"This sort of stupidity, although useful to business advertisement, could really be arrived at, I think, just as correctly by a moment of Chinese common sense and 'intuition.'". ①

In his 1937 bestseller "The Importance of Living", Lin emphasized the "spirit of reasonableness" over logic.

"In contrast to logic, there is common sense, or still better, the Spirit of Reasonableness. ...The Reasonable Age, if that should ever come about, will be the Age of Peace....The Sprit of Reasonableness is the best thing that China has to offer the West....Humanized thinking is just reasonable thinking. The logical man is always self-righteous and therefore wrong, while the reasonable man suspects that perhaps he is wrong and is therefore always right."②

Lin delighted readers around the globe with essays on such profound subjects as his love for loafing, and his insistence that, bottom line, we are all alike: "I am interested only in presenting [in this book] a view of life and of things as the best and wisest Chinese minds have seen it and expressed it in their folk wisdom and their literature. It is an idle philosophy born out of an idle life, evolved in a different age, I am quite aware. But I cannot help feeling that this view of life is essentially true, and since we are alike under the skin, what touches the human heart in one country touches all."③

---

① *My Country and My People*, 85.
② *Importance of Living*, pp. 424-25.
③ *The Importance of Living*, page 1

"在中国人的心灵中,科学方法不能得到发展的原因是很容易理解的,因为科学方法除了要求分析性思维之外,总是免不了要有一些枯燥的工作要做。而中国人则相信自己的庸见与洞察力的闪光。

推理的方法在应用到人际关系(中国人最感兴趣的东西)时,常常导致一种愚蠢的结论,这在美国大学里并不罕见。今天有许多用推理方法写成的博士论文,会使长眠地下的培根感到不安。没有一个中国人会愚蠢到去写一篇关于冰淇淋的博士论文,并且在一系列的观察与分析之后得出令人瞠目的结论说'糖(在冰淇淋的制作中)最重要的功能是使冰淇淋发甜',或者在对'四种洗碟方法的时间与运动方法比较'进行研究之后,很高兴地下结论说'弯腰提取物件的动作是很累人的'……

这种愚蠢的方法也许有助于商业运作,但我想中国人如果用片刻的直觉与常识,也完全能得出同样正确的结论。"①

在1937年出版的畅销书《生活的艺术》中,林语堂强调了"近情精神"比逻辑重要。

"与逻辑相对的有常识,或更好一些的说法:还有近情的精神……这近情的时代,如果有来临的一天,则就是和平时代的来临……近情精神是中国所能贡献给西方的一件最好的物事……人性化的思想其实就是近情的思想。专讲逻辑的人是永远自以为是的,所以他是不近人情,也是不对的;至于近情的人则自己常疑惑自己是错的,所以他永远是对的。"②

林语堂那些主题深刻的文章受到全世界读者的喜爱,例如他热爱闲游,以及他坚信从根本上看,人们都是相似的。

Chinese Typewriter (Lin Yutang's Invention)

"我只想(在书中)表现一种中国最优越最聪慧的哲人们所见到而在他们的文字中发挥过的人生观和事物观。我知道这是一种闲适哲学,是在异于现代时代里的闲适生活中所产生。我总觉得这种人生观是绝对真实的。人类心性既然相同,则在这个国家里能感动人的东西,自然也会感动别的国家的人类。"③

---

① 《吾国与吾民》,第85页。
② 《生活的艺术》,第424~425页。
③ 《生活的艺术》,第1页。

Lin wrote widely in the 20s and by 1930, the NY Times wrote commentaries on his works. Lin worked with Song Qingling (宋庆龄), widow of Sun Yat-sen (孙中山), to create the China Democratic Rights Insurance League, and after 1938 he lived and traveled in Europe, where he wrote the trilogy of "Peking Cloud" (京华烟云), "Wind and Crane's Tear" (风声鹤泪), and "The Red Door" (朱门). Lin returned to the U.S. in 1936 and in 1959 began attending New York City's Madison Avenue Presbyterian Church.

He wrote:
Looking back on my life, I know that for 30 years I lived in this world like an orphan. I am an orphan no longer. Where I had been drifting, I have arrived. The Sunday morning when I rejoined the Christian church was a homecoming.①

Lin settled down in Taiwan in 1966 and passed away in March, 1976, at age 80. The NY York Times obituary noted,

Lin Yutang, poet, novelist, historian and philosopher, had no peer as an interpreter to Western minds of the customs, aspirations, fears and thoughts of his people and their country, China, the great and tragic land.②

Mickey Mouse in "With Love and Irony"
Lin Yutang

> "One of the most difficult things for me to put over to my Chinese-reading public is to convince them that humor is a part of life and therefore should not be shut out even from serious literature. This is as difficult as it has been for me to convince them that Confucius was a human being and always loved a good joke, even at his own expense."
> Lin Yutang, "With Love and Irony."

---

① "Why I Came Back to Christianity," in Presbyterian Life (April 13, 1959), 13-15.
② "Lin Yutang, 80, Dies; Scholar-Philosopher," New York Times, 27 March 1976

第 27 章 人文学院

在 20 世纪 20 年代林语堂著述广泛,到了 30 年代,对他作品的评论文章不时见诸《纽约时报》报端。林语堂和孙中山的遗孀宋庆龄合作,成立了中国民权保障同盟。1938 年以后他在欧洲游历,写下小说三部曲《京华烟云》、《风声鹤唳》和《朱门》。

1936 年,林语堂回到美国。从 1959 年起,定期去纽约麦迪逊大街的长老会教堂。他写道:

"回顾我的一生,30 年来我就像个孤儿般活在人世。从现在起我不再是孤儿了,我又回到迷失的起点。重新参加礼拜的那个星期天早晨,对我而言就像回到家一样。"①

林语堂 1966 年在台湾定居,1976 年 3 月逝世,享年 80 岁。《纽约时报》的讣告这样评价他:

"林语堂,诗人,小说家,历史学家,哲学家。他向西方诠释中国这个多灾多难大国的风土人情,以及中国人的所盼、所虑和所思,在这方面他成绩卓著,无人能比。"②

TV Interview of Lin Yutang 林语堂接受电视台采访

> "最难的事之一就是让我的中国读者们接受这样的观念:幽默是生活的一部分,即使在严肃文学中也应该占有一席之地。这和下面这件事一样困难重重:我一直在说服他们相信孔子是个爱开玩笑的普通人,甚至会拿自己开涮。"
>
> (摘自林语堂的《讽颂集》)

---

① 《我为什么回归基督教》,1959 年 4 月 13 日出版的《长老会教徒生活》,第 13~15 页。

② "Lin Yutang,80,Dies; Scholar-Philosopher",《纽约时报》1976 年 3 月 27 日。

Chapter 28

School of Journalism & Communication

News Flash! Double Chinese & British Degrees for Journalism Majors. Junior students from XMU's Dept. of Journalism and Communication can apply for studies at the U.K.'s Luton Univ. and acquire bachelor degrees from both XMU and Luton if they have earned enough credits and completed their thesis at Luton. These students may stay their fourth year at Luton to acquire a master degree.
Adapted from Common Talk, Xiamen Daily, June 23, 2004

Journalistic education has a long history at Xiamen University, with the "Department of Journalism" established in 1922. The "Department of Journalism & Communication", founded in 1983, was China's first Journalism program to use "communication" in the name, and that year began to enroll Master's students. The Master's in journalism started in 1994, and the Master's in communication in 2002. In 2002, the School was authorized to confer PhD degrees. In 2007, the School of Journalism & Communication was founded, and Dr. Zhang Mingqing was appointed the first dean.

Tel: 0592-2180475
Fax: 0592-2186382
Email: comm@xmu.edu.cn
Address: 福建省厦门市厦门大学新闻传播学院
P.C: 361005

Another News Flash! Xiamen University faculty and students to embark on internship in the Philippines Under a goodwill partnership agreement recently signed by the Xiamen University Department of Journalism & Communication and the Philippines-based World News, the department will send several faculty members and students to the Philippines each year for research and internships. They hope to develop a more intimate understanding of the Chinese-language media in the island nation. Common Talk, Xiamen Daily, Sept. 28, 2005

第28章

新闻传播学院

快讯！ 赴英学新闻拿两国学位 厦门大学新闻传播系的三年级学生可以申请去英国鲁顿大学继续学习，修满学分并在那里完成毕业论文后可获得两所大学的学士学位。此外，这些留英学生毕业后还可以在鲁顿大学继续第四年的学习，获得硕士学位。

《厦门日报·双语周刊》2004年6月23日

厦门大学新闻教育历史悠久。早在1922年，厦门大学就设立了"新闻学部"，1983年，厦门大学新闻传播系正式成立，在国内新闻院系中率先以"传播"冠名。同年，开始招收首批硕士研究生，1994年，厦门大学新闻传播系设立新闻学硕士点，2002年，设立传播学硕士点，2006年，获得传播学博士点学位授予权。2007年，新闻传播学院成立，张铭清为首任院长。

联系方式
电话：0592-2180475
传真：0592-2186382
Email: comm@xmu.edu.cn
地址：福建省厦门市厦门大学新闻传播学院
邮编：361005

快讯！厦大师生将赴菲实习

最近，厦门大学新闻传播系与菲律宾《世界日报》签订了一项友好合作协议。今后新闻传播系每年将选派一些师生去菲律宾进行研究或实习。这家媒体希望能够对菲律宾群岛内的中文媒体有更深刻的了解。

《厦门日报·双语周刊》2005年3月28日

Chapter 29

School of Sinology Research

The preparation for the establishment of Xiamen University School of Sinology Research started in 1925. In 1926, Lin Yutang was appointed Director of Art studies of XMU and secretary of the School of Sinology Research. Lin hired some of the most well-known minds of the time such as Shen Jianshi, Lu Xu, Gu Jiegang, Zhang Xinglang and Chen Wangli, and together they started the full preparation for the foundation of the school.

During the opening ceremony on October 10, 1926, XMU's president, Lin Wenqing, was appointed as dean, Shen Jianshi as director, and Lin Yutang as general secretary.

XMU restarted the School of Sinology Research at its 80th anniversary in 2006, with the intention of seizing the opportunity of China's rise to promote sinology and Confucianism, and carry forward China's rich inheritance of traditions and classic culture.

第29章

厦门大学国学研究院

厦门大学国学研究院于1925年开始筹办。1926年,林吾堂出任厦门大学文科主任兼国学研究院秘书,招揽了沈兼士、鲁迅、顾颉刚、张星烺、陈万里等一批著名学者来厦门大学任职,全面展开筹备工作。

1926年10月10日,厦门大学国学研究院举行成立大会,校长林文庆任院长,沈兼士任主任,林语堂任总秘书。

如今,厦门大学在国学研究院成立80周年之际,复办国学研究院,抓住中华民族面临全面振兴的历史机遇,重振国学、弘扬中华文化,以发扬历史传统,复兴中华文化。

Chapter 30

XMU Arts College

> **News Flash!** **CLAREMONT, CA (January 23, 2006)** "The Scripps College Department of Music and the Gould Center of Claremont McKenna College present a concert performance with a Chinese music delegation from Xiamen University, Fujian, China, celebrating the traditional music and dance of Inner Mongolia on Sunday, February 5, at 3 p.m. in Balch Auditorium of Scripps College."

XMU's Art College, while relatively young (founded in 1983), is fortunate to be located in Xiamen, "City of the Arts," because Xiamen is unique in its preservation of both Chinese and international arts. Xiamen has preserved the 1,000-year-old Nanyin Opera, but it is also famous for its international musical and art heritage as well. Gulangyu Islet is known as Piano Islet, with more pianos per capita than anywhere else in China (1 in 5 families). It has the best piano museum in Asia and the organ museum is expected to become the best in the world. Xiamen has been the home of 100s of well know musicians, and has also produced internationally famous artists like Teng Hiok Chiu (周廷旭).

In Xiamen, City of the Arts, art is not only an issue of aesthetics but also quickly becoming big business as well. Xiamen is one of the largest producers of oil paintings in China, accounting for roughly 18% of the globe's output! (See www.amoypaintings.com)

The Art College has 4 primary divisions:
    The Fine Art Department   The Music Department
    The Art Research Institute   The Art Company

第30章

厦门大学艺术学院

> **快讯：克莱蒙，加利福尼亚**（2006年1月23日）
> "2月5日（星期日）下午3点，在Scripps大学的巴赫大礼堂里，Scripps大学的音乐系和Claremont McKenna大学的古尔德中心，将和来自中国福建的厦门大学的音乐代表团，为大家奉献上一场音乐会，弘扬中国内蒙古的传统音乐和舞蹈。"

厦门大学艺术学院是相对来说比较年轻的学院（创办于1983年），而能够坐落于"艺术之城"厦门——这座对于中国和世界艺术的保护和珍藏有着特殊地位的城市，则是她的荣幸。厦门不仅保留着有着千年历史的南音，还珍藏了世界的其他众多音乐和艺术瑰宝。鼓浪屿有"钢琴之岛"的美称，岛上钢琴的人均拥有量比中国任何其他地方都高（平均每5户家庭就有一架钢琴）。鼓浪屿还拥有亚洲最好的钢琴博物馆，并有望建成世界上最好的钢琴博物馆。鼓浪屿上有100多个音乐世家，也诞生过画坛奇才周廷旭等世界闻名的艺术家。

在厦门这座"艺术之城"，艺术不仅仅是关于审美，它还正在迅速地发展成为一项巨大的商业。厦门是中国油画作品的最大的生产基地之一，每年出口的油画作品大约占了全球市场份额的15%（参照www.amoypaintings.com）。

厦门大学艺术学院下设：
　　美术系、音乐系、艺术研究所、艺术公司

The Arts College's numerous courses cover the fields of Musicology, Music Performance, Fine Arts, and Artistic Design (which includes everything from landscape design to commercial photography and history of architecture). The Sino-European Art Center, hosted by the Art College and located on campus, holds frequent exhibitions by both European and Chinese artists.
Contact Tel: 218-2404 Fax: 218-1499
E-mail: ysxy@xmu.edu.cn Website: http//:art.xmu.edu.cn

Will XMU get its own Orchestra? On the plane back from Beijing last week I was delighted to sit next to none other than "the best woman conductor in the world," Madame Zheng Xiaoying! [1] For much of the 2½ hour flight she told me about her family's background, her experiences with her Xiamen Orchestra—and a funny story about XMU.

Madame Zheng said that while attending a dinner with various big potatoes in Xiamen, she told one man she was frustrated with XMU. "They spend lots of money inviting pop and rock stars from all over China, but never bother to invite our own Xiamen orchestra to perform on campus!" Madame Zheng of course had no idea she was talking to none other than Prof. Zhu Chongshi, who immediately afterwards became President of XMU!

She said, "After Professor Zhu became president of XMU, one of the first things he did was say, "Quick! Invite Xiamen Philharmonic Orchestra to perform at XMU!"

Happily, our Xiamen Orchestra's relationship with XMU has grown closer ever since, with many of the members lecturing at XMU, and now they have been invited to become our university orchestra. Few, if any, universities in the world have their own orchestra!

"Will that happen?" I asked Madame Zheng.

She smiled slyly. "Well, that depends on how well they sponsor us!"

---

[1] Read "Discover Gulangyu" for a biography of Madame Zheng.

第 30 章 厦门大学艺术学院

DISCOVER Xiamen University

艺术学院设置的专业包括音乐学、音乐表演、美术学和艺术设计（其中包括了环境艺术、视觉传达、综合材料与多媒体、雕塑等方向）。隶属于艺术学院的"中国欧洲艺术中心"，就设在厦大校园内，还经常举办欧洲和中国艺术家的作品展览。

联系方式
电话：218-2404 传真：218-1499
电子邮件：ysxy@xmu.edu.cn
网址：http://art.xmu.edu.cn

厦大会拥有自己的乐团吗？

在上个星期从北京回来的飞机上，我有幸坐在"世界上最棒的女指挥家"旁边，对，正是郑小瑛女士[①]！在接下来的两个半小时的航程中，她谈了她的家庭背景、她和厦门爱乐乐团的经历以及一件和厦门大学有关的趣事。

郑女士说，那是在一个晚宴上，有厦门不少"大人物"参加。她向一位先生抱怨说："厦大总是花大把的钱到处去请流行和摇滚明星，却从来不邀请我们自己的厦门爱乐乐团在学校演奏！"郑女士当时根本不知道，这位先生不是别人，正是不久后就成为了厦大校长的朱崇实！

她说："朱崇实教授当了厦大校长之后，立刻就告诉大家，'快快快！赶快去邀请厦门爱乐乐团到厦大来演出！'"

从此以后，厦门爱乐乐团和厦门大学的关系更近了。乐团的很多成员在厦大授课，也有的被邀请参加厦大自己的乐团。厦大将是世界上少有的拥有自己的独立乐团的大学了。

"真会这样吗？"我问郑女士。

她狡黠地笑了笑，说："那得看他们赞助的情况怎样了！"

---

① 详细请参照《魅力鼓浪屿》中关于郑小瑛女士的传记。

An Amoy University Concert
by Anne Averil McKenzie, Gulangyu resident in the 1920

"The University looked quiet and purposeful in the grey afternoon. The large plain blocks were lifted from monotony by the upcurved, green-tiled roofs, an excellent blend of Eastern and Western idioms. Its situation, between the granite rocks and the sea, had an austere dignity. It was hard to associate the place and the quietly animated students, drifting about the still raw quadrangle and gardens, with riots and rabbles; with histrionics perhaps, but not with hysterics. Yet, all over China, it was the students who supplied the most ardent and fanatical agitators, as well as the political spearheads of revolution...

(Dukes, 1885)

"In one of the smaller halls we gathered to hear the 'se' players. The first performer already sat behind the table which bore his instrument, a kind of psaltery, and was there a single orchid in a vase--or am I in another picture? He wore grey brocaded silk beneath his short black satin jacket and bent gravely over the silk strings.

"'I hope,' he eyes us solemnly, 'you, my honoured audience, will not emulate the Emperor Huang Ti who, you will remember, was so deeply moved by the Lady Su's playing of the "se" that he forthwith ordered the number of strings to be halved in order that he might suffer less.'

"The audience was delighted.

"From the first, the music was between the player and his 'se.' He seemed to be privately communing with the strings. Then I had the sensation that he and the "se" were one, and that their utterances were too subtle for me to understand... Its idiom was entirely strange, too baffling for immediate enjoyment, but it left us both with an aftermath in memory as strong and elusive as the aroma of Chinese tea on the palate.

"In China, from legendary times, music was written for poetry and poetry written to be sung. Both spoke a language I could not understand, using age-old symbols, classic repetitions and allusions to which I had not been educated to respond either intellectually or emotionally."

第30章 厦门大学艺术学院

一场厦门大学的音乐会
(Anne Averil McKenzie 著,1920年居于鼓浪屿)

这是一个灰蒙蒙的下午,学校显得安静又有意境。简朴的大楼因向上弯曲的绿瓦屋顶而不再单调,体现了东西方智慧的完美融合。它位于花岗岩石和海之间,彰显出一种简朴的高贵。活泼的学生们安静地出入于庭院和花园,很难把他们及这样一个地方与暴乱闹事联系起来,就算有大概也是演戏,而不是真的歇斯底里。然而在全中国,确实是学生们充当了革命最狂热的鼓动者和政治先锋。

Roadside Theater (MacGowan 1912)

我们聚在一个稍小的礼堂里准备听瑟的演奏。第一个表演者已经坐在桌子后面,桌上摆放着他的乐器,这是一种古代弦乐器,边上一朵兰花插在花瓶里——莫非我是置身在画中吗?他上身穿着黑色缎子短袄,下身是灰色锦缎马褂,神情庄严地专注于琴弦。

"我希望大家,"他说话时眼神严峻,"我尊敬的听众,不要像黄帝一样。众所周知,他被苏夫人的瑟深深打动之后,立刻命令将琴弦的数量减半来减少自己的痛苦。"

听众都笑了。

演奏一开始,音乐存在于演奏者和"瑟"之间,他似乎在和琴弦喁喁私语。后来我感觉他和"瑟"融为了一体,两者间的交谈太玄妙令我难以理解……这种语汇是全然陌生,令人困惑的,不能给人即时的愉悦,但却给我们留下一段回忆,就像中国茶留在腭间的芳香一样强烈而又难以捉摸。

在中国,从有传说的年代开始,音乐就为诗而作,诗又为了歌而作。它们都传递着我无法理解的语言。对于那些古老的符号、经典的重复和暗示,在理性上和感性上我都不知如何产生共鸣。

Chinese European Art Center (中国欧洲艺术中心) (Adapted From "Amoy Magic—Guide to Xiamen")

Seeing as how it was the Dutch who opened up Xiamen back almost 500 years ago, its appropriate that they are in the forefront of opening Xiamen yet again as they help Chinese Laonei and European Laowai better understand one another's culture and arts.

Ms. Ineke Gudmundsson iniated the Art Center in 1999 as a joint venture with XMU Art College. Works by well respected European artists have included Teun Hock's painted photographs ("stills of the theater of life"), JCJ Vanderheyden's "fragments of reality," Pieter Holstein's drawings, Marcel Kalksma's handmade prints, Arni Gudmundsson's sculptures, as well as the works of Chinese artists like Xie Lai, Wu Yiming and Wen Bin.

When I visited the art center this morning, Jean Bernard Koeman was busy, drill in hand, setting up his exhibit entitled, "Mental Architecture (a travel survival kit), which included photos, Chinese characters, and oddly designed cubicles (designed, he said, to fit well in planes, and to form a sphere when stacked). It was a bit too much architecture for my mental capacities (or lack of them), but I enjoyed the photos, and his infectious enthusiasm. I did ask one person why XMU doesn't have an American-Chinese Center and they said it was because we Americans don't have any culture. That isn't true. I've had cultures[①] many times (I use them to make yogurt).

Exhibits change frequently, so check out the latest offerings at their website, or phone.   Tel: 218-0850, 218-5860

website: **http://www.ceac99.com**   E-mail: **ceac99@public.xm.fj.cn**

Center Hours: Wed. thru Sunday, 10 AM – 12 Noon, 3 – 5 PM

---

① Culture: colony of bacteria, such as the lactobacillus used to make yogurt.

第30章 厦门大学艺术学院

厦门大学艺术学院中国欧洲艺术中心
——摘自《魅力厦门》

公元 1500 年前后,荷兰人打开了厦门的门户。500 年后,荷兰人再次出现在厦门对外开放的潮头看来是再合适不过的了。他们可以让中国的老内和欧洲的老外更好地了解对方的文化和艺术。

1999 年,荷兰人伊尼卡·顾蒙逊女士与厦门大学艺术学院合作建立了中国欧洲艺术中心。这里收藏了许多欧洲知名艺术家的作品,其中包括了特恩·霍克的摄影画("人生舞台的静止艺术")、JCJ·范德海登的"现实的碎片"、皮耶特·霍尔斯坦的画作、马赛尔·卡尔斯马的版画和阿尼·顾蒙逊的雕塑。当然也有诸如谢来、吴益明和闻斌等中国艺术家的作品。

今天早上,我刚去过艺术中心。当时,让·勃纳德·寇曼正手拿钻子,忙着把他的展品挂起来。展品是一个旅行求生背包,名叫"精神建筑",里面有些照片和中文字,并且有着奇特的外形设计。寇曼说,这种设计是为了在飞机上使用方便,折叠起来时可以形成一个球形。或许是我缺乏想象力的缘故吧,反正这种"建筑"设计实在有点儿超乎我的想象。不过,我还是蛮欣赏那些照片和他的这股热情。我曾经问过别人,为什么厦门大学没有中美艺术中心。他们说,那是因为我们美国人缺乏文化修养。其实不是那么回事,我就挺有文化修养的。(只是用错地方罢了。)

中欧艺术中心的展品经常更新。因此,你可以致电或者登陆他们的网站了解最新的动态。

电话:218-0850 218-5360
电邮:ceac99@public.xm.fj.cn 网址:http://www.ceac99.com
开放时间:周三至周日,上午 10 时—中午 12 时,
下午 3 时—5 时

Professor Tang Sao Yun 唐绍云教授

I just landed a copy of one of China's bestselling new art books, "Tang Shaoyuan Oil Painting Techniques 《唐绍云谈油画技法》. Now I just need him to autograph it!

Prof. Tang and his wife are both professors in XMU's School of Art. . Tang's works were selected for the 6th, 7th, and 8th National China Art Exhibition, and have been shown in the U.S., Japan, Hong Kong and Taiwan.

The Tang's two daughters are also making their marks in the world. The younger daughter, May, graduated from XMU with an English degree, but taught herself computers, became an internet expert, and is now manager of a large department in Chinabyte.com

The oldest daughter, Rose, was a producer for CNN International and CNN Hong Kong, a reporter/producer/presenter for the Australian Broadcasting Corporation, and an award-winning correspondent for such publications as Asiaweek, Finance Asia, and The Standard (HK). But like parents, like daughter. She recently gave up her successful career for marriage, motherhood, and a return to her paintbrush and canvas. In this Rose reminds me of her idealistic father, of whom she once wrote to me,

"In my biased view, I think the best quality of my dad is that he refuses to bow to pressures from fellow painters or the money driven culture in general to paint for the market or paint to get famous. He sticks to his passion…and he refuses to play politics or whatever power games to… "

Well, enough of that letter! Let me close this chapter with an article I wrote a few years ago about this "Sherlock Holmes of the Canvas"…

唐绍云教授

我最近刚拥有了一本立于中国的畅销书排行榜上的新书《唐绍云谈油画技法》。现在我只需要他的亲笔签名啦!

唐教授和夫人都是厦门大学艺术学院的教授。唐教授的作品曾参加第六、七、八届全国美展,并在美国、日本、香港和台湾等国家和地区展览。

唐教授的两个女儿也成就斐然。小女儿 May,厦门大学英语专业毕业,自学了电脑,现在是一个互联网专家,也是天极一个大部门的经理。

大女儿 Rose,曾经是 CNN 国际频道和 CNN 香港频道的制片人,也曾是澳大利亚广播公司的记者、制片人和主持人,还曾是《亚洲周刊》、《财富》亚洲版、《英文虎报》等出版物的一名出色的记者。但是正所谓"有其父必有其女",最近她为家庭放弃了这些,又回到了由画笔和帆布组成的世界。在这里,Rose 让我想起了她唯美的父亲,她曾经这样向我描写她的父亲:

"作为女儿,在我眼里,父亲最高贵的品质是,他与世俗不同,从不向来自同行的压力屈服,从不为迎合市场而作画,从不为金钱或出名而弯腰,他坚持为自己的那份热情而创作……他还拒绝用政治把戏或任何权力手段去……"

信就引用到这里吧。让我用下面这篇我几年前写的关于唐先生这位"画坛的福尔摩斯"的文章来给为本章画上一个句号吧……

Tang Shaoyun—Sherlock Holmes of the Canvas
(Originally in "*China Today*," April, 1998)

When I attended an art exhibition by XMU's Professor Tang Sao Yun, I expected paintings of archetypical Chinese fishermen poling prosaic bamboo rafts past wizened spruce and pagodas perched on cloud covered precipices, but Tang's works defy pigeonholing as Chinese or Western, classical or contemporary.

Tang's genius is in manifesting the magic of the mundane, in capturing on canvas what we take for granted. In this Tang reminds me of Western literature's most famous sleuth, Sherlock Holmes, who once chided his assistant Mr. Watson, "People see but they don't observe."

I suspected that Tang's rendition of a country road at sunset depicted an exotic locale like Southern France or Wales, but Tang assured me that it was simply the beach road I had cycled down minutes earlier. He explained, "I often travel this road in the evening to market. I like the moon hovering over the trees, and the gentle glow of street lamps at dusk." Tang pointed to a courtyard wall smothered in snarled vines and arthritic tree branches seeking escape from the crowded enclosure. He said softly, "I've always wondered who lives behind that wooden gate. It is mysterious."

From Tang's perspective the gate was indeed mysterious, though to my chagrin, during my many years in Xiamen I had never noticed either the gate or the wall.

I had also never thought twice about the wizened tree at the ancient Huli fort until I saw Tang's "Vicissitudes." Tang noted the gnarled roots, tangled like a wooden web in their suffocating death grip upon the obstinate boulder, and said, "The roots resemble Chinese grass-style characters, don't they? This tree has seen a lot of history."

Tang's magic brush had transformed the tenacious tree into an ancient historian who had recorded in roots upon rock the rise and fall of tides and men, of oppression and deliverance. I could almost fancy young scholars sitting at this ancient academic's feet. I determined to revisit the tree. Perhaps it might speak to me as well?

While the Huli tree evokes China's past, the stately subject of "Pigeon Whistle" embodies China's future. Tang spoke reverently of the tree towering over the courtyard of his old Beijing apartment, "This tree is China. She changes with the seasons, slow or dormant in winter, but in spring, gaining a new lease on life -- 枯木逢春. Always changing, but ever reaching upward.

第30章 厦门大学艺术学院

化世俗为神奇的画家唐绍云

（原载《今日中国》1998年4月，潘维廉）

去看厦门大学唐绍云教授的画展前,原以为会是原汁原味的中国丹青：落木萧萧中,渔夫举篙撑着竹排,高崖峭壁上,云深不知处,有小亭翼然。待看完画展才发现,唐的作品迥异中西,非类古今。

通过在画布上表现我们熟知而又淡漠之物,化世俗为神奇,这就是唐的超凡不群之处。唐这点让我想起了西方文学中著名的侦探夏洛克·福尔摩斯,他曾经责怪助手华生："人们虽会看却不懂得观察。"

我本以为唐画的那条夕阳余辉下的乡村小路表现的是诸如法国南部或威尔士的异国风情,但是唐告诉我,其实它只不过是我刚刚骑车经过的那条海边小道。他解释说："我常在傍晚走这条路去市场。我喜欢月上枝头和薄暮迷蒙中街灯散漫出的柔光。"唐指着一堵藤蔓滋弥的院墙,从那密密层层的禁锢中,有一虬突的树干向外探出了身子。他轻声低语道："我一直想知道在那扇掩映的木门里住着的究竟是谁。这真是神秘。"

在唐看来,这扇门的的确确是神秘莫测的,而令我汗颜的是,在厦门九年,我对这门和墙从不曾留意。

我对胡里山古炮台那棵凋敝的古木同样未多作留意,直到看到唐的《沧桑》。唐指着这根须缠结如网、紧咬顽石的树说："这根须像不像中国的草书？这树可是阅尽人世沧桑了。"

唐出神入化之笔把这棵顽强不屈的古树变成了一个饱经风霜的史学家。在那植于坚石的根须中,记录着潮涨潮落,世事浮沉。我几可想象年轻的学子们围坐于这位耄耋学者脚下的情景,决意再去拜谒这株古树。或许,它也会给我以启示吧？

如果说胡里山的古树让人回想起中国的过去,那么,《鸽哨》这一庄严的主题是则象征着中国的未来。唐近乎虔诚地提到他北京旧寓所院中那棵参天的大树,"这棵树就是中国,她随四时节气变换而变化,严冬来临,凋零敝落,而春风一度,新枝又发。始终生生不息,蓬勃向上。"

"沧桑—胡炮台系列之一" 唐绍云 145×112CM

For Tang, even an old nondescript window tells tales. "A Modern History of China – Stirred by the Sea Wind" portrays the harbor through the window of Xiamen University's old library. On the wooden ledge is a yellowed copy of "A Modern History of China," opened to the chapter on the second opium war. A scholar's candle drips waxen tears, evoking images of the grievous century of opium trade conducted at gunpoint by foreign ships traveling the now tranquil waters below. Yet this art, like the artist, emanates not melancholy but hope, for as Tang explained, "The Sea has influenced all changes in modern China, both good and bad. Today, as China opens to the world, most of the influence is good." The rising sun of a new day casts beams of golden light upon the window frame, and freighters, not warships, ply the harbor. It is a moving work, and reminds us to learn from the past that we might forge a brighter future.

Everyone does a double-take at "The Classroom Corridor Facing the Sea." The Xiamen University Art College's walls, columns and floors are transparent, allowing the chimerical architecture to frame the natural beauty rather than detract from it. Through the ghostly structure one sees the gentle hills rolling into Xiamen harbor, where boats bob like fishing floats and scenic Gulangyu Island floats across the port from busy downtown Xiamen. Tang explained, "I wasn't seeking mere realism – a camera or draftsman could do that."

Tang has a special interest in patriotic art, heedless of whether 'political' art is in vogue or not. He reminisced with me how as a child of 3 or 4 he fled with his family from strafing Japanese bombers, and of his experiences before and after liberation. Like many Chinese, Tang suffered during the Cultural Revolution, but he emerged from the tumultuous decade with a more mature appreciation of those who sacrificed to transform New China from vision into reality.

抗日战争中华侨在滇缅公路——离别、征程、劫难 　　油画 1996
Overseas Chinese on the Burma Road during the War
of Resistance against Japan　　　　oil on Canvas 186 × 186cm

第30章 厦门大学艺术学院

对唐来说,即便一扇寻常老旧的窗子也别有深意。《破海风掀动的一本中国近代史》展现的就是通过厦门大学旧图书馆的一扇窗户看厦门港的景象。窗台上放着的是一本泛黄的、翻至第二次鸦片战争这一章的《中国近代史》。烛泪涟涟,令人遥想在今日平静的海面上,当年列强凭借船坚炮利贩卖鸦片给中国制造苦难的历史。然而画如其人,这幅作品弥散的绝非感伤颓废之气,而是充溢张扬着希望之情。正如唐所说:"受西方影响,近代中国发生了各种变化,这些变化有好有坏,现在中国对外开放,西方的影响大部分还是好的。"旭日初升,新的一轮曙色给窗棂抹上金光,在港湾中游弋的已不再是战舰而是货轮了。这是幅感人至深的画作,它昭示我们要创造一个美好的未来就当以古为鉴。

谁都会忍不住对《临海的教室走廊》多看一眼。厦门大学艺术学院的墙体、廊柱、地面均澄明剔透,这如梦似幻的建筑不但未使自然之美稍减一分,其本身亦成为自然美的一部分。透过这缥缈虚幻的楼体,你可以看到柔曼的群山绵延入港,港湾内船只点点如浮漂着的钓浮,而风光旖旎的鼓浪屿,便栖身在繁华的市区和厦门港间。唐解释说:"我追求的不是纯粹的现实主义————那是照相机或制图员的事。"

唐对爱国主义题材的作品情有独钟,而对"政治性"艺术是否入时并不在乎。他曾向我忆起在他还是一个三四岁的小孩时,为避日机轰炸,如何举家逃难,以及解放前后的经历,如同许多中国人一样,唐在"文化大革命"中历经磨难,但是作为十年动乱的过来人,他对那些流血牺牲把新中国从理想变成现实的先烈反而有了一层更成熟的理解。

One such patriotic work, which has been exhibited throughout Asia, is "Overseas Chinese on the Burma Road during the War of Resistance against Japan." Four war-weary but resolute Chinese volunteers stand before a camouflaged truck, the serpentine Burma Road winding into the mountains and clouds behind them. The curved horizon behind the strafing Japanese bomber conveys not only the global proportions of the war but also the pivotal role that overseas Chinese' sacrifices played for world peace and freedom. As Tang said, "There would have been no Socialist China as we know her without such sacrifices."

Tang has also found inspiration from one of New China's most well known poets -- Mao Ze Dong. We could appreciate the full beauty of Chairman Mao's poem "Lou Mountain Pass" (娄山关) only in Chinese until Tang's magic brush transcended language and culture. In this monochromatic study, a horseman blows reveille at daybreak, and the phantasmal outline of soldiers breaks the blanket of morning mist. One can almost hear the stalwart remnant of soldiers as they rub chilled hands and discuss hopes for a decisive victory that morning.

Professor Tang enthusiastically embraces many schools of art but owes allegiance to none, his priority being message, not method. In "Plateau Horse Racing," lusty stallions painted in violent sweeps of white, brown and ocher threaten to gallop right off the black wooden frame. In an impressionist exercise, dollops of bright blues and reds and greens immortalize the essence of the bougainvillaea that splashes our campus with color year round. An elderly man and woman from Tang's home province of Sichuan were so lifelike that I could feel their eyes following me curiously, a shy greeting on the tips of their unmoving tongues.

Tang said, "There is much to learn from foreign art, but we must also take care not to abandon China's own rich traditions and techniques."

This Sherlock Holmes of the Canvas has given me a greater appreciation of both Western and Chinese art. And he has motivated me to observe life, and to internalize what makes this brief sojourn so beautiful and rewarding -- historian trees, mysterious gates, street lamps at dusk, a Tibetan child serving butter tea, and the gnarled, gentle hands of my sons' adopted Chinese grandfather.

第30章　厦门大学艺术学院

此类爱国主义题材作品中的一件就是曾在亚洲许多国家都展出过的《抗日战争中华侨在滇缅公路》。四名饱受战火洗礼、依然坚强刚毅的华侨机工站在一辆涂有迷彩的卡车前，在其身后，云雾缭绕的崇山峻岭间，是蜿蜒盘旋的滇缅公路，狂轰滥炸的日机后的一条弧线象征着全球范围的战火和华侨对争取世界和平和自由所做的牺牲及奉献。正如唐所说："没有这些牺牲奉献，就不会有我们今天的社会主义中国。"

唐从新中国缔造者、著名诗人毛泽东那里也获得了不少灵感。在唐用其超越语言文化的生花妙笔把毛泽东的《娄山关》画出之前，这首诗之大美只可在中文里细嚼慢品。在这幅单色调的作品中，天方破晓，马背上一名号手正在吹起床号，晨雾如洗，战士们的身影若隐若现。他们搓着冻僵的手摩拳擦掌地讨论着一场重大战役的取胜之机，你似乎仍可以听到他们当时的铮铮之言。

这位朝气蓬勃的艺术家，孜孜不倦地博采各家之长，但又不拘泥于一派一门，他重表现内容而轻表现手法。在《高原赛马》中，粗犷的白、棕、赭三色勾勒出的骠骑烈马在黑木框中呼之欲出。在一幅印象派的画作中，寥寥几笔浓墨重彩的蓝红绿便把终年为我们校园增色添彩的三角梅之神表现得活灵活现。来自唐故乡四川省的老大爷老大娘画得是如此栩栩如生，我可以感觉到他们的目光始终好奇地追随着我，嘴虽未张，但一个羞赧的问候已挂在了舌尖。

唐说："国外艺术中有许多值得我们学习，但我们也不应摒弃中国传统中丰富的表现技法。"

这位画坛的福尔摩斯使我提高了对中西艺术的鉴赏水平。同时他还促使我去观察生活，去发现使这瞬间变得如此美丽如此颇具深意的种种内在联系——垂垂老矣的树、神秘莫测的门、暮霭中的街灯、端着奶茶的藏族小女孩、还有我儿子的中国干爷爷那双骨节粗大而又温柔的手。

Chapter 31

Software School

XMU's Software School (SS), one of 35 approved by the Ministry of Education, is near the Xiamen Software Park on the scenic Island Ring Road.

During the two years prior to the Software Park opening, over 100 new software firms had opened, with annual output exceeding 500 million Yuan. A Software School was a natural, and many of its graduates are helping Xiamen carve a growing niche in China's software industry by starting up their own companies.

SS's staff of highly experienced Chinese and foreign professors use advanced teaching practices, textbooks and software to teach bilingual grad and undergrad programs to over 1000 students. SS emphasizes both theory and practice, and has numerous cooperative activities with such domestic and overseas IT firms as IBM, BEA, ORACLE, SYBASE, DELL and SUN (which designated SS a Sun Microsystems Academic Initiative Institution). Activities include research and development; technical certification; study, teaching and research scholarships; on-campus scientific and technological activities, graduation internships, and technical support services. The school also helps graduates seek employment.

Two teams placed in the 2002 ACM Asia Programming Contest sponsored by IBM in Beijing, and in that same year IBM joined forces with the School to set up a program to train IT professionals. Tony Chen, manager of IBM China Region's Learning Services, said China lags behind India in the software industry because China lacked software engineers, whereas India invests heavily in training.[1] Chen added, "Both the central government and local governments should immediately introduce efficient support, in terms of policies and capital, to upgrade the overall technology level of the sector and take advantage of the bright prospects."

Fortunately, Xiamen government and XMU Software School are working to bring China up to par!

---

[1] "Xiamen Gets IBM Training," *China Daily*, September 9, 2000.

第 31 章　软件学院

第 31 章
软件学院

厦门大学软件学院是教育部和国家计委批准的 35 所示范性软件学院之一，紧邻坐落在风景优美的环岛路上的厦门软件园。

在厦门软件园成立之前的两年里，就已经有超过 100 家的软件公司成立了，并且年产值超过人民币 5 个亿。软件学院应运而生，它许多的毕业生开始开办自己的公司，试图帮助厦门在中国的软件产业中找到一席之地。

软件学院拥有一支高素质的师资队伍，包括国内外具有丰富教学经验的教授和专家。学院设有先进的教学手段和设备，并针对 1000 多名本科生和研究生实行双语教学计划。学院不仅强调理论学习，还注重实际运用，学院与 IBM、BEA、ORACLE、SYBASE、DELL 以及 SUN（SUN 已和软件学院签署协议，共建 SUN 开放技术实验室）等国外著名 IT 企业开展合作办学。这些项目包括联合研究开发、专业技术认证、奖学奖教奖研、校园科技活动、毕业实习、技术支持服务等。学院还为毕业生的就业提供帮助。

学院的两支代表队参加了在北京举行的由 IBM 赞助的 2002 年的亚洲程序设计大赛。同年，IBM 联合学院共同开展培训 IT 专业人才的项目。IBM 中华片区培训中心陈经理说："中国在软件产业落后于印度是因为中国缺乏软件工程师，相反印度在培训上投入了很多。"[①]陈经理还说，"中央政府和地方政府都应该根据政策和资金情况立即提供高效的支持，全面提升地方的技术水平，以期在未来的软件光明前景中掌握主动权。"

幸运的是，厦门政府和厦门大学软件学院都在努力地使中国达到标准！

联系方式：
电话：258-0600　传真：258-0500
电子邮件：software@xmu.edu.cn
网址：http://software.xmu.edu.cn

---

① 《厦门得到 IBM 公司培训支持》，《中国日报》2000 年 9 月 3 日。

Chapter 32

School of Law

China's 1st Degrees in International Law   One of the first Law Schools in China, SL was founded in June, 1926 as the "Law Section". The three departments of Law, Politics, and Economics combined in 1930 to form the School of Law. SL re-opened in 1979, shortly after the Cultural Revolution, and in 1981 became the first Chinese institution to offer a Master of Law (LL.M) for students of International Law. In 1985 it was the first to recruit undergrads in this field, and in 1986 the first to grant the Doctor of Law (LL.D) in International al Law.

In 2003, SL was ranked #9 in the nation, and it is now one of XMU's key programs, with such distinguished professors as our university president Zhu Chongshi.

SL's institutes include the International Economic Law Institute, the Civil and Commercial Law Institute, the Roman Law Institute and the Center for Oceans Policy and Law, as well as the Center for JM Education and the Teaching and Experiment Center.

SL's International Law program and "Law of Hong Kong, Macao and Taiwan" program are key items under the State's "211 Project", and the Civil & Commercial Law Studies is a Provincial Key Discipline.

SL has links with numerous overseas institutes and has hosted various international programs, such as the "Recent Developments in the Law of the Sea and China" (March, 2005).

第32章 法学院

第32章

法 学 院

中国最早的国际法学位

厦门大学法学院是中国第一批法学教育院校之一,成立于1926年6月,当时名为法科,下设法律学、政治学、经济学三系,到1930年三系合并组成了现在的法学院。法学院在1979年即"文革"结束后不久又重新开办,并在1981年成为中国最早设有国际法专业硕士学位点的教育机构;1985年,在全国率先招收国际经济法专业本科生;1986年,又最早获得国际法专业的博士授予权。

2003年,厦门大学法学院全国专业排名第九,现今是厦门大学的重点学科之一,院内汇集了杰出的教师,其中包括了厦大的校长——朱崇实。

法学院现设有国际经济法研究所、民商法研究所、罗马法研究所、海洋政策与法律研究中心等4个研究机构,并成立了法律硕士教育中心和教学实验中心。

"国际经济法与台港澳法研究"项目是国家"211工程"的重点建设项目,另外民商法学为福建省重点学科。

法学院和很多的海外院校都建立了联系,并举办了很多国际性的活动,比如2005年3月举办了"海洋法的新发展与中国"国际学术会议。

SL's widely read academic journals include, "Xiamen University Law Review", "Journal of International Economic Law", and "Roman Law and Modern Civil Law".

The SL's new 10,000m^2 teaching and research center has an idyllic setting on the Island Ring Road, overlooking the sea, with central administration building and two buildings with classrooms, case study room, and faculty offices.

UN Depository Library The International Economic Law Institute, established on October 5, 1957, has a UN depository library[1].

Contact Tel: 218-5983   218-6991   Fax: 218-6154
Email: sppan@xmu.edu.cn,   lqy@xmu.edu.cn
fashuo@xmu.edu.cn   Website:http://law.xmu.edu.cn

Prof. Liao Yixin, Dean, School of Law
E-mail: law@jingxian.xmu.edu.cn

Prof. Zeng Huaqun, Director, Institute of International Law
E-mail: zenghuaqun@163.com

Zeng Huaqun

---

[1] The UN has over 400 depository libraries in over 140 countries maintaining United Nations material; all are open to the public free-of-charge.

第 32 章 法学院

法学院被广泛阅读的学术论丛包括：
《厦门大学法律评论》
《国际经济法学刊》
《罗马法与现代民法》

厦门大学法学院大楼占地 10000 多平方米，坐落在风景如画的环岛路，眺望大海。学院不仅拥有独立的中央办公楼和两栋教学楼，而且建设有标准化的案例教学讨论室以及教师工作室。

联合国托存图书馆[①]

建立于 1957 年 10 月 5 日的国际经济法研究所，拥有一个联合国托存图书馆。

Liao Yixin

联系方式

电话：+86(0)592-2185933, +86(0)592-2186991
传真：+86 (0)592-2186154
电子邮件：sppan@xmu.edu.cn, lqy@xmu.edu.cn, fashuo@xmu.edu.cn

廖益新教授（法学院院长）：
E-mail: law@jingxian.xmu.edu.cn

曾华群教授（国际经济法研究所所长）：
E-mail: zenghuaqun@163.com

---

① 联合国在 140 多个国家拥有 400 多个托存图书馆，收藏联合国的资料文献，这些资料文献对公众是免费借阅的。

Chapter 33

School of Information Science & Technology (SIST)

News Flash! "Crime doesn't pay," especially nowadays, thanks to three XMU computer science professors. Ke Yu, Li Shengrui, and Li Cuihua have developed an innovative adaptive-oriented filter[①] for enhancing fingerprints."

'In the Dark!' No Longer! It's hard to believe that in the early 1990s we usually did not have electricity in our classrooms, and on overcast days it was so dim I could barely see the blackboard. No computers either. The Foreign Affairs Office' first computer was one I put together from parts I bought in Hong Kong (I knew nothing about computers, but I could read the English instructions, so I was the computer "expert" by default).

I'd have never imagined that a decade later XMU would have China's most advanced university high speed information network, and one of China's leading information science programs. And today our classrooms not only have electricity but teleconferencing, so I can give lectures to students in many cities at the same time. We even have telephones nowadays! (I made only 3 phone calls my first two years at XMU, and none went through—and my first phone cost USD $450 and a 3-year wait! Nowadays people don't even bother with them because cell phone service is so cheap in China).

---

① "Design of Fingerprint Adaptive Enhancement Filter" research supported by grants from National Natural Science Foundation of China, Ministry of Education's Foundation for Key Teachers, and Natural Science Foundation of Fujian Province

第 33 章　信息科学与技术学院

第 33 章

信息科学与技术学院

快讯！　"罪犯无法逍遥法外！"多亏了三名厦大计算机科学系的师生柯渝、李胜睿、李翠华，他们发明了一种改进版的指纹适应性过滤器。①

告别"黑暗"！ 说出来令人难以置信，上世纪 90 年代初我们的教室常常停电，一到阴天我几乎看不清黑板。当时，我们也没有电脑。外事办公室的第一台电脑是我用从香港买回来的零件拼装而成的（那时，我对电脑一无所知，但却因为看得懂英文说明书，理所当然地成了电脑"专家"。）

没想到，十多年后的厦大拥有中国最先进的高速校园信息网络以及一流的信息科学学科。今天，教室里不仅有电，而且还有电视会议系统，通过它我可以同时给很多身在外地的同学上课。我们也装上了电话！（刚到厦大那两年我就只打过 3 个电话，还都没通。装第一部电话的时候，我不仅花了 450 美元，还等了 3 年！如今，人们都懒得用固定电话了，因为手机费用在中国很便宜。）

---

①　"适应性过滤器"的研究是由中国国家自然科学基金会、教育部重点教师基金会以及福建省自然科学基金会批准、资助的。

SIST now has a staff of over 200, and 80% of the teaching staff are under the age of 45. The young and energetic researchers have been behind some amazingly diverse technological breakthroughs.

Four departments: Computer Science, Automation; Electronic Engineering; and Communication Engineering.

SIST institutes include: Electronic Information Institute, Image and Information Systems Institute, the Population Resources, Environment and Geography Information Systems Institute, Language Technology Institute, the System and Control Theory Institute, Institute of Artificial Intelligence

"The Chinese Association for Artificial Intelligence was formed with the aim of exploring the deep secrets of human wisdom and transplanting it into machines." Professor Yixin Zhong

The Institute of Artificial Intelligence (IAI) was founded in 1998 and the first director was the famous academician Qinshi Gao. The IAI has received 3 grants from the Chinese national science foundation and 3 grants from the 863 national hi-tech program. One of their most practical applications has been a system for recognizing handwritten Chinese characters (I can't do that myself!). IAI has also cooperated with the Department of Chinese Language and Literature, School of Foreign Languages, the OEC, and the School of Software to found the Center for Language Technology, which is doing research on multilingual machine translation.

International Cooperation
SIST has many links with such overseas institutes as the University of Ulster's School of Computing and Information Engineering. SIST has also hosted numerous hi-tech conferences and workshops. In September 2005, a delegation from the Furtwangen University of Applied Sciences, led by their president, visited XMU. This university specializes in information technology, economics and industrial and commercial management, and is planning cooperation with XMU.

Contact Information Tel: 592-0188 Fax: 592-0258
E-mail: cies@jingxian.xmu.edu.cn
Website: http://ist.xmu.edu.cn

第33章　信息科学与技术学院

信息科学与技术学院现在有教职工200多人，80%的教师年龄在45岁以下。这些朝气蓬勃的研究人员在许多技术领域已经取得了一些重大的突破。

四大系　计算机科学系、自动化系、电子工程系、通信工程系。

研究机构　电子信息研究所、智能图像与信息系统研究室、人口资源环境与地理信息系统中心、语言技术中心、系统与控制研究中心、人工智能研究所。

> "中国人工智能学会成立的目的旨在探索人类智慧的深层奥秘并将其运用到机器当中。"
> ——钟义信教授

人工智能研究所（IAI）　成立于1998年，第一任所长是著名的高庆狮院士。人工智能研究所已承担3项国家自然科学基金项目，3项国家863高科技计划项目。他们研究的一项非常实用的项目是手写汉字识别系统（汉字识别？这个我就不行啊！）。该研究所已经与汉语语言文学系、外文学院、海外教育学院、软件学院等单位展开合作建立一个语言技术中心，从事多语种机器翻译的研究。

国际合作

信息科学与技术学院与多个海外研究机构都保持学术联系，如阿尔斯特大学的计算机与信息工程学院等。学院还曾主办过多次高科技会议和研讨会。2005年9月，由其校长亲自率领的福特万根应用技术大学代表团访问厦门大学。这所大学以信息技术、经济学以及工商管理专业为办学特色，计划与厦大开展合作。

联系方式
电话：592-0188　　传真：592-0258
电子邮箱：cies@jingxian.xmu.edu.cn
网址：http://ist.xmu.edu.cn

Chapter 34

School of Public Affairs (SPA)

SPA was founded in November 2003 by Professor Chen Zhenming, the current dean, and has 5 key units:
Political Science Dept.   Public Administration Dept.
Sociology Dept.   MPA Education Center
Institute of Population Studies (includes Professor Zheng Qiwu, who contributed much to this book).

The SPA's MPA Center, recognized as one of China's best, is rapidly gaining ground in public policy analysis, comparative government studies and public management theories. SPA has over 1200 students taking 4 undergraduate programs, 10 Master's programs, and 4 PhD programs, and students enjoy academic exchange programs with prestigious institutions in China and in the U.S.A., Canada, the Netherlands and Hong Kong SAR.

Contact   Tel: 218-2783   Fax:218-3191
Email: ggsw@xmu.edu.cn
Website: http://spa.xmu.edu.cn

Ancient Politician (old Chinese tale) A new official tried to impress folks with his moral virtues by writing three phrases on his office wall:
1. Don't covet money.
2. Don't desire promotions.
3. Don't fear death.
A few days later some wit added two characters to the bottom of each:
1. ...in small quantities.
2. ... unless it's much higher than this one.
3. ...but I want to live as long as I can.

 第34章 公共事务学院

第34章

公共事务学院

厦门大学公共事务学院成立于2003年11月,现任院长为陈振明教授,下设:

政治学系　　公共管理系　　社会学系　　MPA教育中心

人口研究所(郑启五老师就在这里工作,他为本书帮了不少忙)

公共事务学院的MPA教育中心处于全国前列,学院在公共政策分析、比较政府研究和公共管理理论方面迅速发展。

公共事务学院现有四个本科专业,本科生超过1200多人,设有10个硕士点,4个博士点,并与美国、加拿大、荷兰、香港等国内外知名的大学开展了各种学术交流活动。

联系方式　电话:218-2783　传真:218-3191
电子邮件:ggsw@xmu.edu.cn　网址:http://spa.xmu.edu.cn

中国古代传说——人民公仆

新官刚一上任,决定让他的人民知道他所具有的美德。于是,他在办公室的墙上写下三行字:

1. 不要钱。

2. 不要官。

3. 不怕死。

几天后,某位智者在每一行的后面添上两个字。结果,变成了——

1.不要钱,嫌少。

2.不要官,嫌小。

3.不怕死,嫌老。

Chapter 35

College of Architecture and Civil Engineering

The College of Architecture and Civil Engineering (CACE) has been growing faster than Xiamen's mushrooming skyline since it was established in April 2004. It consists of the Department of Architecture and the Department of Civil Engineering, with over 50 faculty members engaged in teaching and research.

The college enjoys excellent teaching and research facilities, with laboratories of architectural physics, CAD, model testing, building materials, mechanics, and structural and geo-technical engineering.

The college has classrooms dedicated to design, painting, architectural drawing and multimedia applications. Their library has over 8,000 books in Chinese and foreign languages, subscriptions to nearly one hundred different domestic and international journals, and extensive electronic resources. The Institute of Architectural Design & Research, a national first-class design institute affiliated with the college, gives students an ideal environment to put theory into practice.

Contact   Tel: 218-3505   Fax: 218-6421
Email:archt@jingxian.xmu.edu.cn
Website:http://archt.xmu.edu.cn

第35章

建筑与土木工程学院

厦门大学建筑与土木工程学院自 2004 年 4 月成立以来处于飞速发展中。学院设有建筑系和土木工程系，从事教学和科研的专职教师达 50余人。

学院现有设备齐全且先进的建筑物理、建筑 CAD、建筑造型、建筑材料、建筑力学、结构工程和土工等实验室。

学院配备有专业教室、美术教室、制图教室和多媒体专用教室等教学场所；学院专用资料室藏有中外文图书资料 8000 余册、中外文期刊近百种及大量的声像资料；学院设有全国一流的建筑设计研究院，为学生提供了理想的实践场所。

联系方式

电话：218-3505　传真：218-6421

电子邮件：archt@jingxian.xmu.edu.cn

网址：http://archt.xmu.edu.cn

Chapter 36

Tan Kah Kee College

News Flash! "Open House" at Tan Kah Kee College.

Xiamen University's Tan Kah Kee College held its first Open House on June 19, 2005. Over 1,500 visitors, including prospective students and their parents, came to the campus. The college took the opportunity to display the achievements of its educational reform. Visitors commented that this Open House activity is very helpful for decision-making as to which university to choose after taking the national college entrance examination.

Common Talk, *Xiamen Daily*, June 29, 2005[①]

Tan Kah Kee College (TKKC), an independent subsidiary of XMU, is across the bay from XMU. This 4-year college, named after XMU's founder, offers an amazing diversity of programs—everything from music and art to architecture and computers. TKKC has one of China's most attractive campuses, as well as numerous innovative incentives to attract and keep talented undergraduate students. For example, Common Talk[②] reported that in 2005 TKKC offered 700,000 RMB in scholarships, including 40,000 RMB each to the most 13 outstanding freshmen (Kind of makes me want to sign up myself!).

For such a young school, TKKC also has numerous activities, such as the contemporary art exhibition "Via." Held Feb. 25 to March 2, 2005, it included works by nine young artists from the Netherlands, America, Germany, Canada and China.[③]

---

① By Zhu Zhiqiang and Zhou Fei.
② Oct. 19, 2005.
③ Common Talk, *Xiamen Daily*, February 23, 2005.

第 36 章

嘉 庚 学 院

快讯！嘉庚学院首个校园开放日 厦门大学嘉庚学院于 2005 年 6 月 19 日举办了首个校园开放日。1500 多参观者，其中包括考生以及他们的家长，来到了校区。学院借此机会向社会展示了它教育改革的成果。参观者评论校园开放日此举对于学生参加高考后在填报大学的选择上非常有帮助。

(《厦门日报·双语周刊》2005 年 6 月 29 日[①])

嘉庚学院是厦大本科层次的独立学院，与厦门大学隔海相望。这个以厦大校主陈嘉庚先生名字命名的四年制学院，自创办以来呈现了惊人的专业多样性——专业从音乐、艺术到建筑、计算机，门类齐全。嘉庚学院同样拥有中国最迷人的校园之一，以及许多创新激励机制，以吸引和留住才能出众的本科生。《厦门日报·双语周刊》[②]曾报道，2005 年嘉庚学院提供了 700000 元的奖学金，奖励给 13 名优秀的新生每人 40000 元。（让我也有点儿想进嘉庚学院了）

虽是一个如此年轻的学院，嘉庚学院也展开了丰富多彩的活动。例如从 2005 年 2 月 25 日到 3 月 2 日，学院举办了以"经过"为主题的当代艺术展，展出了来自荷兰、美国、德国、加拿大和中国的 9 位年轻艺术家的作品[③]。

---

① 作者：祝自强、周菲(音译)。
② 2005 年 10 月 19 日。
③ 《厦门日报·双语周刊》2005 年 2 月 23 日。

The school's success can be attributed in part to outstanding leadership, such as Professor Ji Yuhua (see Foreign Languages chapter) and President Wang Ruifang.

President Wang Ruifang graduated from XMU's Department of Economics in 1982 and in 1994 received his Ph.D in Economics from the University of Strathclyde in Glasgow, Scotland. He taught at Nanyang Technological University, Singapore, from 1994 to 2003, where he supervised masters and doctoral candidates. Since 2003, he has shouldered two responsibilities—professor of the Department of Economics and president of Tan Kah Kee College.

Prof. Wang's academic papers have been published in English language academic journals and international conferences. His primary research has been in economic modeling and exchange rate policy, and macro-monetary theory (a discipline that might explain my wife's spending habits!).

Excerpt from President Wang's Letter

"During this time of revival and flourishing development of our great nation, I am honored to return to my motherland after a long absence and to be appointed as the first President of Tan Kah Kee College. I am motivated by responsibility and obligations. Under the leadership of the College Board of Directors and support from our parent university, Xiamen University, I vow to cooperate with my colleagues, to embrace the patriotic spirit of Mr. Tan Kah Kee and the motto of "Pursue Excellence and Strive for Perfection", and to adhere to the concepts of Responsibility, Pragmatism, Innovation, and Cooperation. We are endeavoring to establish a new-style college for four-year undergraduate courses. It will be a top-ranking college enjoying an extensive reputation both at home and abroad and will be known for its efficient educational system."

Getting to that Campus across the Sea
By Gary Proctor

As a 'Foreign Expert' teaching for XMU, I have some thoughts regarding the school and my participation in this beautiful place. I've taught in several countries and territories over the years, and encountered institutions with more than one campus, but never have I even heard of one with campuses in the same locality separated by the sea. Methinks having the largest university auditorium in China is not the only distinction unique to XMU.

第 36 章　嘉庚学院

学院的成功部分要归功于杰出的领导班子，比如纪玉华教授（在外文学院章节中更多介绍）和王瑞芳院长。

王瑞芳院长 1982 年毕业于厦大经济系，1994 年获得英格兰格拉斯哥斯托拉斯大学的经济学博士学位。他曾于 1994 年到 2003 年在新加坡南洋理工大学任教，指导硕士和博士研究生。2003 起，担任两个职务——经济系教授和嘉庚学院院长。王教授的学术论文曾经在英文学术刊物和有关国际学术会议上发表。他的研究方向主要集中于经济建模，汇率政策和宏观货币理论（一个也许能解释我妻子消费习惯的理论！）。

院长寄语
（摘自王教授的信）

在中华民族伟大复兴的事业蓬勃发展之际，我有幸回到阔别多年的祖国，出任厦门大学嘉庚学院的首任院长，深感重担在肩，不敢懈怠。在学院董事会的领导下，在母体学校厦门大学的倾力支持下，我愿和全体同仁一道，秉承嘉庚先生爱国主义精神和"自强不息，止于至善"的办学精神，怀着敬业、务实、创新、合作的共同理念，用质量打造品牌，以创新推动发展，努力将嘉庚学院办成国内一流的、获得国际广泛认可的、以有效教学见长的一所新型的本科独立学院。

Ferry to Zhangzhou Campus

跨海到校区

[美]Gary Proctor 著

作为在厦大任教的一个"外国专家"，身在其中，这魅力之所在让我产生了一些想法。这些年来，我在很多国家和地区教过书，也见过很多不只一个校区的大学，但是在我来厦大之前甚至还没听说过一所被大海分隔的大学。看来拥有全国高校中最大的礼堂不是厦大的唯一独特之处。

Teaching four forty-five minute classes to students from two different college majors per day requires just over six hours all told. Let's follow me on a typical teaching day:
 Catch one of three university buses departing at 7:00AM sharp.
 Exit the East Gate at 7:04 for the ride to the ferry dock.
 Arrive at the ferry dock 7:12-16.
 Board chartered ferry and depart Xiamen 7:20-25 (there's a story hidden here as well[①]).
 Arrive at Zhangzhou and board one of four ancient chartered local buses to the lower division campus 7:45.
 Arrive at the teaching buildings 7:50-55.
 Teach two sessions from 8:00 until 11:40.
 Return to campus hotel on one of two buses 11:45.
 Board 1 of 4 worn out chartered local buses back to dock 12:30.
 Board ferry for Xiamen 12:35.
 Depart Zhangzhou 12:38.
 Arrive Xiamen, board one of three university buses 1:00 PM
 Arrive back to XMU main gate starting point 1:10.

 One feature of the 'school ferry' that I like is the pitching from side to side in heavy seas. Whereas some may get a bit nauseous, it is a very short trip and I've not seen anyone, even with a hangover, get sick. It's just part of the fun of the trip.
 The boat ties up to a floating concrete dock that misleads one into thinking it is more stable than it actually is. Oh it's safe enough, but unsteady, especially at high tide. I recall my first experience with lighting onto a swelling landing and wondering if I'd had too much Chinese white liquor (白酒) the night before. Now that I've found my sea legs and know to look out for it there is no more wooziness.
 Low tide carries yet another feature of interest. Going *down* to the sea in ships is easy enough with gravity's help, but at high tide the ascent upon arrival gives the legs a good mountain work out.
 All told, the ferry experience is one of several special aspects of teaching at one of the more beautiful premier universities in this largest of countries that makes Xiamen stand out for me.

---

 ① I've ridden ferries to work before when I lived in the Puget Sound of western Washington State. Those boats were much larger and similar to the vehicle ferries here. The boats we ride to school hold 96 or 100 passengers on two decks. While the lower deck has sea spray flying past the forward windows, they don't use portholes anymore; the upper seating area offers better viewing of the scenery.

第 36 章 嘉庚学院

每天给两个不同专业的学生上四节 45 分钟的课合计需要 6 个小时的时间。下面跟随我来经历这样典型的一天吧：

三辆校车 7 点准时出发，赶上其中一辆
7:04 离开东校门开往轮渡码头。
在 7:12—7:16 之间到达码头。
登上学校包的船，在 7:20 到 7:25 之间驶离厦门（这里还有个故事①）。
到达漳州后有 4 辆专用的旧公交车将我们于 7:45 分送到分校区。
7:50—7:55 到教学楼。
8:00—11:40，上两节课。
11:45 有两辆公交车送我们到校区宾馆。
有 4 辆专用公车将我们于 12:30 送回到码头。
12:35 登上回厦门的渡船。
12:38 驶离漳州。
到达厦门，下午 1:00 有 3 辆校车接我们。
1:10 回到厦大主校门的出发点。

我喜欢"校船"的一点就是坐在笨重的座位上感受在海上左右摇晃的感觉。虽然有的人会有些不舒服，可这是非常短的旅程，我还没有见过有人，即使是宿醉的人晕这个船的。当然，这只是旅程中的部分乐趣。

船会被拴在一个混凝土制造的、让人误以为比实际更稳固的浮动船坞上。对，够安全了，但是会晃动，尤其在涨潮的时候。我回想到我第一次在海水涨得很厉害的时候在灯光下下船的经历，开始怀疑我前晚是不是喝了太多的中国的白酒。现在我既然已经知道摸索出如何做才能不晕船了，每次也就再不会不舒服了。

低潮的时候也是另有一番乐趣的。有地球引力的帮助下海是很容易的，但到了浪高处"爬坡"可就不容易啦，这样的时候船可是做够了"登山运动"了。

所有的都算进去的话，我们的"跨海之旅"是我在这个大国最美丽的高校教书生活中诸多的独特经历之一，也是使我格外喜爱厦门的原因之一。

---

① 以前我住在华盛顿州西部的 Puget Sound 的时候也坐船去工作。那些船和这里的轮渡相似，但要大很多。我们去学校坐的船有两层，能容纳 96 或者 100 名乘客。海浪会飞溅到底层的窗户，现在不用舷窗了；上层则能让人看到不错的风景。

Chapter 37

"Beautiful Minds of XMU"

"All talents, young and old, converge here; bright stars have filled the skies of XMU for 85 years…"

We had planned to interview many professors but our tight deadline prevented this. However, we did have a delightful time interviewing one of XMU's "Beautiful Minds," the famous economist Prof. Deng Ziji. And now that this book is behind us, we hope to interview more such academic legends for a book entitled, "Beautiful Minds of XMU." If our experience with Prof. Deng is any indication, it will be fun to write—and hopefully fun to read as well.

So until next time, Enjoy Amoy, and Enjoy XMU, our home!

Bill and Robin

"Charming Deng Ziji"
——Face-to-face with Pro. Deng

Hailed as "The Giant of Finance" and "An all-time Master", this famous senior economist, financier and educator, has devoted himself to education for almost 60 years and has cultivated countless outstanding talents, including over 300 masters, almost 100 PhDs and 3 post-doctoral students, some of whom have gone on to become local and national government leaders, professors, PhD supervisors, vanguards of academia, presidents of universities, deans of schools, leaders of banks and stock companies, etc… Many of his theories and proposals have been adopted by central, provincial, and municipal governments to direct the regulation and execution of related policies. He has published 56 monographs, translations and textbooks, over 370 papers, and has composed works of some 20 million characters. His name is listed in over 40 dictionaries and biographies of world and domestic celebrities, including Biography of 500 World Celebrities (UK) and Biography of 500 International Influences (US). He was also awarded the Medal of 500 World Celebrities (UK), the International Medal of Honor, and Lifetime Outstanding Achievement Medal (UK).

第37章 厦门大学的"美丽心灵"

第37章

厦门大学的"美丽心灵"

"群贤毕至,少长云集",厦大的天空繁星闪烁,照彻风雨辉煌的85年。我们渴望采访更多的厦大人物,探寻更多盏点亮历史星空的明灯,但是校庆的一天天临近使我们不得不暂时推迟这个想法。于是对邓老的采访便成了此次《魅力厦大》的总结。

但在此真诚地希望,今后的日子里能触摸到更多颗美丽的繁星——厦大人物,并以一本书专门撰写他们,题为《美丽心灵》。如果说我们与邓老的面对面是个很好的开头的话,那么这本厦大"美丽心灵"的成书过程对于我们一定是收获无穷的,希望,对于读者也将是如此。

那么下次见喽!享受厦门,热爱我们共同的家——厦门大学吧!

潘维廉　费菲

"魅力邓子基"——与邓老面对面

他是厦门大学文科资深教授、是被誉为"财政学泰斗"、"一代大师"的著名资深经济学家、财政学家和教育家;他从教近60年,为国家培养出大量的专业人才,其中硕士300多人,博士近100人,博士后3人。他们中有国家和地方省部级领导,有教授、博士生导师、学术带头人,大学校(院)长或银行证券公司领导者……他的许多理论与主张被中央、省、市政府采用,指导相关政策的制定与执行。他出版专著、译著和教材56本、发表主要论文370多篇,著述近两千万字;他被英国剑桥国际传记中心授予"世界500名人"称号、美国国际传记协会授予"国际500名有重大影响人物"称号,并获"世界500名人勋章"、"国际荣誉勋章"(英)、"终身杰出成就金人奖"(美)等;他的名字被列入国内外40多部辞典、传记之中……他的名字,邓子基。

His academic achievements, his devotion to education, his continued work into his 80's, and his contribution to the country's economic development not only thrilled me but also intimidated me as I prepared for my interview with him. How could my limited words possibly describe a person like Dr. Deng, who is rich in knowledge and life? I was fearful, but looked forward to this challenging and most precious experience.

We Set Out   At 9:50 am, at Sanjia Cun, I hopped into Dr. Bill Brown's van and said, "Dr. Deng lives at Haibin #26. Know where that is?"

"Hmm, it's probably near #25", Dr. Brown answered, and drove towards the teacher's housing area along the tidy road threading through the green mountains, above the vast sea. I was all the more anxious to meet Prof. Deng and at 10:00 AM sharp we rang his doorbell.

The Interview   The gray haired Dr. Deng invited us into his home, face glowing, and he shook hands warmly, especially happy to see Dr. Brown. "How's your house on the mountain?" he asked.   Dr. Deng turned to me and said, "Dr. Brown's house at Lingfeng is where we lived for eight years. Now he's lived there for 18 years!"   I did not know this  and was all ears, because I had a strong feeling that today I would be honored to get to know not just about his famous career but also something about his daily life.

Deng: "The house wasn't very nice when we lived there, but I read in the paper that now you've changed it into "the best house on the planet!"

Dr.Brown: Well, it's still a little messy."

Deng: "It's hard to believe you've lived there for 18 years. How's your family? Still have two kids?" he asked, jokingly.

Dr.Brown: Yes, two kids, but only one wife.

Deng: Are the kids going to school here?

Dr. Brown: The elder one returned to America for college, and the younger one is here in senior high. But both say that after graduation they want to return home—to China.

第37章 厦门大学的"美丽心灵"
DISCOVER Xiamen University

他的学术成就,他的教书育人,他的倾情祖国经济腾飞,他的年过 80 仍不辍耕耘,他的"青春献事业,奉献写人生"……,使我这个"小字辈"在准备采访时,既兴奋不已又战战兢兢。他的丰富和内涵,有限的文字怎么可能全面地表达?我怀着忐忑不安的心情,期待着这次极富挑战性而又将是无比珍贵的经历。

序曲

上午 9:50 分,三家村,我上了潘维廉教授的面包车。

"He lives at Haibin 26#, do you know where that is?(住址是海滨东区 26 号,你知道在哪里吗?)",我问。

"Hmm, it's probably near 25#(嗯,就挨着 25 号)",潘答。

车在海滨公寓区内的公路上前行,远处巍巍青山挺拔,茫茫大海辽阔无边。这一切都使我心中的企盼更加强烈。终于,10 点整,我们按响了门铃。

采访

鹤发童颜、精神矍铄的邓老一见我们,便热情地握手。见到潘维廉教授,他更是格外高兴。一番寒暄之后,开始了以下的对话:

"你山上的房子怎么样了?"他先问潘,然后转头跟我说,"潘教授'凌峰'的房子以前是我住的,我住了 8 年,然后就是他住,他住了 18 年啊!"对此,我可是一无所知,于是就饶有趣味地仔细聆听。我强烈地预感到,今天我将有幸认识生活之中的"有血有肉"的邓老。

邓:"我们那时候不行,现在你改造好了,变成了'全世界最好的房子'。"

潘:"呵呵,有点儿乱。"

"哎呀,没想到你一住就是 18 年啊,家里怎么样?还是两个孩子吗?"邓老风趣幽默地问。

潘:"对。两个孩子,只有一个夫人。"

邓:"都在这里上学吗?"

潘:"老大回美国上大学了,老二在这里念高中,但是他们都说毕业后'回家',回中国来。"

Deng: Wow, that's great! I also just read that Premier Wen Jiabao has just seen you and shook hands with you.
Dr. Brown: Yeah. I haven't washed my right hand for days.
Deng: You haven't? Oh, don't…
"Which department are you from?" Pro. Deng then asked me.
"International Economics and Business," I answered hurriedly.
"Oh, my kid teaches there, does he teach you?"
"I've met Pro. Deng Liping at National Accounting Institute. But he doesn't teach undergraduates now so he doesn't teach me." I said.

Pro. Deng Liping is president of Xiamen National Accounting Institute, a professor of XMU Economics Dept., a PhD supervisor, and a deputy to the 9th and 10th Session of the National People's Congress. I met him once at Xiamen National Accounting Institute, and I remembered that his eyes were red and it seemed like he had not rested for days. I couldn't help but think, "Like father, like son," dedicated to work and research. How I admire these people who have devoted their lives to their careers!

Deng pointed to the family picture on the wall behind him, which I'd noticed when I walked in. "This is my entire family." Deng said.

Dr. Bill Brown stood in front of it holding a camera and asked: "May I take a picture of you with that family picture?"

Deng: "Oh, then I have to get changed."

Dr. Brown: "Not necessary, professors are supposed to dress like this." The camera flashed repeatedly and whirred as he snapped photos. .

Deng: "It's my honor to have you in my home."

Dr. Brown: "I am just a layman at photography, so I need to take more pictures."

Deng: "I think you're an expert at everything."

第37章 厦门大学的"美丽心灵"

邓:"哦,真是幸运啊,刚刚温家宝总理还接了见你啊,还跟你握手了呢。"

潘:"对,还没洗手。"

邓:"还没洗?哦,不要洗……"

"你是哪个系的?"邓老把问题转向我。

"国际经贸系",我忙答。

"哦,我孩子就在那里呀,教不教你?"

"我见过邓力平教授,是在国家会计学院那里。不过他现在没有给本科生上课了,所以不教我,"我说。

邓力平教授是厦门国家会计学院院长,厦大经济学教授、博士生导师,第九、十届全国人大代表。我在国家会计学院见过他一次,记得当时他两只眼睛布满了血丝,看上去好像几天几夜没有休息。我心里想,"有其父必有其子",做学问忙工作,这些倾尽精力奉献于事业的人们是多么值得敬佩啊!

邓老回头指了指身后一张"全家福",其实我一进门就已经注意到了。他说:"这就是我全家。"

潘维廉教授拿着相机站到对面,说:"能不能让我拍个照,就是您和那张全家福。"

邓:"哦,那我要换件衣服。"

潘:"不要换,教授就是穿这样的衣服。"他开始拍照,闪光灯"咔咔"地闪。

邓:"你能到我家来,我很光荣啊。"

潘:"我是外行,所以要多拍几张。"

邓:"你是全面专家……"

— 359 —

During the entire interview, Pro. Deng's modesty made me look up to him even more. He didn't want to talk about his academic achievements. Indeed, there are numerous articles about his achievements all over the world, so what does reputation matter for a senior who has devoted his entire life to education and the flourishing of his country?

Pro. Deng told us his motto, "Teaching and educating, cultivating talent, and attaining achievements". Simple philosophy, simple words. "I'm 84 years old now, but in fine shape and I'm still supervising doctors. My hair is gray, but I hope I can still contribute to society."

In 2007, it will be 60 years since Pro. Deng started teaching. By then this professor who has devoted himself to education for more than half a century will have mentored over 100 doctors. "Pro. Deng, you've had so many students. I heard president Zhu Chongshi was your student too?"

"Yes. He is 50 years old now."

"He is just 50?" I was surprised.

Dr. Brown said, "At 50 he's already the president of the university. I'm 50 too but I'm just a French fry (In English, important people are called a "big potato", and Dr. Brown was saying he was just a "small potato.")

"Anyway, I have no weekends now," Pro. Deng said.

Hearing that, Dr. Brown asked Mrs. Deng, who was sitting beside us, "He even works weekends? And you're ok with that?"

"Yes," She said. "He enjoys what he is doing, so I let him."

"So you're not henpecked," Dr. Brown said to Pro. Deng, with envy.

"How have you been preserving your health?" I asked him. "You're still fit as a fiddle and do so much work!" I knew he was modest and didn't want to talk about his achievements, so I asked this instead.

"This, I know…" He was obviously happy with this question and ready to expound upon his views of health, but the modest Mrs. Deng urged him to drop it, and not let his "theory" be put in print. Prof. Deng retorted, "Don't interfere! Let them have it!"

Prof. Deng then proceeded to say, "Do a better job in teaching, engage in research, keep happy, eat well, exercise, think hard, talk more, write a lot, walk a lot. I tell people this all the time, and I don't need to worry about being a patient. I always think about this to encourage myself, "Eighty years in age, but a 60 year old body and a 40 year old heart and mind!" Of course I just say this to encourage myself, but I am like this old cow plowing the field, and sometimes I too need to get fixed up, so I then go to the doctors to get treated…"

"So many schools and institutions around China must be begging for you to work for them," Dr. Brown said. "Why have you chosen to stay here at XMU?"

"Because I'm a student of Wang Yanan's…"

第37章 厦门大学的"美丽心灵"

整个采访过程中邓老的谦虚令人钦佩,他不想谈学术成就,的确,海内外介绍他成就的文章不胜枚举,而"功名"对于一位早已决定将毕生心血奉献给教育事业和祖国经济繁荣的长者来说,又算得了什么呢?

邓老紧接着谈到了他一生的座右铭:"教书育人,出人才,出成果。"没有华丽的语言,他说:"今年84啦,身体还好,还在继续带博士。白发苍苍,希望还能发挥余热。"

2007年将是邓老从教60周年,到那时,这位半个多世纪奉献教育事业的老教授将培养出100个博士!

"邓老'桃李满天下',听说朱崇实校长也是您的学生?"

"对,他是我的高材生,50岁啦。"

"朱校长才50岁?"我很惊讶。

潘:"他50岁是校长,我也50岁,还是个'薯条'呢"。(英文里面"大牌"人物叫"big potato",直译过来就是"大土豆"的意思,那么维廉教授的意思大概就是自己还是个"小土豆"吧)

"反正没什么礼拜六礼拜天,"邓老说。

潘听了此语,忙问坐在一旁的邓老夫人:"他没有周末,你没意见?"

"我没意见。"她摇摇头。

"那你不是'气管炎'(妻管严)。"潘冲着邓老羡慕地说。

"邓老有什么养生之道啊,身体这么硬朗,还做那么多工作?",我看邓老很谦虚,不想谈自己的成就,于是问了这个问题。

"这个我有总结……",邓老听到这个问题显得十分高兴,准备和我分享他的一套理论了,可是邓夫人在这方面倒更显谦虚,想阻拦这套"理论"的"发表",邓老却说:"你不要干预嘛。"

他接着说:"搞好教学,从事科研,要心情舒畅,饮食得当,锻炼为上;要'四动',动脑多思,动口多讲,动手多写,动脚多走。我到处宣传这个,没有专利的问题。我就经常自勉,说自己是'80岁的年龄,60岁的身体,40岁的心态'。当然,只是自勉而已。其实我是'老牛拉破车',这'破车'坏了也得要修一下,所以有病要'必要治疗'……"

"过去许多部门和高校请您去工作,您为什么留厦大教书?"潘问。

"因为我是王亚南的学生……"

— 361 —

Prof. Deng had a really tight schedule. Another group came to visit him while we were interviewing him, so we prepared to leave. The following is the conversation between Dr. Brown and Prof. Deng, an American professor and a Chinese professor, just as we were leaving:

Deng: "I stayed here at XMU to devote myself to education, to develop our country, in this splendid place, XMU. You and I have the same reasons for staying here. But you are wiser."

Dr. Brown: (waving his hands) "No, No..."

Deng: "To have an American friend devoted to China and the Chinese, I admire you. You've really done a lot!"

Dr. Brown: "Huh, I guess I've fooled you!"

Deng: "The title of your new book Meili XMU is delightful itself, but XMU is even more charming."

Dr. Brown: "We are rushing for the 85th anniversary deadline. I hope Robin and I can do a better job of the book next time."

Deng: "'Meili' keeps coming, so you can't have them all at once. You're writing an entire Meili series."

Dr. Brown: "But today we're writing 'Meili Deng Ziji...'"

Epilogue:

After leaving Prof. Deng's apartment, I boarded Dr. Brown's van, "Toy Ota." Dr. Brown seemed as if he had lots to say but he said only one word. "Wow!"

"I'll write the article based on my notes. Any suggestions?" I asked.

"No," Dr. Brown said. "I like everything you've written... But don't forget to say that I kicked him out of his house..."

I laughed. He never forgets to use his great sense of humor.. But I knew we were both thinking the same thing: We had no idea where to start when portraying such a personage as Prof. Deng. There was so much about him worth writing about. It was a shame we had such limitations in time, skill, and the number of pages we could allot. I was deep in thought. So much has already been written about Prof. Deng. As the van pulled out of the housing area, I was again carried away by the beautiful scenery, and I thought that Prof. Deng had a heart as broad and splendid as the towering Five Peak Mountain. And Prof. Deng's thoughts reminded me of the sea—peaceful and deep. Prof. Deng has devoted his entire life to his country and university.

"Meili Deng Ziji!" How could such a life have been!

第37章 厦门大学的"美丽心灵"

邓老的时间排得非常满，我们采访中又有人来访，于是我们打算离开，以下是临走前潘维廉和邓老这一中一美两位教授的对话：

邓："我留下来搞教育，教育兴国啊，厦大这里好山好水好地方。其实和你留下来的心情是一样的。但是你比我更高明。"

潘：（忙摆手）"乱讲。"

邓："有这样一个美国友人献身于中国事业，很佩服你啊，你做了很多贡献啊！"

潘："呵，你被我骗了。"

邓："'魅力厦大'的题目本身就很有魅力，厦大更有魅力。"

潘："这次为赶85周年，写得很快，下次希望写丰富一点。"

邓："魅力是不断闪现的，不可能一次写完。你写的是'魅力'系列专著啊。"

潘："但今天要写'魅力邓子基'……"

尾声

离开邓老寓所，我又上了潘教授的车。

"Wow…（哇！…）"他看起来十分感慨，但只说了这一个字。

"I'll write it, any suggestions? （我来写吧，有什么建议吗？）"，我问他。

"No…I like everything you've written…But don't forget to say that I kicked him out of his house…（没有，你写的东西我都喜欢，但千万别忘了写是我把他'赶出'原来那个家的……"

我笑了，他什么时候都不会忘记幽默。但我知道他和我一样，对于这样一个鲜活生动、"有血有肉"的长者形象，因为有了太多的东西要说反而不知从何去着手刻画。只可惜篇幅有限，时间仓促，文字功底太浅……手中抱着厚厚一摞描写过邓老的文章，我陷入了沉思……

车子驶出海滨东区26号寓所，眼前的景色美得令人陶醉。邓老的胸怀就像那巍峨挺拔、郁郁葱葱的五老峰，博大而壮观，他的思想就像面前蔚蓝无垠、苍茫辽阔的大海，平静而深邃；他一生心血倾情祖国，倾注于厦大……

"魅力邓子基"，应该是怎样一种人生？！

图书在版编目(CIP)数据

魅力厦大/(美)潘维廉,费菲著.—2版.—厦门:厦门大学出版社,
2007.8(2019.2重印)
(魅力·老潘)
ISBN 978-7-5615-2548-7

Ⅰ.①魅… Ⅱ.①潘…②费… Ⅲ.①厦门大学—校史—汉、英
Ⅳ.①G649.285.73

中国版本图书馆 CIP 数据核字(2006)第 020077 号

出 版 人	郑文礼
责任编辑	施高翔

出版发行 *厦门大学出版社*

社　　址	厦门市软件园二期望海路 39 号
邮政编码	361008
总 编 办	0592-2182177　0592-2181406(传真)
营销中心	0592-2184458　0592-2181365
网　　址	http://www.xmupress.com
邮　　箱	xmup@xmupress.com
印　　刷	厦门集大印刷厂

开本	880 mm×1 230 mm　1/32
印张	12.5
插页	11
字数	430 千字
版次	2007 年 8 月第 2 版
印次	2019 年 2 月第 2 次印刷
定价	30.00 元

本书如有印装质量问题请直接寄承印厂调换

厦门大学出版社
微信二维码

厦门大学出版社
微博二维码